Illustrated Ventura 2.0

George Sheldon

Wordware Publishing, Inc.

Library of Congress Cataloging-in-Publication Data

Sheldon, George.
Illustrated ventura 2.0 / by George Sheldon.

Includes index.
ISBN 1-55622-104-5
1. Ventura publisher (Computer program) 2. Desktop publishing.
I. Title.
Z286.D47S574 1989 686.2'2—dc19 89-5289

1506 Capital Ave.
Plano, Texas 75074

Printed in the United States of America

ISBN 1-55622-104-5

10 9 8 7 6 5 4 3 2 1
V8902

All inquiries for volume purchases of this book should be addressed to Wordware Publishing, Inc., at the above address. Telephone inquiries may be made by calling:

(214) 423-0090

Contents

Contents Continued

Recommended Learning Sequence

Recommended Learning Sequence (Cont.)

Module 1
ABOUT THIS BOOK

INTRODUCTION

Illustrated Ventura 2.0 is a reference and self-instruction book for Xerox Ventura Publisher 2.0, an electronic page composition program for PC-DOS-, MS-DOS-, and OS/2-compatible computers. This book is designed for a wide range of Xerox Ventura Publisher users—first time users who want to learn Xerox Ventura Publisher from the very beginning, experienced users who need an easy-to-use reference containing examples of every Xerox Ventura Publisher command, and classroom instructors who want an instructionally designed text for Xerox Ventura Publisher.

ORGANIZATION OF MODULES

Illustrated Ventura 2.0 is divided into 78 modules. The first three modules contain a general introduction to Xerox Ventura Publisher 2.0.

Module 1 describes how to use this book as a reference manual or a self-instructing educational handbook. *Illustrated Ventura 2.0* can also be used as a textbook in a classroom environment.

Module 2 contains an overview of Xerox Ventura Publisher. With text, pictures, and illustrations, this module describes the features of Xerox Ventura Publisher. This module also demonstrates how all the pieces of a Xerox Ventura Publisher document fit together. The description places emphasis on the use of Xerox Ventura Publisher's frames and style sheets, as these two features control the power and usefulness of the program. To master these two main concepts is to master Xerox Ventura Publisher. Although there are many other things to learn about using the program, once you master the principle of using Xerox Ventura Publisher's frames and style sheets, you will find your work with the program to be much smoother and faster. Module 2 also discusses the user interface with the program, which is how you communicate and control Ventura's various commands. You will learn about using the mouse, pull-down menus, dialog boxes, and control keys. Although this may seem elementary, it is important to master this information if you are ever to become proficient at using Xerox Ventura Publisher.

Module 3 presents a sample session with Xerox Ventura Publisher. Easy-to-follow step-by-step instructions take you on a tour through Xerox Ventura Publisher. This module leads you through the creation, saving, editing, and printing of an entire document.

Modules 4 through 78 are self-contained descriptions of each Xerox Ventura Publisher command and feature. The modules are in alphabetical sequence for easy reference. You can follow the Recommended Learning Sequence for a step-by-step learning guide through the program. After completing the Recommended Learning Sequence, this book can then be used as a reference guide.

Appendix A contains a glossary of terms and definitions for quick reference. Most of the terms listed in the glossary are not covered by their own module within this book.

Appendixes B, C, D, and E provide additional information and reference resources for you when using Xerox Ventura Publisher.

Appendix F is provided for both classroom and self-teaching exercises. It presents questions about each module, which, if correctly answered, indicate you are ready to move on to the next module. Classroom instructors may want to include these as part of assignments. If you are studying alone, these questions will help you realize if you have clearly grasped the important concepts of each module.

CONTENT OF MODULES

Beginning with Module 4, each module follows a consistent format to make this book easy to use. The parts of each module are:

Description
Applications
Typical Operation

The Description section of each module contains general information about a command. The Applications section describes the different ways to use a command. The Typical Operation section contains an example related to the module topic and the learning sequence of this book. Most of the examples provided in the Typical Operations are simple and easy-to-follow, to minimize the amount of time it takes for you to master the program.

Each module provides insight into Xerox Ventura Publisher's use in solving practical, everyday publishing problems or needs. Hundreds of useful examples and illustrations are presented within the Description, Applications, and Typical Operation sections of the modules. These examples help you master Xerox Ventura Publisher quickly.

By first following these examples, you will be able to design, create, and publish your own documents to meet your own needs. The examples permit you to experiment with the special features of Xerox Ventura Publisher and remove the mystery from what may at first look like difficult, confusing, or impossible operations. As you conduct and learn from the actual hands-on experiments, do not be surprised if you are suddenly having fun with the program. Not only is Xerox Ventura Publisher a powerful page composition program, it is also fun to use, once you master it.

WHAT YOU NEED

To use this book to its greatest potential, you will need a PC-DOS-, MS-DOS-, or OS/2-compatible computer with at least 640 Kbytes of RAM (memory), a fixed disk with at least 7 megabytes of storage capacity available, a high resolution monitor, a graphics board, a mouse, and a current copy of Xerox Ventura Publisher 2.0. In addition to this minimum hardware configuration, you also need a full featured word processor.

NOTE

Although Xerox Ventura Publisher can be used without a mouse, it is not recommended. Trying to do so greatly decreases your productivity. This book assumes you will be using a mouse, and if you choose not to use a mouse with your computer, you should reconsider that decision.

WHAT YOU SHOULD KNOW

The descriptions and examples in this book assume you know how to use your PC-DOS-, MS-DOS-, or OS/2-compatible computer. You should be familiar with your computer's operating system, the keyboard, and the mouse. You should know simple DOS commands, such as DIR, COPY, REN, and CD \. You should have a good working knowledge of creating, using, removing, and making directories. Further, you should have developed some expertise with at least one powerful word processor, such as WordPerfect, Microsoft Word, WordStar, XyWrite, or DisplayWrite 4. If you know all of these things, you are ready to proceed with Xerox Ventura Publisher. If not, you should read the appropriate user manuals, or refer to the related book in the Illustrated series from WordWare Publishing, Inc. before attempting to move on to Xerox Ventura Publisher.

PROPER INSTALLATION

In Module 2, information is provided about how to install Xerox Ventura Publisher. To use this book, you must have first properly installed the program. In addition, it is assumed that you have installed and still have on your hard disk the sample documents and chapters that are included with your copy of Xerox Ventura Publisher 2.0. These documents should be located in the TYPESET directory. These samples are the files and documents that are used in the Typical Operation sections of the modules.

NOTE

If you have altered, changed, or deleted these original samples supplied by Xerox, you should copy them from diskette #4 into the TYPESET directory. To do so, insert diskette #4 in the A drive, and at any DOS prompt, type: COPY A:*.* C:\TYPESET

THE THREE XEROX VENTURA PUBLISHER PRODUCTS

With the release of Xerox Ventura Publisher 2.0, there are now three versions of the product available. They are Xerox Ventura Publisher 2.0, Xerox Ventura Publisher 2.0 Professional Extension, and Xerox Ventura Publisher 2.0: Network Server. No matter which version of Xerox Ventura Publisher 2.0 you might be using, this book will get you started.

Appendix F provides additional information about Xerox Ventura Publisher 2.0 Professional Extension.

For your information, the Xerox Corporation attained the rights to distribute and market the program, and accordingly, that is why it is called Xerox Ventura Publisher.

Should you be using a release of Xerox Ventura Publisher earlier than 2.0, you may still find this book helpful, particularly in the beginning modules. Many of the basic features and modes are the same from the earlier to later releases. Some of the more advanced features, however, are not available on earlier releases of Xerox Ventura Publisher.

Module 2
XEROX VENTURA PUBLISHER OVERVIEW

XEROX VENTURA PUBLISHER AND DESKTOP PUBLISHING

Xerox Ventura Publisher is a high-end desktop publishing computer program. Today, the term "desktop publishing" is a muddied, confused phrase and means many different things to many different people. Even some high-end word processors are now self-proclaimed desktop publishing packages.

This book was prepared with the approach that desktop publishing refers to the use of a personal computer to create near-typeset-quality documents that are "camera-ready." In other words, the documents you create with Xerox Ventura Publisher are of such high quality that they will look like they were created with a commercial typesetter and are ready to be turned over to a printer, so they can be mass reproduced. Sometimes, the mass reproduction is done with a printing press, and other times, the reproduction may be done with a standard photocopying machine.

Desktop publishing is also called *electronic page composition*. Xerox Ventura Publisher was designed to be the electronic equivalent of the layout table used by a graphic artist. Xerox Ventura Publisher contains many different types of tools that allow you to perform the electronic composition of your documents. Some of these tools are equivalent to the tools used by graphic design layout artists and designers as well as typographers. And, in some special instances, these electronic tools permit you to create documents that will have a better appearance than if they were produced by traditional methods. If you are currently using a typewriter or a computer and dot matrix or letter-quality printer, you will be amazed and more than satisfied with the new quality appearance of your documents.

By using Xerox Ventura Publisher to produce these materials, you save time (by eliminating the waiting period when you send your job to a typesetter for completion), and you cut costs (by eliminating the expense of commercial typesetting). You can produce a wide array of documents—everything from raffle tickets to books, from business reports to luxurious sales brochures. You will soon be able to produce just about any type of document you may want or need—the only thing that limits you when using Xerox Ventura Publisher is your imagination.

One of the very best things about Xerox Ventura Publisher is the simple fact that it is available to everyone. You need not be a graphic designer or a commercial typesetter to create decent, graphically correct documents. Even though you may not have "gifted talents" or the natural ability to design outstanding documents, almost everyone can master the design, layout, and production of basic, high-quality, camera-ready pages.

LEARNING XEROX VENTURA PUBLISHER

Learning Xerox Ventura Publisher takes time, patience, and a willingness to experiment. The program is not intuitive, but if you follow the learning sequence of this book, you will be able to produce documents in a short time.

Xerox Ventura Publisher is not the sort of program in which you can learn only a "few pieces" and then try to pick up the rest later or as you work in a document. You will probably be disappointed with your results if you do not learn most of the features of the program before attempting to produce your own documents. Unlike a word processing program, where you can learn the basics, such as cursor movements, spell checking, printing, and block movements, to effectively use Xerox Ventura Publisher you must learn most of the features of the program first.

If you take the time to learn Xerox Ventura Publisher, it will have taken a lot of effort, but the results you achieve with your document will prove it was worth undertaking.

As mentioned in Module 1, to use Xerox Ventura Publisher effectively, you should be comfortable and experienced with MS-DOS or PC-DOS as well as with one powerful word processor, such as WordPerfect, Microsoft Word, WordStar, XyWrite, or Multimate. Unless you know DOS and a word processor very well, you are limiting your use of Xerox Ventura Publisher.

"WYSIWYG"

Xerox Ventura Publisher offers what is called WYSIWYG (pronounced wizz-ee-wig). The term WYSIWYG is an acronym which stands for "What You See Is What You Get." It means that what you see on your screen is what you get when you print your document. Although this is the principal of how Xerox Ventura Publisher works, there is no such thing as true WYSIWYG. Since the method of displaying graphics and text on your screen is different from the technique used to print them, and because of the differences between your screen and printer resolution (the number of dots per inch is different on each), there is no true WYSIWYG.

So what you see on your screen is not what you will really get, but it will be fairly close. Do not be surprised if you find some differences between what you create on your screen and what you receive from your printer. But in most cases, it will approach WYSIWYG.

Xerox Ventura Publisher 2.0 drives and supports color displays if your computer equipment includes a color monitor and a VGA, EGA, or DEB graphics adapter. Of course, even if you are using a monochrome monitor with Xerox Ventura Publisher, the text prints in the chosen color if a color printer is used. The user interface, which means the menus, side bar, rulers, and dialog boxes, displays in monochrome even on a color monitor. Text, graphics, and other page elements appear in the color assigned to each.

PRINTER LIMITATIONS

Most laser printers are not capable of printing to the edge of the standard size paper. Accordingly, if you place text, pictures, or graphics near the edge of the page, they may not print properly, even though they show correctly on the screen. In the next module, you will be instructed to print a file called CAPABILI.CHP so you can see exactly what your printer can and cannot do.

INSTALLING XEROX VENTURA PUBLISHER

Before you can begin the sample session or the learning sequence presented in this book, you must make certain that Xerox Ventura Publisher has been properly installed on your computer. It must be installed for your individual system, including the type of monitor, graphics adapter board, mouse, and printer you have.

If you have not yet installed Xerox Ventura Publisher, you should do so now. Before starting the installation, you should:

- Make backup copies of your master disks received in the Xerox Ventura Publisher package. Read the Software License and Warranty Agreement included within your copy of Xerox Ventura Publisher to understand the legal restrictions governing copying and installing Xerox Ventura Publisher.
- Be aware of the type of computer hardware you will be using. You must know what type of printer you will be using, what type of graphics board is installed within your computer, and how your mouse is installed.
- Make sure you have between 4 and 5 megabytes of space on your computer's hard disk to hold all the printer fonts, screen fonts, program software, and examples provided with Xerox Ventura Publisher. You will use another 1 to 3 megabytes for the program (depending on the type and number of printers installed). You should have another 2 or 3 megabytes available to hold document files and any additional fonts you might add later.
- Make sure MS-DOS or PC-DOS version 2.10 or higher has been installed on your computer.

You can proceed with the installation by inserting the Xerox Ventura Publisher Disk #1 into the A drive. Close the drive door, type A:VPPREP, and press Enter. If you must use the B drive because of incompatible disk size on your A drive, type B:VPPREP B: and you can install Xerox Ventura Publisher from the B drive.

When the Installation screen appears, answer the questions and follow the instructions. You will be making selections by typing individual letters. After you have told Xerox Ventura Publisher what type of system you are using, you will then be instructed to insert some of the disks into your drive so the files can be copied. Simply follow Xerox Ventura Publisher's instructions, and within 15 to 20 minutes, the installation will be complete.

CHECKING YOUR INSTALLATION

The instructions in this book assume you are using a standard Xerox Ventura Publisher installation, which includes two standard Ventura directories, VENTURA and TYPESET. Xerox Ventura Publisher places the programs and associated files in the VENTURA directory and places the style sheets and sample text and graphic files in the TYPESET directory. Check whether these directories are on your hard disk by typing DIR at the DOS command line.

Also, make sure you have a copy of the original default style sheet called DEFAULT.STY installed in the TYPESET directory. If you have altered or changed this style sheet, then recopy it from the working copy master diskette into the TYPESET directory.

STARTING XEROX VENTURA PUBLISHER

Before starting Xerox Ventura Publisher, make sure you are logged on to your computer's hard drive (usually C), and you have changed to the root directory. To do this:

1. Type **C:** and press **Enter**.
2. Type **CD** \ and press **Enter**. (Make sure you typed \ and not /.)

To begin running Xerox Ventura Publisher,

1. Type **VP**.
2. Press **Enter**.

Depending on your computer, Xerox Ventura Publisher takes anywhere from 10 to 60 seconds to load.

You can also specify the name of a chapter to open when you start Xerox Ventura Publisher. You type the name of the chapter, as well as the directory where it is resting, on the same line as the VP command. For example, to open SCOOP.CHP located on the C drive in the TYPESET directory, you type: VP C:\TYPESET\SCOOP.CHP and press Enter.

Xerox Ventura Publisher can also be run under Microsoft Windows. Before doing so, you should copy the VP.PIF file from the Xerox Ventura Publisher Utilities Disk to the WINDOWS\PIF directory by typing: COPY A:\VP.PIF C:\WINDOWS\PIF

Start Microsoft Windows, and run Xerox Ventura Publisher by double-clicking on the VP.PIF in the WINDOWS\PIF directory.

XEROX VENTURA PUBLISHER MAIN SCREEN

After starting Xerox Ventura Publisher, the first thing you see is the main screen:

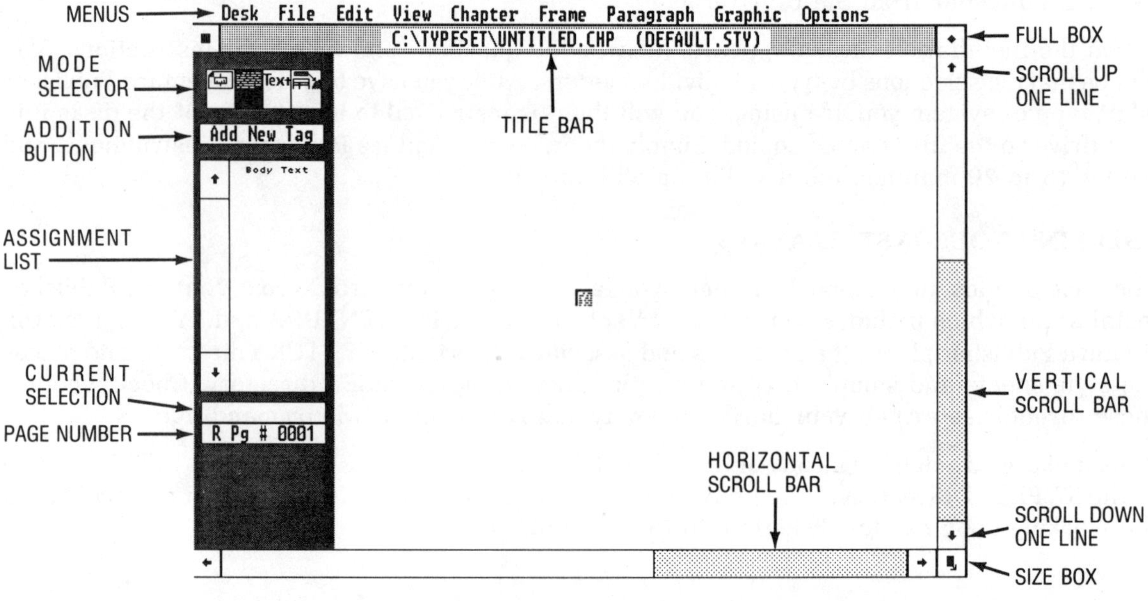

This screen provides the user interface (how you work with, command, and control Xerox Ventura Publisher).

The parts of the screen are:

1. Menus — At the top of your computer screen, the various menu names are displayed. When you point the mouse cursor at one of the menu names, the menu drops down. As you move the mouse cursor down through the menu, the available menu options change appearance from black on white to white on black. This reverse highlighting indicates that the item is available for selection.

2. Title Bar — Located just below the menu names, the Title Bar displays the name of the current Xerox Ventura Publisher document and the name of the current style sheet.

3. Full Box — Located in the upper right corner, this feature returns Xerox Ventura Publisher to the full screen size. (Xerox Ventura Publisher appears in a window on the screen, much like programs do in Microsoft Windows applications.) Although Xerox Ventura Publisher uses a different graphics environment called GEM, the window can be sized.

4. Scroll Up One Line — Located just below the Full Box, this feature moves the screen up over the page in increments of approximately one line at a time. Point the mouse cursor to this feature and click once to move the screen one line. To continue scrolling, press and hold the mouse button until the display is where you want it, then let go. For large screen movements, use the Vertical Scroll Bar.

5. Vertical Scroll Bar — Located on the right side of the screen, the Vertical Scroll Bar moves the screen up or down over the page. The grayish area in the scroll bar indicates the portion of the page that is not visible. Move the mouse cursor to the scroll bar and press and hold the mouse button to drag the scroll bar up or down, depending on which direction you want the screen to move over the page. When you see the area of the page that you want, release the mouse button. You can also reposition the page by moving the mouse cursor to the gray area in the scroll bar and clicking once. The page will move approximately one screen length. (This operation is quite similar to using PgDn in most word processing programs.)

6. Scroll Down One Line — This works like Scroll Up One Line, described before, except that the screen moves down.

7. Size Box

Located in the lower right corner, this feature adjusts the screen size within Xerox Ventura Publisher. Just like the Full Box, within the current release of Xerox Ventura Publisher, the Size Box command has no pertinent application since you will want to always have the screen adjusted to it largest, full size.

8. Horizontal Scroll Bar

This works like the Vertical Scroll Bar, except it moves the screen horizontally.

9. Mode Selector

Located in the Side Bar, the Mode Selector consists of four icons (pictures) in the upper left corner of the screen. These icons represent the four major operating modes and indicate which is currently enabled and ready for use. You can also change modes by clicking on the icons. The modes are Frame Setting, Paragraph Tagging, Text Editing, and Graphic Drawing. The operation of each of these major modes is described in detail in later modules.

10. Addition Button

Also located in the Side Bar, the Addition Button is positioned just below the Mode Selector. This button allows you to add additional frames, paragraph tags, or text attributes, depending on which mode is selected. Activate the button by moving the mouse cursor to it and clicking once, or by pressing Ctrl-2.

11. Assignment List

Located within the Side Bar below the Addition Button, the Assignment List shows the items that can be assigned to whatever you have selected in the main screen area. In the Frame Setting mode, a list of text and graphic files is displayed. In the Paragraph Tagging mode, a list of tags for the current style sheet is displayed. Text Attributes are listed when in the Text Editing mode. The Assignment List is replaced with graphic drawing tools when the Graphic Drawing mode has been selected. The operation of the scroll bar within the Assignment List is the same as the Vertical Scroll Bar previously described.

12. Current Selection

Also located within the Side Bar, just below the Assignment List, the Current Selection indicator displays which item from the Assignment List is currently assigned to a specific frame, paragraph, text, or graphic that you have selected.

13. Page Number

Located at the bottom of the Side Bar, this shows the page number of the currently displayed page and if the page is a left or right page.

USING THE MOUSE

A mouse is a computer peripheral that connects to your computer. It is called a mouse because it has a long thin wire that looks like a mouse tail which attaches to your computer. A mouse is small and fits within your hand. It is electronically attached to a pointer on the computer screen. The shape of the pointer or cursor on the screen is determined by which Xerox Ventura Publisher function you are currently using. There are currently 13 different shapes for the mouse cursor. They are:

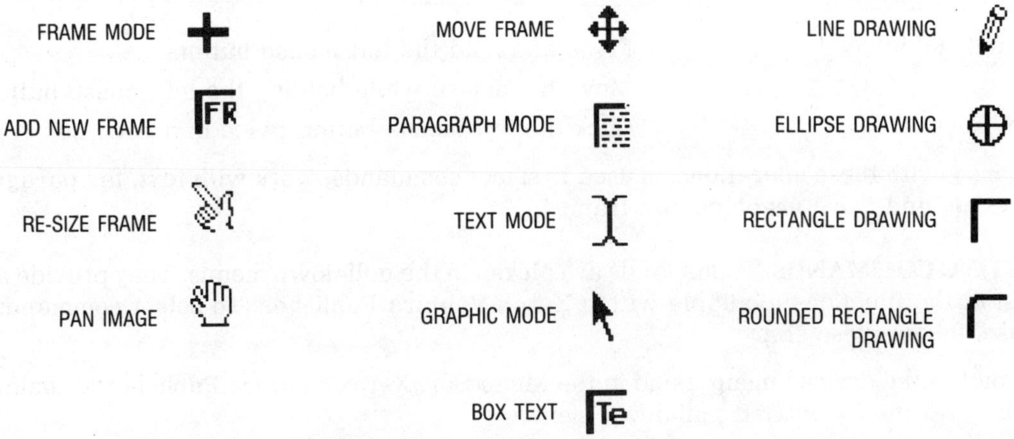

To operate a mouse, you move it around on a flat surface near your computer. Either a ball attached to tiny sensors or a light-emitting diode within the mouse tells the computer which way the mouse is moving. Each time you move the mouse, the pointer or mouse cursor on the screen moves in the same direction.

The mouse has two separate functions within Xerox Ventura Publisher. They are:

- Move the mouse cursor to items on the screen that you want to select and use
- Draw frames and graphics

To select items with the mouse, simply move the mouse cursor to anywhere within the item, and click the left mouse button once. Exact or precise placement of the mouse cursor is not critical as long as the cursor lies within the item you have selected. Pressing the mouse button twice in a row, very quickly, is equivalent to selecting the item and then selecting OK. This is also called a *double click*.

There are five basic operations you do to make the mouse work. They are:

Point	Move the mouse until the pointer rests on an item you want to select or choose.
Click	Press and release the left mouse button.

NOTE

If your mouse has multiple buttons, only the left button works with Xerox Ventura Publisher.

Click and Hold	Press and hold the left mouse button.
Drag	Move the mouse while holding the left mouse button.
Double Click	Click the left mouse button twice in a row.

The mouse, with these operations, is used to select commands, work with text, tag paragraphs, size, resize, and move graphics and frames.

SELECTING COMMANDS Commands are picked in the pull-down menus. They provide access to most of the functions available within Xerox Ventura Publisher. To select commands with a mouse, follow these steps:

1. Point to the desired menu name in the Menu Bar. Xerox Ventura Publisher automatically displays the associated pull-down menu.
2. Move the mouse cursor down through the various options on the menu until you are pointing at the command you want to execute.
3. Click the left mouse button once to finish the selection process.

The following illustration depicts selecting an item within a pull-down menu:

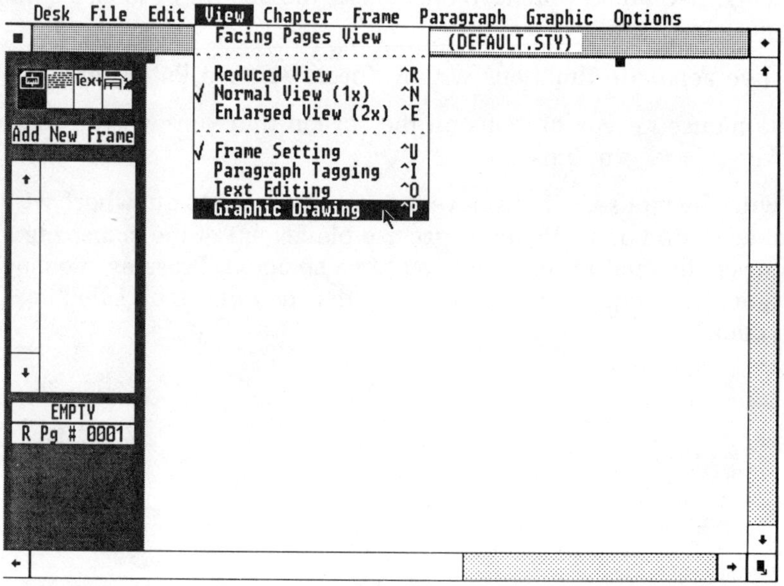

DRAWING, RESIZING, AND MOVING FRAMES Frames hold either text or graphics. In most cases, the text has been imported from a file previously created in a word processor, but text can also be typed directly into a frame within Xerox Ventura Publisher. However, graphics placed within a frame must always be imported into Xerox Ventura Publisher from a graphics file. Frames are easily drawn, resized, and moved. To work with frames, first choose the Frame mode. The mouse cursor changes to its Frame selection shape.

To draw a frame:

1. Click on the Addition button in the Side Bar to select Add New Frame.
2. Point to the position where you want the upper left corner of the frame.
3. Click and hold the mouse button.
4. Drag the mouse cursor to the position where you want the lower right corner of the frame.
5. Release the mouse button.

Your screen will resemble this illustration:

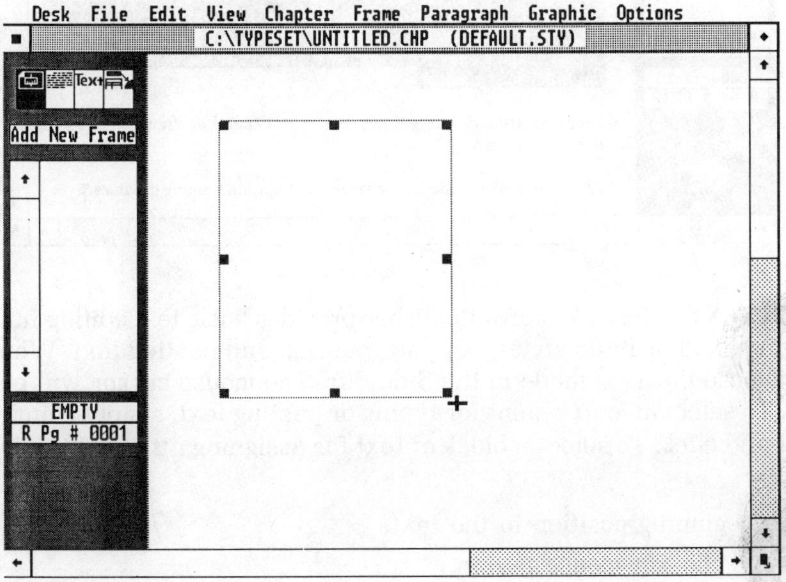

WORKING WITH PARAGRAPH TAGS Paragraph tags are used to define the appearance of any paragraph. In Xerox Ventura Publisher, a paragraph is any text that ends with a required carriage return (which is entered whenever you press Enter.) To tag a paragraph, first choose the Paragraph Tag mode in the Side Bar. The mouse will change to its paragraph tagging shape. Then move the mouse to any point within the paragraph, and click the left mouse button once. The entire paragraph is displayed in reverse or highlighted background and the current tag name is identified in the Current Selection within the Side Bar.

You can select additional paragraphs for the same tag by pressing and holding Shift, then pointing to the next paragraph to be tagged, and clicking the left mouse button. This procedure can be continued until you have selected all the paragraphs you need to change. The word Multiple appears in the Current Selection within the Side Bar. You can then work with all the selected paragraphs at one time, rather than selecting each individually.

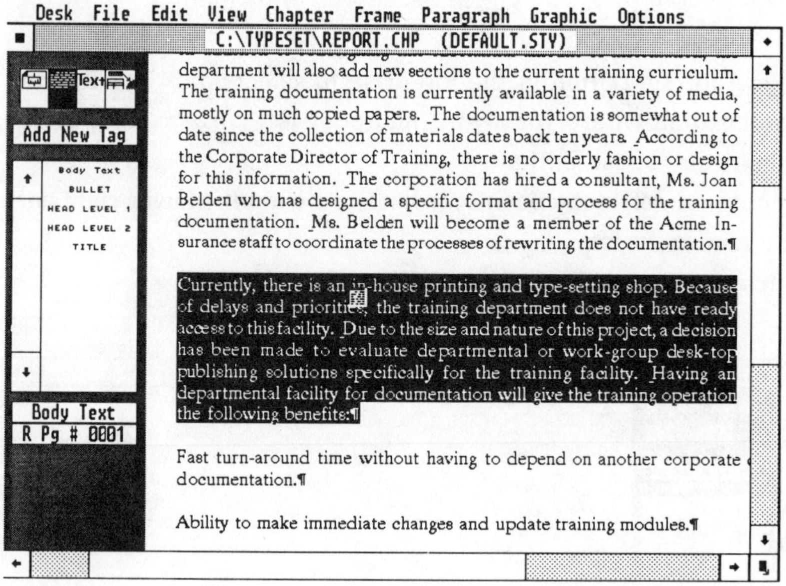

WORKING WITH TEXT Xerox Ventura Publisher provides basic text editing functions including adding text, adding bold or italic styles, copying, cutting, and pasting text. When working with your text, first choose the Text mode in the Side Bar. The mouse cursor will change to its text selection shape. To select an entry point for typing or pasting text, simply point to the beginning place in the text and click. To select a block of text for assigning attributes, copying, or cutting, follow these steps:

1. Point to the beginning position in the text.
2. Click and hold the left mouse button.
3. Drag the mouse point to the ending position within the text. As you drag the pointer, Xerox Ventura Publisher shows the selected text by displaying it on a highlighted background. You can only select text that is displayed on the screen. You cannot select text that is not on the screen, as Xerox Ventura Publisher does not automatically scroll forward or backward.
4. Release the left mouse button.

When text has been selected, your screen will look like this:

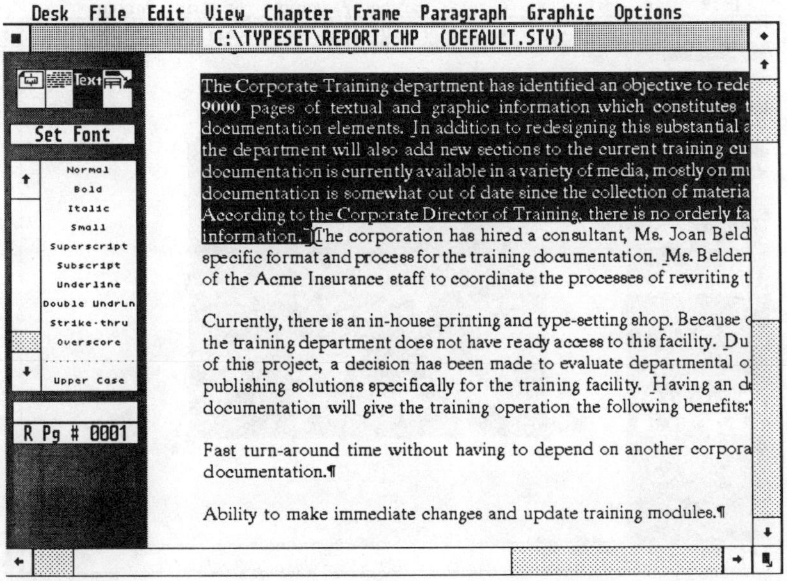

Once the text is selected, the attributes of the text can be changed, deleted, or pasted.

DRAWING, RESIZING, AND MOVING GRAPHICS Graphics consist of boxes, circles, and lines you draw within Xerox Ventura Publisher to enhance the graphic design of your pages. To work with Xerox Ventura Publisher's graphics, first choose the Graphic Drawing mode in the Side Bar. The mouse cursor will change to a pointer. Select one of the graphic drawing tools in the Side Bar. The mouse cursor will change to match the tool selected.

To draw a box, circle, or line:

1. Select on the graphic drawing tools.
2. Point to the position where you want the upper left corner of the graphic.
3. Click and hold the left mouse button.
4. Drag the mouse cursor to the position where you want the lower right corner of the graphic.
5. Release the left mouse button.

After drawing a box, your screen looks like this:

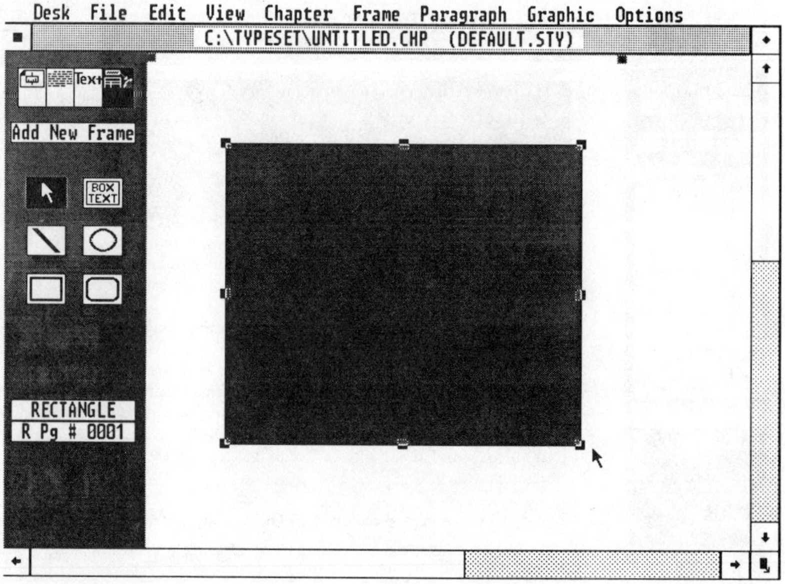

To resize a box, circle, or line:

1. Point to the object you want to resize.
2. Click the left mouse button. Eight dark boxes appear around the edge of the object. The corner boxes permit you to resize the height and width of the box or circle at the same time, while the edge boxes allow you to push or pull the edge of the box or circle to resize it. If the box, circle, or line is extremely small, you may only see the corner boxes.
3. Point to one of the boxes around the edge of the object.
4. Click and hold the left mouse button.
5. Drag the pointer to the new position where you want the corner or edge of the box, circle, or frame.

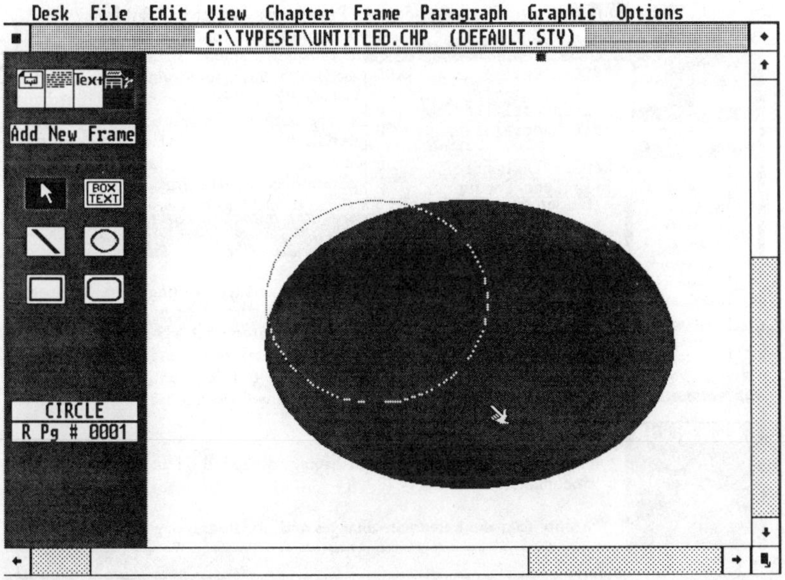

6. Release the left mouse button.

To move a graphic:

1. Point the mouse cursor to the object you want to move.
2. Click and hold the left mouse button. The mouse cursor will change shape.
3. Drag the object to the new position.
4. Release the mouse button.

USING THE PULL-DOWN MENUS

Xerox Ventura Publisher's pull-down menus are the primary means of selecting commands. The following menu names are listed at the top of your computer screen:

Desk	Frame
File	Paragraph
Edit	Graphic
View	Options
Chapter	

When you point the mouse cursor at a menu name, Xerox Ventura Publisher displays the entire pull-down menu. Some items in the menu are solid black, while others are gray. The items displayed in solid black are available as commands. The items displayed in gray are not available in the current mode, but are available when Xerox Ventura Publisher is operating under a different mode. In the following illustration, only Cut Text, Copy Text, and Edit Special Item are available:

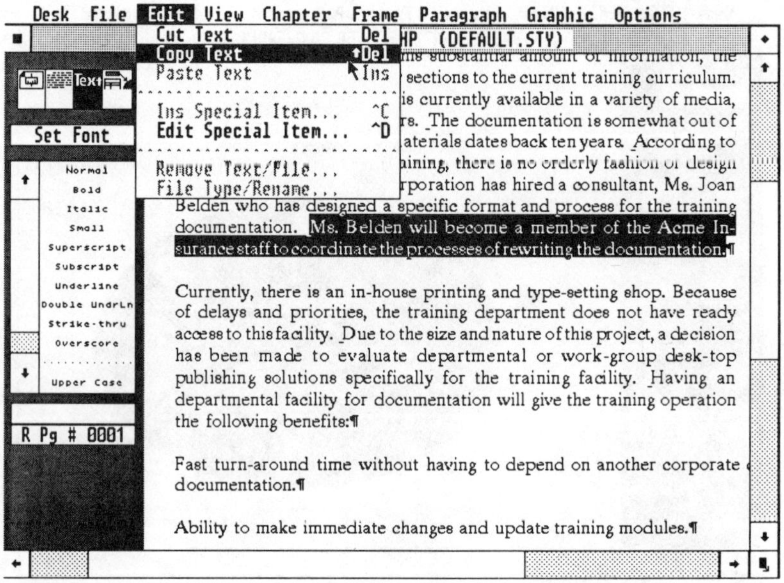

Some of the items on some menus also have keyboard equivalents. Some commands can be executed by pressing Ctrl in combination with other keys. For example, Ctrl-S executes the Save command without using the mouse to make the selection in the File menu.

For a complete list of the various keyboard shortcuts available within Xerox Ventura Publisher, see Appendix D.

SCROLLING AROUND THE PAGE

Xerox Ventura Publisher lets you view the screen in three different sizes: reduced, normal, and enlarged. In the normal and enlarged views, Xerox Ventura Publisher shows only part of the page. To see the other parts of the page, it is necessary to use the scroll bars. To scroll up or down, click on the scroll bar or scroll arrows on the right edge of your computer screen. To scroll to the left or right, click on the scroll bar or scroll arrows on the bottom edge of the screen. You can also click in the gray area of the scroll bar to move the screen a fixed amount with each click. You can click and hold in the solid area of the scroll bar and then drag the mouse to move the screen the amount you want to move it. You can also scroll up one line or down one line by clicking on the Scroll Up or Scroll Down One Line Arrows at the ends of the Vertical Scroll Bar.

USING VENTURA'S DIALOG BOXES

Although some of the menu options within Xerox Ventura Publisher function as simple commands which are executed as soon as you select them, many menu options contain features that require you to specify additional information. To allow you to do so, Xerox Ventura Publisher displays a dialog box.

The following illustration depicts a typical Xerox Ventura Publisher dialog box:

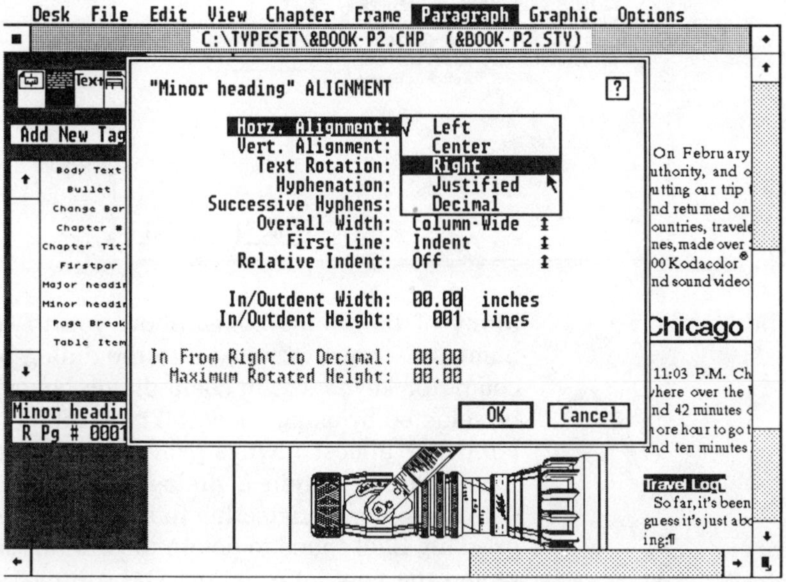

In a dialog box, there can be any one or a combination of the following types of controls and features:

Button Controls — These controls work much like the push buttons on a car radio. You can select any of a series of rectangular boxes. When you make a new selection, the previous selection or button is disabled and no longer active.

Measurement Controls — The measurement system for a dialog box can be changed within each dialog box. When a dialog box allows you to enter a unit of measure, you can change the units of measure by moving the mouse cursor to the word that describes the measurement and clicking the mouse. Each click of the mouse will present another unit of measure. The available units are inches, picas and points, fractional points, and centimeters.

Pop-Up Menus — This is a new feature of Xerox Ventura Publisher 2.0 that was not available in earlier versions of the program. These menus pop up whenever you choose a dialog box option which is followed by the ↕ symbol. Pop-up menus show all the available options for the feature you want to change. You can select only one option from the list that appears in a pop-up menu. This illustration depicts a pop-up menu that has been selected:

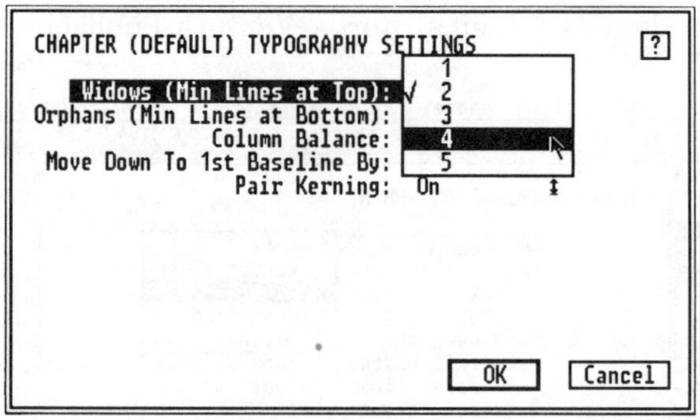

Entering Text and Numbers

Many of the dialog boxes allow you to specify text and numbers. They are typed into the dialog box by using the computer keyboard. In some dialog boxes, some text can be selected by using the scroll bar method. Xerox Ventura Publisher almost always provides a default value in the type-in areas within a dialog box. You can change the default values by selecting the entry area with the mouse, pressing Backspace to delete the default setting, and then typing the new information. Or, you can select the entry area with the mouse, press Esc once to clear the default settings, and then type the new information. A third method of deleting and typing text in a dialog box is to select the entry area with the mouse, use the left or right arrow keys to position the cursor at the edit point (this cannot be done with the mouse), and type the new information on top of the default, deleting any additional text with either Backspace or Delete.

Help Menus

This is another new feature available in Xerox Ventura Publisher 2.0. Help menus and associated help screens provide on-line assistance concerning the functions and operations of each feature within Xerox Ventura Publisher. Help is accessed by clicking on the ? in the upper right corner of a dialog box. The following illustration depicts a Xerox Ventura Publisher Help screen:

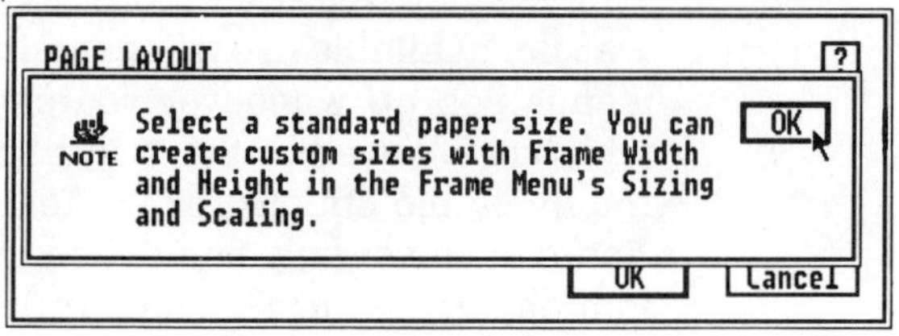

To accept the new settings in a dialog box, move the mouse cursor to the box labeled OK and press the left mouse button. Or, you can press Enter on the keyboard, which is equivalent to selecting OK with the mouse.

To cancel the new settings in a dialog box, move the cursor to the box labeled Cancel and press the left mouse button. Or, you can press Ctrl-X (press and hold Ctrl while you type X) to cancel the new settings. None of the changes will take effect.

PRINTING MEASUREMENTS

In printing, *points* and *picas* are the standard. For those not familiar with points and picas, there are 12 points to a pica, and there are 6 picas to an inch. Accordingly, there are 72 points to an inch. So 6 picas and 72 points each equal one inch.

When setting measurements in picas in Xerox Ventura Publisher, the numbers to the left of the comma are picas and to the right of the comma are points. Thus to set 5 picas and 3 points, type 5,03.

If you were to type 2,12, Xerox Ventura Publisher would change your setting to 3,00, since 2 picas and 12 points actually equals 3 picas.

Sometimes, you may see a tilde character (~) appear in a measurement setting within a dialog box. The reason for this is that the setting is too large to be displayed in the chosen measurement unit. For example, if you set the top margin to 3.00 inches and then change your measurement units to fractional points, you will see only ~ ~ . ~ ~ because three inches is larger than 99.99 points, the largest setting possible with the fractional points measurement unit. When these characters are displayed (~ ~ . ~ ~) the settings are not lost or discarded by Xerox Ventura Publisher. To see them, change the measurement unit to another setting.

STYLE SHEETS

Xerox Ventura Publisher uses *style sheets* to control the appearance of your documents. By mastering the use of Xerox Ventura Publisher's style sheets, you will be able to easily control the appearance of your documents, especially when similar documents need to be produced. For example, if you were to use Xerox Ventura Publisher to produce a magazine, each issue of the magazine would look similar to the others because the same style sheet would be used, the headlines, body text, bylines, justification, line spacing, and so on would always be the same.

You will learn more about Xerox Ventura Publisher's style sheets in later modules, but remember now that by using them, your documents will develop a consistent appearance.

This diagram depicts how a style sheet fits into the Xerox Ventura Publisher document.

XEROX VENTURA PUBLISHER MODES OF OPERATION

One of the sometimes confusing concepts of Xerox Ventura Publisher is the program's use of Modes of Operation. There are four modes of operation, Frame Setting, Paragraph Tagging, Text Editing, and Graphic Drawing mode. In addition, under Xerox Ventura Publisher Version 2.0 Professional Extension, a fifth mode has been added, called Table Edit. For more information about the Professional Extension, see Appendix F.

These modes of operation determine which mouse cursor will be available and which commands can be executed. For example, when in the Text Editing mode, you cannot move or resize a frame. Rather, you would need to leave the Text Editing mode by selecting the Frame mode. Then you could move or resize the frame as well as complete any other command dealing with frames.

You can select a mode of operation in the Side Bar with the mouse, in the View menu, or by entering keyboard commands.

FITTING IT ALL TOGETHER

Each Xerox Ventura Publisher document is comprised of several files. The complete document is called a *chapter*.

Since many different files can make up a Xerox Ventura Publisher chapter, the file that directs, or controls, the final output of the document to the printer is the *chapter file*. Xerox Ventura Publisher creates this file, and it is always assigned the extension .CHP. Each chapter file contains a link, or directions, to Xerox Ventura Publisher, telling the program where to look for the various files that make up the Chapter.

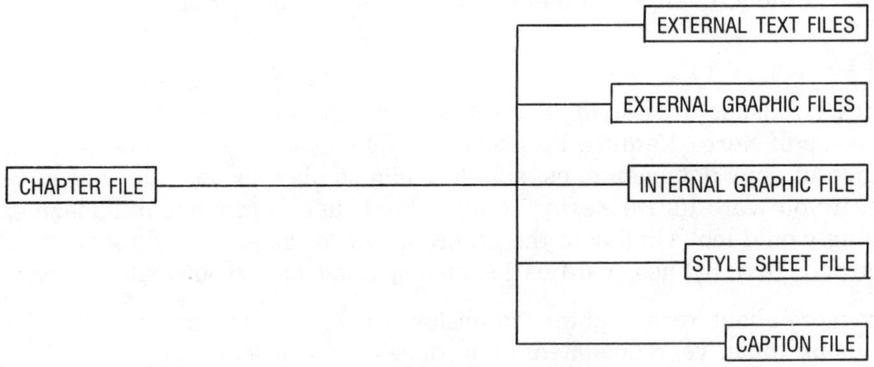

As you can see from reviewing this illustration, many different files are connected or linked to the chapter file. External text and graphic files (those created outside of Xerox Ventura Publisher and imported into the program) are used, as well as files created within Xerox Ventura Publisher. The style sheet file, caption file, and internal graphics file are created within Xerox Ventura Publisher. The style sheet file contains the paragraph tag information. The caption file contains the frame information, including the frame text. The internal graphics file contains the graphics created within the Xerox Ventura Publisher Graphic Drawing mode.

Since the chapter file acts as a director of the various files used to make the final Xerox Ventura Publisher document, all the various files need not be located in any single directory or subdirectory. The chapter file will direct Xerox Ventura Publisher to go to different directories or drives to get the documents required to create the final document. In addition, you can continue to edit or modify the files used within the final document after they have been merged into Xerox Ventura Publisher. For example, no matter how much a graphic has been scaled, resized, or distorted, the original graphic file remains unchanged by Xerox Ventura Publisher.

Module 3
SAMPLE SESSION

INTRODUCTION

Using Xerox Ventura Publisher becomes easy once you have mastered the concepts of using a computer to do page composition. You will also have to learn how to use Xerox Ventura Publisher's various modes, how to enter commands, and how to work with Xerox Ventura Publisher's style sheets. This module is intended to provide a tour through Xerox Ventura Publisher 2.0 and to let you practice using the mouse and entering commands.

CREATE A TEXT FILE WITH YOUR WORD PROCESSOR

Xerox Ventura Publisher has a text editing function, but its word processing capabilities are very limited. Using Xerox Ventura Publisher as a word processor is never recommended. In fact, if you do, you will be disappointed with the results and the limited power of Ventura's text editing function. The program was never intended to be a word processor, rather, it was designed to be used as a page composition program. Accordingly, you should prepare your text with a word processor and import it into Xerox Ventura Publisher.

Review this list:

MicroSoft Word	.DOC
Multimate	.DOC
WordPerfect (4.2 and 5.0)	.WP
Wordstar	.WS
Wordstar UK	.TXT
Xerox Writer	.XWP
Xywrite	.TXT

If the word processor you will be using is on the list, you can save your text document in the standard file format of the word processor. Xerox Ventura Publisher can work with the file created by the word processor. If your word processor is not on the list, then you will need to save your text file in either ASCII (.TXT extension) or DCA (.RFT extension).

Type the following text pressing Enter only where <Enter> appears:

> **Here Comes Desktop Publishing!** <Enter>
> **Page Composition by Personal Computer** <Enter>
> **by George Sheldon** <Enter>
> **Just as Morse changed the world of communications with the invention he called the telegraph, desktop publishing is changing the way we communicate today.** <Enter>
> **Being able to use a personal computer linked to a laser printer to produce near-typeset-quality documents is what desktop publishing promises...and delivers!** <Enter>

Name the file DTP and add the proper extension for your word processor format. For example, if you are using WordPerfect as your word processor, name the file DTP.WP. Place the text file, with the proper filename extension, within the TYPESET directory.

REMOVE THE VP.INF FILE

Xerox Ventura Publisher creates a file called VP.INF to hold the default information you were using during your last session in the program. To make this session easier for you to use and to learn, you should start Xerox Ventura Publisher without a VP.INF file in the \VENTURA directory. By deleting VP.INF, you will cause Xerox Ventura Publisher to start with the DEFAULT.STY style sheet and with all the paths, filenames, and file types set with the installation defaults. To remove the VP.INF file:

1. At the DOS command prompt, type **Del C:\VENTURA\VP.INF** and press **Enter.**
2. Xerox Ventura Publisher will automatically recreate this file for you each time you use the program.

START VENTURA

To start Xerox Ventura Publisher, begin at the DOS command prompt:

1. Type **VP** and press **Enter.**
2. The VP command actually starts the program by running VP.BAT, a batch file that was created during the installation process. DOS displays the contents of the batch file on your computer screen for a few moments, and then you will see Xerox Ventura Publisher's main screen. Depending on your computer configuration, it could take up to 60 seconds to see the main screen.

Xerox Ventura Publisher's main screen looks like this illustration:

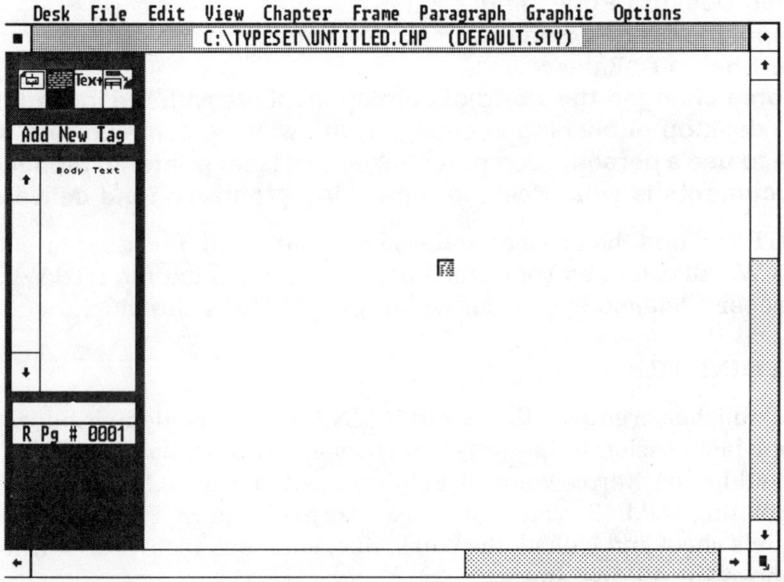

Look at the Title Bar. It shows that you are working with a Ventura file called C: \ TYPESET \ UNTITLED.CHP and that you are using the DEFAULT.STY as your style sheet. (For a detailed description of the parts of this opening screen, see Module 2.)

LOAD THE TEXT FILE

To load the text file that you created with your word processor:

1. Point to the View menu and point to **Frame** setting.

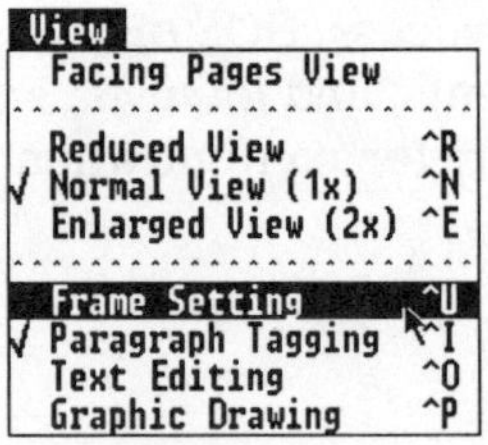

Click the mouse button once to access the Frame Setting mode.

2. Point to the **File** menu and click on **Load Text/Picture**. The Load/Text Picture dialog box is displayed.

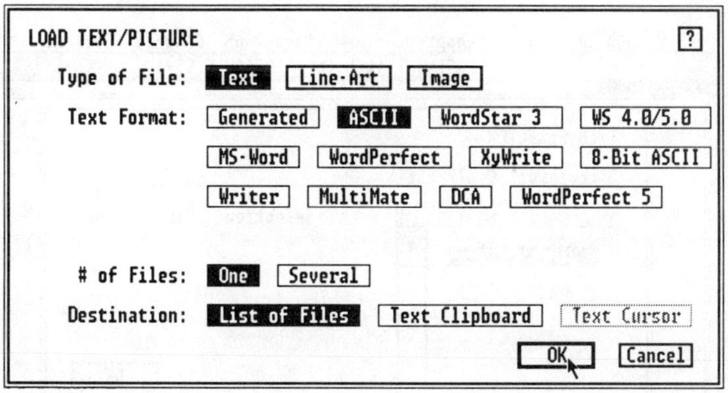

3. Click on **Text** for Type of File, **WordPerfect** (or the word processor you used) for Text Format, and **One** for # of Files.
4. Click **OK** to display the Item Selector dialog box.

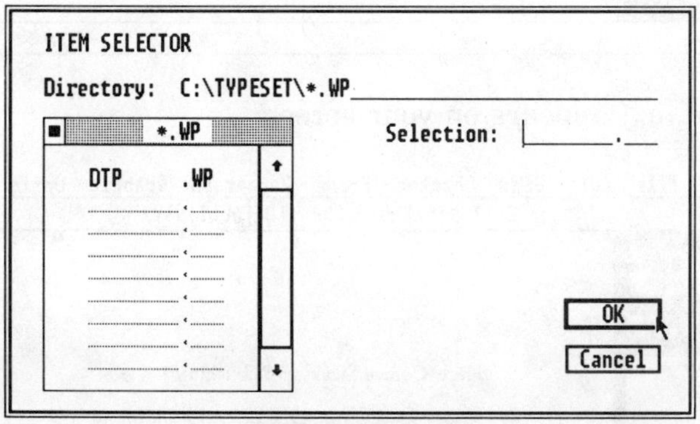

Notice that the Directory entry within the Item Selector dialog box contains the TYPESET path name, the asterisk (*) wild card filename, and the extension associated with the selected word processor file format. The window below the directory displays the list of files with extensions matching the one associated with the word processor file format that was selected.

NOTE

If the path name is not TYPESET, exit from Xerox Ventura Publisher by selecting Quit from the File menu. Delete VP.INF from the VENTURA directory. Be sure that the text file you created is in the TYPESET directory. Start Xerox Ventura Publisher again, repeat steps 1-4 under "load the text file."

5. Click on the text file called DTP.XXX (where XXX is the extension for your particular word processor).
6. Click on **OK**.

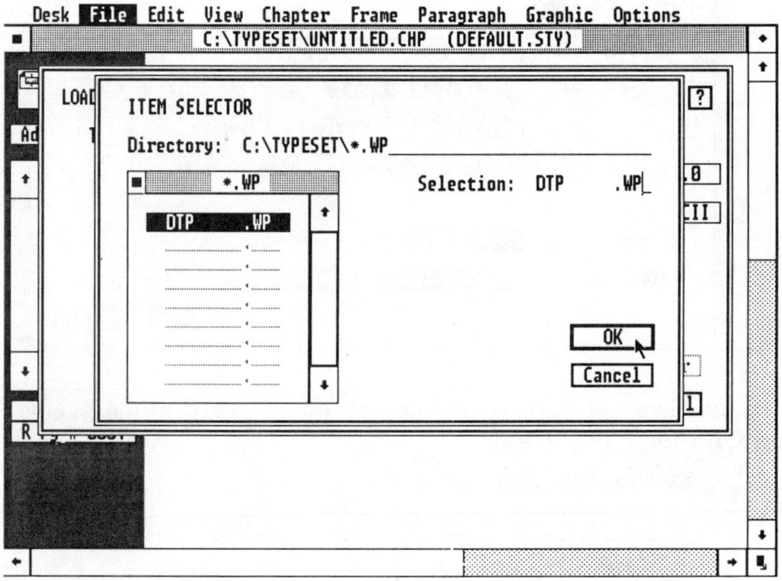

Within a moment, the text appears on your screen:

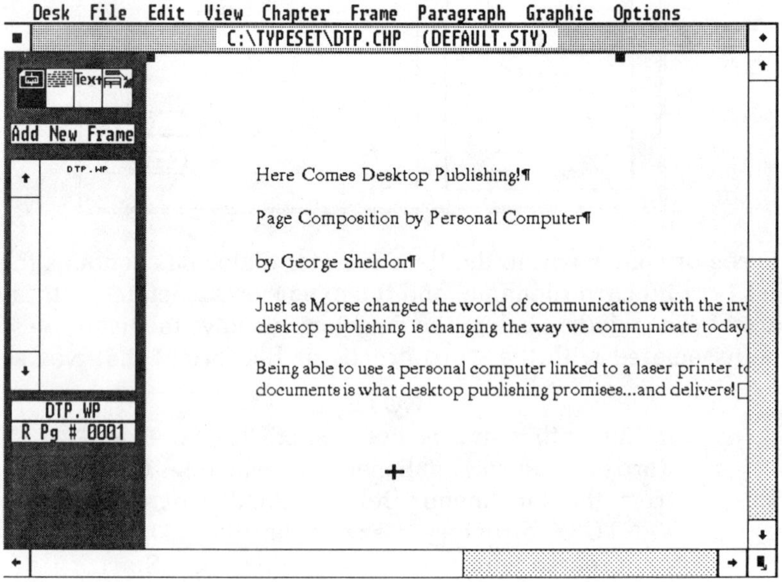

Notice that space appears between the paragraphs, even though there were no blank lines inserted within the text. This space has been created by the paragraph tag for Body Text. Also note that the name of your text file DTP.XXX now appears in the Assignment List within the Side Bar.

NOTE

If the text does not appear on your screen, press Ctrl-U to select the Frame Setting mode. Then click on the middle of the working part of the screen, and click on the name of your text file within the Assignment List. The text should then appear on your computer screen.

7. Press **Ctrl-N** for a normal view of the screen, which will match the illustrations in this module.

SELECT TEXT ATTRIBUTES

To change the attributes of the selected text:

1. Point to the **View** menu and click on **Text Editing** (or press Ctrl-O) to select the Text Editing mode.
2. Select the words **Page Composition by Personal Computer**. To do so, click and hold at the front of the word "Page" and drag to the end of "Computer" and release the mouse button.
3. Point to the Assignment List and click on **Italic**.

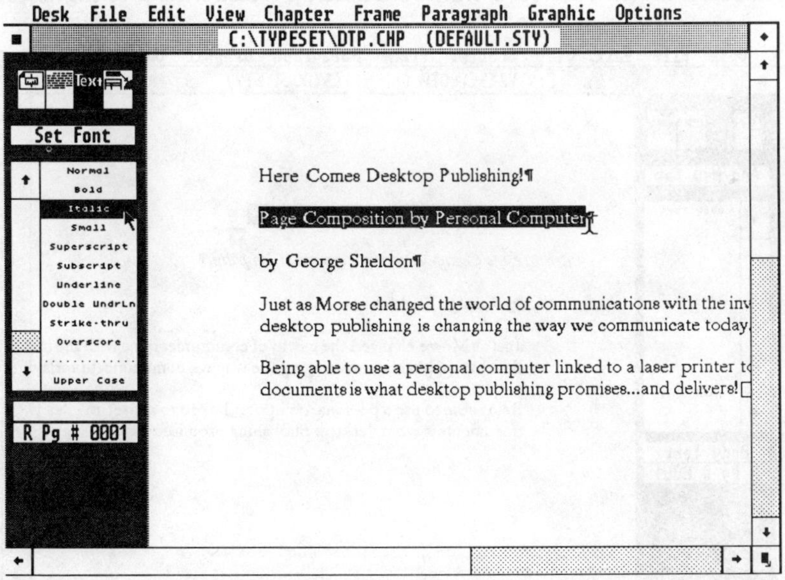

Notice that the text has now changed from normal to italic.

ALTER THE STYLE SHEET

To alter the style sheet:

1. Point to the **View** menu and click on **Paragraph Tagging** (or press Ctrl-I) to select Paragraph Tagging mode.

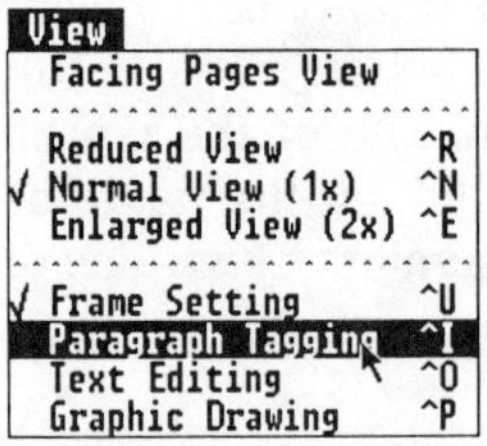

2. Point to the **File** menu and click on **Save As New Style**. Xerox Ventura Publisher displays the Item Selector dialog box.

NOTE
To keep DEFAULT.STY from being altered, it is necessary to create a new style sheet.

3. Type **TEXTDOC1.STY** in the Selection area and press **Enter** or click **OK** to save the new style sheet. Notice that the new style sheet name, TEXTDOC1.STY, is now displayed in the Title Bar on the computer screen.
4. Click anywhere on the words **Here Comes Desktop Publishing!** to highlight the paragraph.

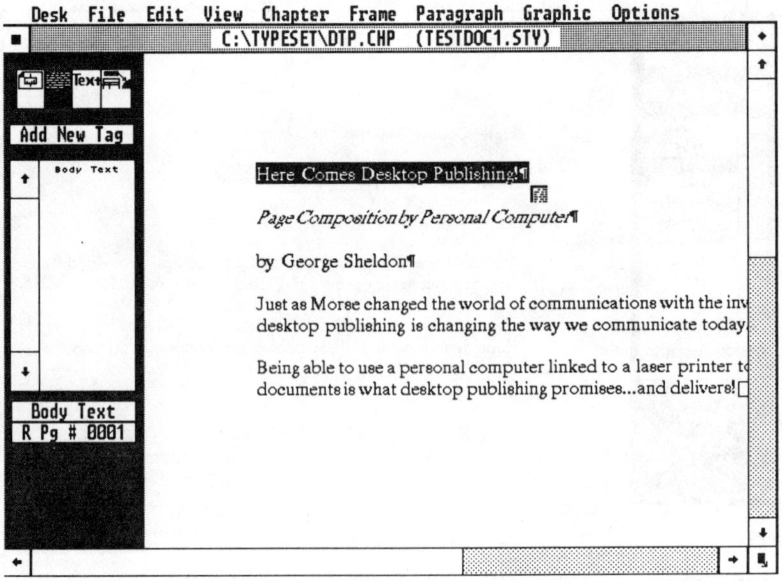

5. Click on **Add New Tag** in the Side Bar to display the Add New Tag dialog box.

TIP: You can also press Ctrl-2 to display the Add New Tag dialog box.

6. Type **Headline** in the Tag Name to Add section of the Add New Tag dialog box.

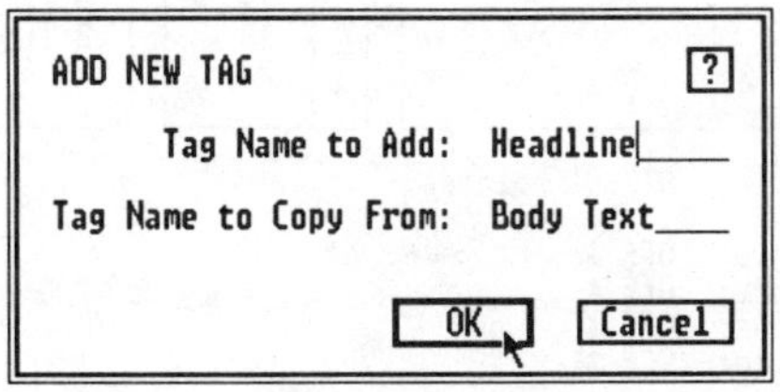

7. Click **OK** or press **Enter**. Notice that Headline now appears in the Assignment List. Headline is also displayed in the Current Selection window within the Side Bar to show that it is assigned to the currently selected paragraph.

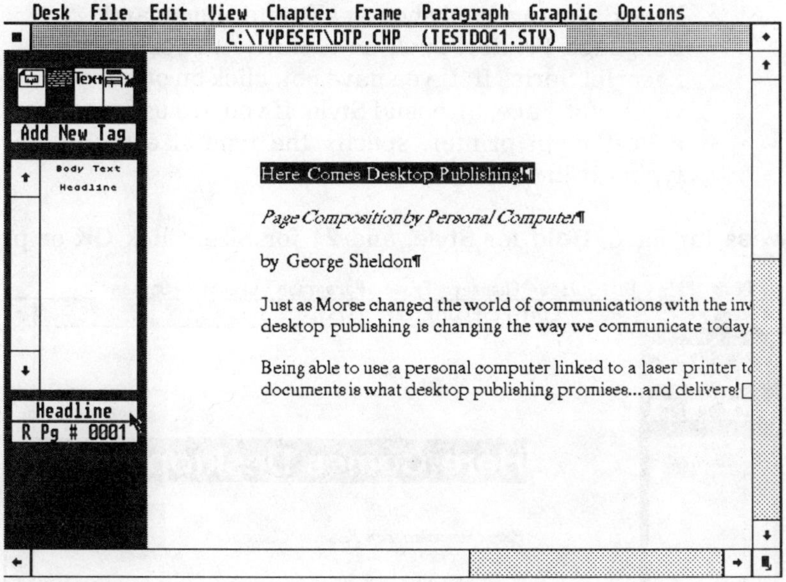

8. Point to the **Paragraph** menu and click on **Font** to display the Font dialog box.

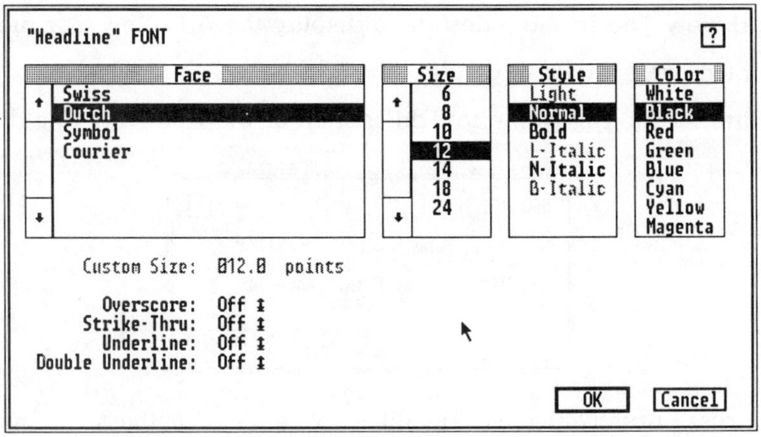

NOTE

The next step assumes that you have installed Xerox Ventura Publisher on a Printer Command Language Printer, such as a Hewlett-Packard LaserJet Series II. If you have not, click on other values for Face, Size, and Style. If you are using a PostScript printer, specify the type size by typing it in the Custom Size area.

9. Click on **Swiss** for Face, **Bold** for Style, and **24** for Size. Click **OK** or press **Enter**.

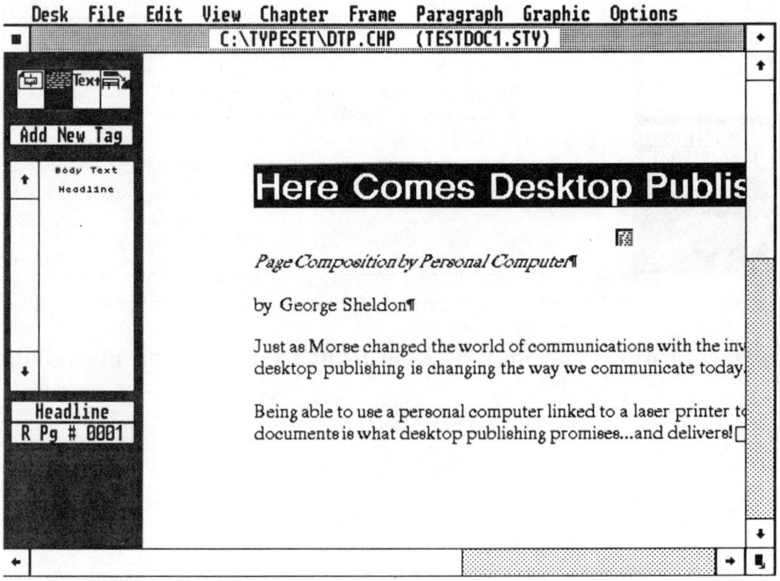

Notice the new appearance of the selected paragraph.

10. Save the changes to the style sheet by pointing to the **File** menu and clicking **Save**.
11. Click anywhere on the words **by George Sheldon** to highlight them.
12. Click on **Add New Tag** in the Side Bar to display the Add New Tag dialog box.
13. Type **Byline** in the Tag Name to Add area and click on **OK**. Notice that Byline is now included within the Assignment List. Byline is also displayed in the Current Selection window to show that it is assigned to the highlighted paragraph.
14. Point to the **Paragraph** menu and click on **Font** to display the Font dialog box.

NOTE

The next step assumes that you have installed Xerox Ventura Publisher on a Printer Command Language Printer, such as a Hewlett-Packard LaserJet Series II. If you have not, click on other values for Face, Size, and Style. If you are using a PostScript printer, specify the type size by typing it in the Custom Size area.

15. Click on **Swiss** for Face, **Bold** for Style, and **10** for Size. Click **OK**.
16. Point to the **Paragraph** menu and click on **Alignment** to display the Alignment dialog box.

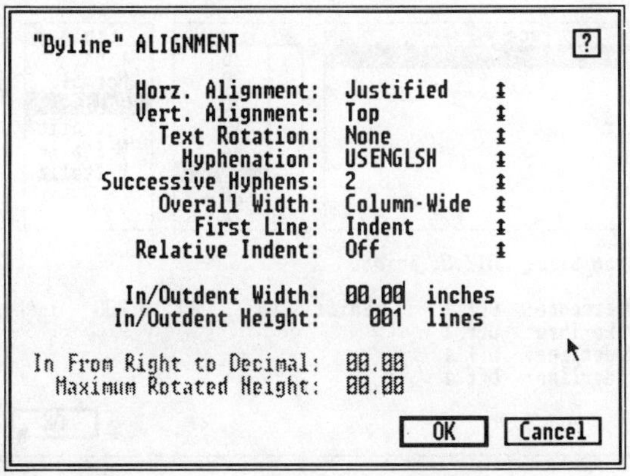

17. Click and hold on the arrow beside **Justified**, drag the pointer up to **Center** in the pop-up menu for Horizontal Alignment and release the mouse button. Do the same to select **Off** for Hyphenation. Click **OK**.
18. Click anywhere on the first paragraph which begins "Just as Morse changed the world of communications..." to highlight and select the paragraph.
19. Click on **Add New Tag** in the Side Bar to display the Add New Tag dialog box.
20. Type **First Para** in the Tag Name to Add area and click on **OK**. Notice that First Para is now included within the Assignment List. First Para is also displayed in the Current Selection window to show that it is assigned to the highlighted paragraph.

21. Point to the **Paragraph** menu and click on **Special Effects** to display the First Para Special Effects dialog box.

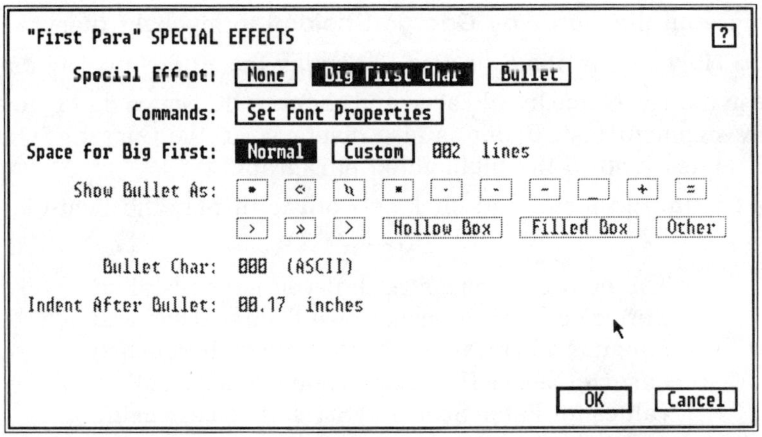

22. Click on **Big First Character** for Special Effects and **Set Font Properties** for Commands. Xerox Ventura Publisher displays the Font Setting for Big First Character dialog box.

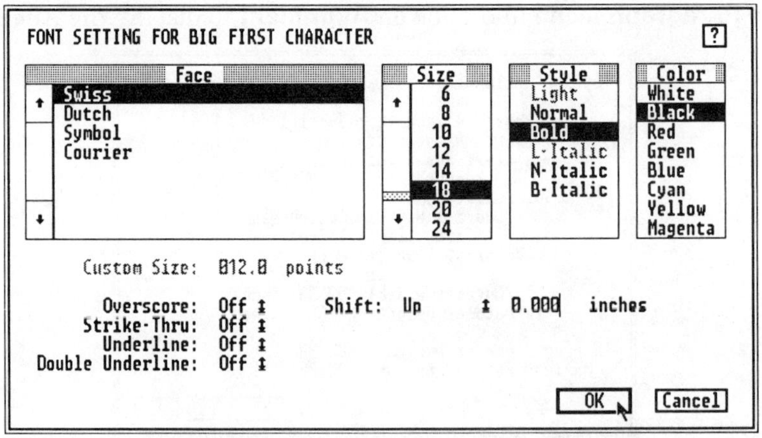

NOTE

The next step assumes that you have installed Xerox Ventura Publisher on a Printer Command Language Printer, such as a Hewlett-Packard LaserJet Series II. If you have not, click on other values for Face, Size, and Style. If you are using a PostScript printer, specify the type size by typing it in the Custom Size area.

23. Click on **Swiss** for Face, **18** for Size, and **Bold** for Style. Click **OK** to redisplay the First Para Special Effects dialog box.
24. Click on **Normal** for Space for Big First, and Click **OK**.
25. Click once anywhere in the margin to remove the highlight from the selected paragraph. Your screen should now resemble this illustration:

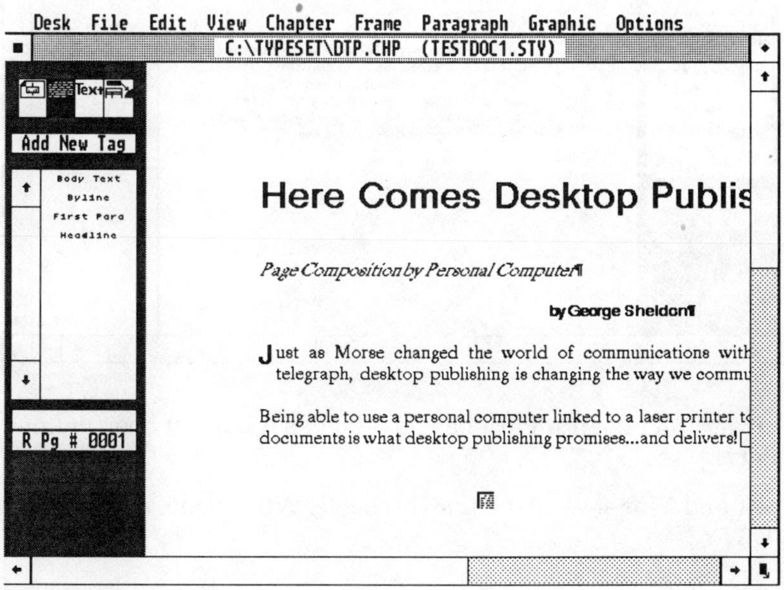

USE ANOTHER STYLE SHEET

To use a different style sheet:

1. Point to the **File** menu and click on **Load Diff. Style** to display the Item Selector dialog box.
2. Double click on **&NEWS-P2.STY**. Notice the changes made to the entire document.

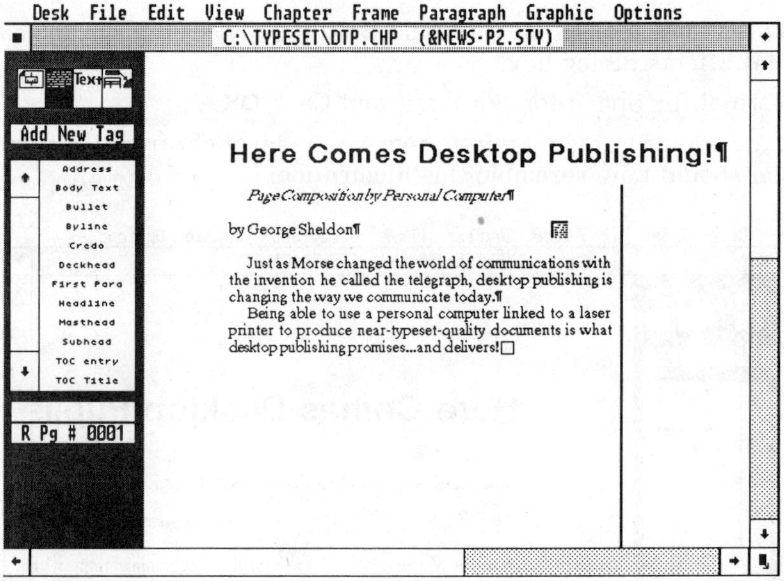

Notice that the paragraph tag First Para has no effect as it has not been defined in the &NEWS-P2.STY style sheet.

3. Repeat steps 1 and 2 for several other style sheets. When done, repeat steps 1 and 2, loading **TESTDOC1.STY**.

LOAD A PICTURE

To load a picture:

1. Point to the **View** menu and click on **Frame Setting** to activate the Frame mode.
2. Click on the **Add New Frame** button in the Side Bar. Move the mouse cursor to the middle of the page and click and hold the mouse button.
3. Drag the mouse button down and to the right to draw a new frame.

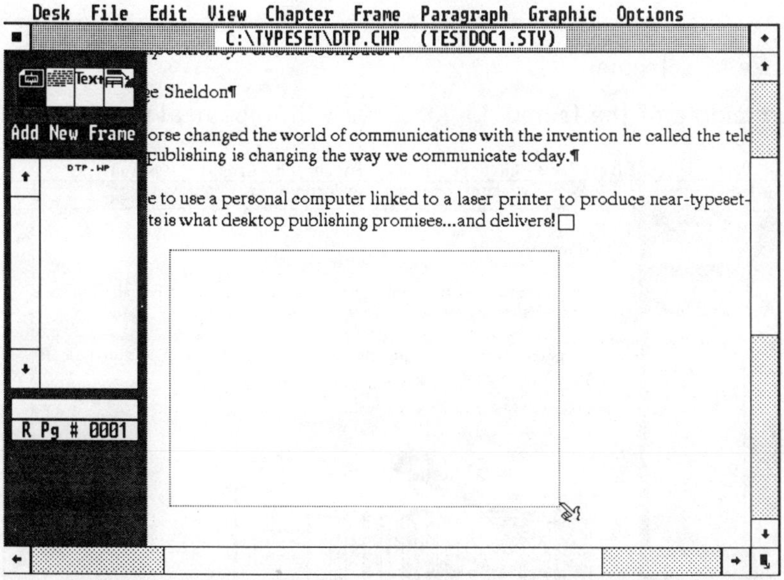

4. Release the mouse button.
5. Point to the **File** menu and click on **Load Text/Picture** to display the Load Text/Picture dialog box.
6. Select **Line-Art** for Type of File, **One** for # of Files, and **GEM** from Line-Art format. Click **OK**. The Item Selector is displayed.
7. Double Click on **NOZZLE.GEM**. The picture of the nozzle will appear in the frame drawn in steps 2 and 3.

NOTE

If the nozzle picture does not appear in the frame, point to the middle of the frame and click the mouse once. Then point to the Side Bar and click on NOZZLE.GEM in the Assignment List. The nozzle picture should then appear in the frame.

SIZE A FRAME

To change the size of a frame:

1. Click in the middle of the frame. Eight boxes will appear along the edge of the frame.

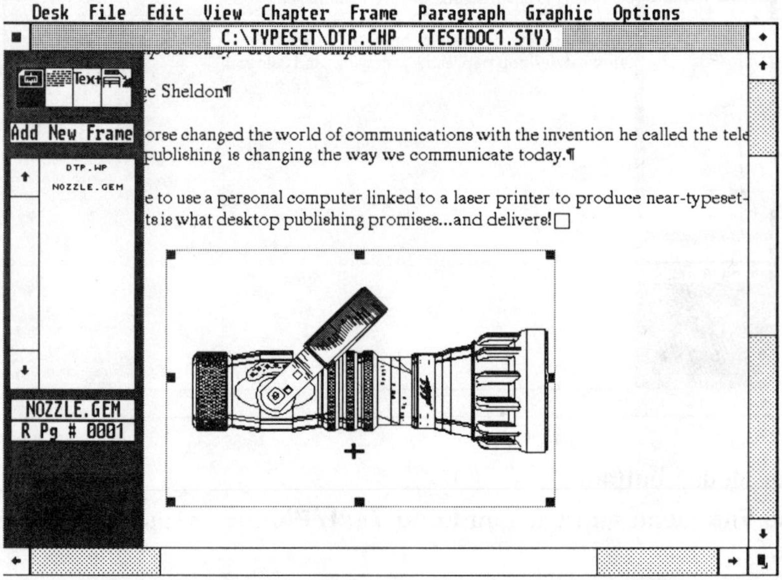

2. Click and hold on the box located in the bottom right corner. Drag the mouse down and to the right to make the frame larger.

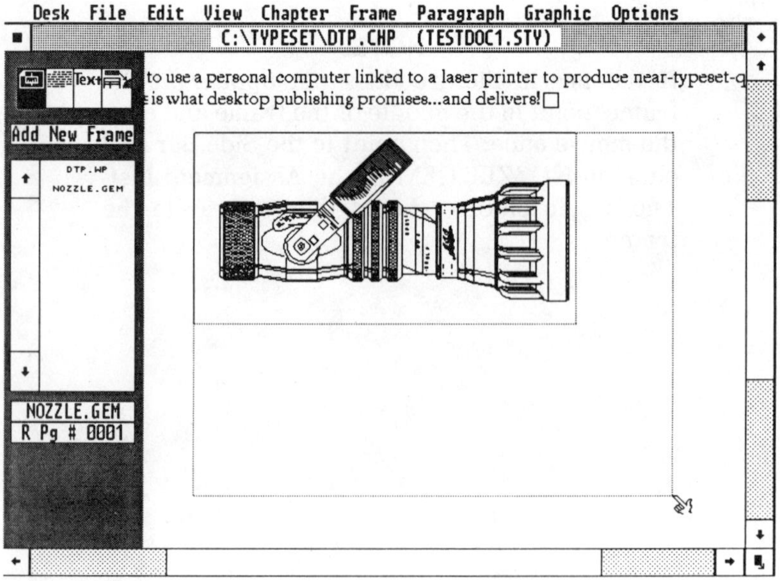

3. Repeat step 1. Click and hold on the box located in the bottom right corner. Drag the mouse to make the frame smaller.
4. Repeat step 1, and click and hold one of the other boxes to practice sizing the frame. Continue practicing sizing the frame until you feel comfortable with the procedure.

CHANGE VIEWS

To change the view of a Xerox Ventura Publisher document:

1. Point to the **View** menu and click on **Reduced View**.

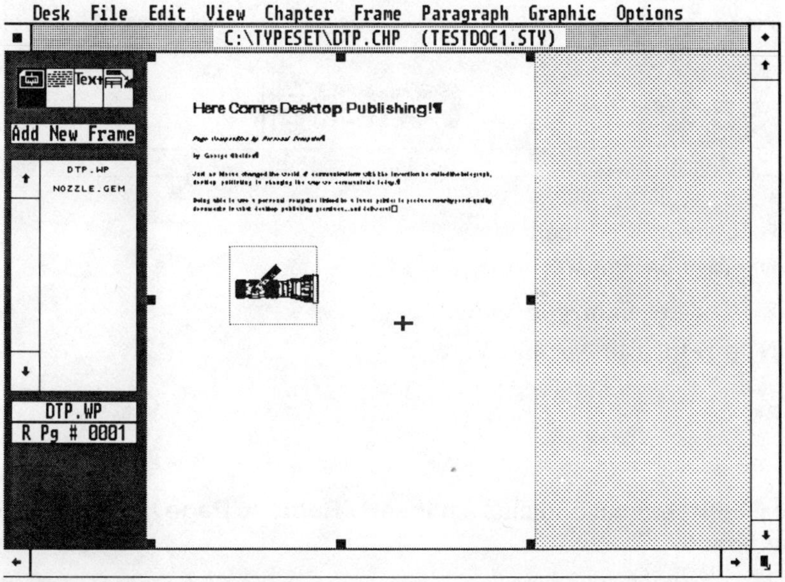

2. Point to the **View** menu and click on **Normal View**.

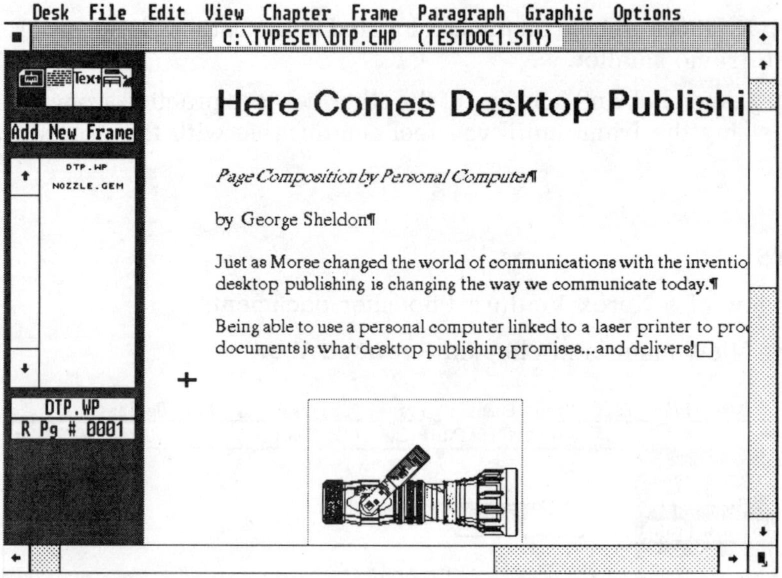

3. Press **Ctrl-R** to select Reduced View.
4. Press **Ctrl-N** to select Normal View.
5. Press **Ctrl-E** to select Enlarged View.
6. Press **Ctrl-N** to return to Normal View.

INSERT A PAGE

To insert a new page:

1. Point to the **Chapter** menu and click on **Insert/Remove Page** to display the Insert/Remove Page dialog box.

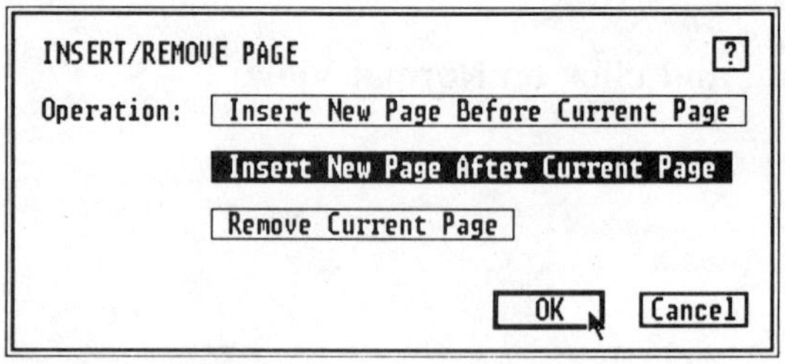

2. Click on **Insert New Page After Current Page** and then click **OK**.

Notice that a new page has been inserted and Xerox Ventura Publisher is now on page 2.

CREATE A GRAPHIC

To create a graphic within Xerox Ventura Publisher:

1. Press **Ctrl-U** to select Frame mode.
2. Click on the **Add New Frame** button in the Side Bar. Move the mouse cursor to the middle of the page and click and hold the mouse button.
3. Drag the mouse button down and to the right to draw a new frame, and release the mouse button.
4. Press **Ctrl-P** to select Graphic Drawing mode.
5. Click on the **Rectangle** drawing tool within the Side Bar.
6. Move the mouse to the middle of the frame and click and drag the mouse. A box appears as you drag.

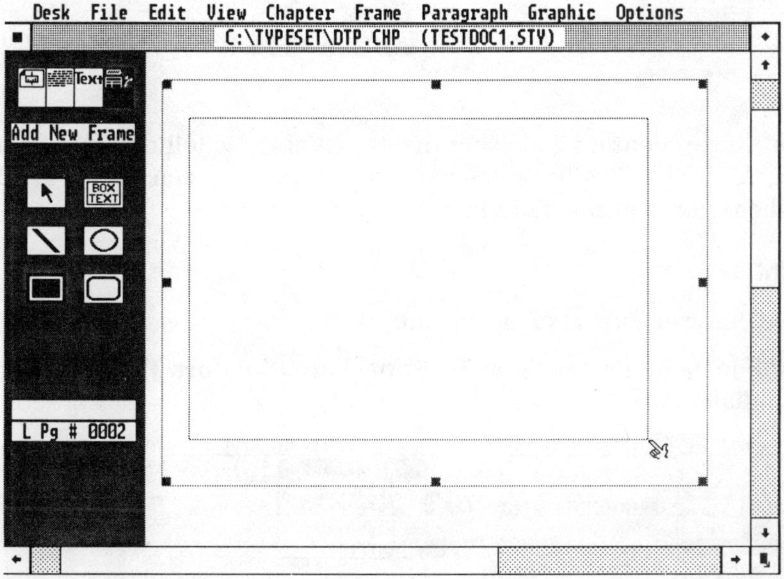

7. Release the mouse button.

SAVE THE DOCUMENT

To save the Xerox Ventura Publisher document:

1. Point to the **File** menu and click on **Save**. Xerox Ventura Publisher displays the Item Selector dialog box.

The Item Selector should display the various chapters located with the TYPESET directory.

2. Type **FIRSTDOC.CHP** as the name of the document you are now saving in the Selection area.

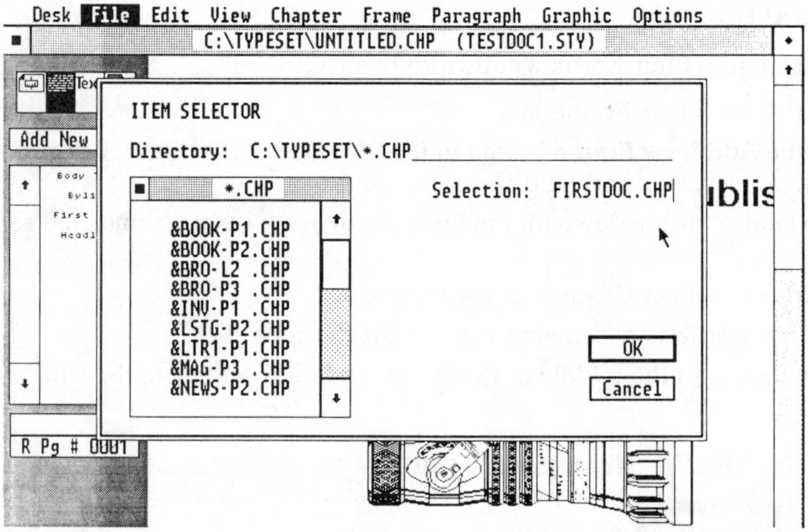

3. Press **Enter**. Xerox Ventura Publisher displays messages telling you what documents it is now saving. After the files have been saved, the main screen shows the document name and style sheet name in the Title Bar.

PRINT A DOCUMENT

To print a Xerox Ventura Publisher document:

1. Point to the **File** menu and click on **To Print**. Xerox Ventura Publisher displays the Print Information dialog box.

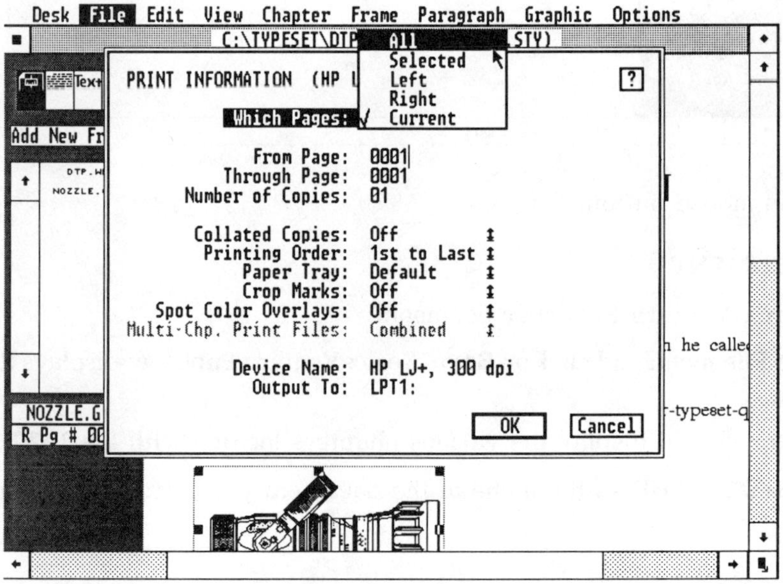

2. Click on the arrow beside Which Pages and slide the highlight up to **All**. Click **OK** to start printing. Xerox Ventura Publisher displays different messages to tell you what it is doing.

QUIT XEROX VENTURA PUBLISHER

To quit Xerox Ventura Publisher:

1. Point to the **File** menu and click on **Quit**. Xerox Ventura Publisher returns you to the DOS prompt.
2. Turn to Module 42 to continue the learning sequence.

Module 4
ABANDON

DESCRIPTION

The Abandon command allows you to revert to the last, most recently saved version of your document. It abandons any changes made during the current session. Abandon reverts to the last saved version of the document, the currently active style sheet, and any external graphic files. You cannot change graphic files in Xerox Ventura Publisher.

The Abandon command is located in the file menu.

APPLICATIONS

Abandon is a useful tool when you choose, for any reason, not to save changes you have made. For example, you might use Abandon if you accidentally removed a page.

You may also want to use Abandon when you are experimenting with a new design on a document. If you do not like your new design, select Abandon to revert back to the original version of your document.

TYPICAL OPERATION

In this example, you make a change to the sample chapter document SCOOP.CHP, then abandon it. The example begins with SCOOP.CHP already open and in use. If you do not have this chapter open, use the Open Chapter command in the File menu to retrieve and open SCOOP.CHP. Press Ctrl-N to show the file in Normal View.

1. Click on the **Text Editing** box to select that mode.
2. Select the word "Ventura" in the second headline by clicking and dragging the mouse cursor across the word. Your screen should look like this:

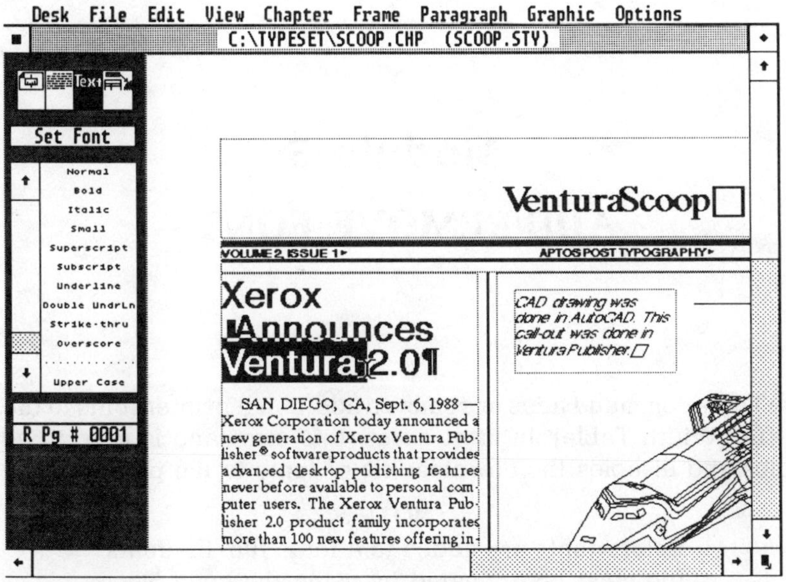

3. Press **Del**.
4. Point at the **File** menu and click on **Abandon**. A dialog box will appear asking if you want to revert to the last saved version.
5. Click **OK** to restore the file. Notice that the word "Ventura" now appears.
6. Turn to Module 17 to continue the learning sequence.

Module 5

ADD/REMOVE FONTS

DESCRIPTION

The Add/Remove Fonts command adds or removes additional printer fonts to the Xerox Ventura Publisher fonts file (Width Table). In most cases, this command is used to add fonts. It also selectively enables and disables the downloading of fonts to the printer.

NOTE

Before fonts are added to a fonts file, the fonts file must be activated by using the Load New Width Table option in the Set Printer Info command.

To use this command, select Add/Remove Fonts from the Options menu.

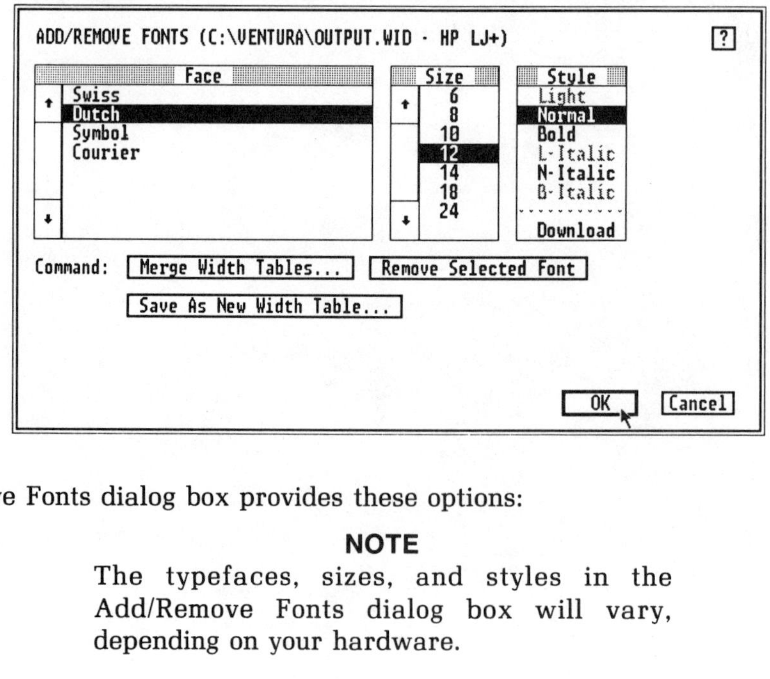

The Add/Remove Fonts dialog box provides these options:

NOTE

The typefaces, sizes, and styles in the Add/Remove Fonts dialog box will vary, depending on your hardware.

Face	Select the type face to either remove from the fonts file or add or remove from being automatically downloaded to the printer.
Size	Select the size of each type face to either remove from the fonts file or add or remove from being automatically downloaded to the printer.
Style	Select the style of each type face to either remove from the fonts file or add or remove from being automatically downloaded to the printer. If the word Resident appears at the bottom of the Style box, the currently selected type face, size, and style of font are already loaded in the printer. If the word Download appears at the bottom of the Style box, the currently selected type face, size, and style of font must be downloaded to the printer from Xerox Ventura Publisher at print time. The download status of a selected face, size, and style can be changed by clicking on the words Download or Resident. However, Xerox Ventura Publisher automatically establishes the correct download status for each font when the program is installed.
Command	Select the function needed to process your fonts.

Select Merge Width Tables to add new fonts to an existing fonts file (width table). Before doing this, use the Save As New Width Table to save the current fonts file under a new name in case something goes wrong when the new fonts are being added. Xerox Ventura Publisher displays the Item Selector dialog box where the name of the new fonts file to be created is typed.

NOTE

When two width tables are merged together, they must both be for the same printer.

Select Remove Selected Font to remove the selected face, size, and style from the fonts file.

If you buy additional fonts to use with your copy of Xerox Ventura Publisher, make sure you read the installation directions thoroughly *before* trying to load the fonts. There are roughly ten different steps, from making the fonts, to installing them in Xerox Ventura Publisher and merging the width tables. If you are going to undertake the task of loading fonts, be sure to read and follow the directions carefully. Doing so will eliminate hours of frustration and aggravation.

APPLICATIONS

The Add/Remove Fonts command allows additional fonts to be added for your use when running Xerox Ventura Publisher. New type faces are being developed and released by software developers each month. By adding additional fonts to your computer, you can create more dynamic, interesting documents.

You can also use this command to remove fonts, particularly if you find you have loaded a font series that you are never using and need additional disk space.

Finally, this command can be used to automatically download fonts to your printer. You can decrease printer time when using either an HP LaserJet or a PostScript driven printer by eliminating automatic downloading. To do this, you must first download the fonts into your printer and make them permanent before running Xerox Ventura Publisher. For more information, see your printer manual and read the information about making fonts resident.

TYPICAL OPERATION

In this operation, you save the current fonts under a new name and then delete a font. (These instructions assume you are using an HP LaserJet Series II laser printer. If you are using another printer, select another face, size, and style to delete.) The instructions begin with Xerox Ventura Publisher running.

1. Point to the **Options** menu and select **Add/Remove Fonts** to display the Add/Remove Fonts dialog box.
2. Select **Save As New Width Table** for Command to display the Item Selector dialog box.
3. Type **FONTTEST** for selection and press **Enter** to create the new fonts file.
4. Select **Swiss** for Face, **14** for Size, and **Bold** for style when the Add/Remove Fonts dialog box reappears.

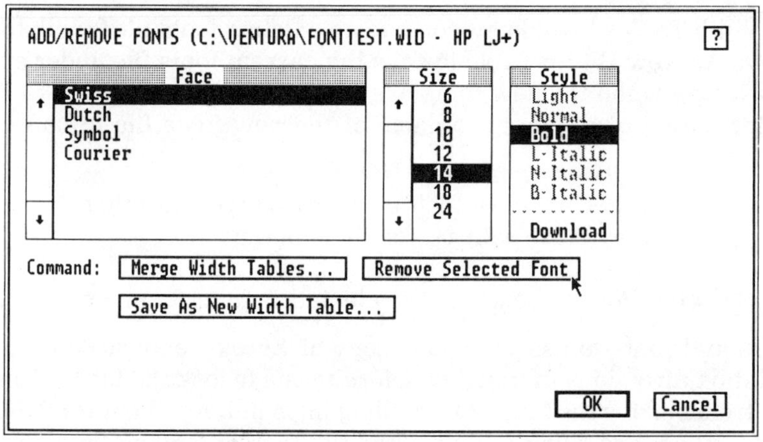

NOTE

The next step causes the Swiss 14-point Bold font to be removed. Do not complete the next step unless you want to remove the font. If you want to stop, click Cancel.

5. Click **Remove Select Font** for Command. Notice that Swiss 14-point Bold is now gray and no longer available for use.

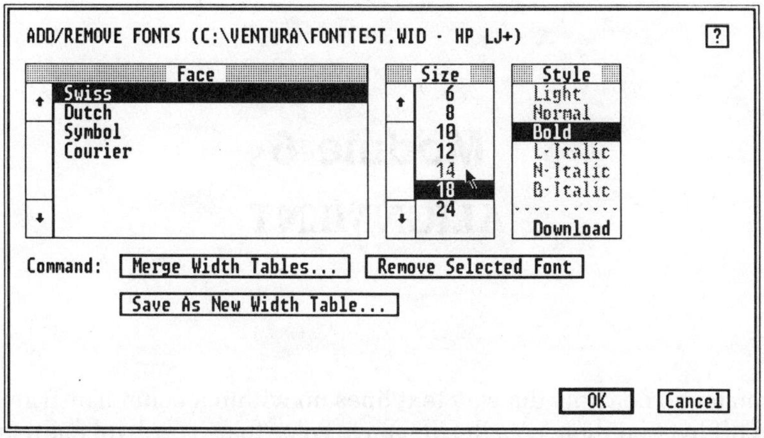

6. Click **OK** to exit the dialog box and click **Abandon** when the message box appears asking if you want to save or abandon the changes to the width table.
7. Turn to Module 9 to continue the learning sequence.

Module 6

ALIGNMENT

DESCRIPTION

The Alignment command controls the way text lines up within a column or frame. This command also turns on and off hyphenation, sets the language rules to use for hyphenation, and determines the number of successive lines that can be hyphenated.

The Alignment command in Xerox Ventura Publisher is accessed by tagging a paragraph and then selecting the Alignment command. The changes made with this command affect the paragraph tag associated with the selected text. When a paragraph tag is changed, it affects all text marked with that paragraph tag in your Xerox Ventura Publisher document as well as in other Xerox Ventura Publisher documents that use the same style sheet.

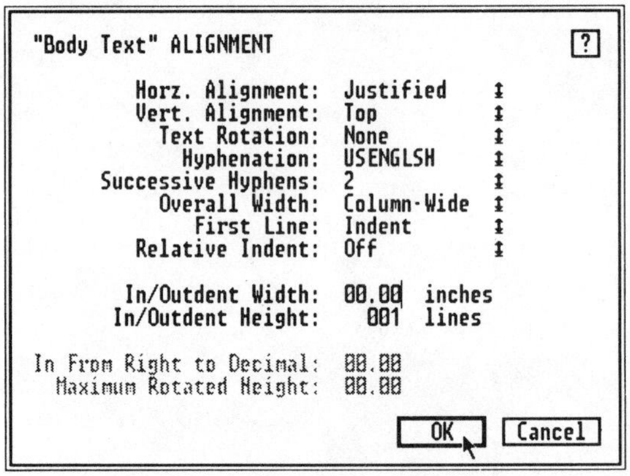

The Alignment dialog box contains these options:

Horz. Alignment — Select how the text lines up horizontally in the column or frame: Left, Center, Right, Justified, or Decimal. The following example illustrates the five types of alignments available in Xerox Ventura Publisher:

Left aligns all the text along the left margin and keeps the right margin ragged.

Center aligns all the text in the middle of the left and right margins and keeps both margins ragged.

Right aligns all the text along the right margin and keeps the left margin ragged.

Justified aligns all the text along the left and right margins. Justified text has no ragged edges. Justified adds spaces between words and letters as needed to align the left and right margins.

You can also select Decimal. This option within the pop-up menu positions the first decimal point in a line at a distance from the right margin specified by In From Right To Decimal (also located within the Alignment dialog box). This setting allows easy alignment on the decimal point.

Vert. Alignment	Text is aligned vertically within a page or frame. This option allows you to position vertical text at the top, bottom, or center of the page or frame. (For some printers, this command does not work.)
Text Rotation	Choose the degree of text rotation desired.
Hyphenation	Choose between the hyphenation rules for US English or another language. Select Off to disable the automatic text hyphenation available in Xerox Ventura Publisher.
Successive Hyphens	Select the number of successive lines that end with hyphens. For example, if you select 3, Xerox Ventura Publisher never hyphenates the last word more than three text lines in a row.
Overall Width	Select whether the text should be aligned within the column or within the frame. By selecting Frame-wide as the Overall Width, column settings are ignored and the paragraph is printed across the entire frame or page.

NOTE

Text after a frame-wide paragraph continues to flow after the frame-wide paragraph. For that reason, frame-wide paragraphs in other columns will print over the paragraphs in the left column. Column Balance should always be turned on whenever frame-wide tags are applied to paragraphs which are not at the top of a frame.

First Line	Select Indent or Outdent if the first line of the paragraph should be offset either to the right (indent) or to the left (Outdent). An outdent is sometimes called a hanging indent. The following text illustrates the indent and outdent: This paragraph is indented text where the first line of the paragraph is offset to the right. This paragraph is outdented text where the first line of the paragraph is offset to the left.
Relative Indent	Select On if you want the indent of the paragraph to be exactly the length of the last line in the previous paragraph. If there is an amount specified in the Indent Width, that amount of space is added in addition to the length of the previous line. Select Off for the last line in the previous paragraph to have no affect.
In/Outdent Width	Select the amount of space desired for the indent or the outdent.
In/Outdent Height	Enter the total number of lines to indent or outdent. In most cases, the typical number of lines is one.
In From Right to Decimal	Enter the amount of distance from the right margin to align the decimal within the text.
Maximum Rotated Height	Enter the maximum height desired for the text that is rotated.

The Alignment command is located in the Paragraph menu.

APPLICATIONS

The text alignment command affects the final appearance of the text. Justified text generally looks neater in appearance.

Center-aligned text is useful for headlines in most publications. Right-aligned text is often used in advertisements and picture captions on the left side of the picture. Left-aligned text is still used in many applications, for both style and for ease of reading. Decimal alignment is used to create easy-to-read tables containing numbers.

This command is also used to create both indented and outdented paragraphs. Such paragraphs are often used to enhance the design of a publication. Outdents are also used in combination with bullets to make items on a list easy to read.

The Alignment command also sets the hyphenation of text within the Xerox Ventura Publisher document. Depending on the width of your columns, you may need more hyphenation to eliminate white "rivers of space" within your text. Also, you should turn the hyphenation off for most headlines.

TYPICAL OPERATION

In this example, you change the alignment of text. The example begins with &LSTG-P2.CHP already open and in use. Use the Open Chapter command in the File menu to retrieve and open &LSTG-P2.CHP. So your view matches the screen depicted in this book, press Ctrl-N. Adjust the scroll bars to make your computer screen look like the illustration.

1. Press **Ctrl-I** to select Paragraph mode.
2. Click on the text "PC-Eye" in the left column.
3. Point to the **Paragraph** menu and select **Alignment**.
4. Click on **Horz. Alignment** and, using the pop-up menu, select **Right**. Press **Enter**. Your screen should resemble this illustration:

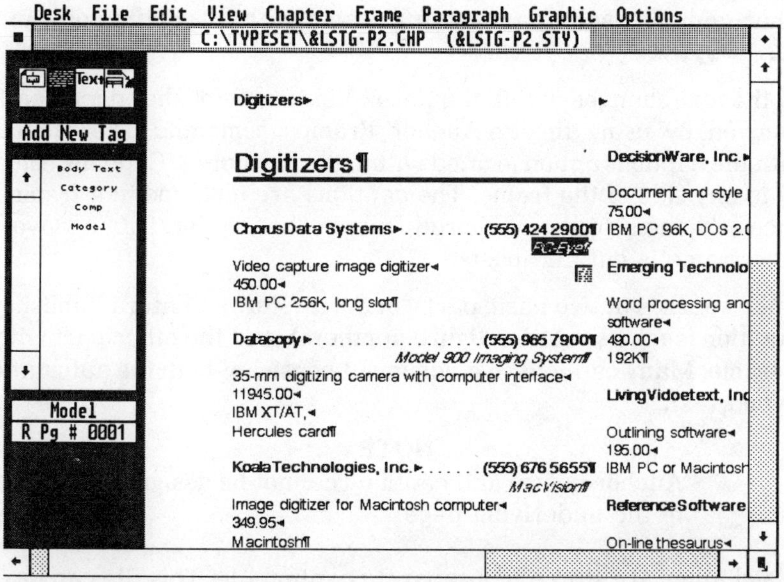

5. Point to the **Paragraph** menu and select **Alignment**.
6. Click on **Horz. Alignment** and, using the pop-up menu, select **Left**. Press **Enter**.
7. Close the chapter without saving any changes.
8. Turn to Module 66 to continue the learning sequence.

Module 7

ANCHORS & CAPTIONS

DESCRIPTION

The Anchors & Captions command assigns an anchor name and creates a caption for any frame. The anchor name is used to associate a frame with a specific point in the text on the underlying page.

If the location of the text changes within the Xerox Ventura Publisher document, the associated frame can be moved by using the Re-Anchor Frames command (see Module 56 for more information). With the captions option located within the Anchors & Captions command, a caption can be attached to any side of the frame. The captions are included in a frame Xerox Ventura Publisher produces adjacent to the anchored frame. The caption frame moves with the main frame, even if the frame is cut and pasted.

Each caption frame consists of two basic parts: one with Xerox Ventura Publisher automatically generated information (such as table or figure numbers), and the other part with the text typed into the caption frame. Many captions in a document consist of both the automatically generated and manually typed text.

NOTE

Anchor names and captions cannot be assigned to the underlying page.

All captions for a chapter are stored in a separate caption file. This file can be edited and even spell checked later in a word processor.

There are two different caption counters used in this command. The Table Counter and the Figure Counter can be used to automatically number frame captions. These counters are automatically updated as captions are deleted or added. See Module 74 for more information about the Update Counter command.

The Anchors & Captions command is accessed from the Frame menu. To access the command, Xerox Ventura Publisher must first be in Frame mode, and a frame must be selected. When the Anchors & Caption command is selected, the Anchors & Captions dialog box appears:

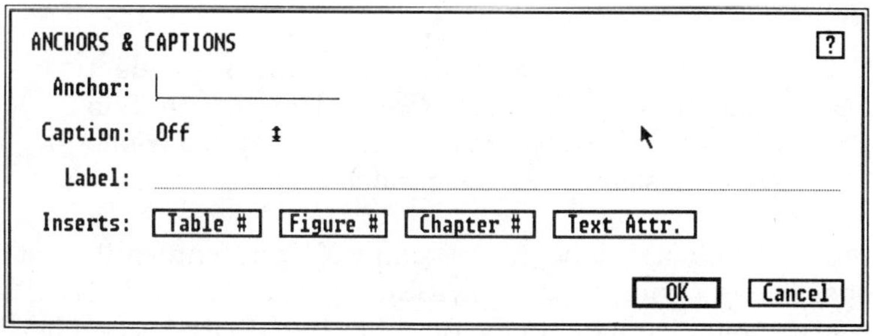

The options in the Anchors & Captions dialog box include:

Anchor — Type the name of the anchor to be assigned to the selected frame. This name must exactly match the anchor name that was inserted in the text with the Insert/Edit Anchor command (see Module 35 for more information about Insert/Edit Anchor).

Caption — Select the location where the caption is to appear in relation to the frame. The choices are: Above, Below, Left, and Right.

Label — Type the information Xerox Ventura Publisher is to enter automatically into the frame caption. The information can include the inserts described below.

TIP: If you are creating a series of figures or tables, enter this generated information in the same format for all figures and tables to create a uniform appearance.

Inserts — Select the type of information Xerox Ventura Publisher is to enter automatically into the caption. Also, the appearance of the caption can be defined. The information Xerox Ventura Publisher inserts into the Label area each time an item is clicked in the dialog box is:

Item	*Inserted Characters*
Table #	[T#]
Figure #	[F#]
Chapter #	[C#]
Text Attr.	<D>

For [T#], Xerox Ventura Publisher substitutes the current table number.

For [F#], Xerox Ventura Publisher substitutes the current figure number.

For [C#], Xerox Ventura Publisher substitutes the current chapter number.

For <D>, you must substitute for "D" the characters associated with the various text attributes Xerox Ventura Publisher supports. The letters and attributes are described in Appendix B.

NOTE

If no text appears in the caption frame, select the Frame mode and then select the caption frame. Then lengthen or widen the caption frame as necessary until the caption text can be seen.

Two paragraph tags are automatically generated by Xerox Ventura Publisher when a caption is added to a frame. The tag names are Z_LABEL FIG and Z_CAPTION. The basic attributes for these two tags are copied from the Body Text, but the attributes can be changed if desired.

APPLICATIONS

The Anchors and Caption command provides several useful tools when working with frames. The first is that it assigns an anchor entered into the text to a frame. By doing so, this completes the process and allows a frame to be anchored to specific text within the Xerox Ventura Publisher document. Then, as the text moves through editing, formatting, or realignment, the frame moves with the text.

The Anchors and Captions command also provides a way to add captions to the frames created within the Xerox Ventura Publisher document. Captions make illustrations, tables, and charts easier to understand for the reader of documents. Xerox Ventura Publisher can automatically number the captions, such as Figure 1-1, Figure 1-2, etc.

This command also allows you to decide where the captions should appear on your document. A caption can be on either side of a frame, or the top, or bottom.

TYPICAL OPERATION

In this example, you change a caption and insert an anchor. The Xerox Ventura Publisher sample chapter &BOOK-P1.CHP is used. The example begins with &BOOK-P1.CHP already open and in use. If you do not have this chapter open, use the Open Chapter command in the File menu to retrieve and open &BOOK-P1.CHP. So your view matches the screen depicted in this book, press Ctrl-N. You may need to adjust your screen using the scroll bars to make your computer look like the illustrations.

1. Press **Ctrl-U** to select Frame mode.
2. Click in the middle of the frame containing the nozzle to select it.
3. Point to the **Frame** menu and select **Anchors & Captions** to display the Anchors & Captions dialog box.
4. Press **Esc** or **Backspace** over Map and type **Nozzle** in the Anchor section.
5. Press **Esc** or **Backspace** enough times to erase the text in the Label section.
6. Click on **Figure #**, press **Spacebar** once, and type **An Example of a Graphic**. Press **Enter**. Your screen should resemble this illustration:

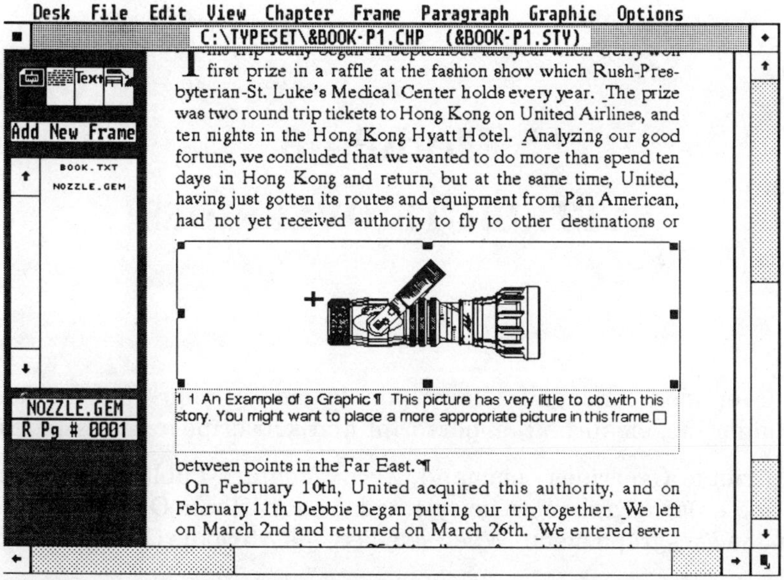

7. Point to the **File** menu and click on **Abandon**. Click on **OK** when prompted to revert back to the last saved version.
8. Turn to Module 78 to continue the learning sequence.

Module 8
ATTRIBUTE OVERRIDES

DESCRIPTION

The Attribute Overrides command allows you to modify your text by adding overscore, strikethrough, underline, small text, superscript and subscript text attributes.

To select the Attribute Overrides command, Xerox Ventura Publisher must be in Paragraph Tagging mode, and a paragraph must be selected. The Attribute Overrides command can then be selected from the Paragraph menu. When selected, the Attribute Overrides dialog box appears:

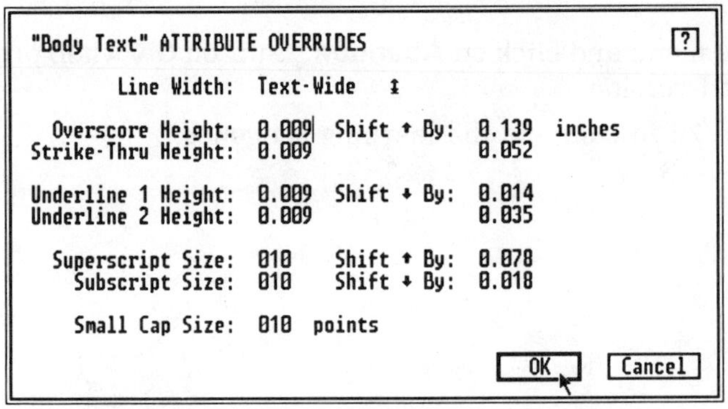

The following options are available within the Attribute Overrides dialog box:

Line Width	Select Text-Wide to set the length of lines to the width of text. Select Margin-Wide if the line is to extend from the left margin to the right margin.
Overscore Height	Type in the height or thickness of the overscore height and the amount of distance the overscore is to shift from the text baseline.
Strike-Thru Height	Type in the height or thickness of the Strike-Thru height and the amount of distance the Strike-Thru height is to shift from the text baseline.
Underline 1 Height	Type in the height or thickness of the Underline 1 height and the amount of distance the underline is to shift from the text baseline.

Underline 2 Height	Type in the height or thickness of the Underline 2 height and the amount of distance the underline is to shift from the text baseline.
Superscript Size	Type in the font size of the Superscript and the amount of distance the superscript is to shift from the text baseline.
Subscript Size	Type in the font size of the Superscript and the amount of distance the superscript is to shift from the text baseline.
Small Cap Size	Type in the font size to be assigned to the Small Cap setting.

APPLICATIONS

The Attribute Overrides command provides several different ways to fine-tune the typography of your Xerox Ventura Publisher document. For example, you can precisely adjust the super and subscript characters of your document to prevent them from touching the adjacent lines of type.

The Attribute Overrides command allows you to determine how thick or thin an underline should be, and how far under the word it should be placed. This precise control is available to you with this command.

TYPICAL OPERATION

In this example, you change the attributes of selected text within the Xerox Ventura Publisher sample chapter &LTR1.P1.CHP. The example begins with &LTR1.P1.CHP already open. Use the Open Chapter command in the File menu to retrieve and open &LTR1.P1.CHP.

1. Press **Ctrl-O** to select the Text Editing mode.
2. Select the phone number within the letterhead.
3. Click on **Underline** in the Side Bar.
4. Press **Ctrl-I** and click on the phone number paragraph.
5. Select **Attribute Overrides** from the Paragraph menu.
6. Type **0.016** inches for Underline 1 Height and **0.050** inches for Shift Down By.
7. Click **OK**. Notice the change in the underline's position and thickness.
8. Point to the **File** menu and click on **Abandon**. Click on **OK** when prompted to revert back to the last saved version.
9. Turn to Module 18 to continue the learning sequence.

Module 9
AUTO-NUMBERING

DESCRIPTION

The Auto-Numbering command defines the automatic numbering of tagged paragraphs in the underlying page. With automatic numbering, you create numbered headlines and paragraphs, such as those used in technical manuals, scholarly outlines, and business documents.

Auto-Numbering automatically inserts the section numbers for you. These section numbers can contain combinations of numbering styles as well as punctuation.

NOTE

Only text in the underlying pages can be auto-numbered. Text in frames and box text cannot be auto-numbered. This command never affects the text in regular frames.

A computer training manual might have these headlines:

1.0 Personal Computers
    1.1 Major Components
        1.1.2 C.P.U.
        1.1.3 Input Devices
        1.1.4 Output Devices
    1.2 How They Work
2.0 Main Frame Computers

As a scholarly outline, these topics might use this numbering scheme:

A. Personal Computers
    1. Major Components
        a. C.P.U.
        b. Input Devices
        c. Output Devices
    2. How They Work
B. Main Frame Computers

The numbers or letters can be any variety of styles such as legal (1.0, 1.1., 1.2, and so on), Harvard (I. II. III. and so on), or numeric (1, 2, 3, and so on).

Your numbering scheme is associated with a particular paragraph tag (see Module 50 for a description about paragraph tags). When the paragraph tag is assigned to a paragraph, Xerox Ventura Publisher precedes the paragraph with the numbering scheme. Xerox Ventura Publisher automatically increases the number or letter by one each time it encounters a paragraph marked with the paragraph tag. For example, if the first paragraph is numbered with I, the second paragraph is automatically numbered with II.

The numbering scheme is created by typing information in the Auto-Numbering dialog box.

The Auto-Numbering dialog box contains these options:

Usage	Select On or Off. To use the auto numbering, Usage must be On.
Level 1 through 10	The multiple levels establish different numbering definitions for different paragraph tags. You can create a maximum of 10 levels of section numbering by typing a different tag name on each level line. The tag names entered in the different levels must match paragraph tags associated with the current style sheet.
Inserts	Select the type of numbering scheme Xerox Ventura Publisher is to place into the auto-number definitions. Also, define the appearance of the numbers. The information Xerox Ventura Publisher inserts into the auto-numbering definition each time you click on the item on the dialog box is:

Item	*Inserted Characters*
Chapter #	[C#]
1,2	[*tag name,1]
A,B	[*tag name,A]
a,b	[*tag name,a]
I,II	[*tag name,I]
i,ii	[*tag name,i]
Suppress Previous Level	[-]
Text Attr.	<D>

For [C#], Xerox Ventura Publisher substitutes the current chapter number.

For any definitions containing [*tag name,X], replace "tag name" with the name of the paragraph tag you are associating with the numbering scheme. For example, if you want to define a numbering scheme for the paragraph tag named Headline, replace [*tag name,x] with [*Headline,x]. The x in [*tag name,x] is the type of numbering scheme to use.

The following table shows the different types of numbering schemes available:

What You Enter For Tag Definition	*What You Get For First Headline*	*What You Get For Second Headline#*
[*Headline,1]	1	2
[*Headline,A]	A	B
[*Headline,a]	a	b
[*Headline,I]	I	II
[*Headline,i]	i	ii

Xerox Ventura Publisher precedes the numbering scheme for lower level definitions with the numbering schemes for higher level definitions. Each time a paragraph tag specified in the Auto-Numbering dialog box is encountered, the numbers for all lower level paragraphs are reset to their starting number. For example, if Level 1 generates a 1. and Level 2 generates a 2., Xerox Ventura Publisher would print the Level 2 definition as 1.2., preceding the Level definition with the Level 1 definition. This, in fact, creates headings for many technical manuals. For example, if you are creating an outline with a Level 1 of capital letters and a Level 2 of Arabic numerals, Ventura prints the first level similar to this:

A. Headline

and the second level similar to this:

A.1. Headline

The final output would look similar to this:

A. Personal Computers
    A.1. Major Components
    A.2. How They Work

To suppress the printing of the previous level and to prevent the A. from printing on the lower levels and present a more traditional outline appearance, begin the definitions for the lower levels with the Suppress Previous Level characters, [-]. For example, Level 1 and 2 entries should look like this:

[*Headline, A].   (to print capital letters)
[-][*Headline, 1].   (to suppress the previous level and print Arabic numbers)

The output looks like this:

A. Personal Computers
    1. Major Components
    2. How They Work

Auto-Numbering automatically creates a paragraph tag for each of the 10 levels. The automatically generated tags are named Z_SECn, where n is the level number. All the attributes of these tags can be changed to control the appearance of the automatically generated numbers.

When Auto-Numbering creates the labels, they are located on the line above the associated tagged paragraph. To place the auto-number and paragraph on the same line, enter these values for the number tag and the paragraph tag.

Item to Change	*Auto-Numbering Tag*	*Text Tag*
Font	Same As Text Tag	Same As Auto-Numbering Tag
Alignment	Left	Indent relative to previous line, plus Relative Indent: On First Line: Indent In/Outdent Width: 1,00 picas and points
Spacing	Above: Normal Below: 0.000	Above: 0.000 Below: Normal
Breaks	Line Break: Before	Line Break: After
	Keep with next: Yes	Next Y Position: Beside Last line of Previous Para
Ruling Line Above	As desired	None
Ruling Line Below	None	As desired

Text Attributes define the appearance of the generated numbers. Selecting Text Attribute places the characters <D> on the line. Substitute the characters for "D" associated with the various text attributes Xerox Ventura Publisher supports. For example, place the characters <B> in front of the paragraph numbers to make them bold and place the characters <I> in front of the paragraph numbers to make the numbers italic. The complete list of letters and attributes are described in Appendix B.

You can also add any additional text to a numbering scheme by typing it outside the left and right brackets. For example, if you want to include the word "Headline" at the beginning of the Level 1 definition, type:

Headline [*Headline,1]

Each time Xerox Ventura Publisher encounters text marked with the Headline, it now adds

Headline n

to the front of the text, where "n" is the paragraph number.

If you want to place periods between the level numbers in a technical document, type for Levels 1, 2, and 3:

[*Headline 1,1].
[*Headline 2,1].
[*Headline 3,1].

For a Headline 3 paragraph tag, Xerox Ventura Publisher adds a number similar to this to the front of the text:

1.1.2. How A C.P.U. Really Works

Without the periods at the end of the brackets, the headline would look like this:

112 How A C.P.U. Really Works

Section numbers are added, deleted, or changed only when a change is made in the Auto-Numbering menu or when the Renumber Headline option is selected within the Chapter menu.

APPLICATIONS

This command is used to automatically number sections within a technical manual or an outline. Being able to automatically number your headlines permits easy revisions when the additional text is added or deleted during editing.

You can also automatically number chapters. If your document is made up of many small sections, you could group them together into one Xerox Ventura Publisher chapter and automatically number the chapter numbers.

TYPICAL OPERATION

In this operation, you add numbering schemes to the &BOOK-P1.CHP sample chapter. The operation begins with the &BOOK-P1.CHP already open and in use.

1. Point to the **Chapter** menu and click on **Auto-Numbering** to display the Auto-Numbering dialog box.
2. Click **On** for Usage. The auto-numbering function is now activated.
3. Click on the **Level 1** line and Click on **[I,II]** for inserts.
4. Press **Left Arrow** three times, and press **Backspace** enough times to erase tag name.
5. Type **Chapter**, press **Right Arrow** to move the cursor to the end of the line, and type a period.
6. Click on the **Level 2** line, click on **Suppress Previous Level** for Inserts, then click on **[i,ii]**.
7. Press **Left Arrow** three times, and press **Backspace** enough times to erase tag name.
8. Type **Chapter Title**, press **Right Arrow** to move the cursor to the end of the line, and type a period. Your screen should resemble this illustration:

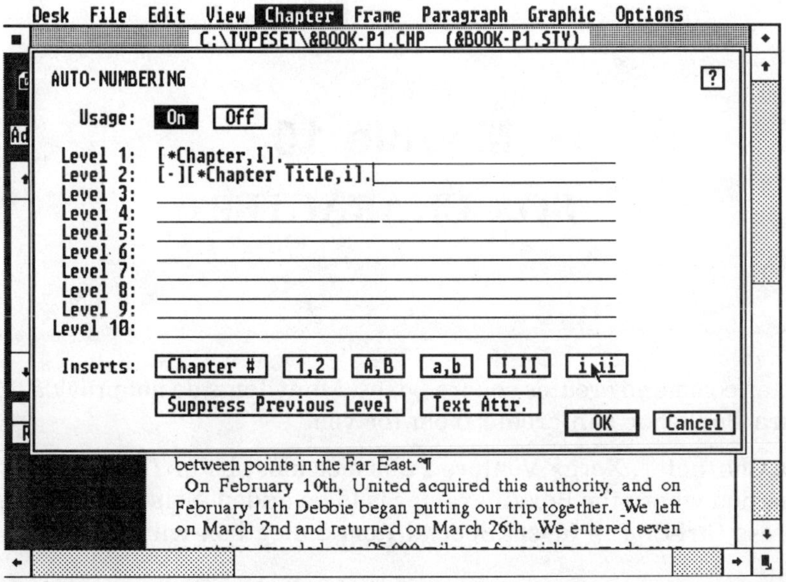

9. Click **OK**. Notice the automatically created levels are on the line above the Chapter and Chapter Title tagged paragraphs.
10. Press **Ctrl-S** to save the changes.
11. Turn to Module 55 to continue the learning sequence.

Module 10

BOX CHARACTER

DESCRIPTION

The Box Character command creates square boxes. Many fonts do not provide these characters, so Xerox Ventura Publisher can create them for you.

To create a Box Character, Xerox Ventura Publisher must be in Text Editing mode. Place the cursor at the position where the Box Character is to be added. Select Insert Special Item in the Edit menu or press Ctrl-C. The Insert Special Item dialog box will appear.

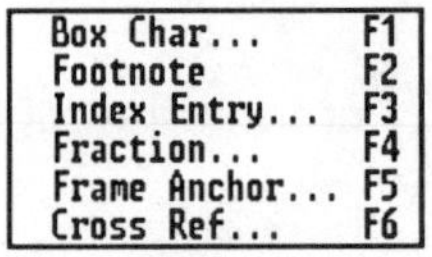

Select Box Char with the mouse or press F1. The Box Char dialog box appears:

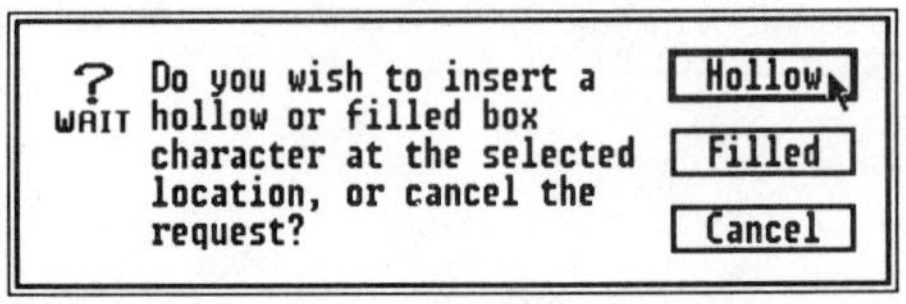

Select the type of box to be created by selecting either Hollow or Filled. Select Cancel to cancel the creation of the Box Character.

TIP: Once the Box Character has been created, use the Text mode Set Font button to change the size of the box character, shift it up or down, or move it left or right with kerning.

APPLICATIONS

The box character is used in many different forms and can enhance the appearance of many documents. For example, a check-off type form can be created, or a box character can be placed at the beginning of a paragraph to create a different look to your document.

Without this command, the box character is not available in most fonts.

TYPICAL OPERATION

In this operation, you create a special box character. The Xerox Ventura Publisher sample chapter &LSTG-P2.CHP is used. The example begins with &LSTG-P2.CHP already in use. Use the Open Chapter command in the File menu to retrieve and open &LSTG-P2.CHP. So your view matches the screen depicted in this book, press Ctrl-N. You may need to adjust your screen using the scroll bars to make your computer look like the illustrations.

1. Press **Ctrl-O** to activate the Text Editing mode.
2. Move the mouse cursor to in front of the "E" in "Editorial Software" located in the left column.
3. Point to the **Edit** menu and click on **Insert Special Item** to display the Insert Special Item dialog box.
4. Press **F1** to access the Box Char... dialog box.
5. Select **Filled** to create a filled box.

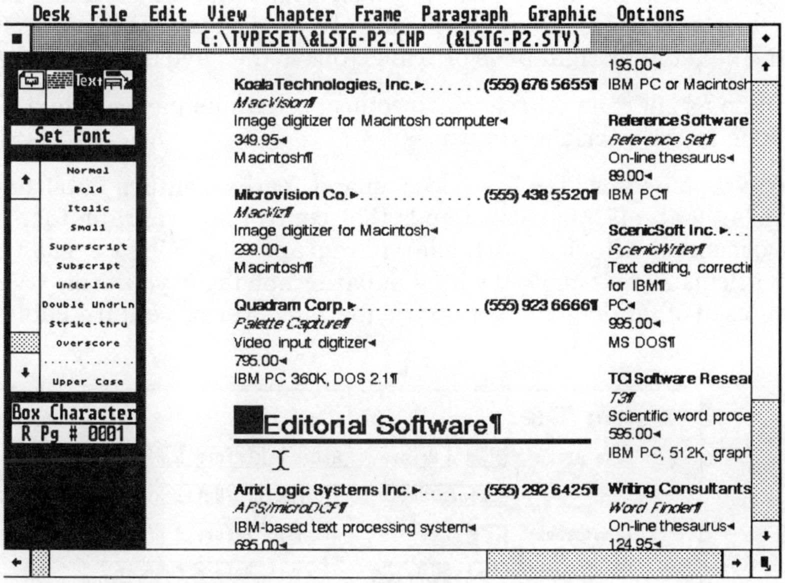

Notice the filled box character that has been created.

6. Point to the **File** menu and click on **Abandon**. Click on **OK** when prompted to revert back to the last saved version.
7. Turn to Module 54 to continue the learning sequence.

Module 11
BREAKS

DESCRIPTION

The Breaks command adjusts the way paragraphs are grouped and separated on a page. The command controls the flow of text between paragraphs.

Following a break, the next paragraph can begin on a new line (this is a line break), at the top of a new column (this is a column break), at the top of a new page or frame (this is a page break), or at the top of the next left or right page or frame (this is the page break before/until left/right).

A paragraph can be as short as one carriage return, or can be pages of text. What marks the end of a paragraph is the carriage return.

To select the paragraph and use the Breaks command, Xerox Ventura Publisher must be in the Paragraph mode. As with all other commands that control a paragraph tag, the changes you make with this command affect a particular paragraph tag. When a change is made to a paragraph tag, it affects all text marked with that paragraph tag in your Xerox Ventura Publisher document as well as in other documents that use the same Xerox Ventura Publisher style sheet.

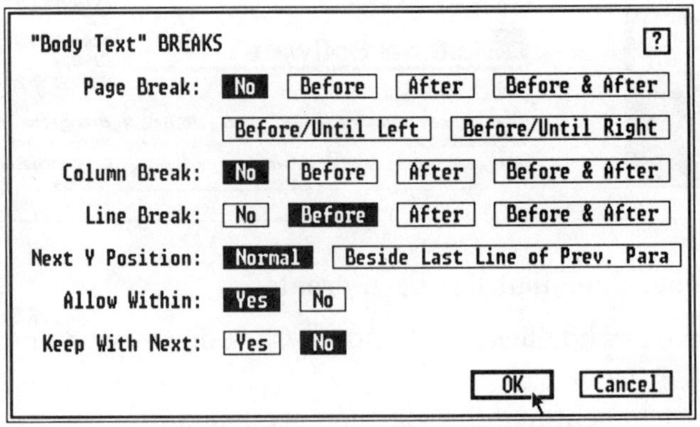

The Breaks dialog box contains these options:

Page Break — Select where the page breaks should occur in relation to the tagged paragraph. Use No if you do not want the paragraph to create a page break. Before places a page break in front of the paragraph. After places the page break following the paragraph. Before & After places a paragraph on a page by itself. Before/Until Left locates the page break at the top of right-hand pages within the Xerox Ventura Publisher document. Before/Until Right locates the page break at the top of left pages within the Xerox Ventura Publisher document.

TIP: The Page Break Before/Until Left or Right forces the text to the next left or right page. Xerox Ventura Publisher will automatically insert a blank page if necessary.

Column Break — Select where the column breaks occur in relation to the tagged paragraphs. (This option works the same way as the Page Break option, except it forces the text to the top of the next column, rather than the next page.) Use No if you do not want the paragraph to create a break. Before places a column break in front of the paragraph. After places the column break following the paragraph. Before & After positions a paragraph in a column by itself.

Line Break — Select where the line break occurs in relation to the tagged paragraphs. Use No if you do not want the paragraph to force a line break.

NOTE

If you select No, all successive paragraphs marked with this tag will run together.

Before positions a line break in front of the paragraph. After positions a line break following the paragraph. Before & After positions the paragraph alone.

Next Y Position — Select either Normal or Beside Last Line of Prev. Para. In most cases, select Normal. The Beside Last option allows you to place the text of the next paragraph on the same line as the previous paragraph. This is useful if your layout requires multi-columns tables or if you need to specify a portion of a paragraph as a different tag name.

Allow Within — Select Yes to have Xerox Ventura Publisher break paragraphs between columns or pages. Select No to have Xerox Ventura Publisher keep a paragraph in one page or column. If Xerox Ventura Publisher cannot fit the paragraph into the current page or column, it pushes the entire paragraph to the top of the next page or column.

TIP: In most cases, it is best to use Yes for Allow within.

Keep With Next — Select Yes to have Xerox Ventura Publisher keep the current paragraph and next paragraph in the same page or column. (This feature is extremely useful to keep headings with body text.) Select No if you always want Ventura to be able to break up the current paragraph and next paragraph between succeeding pages and columns.

The Breaks command is accessed by first selecting a paragraph and then selecting the Breaks command from the Paragraph menu.

APPLICATIONS

Breaks is an extremely powerful tool that will make your work with Xerox Ventura Publisher much easier. You can keep a paragraph from being split across a column or a page. Or you can allow the paragraph to be split across the column or the page.

The Breaks command also allows you to make settings that keep certain paragraphs together. This is useful for headings, caption numbers, or even bylines, where the paragraphs must be kept together to make sense in the publication. For example, you would not want the headline to appear on the bottom of the page, orphaned from the rest of the text.

The Breaks command also allows you to have certain paragraphs start at the top of a new page. For example, book chapters always start on the top of a page. Using this book as an example, suppose you create a paragraph tag called Module. You would assign Page Break Before to the tag. Then that tag would be assigned to each Module heading. Xerox Ventura Publisher would automatically push the text to the top of the next page.

The Breaks command can also be used in conjunction with the Spacing commands to create a table using vertical tabs. To do so, first type the text in your word processor like this:

PART NUMBER
DESCRIPTION
PRICE

A123
Eight-Inch Elastometer
$123.99
B456
Twelve-Inch Hydrometer
$454.87
C789
Fourteen-Inch Ohm Meter
$321.21

The paragraph tags (with proper spacing and settings) would make the text look like this:

PART NUMBER	DESCRIPTION	PRICE
A123	Eight-Inch Elastometer	$123.99
B456	Twelve-Inch Hydrometer	$454.87
C789	Fourteen-Inch Ohm Meter	$321.21

Each category in the vertical tab table would be assigned its own paragraph tag within the Xerox Ventura Publisher style sheet. For example, there would be three paragraph tags created, one each for Part No, Description, and Price.

In the Breaks dialog box, the Line Break settings for each Xerox Ventura Publisher paragraph tag would be:

Paragraph Tag	Line Break Settings
Part No	Before
Description	No
Price	After

To complete the vertical tab table format, you must access the Space dialog box and use the In From Left and In From Right settings. When completed, those settings should be similar to these:

Paragraph Tag	In From Left	In From Right
Part No	0	6
Description	1.5	3
Price	4	2

TYPICAL OPERATION

In this example, you use Breaks to change the attributes of Body text within the Xerox Ventura Publisher sample chapter document called SCOOP.CHP. The example begins with SCOOP.CHP already open. If you do not have this chapter open, use the Open Chapter command in the File menu to retrieve and open SCOOP.CHP. So your view matches the screen depicted in this book, press Ctrl-R.

1. Press **Ctrl-I** to select Paragraph mode.
2. Click on the first paragraph in the left column. In the Side Bar, Xerox Ventura Publisher indicates this is Body Text.
3. Point to the **Paragraph** menu and click on **Breaks**. The Breaks dialog box appears.
4. Select **After** in the Page Break option. Your screen should look like this:

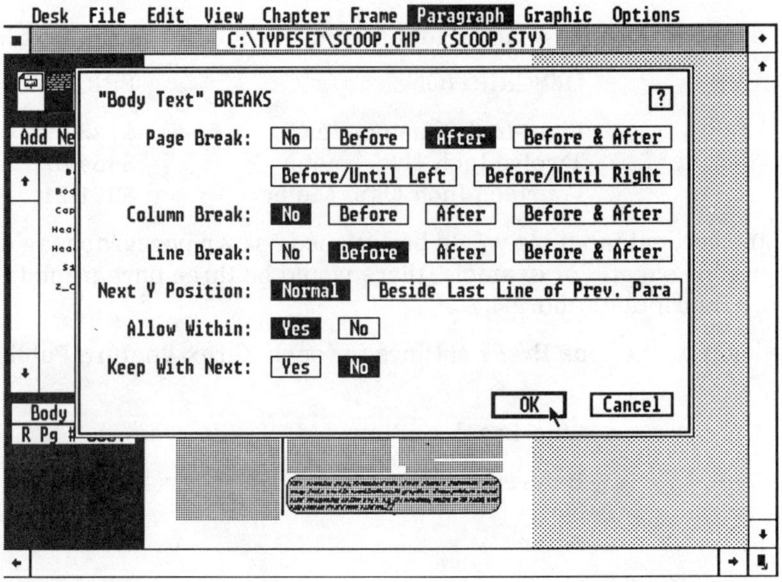

5. Click **OK**. Notice that Xerox Ventura Publisher has redrawn the screen, and the text following the selected paragraph is now on a separate page. Your screen should look like this:

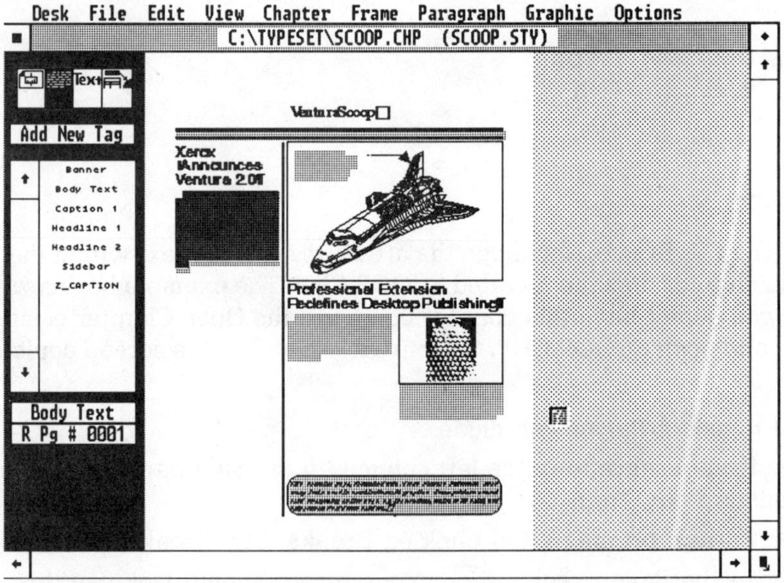

6. Point to the **Paragraph** menu and click on **Breaks**. The Breaks dialog box appears.
7. Select **No** in the Page Break option. Click **OK**. When Xerox Ventura Publisher redraws the screen, the document returns to normal.
8. Abandon the chapter without saving any changes.
9. Turn to Module 38 to continue the learning sequence.

Module 12

BRING TO FRONT, SEND TO BACK

DESCRIPTION

The Bring to Front and Send to Back commands allow you to change the stacking or layering of the graphics that overlay each other.

You can Bring to Front or Send to Back one graphic or multiple graphics at a time.

The Bring to Front command is accessed in the Graphic menu (you must be in the Graphics Drawing mode to access it) or by pressing Ctrl-A. The Send to Back command is also accessed in the Graphic menu or by pressing Ctrl-Z.

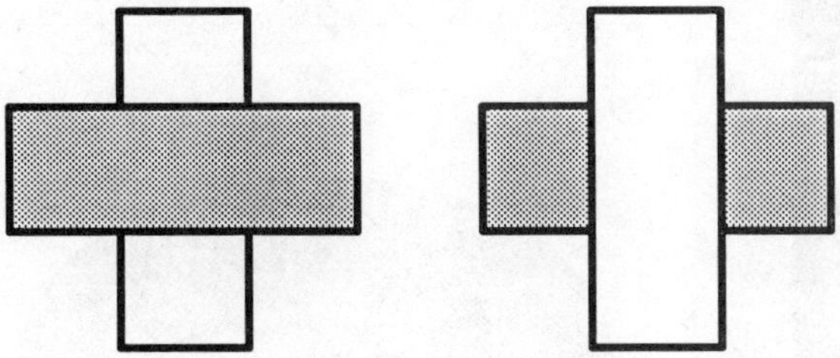

APPLICATIONS

These two commands are useful when you need to cover part of a graphic with another graphic.

For example, if you were drawing a simple block diagram, you could place the boxes and then connect them with a line. Then you could make the line look segmented by either bringing the blocks front, or by sending the lines back.

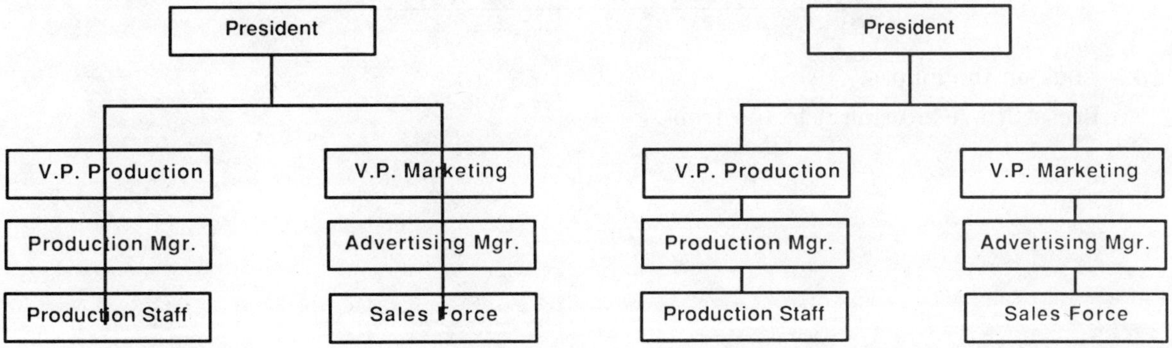

TYPICAL OPERATION

In this exercise, you create selected graphics and move them from the front to the back, and again from back to the front. Load the default style sheet and select normal view.

1. Point to the **File** menu and select **New.**
2. Press **Ctrl-U** to select the Frame mode.
3. Point to the **Add New Frame** button in the Side Bar and then create a new frame in the middle of the page.
4. Press **Ctrl-P** to select the Graphic Drawing mode.
5. Select the **Circle** tool from the Side Bar and click and drag the mouse down and to the right to create an ellipse. Release the mouse button.
6. Point to the **Graphic** menu and select **Fill Attributes**. Select **Black** for color and **3** for Pattern. Click **OK**.
7. Select the **Line** tool from the Side Bar, and draw a line over the top of the circle. Your screen should resemble this illustration:

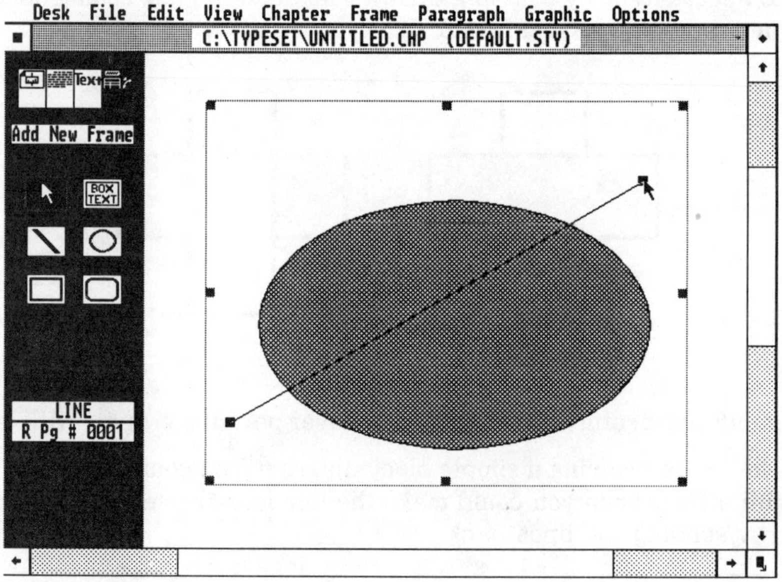

8. Click on the ellipse.
9. Press **Ctrl-A** to bring it to the front.

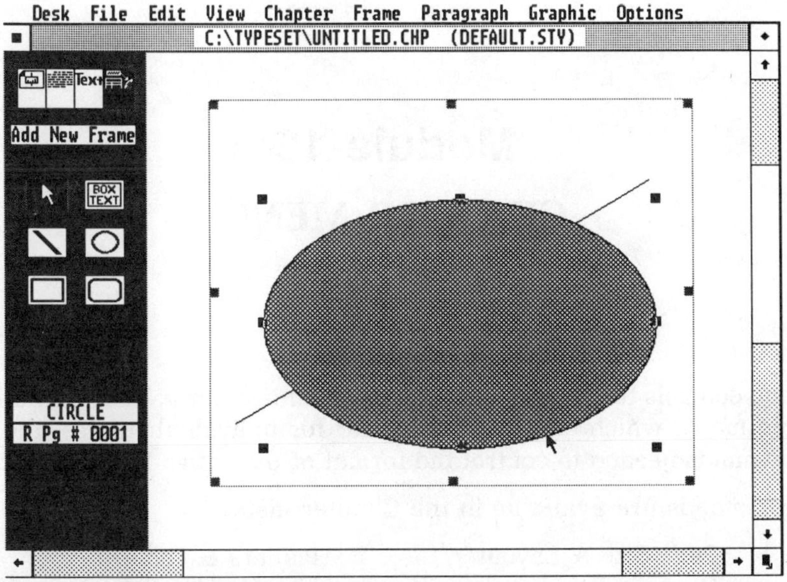

10. Press **Ctrl-Z** to send it to the back.

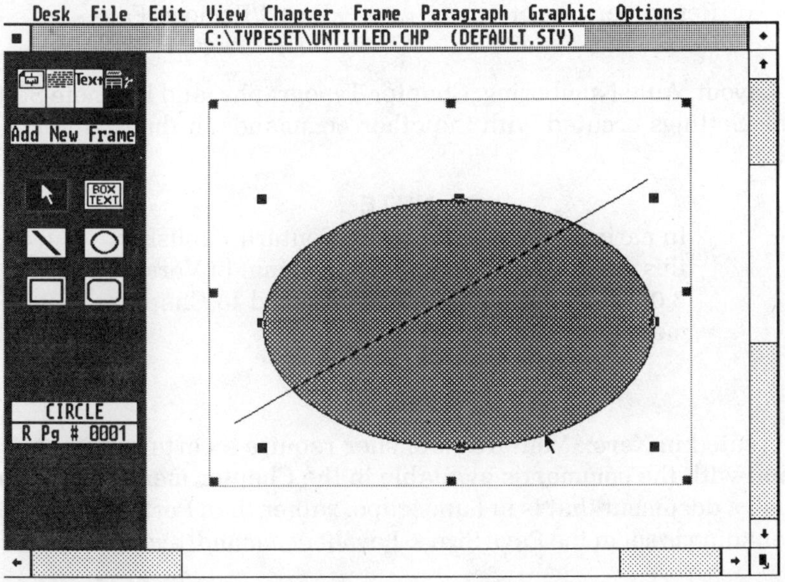

11. Point to the **File** menu and click on **Abandon**. Click on **OK** when prompted to revert back to the last saved version.
12. Turn to Module 16 to continue the learning sequence.

Module 13
CHAPTER MENU

DESCRIPTION

The Chapter menu controls the page formatting for an entire Xerox Ventura Publisher chapter. Unlike the Frame menu, which controls the format for individual frames, the Chapter menu provides the commands needed to control the format of the entire Ventura Publisher chapter.

The following commands are available in the Chapter menu:

Page Size & Layout	Headers & Footers
Chapter Typography	Turn Header On
Update Counters	Turn Footer On
Auto-Numbering	Footnote Settings
Renumber Chapter	Insert/Remove Page
Re-Anchor Frames	Go To Page

The Page Size & Layout, Auto-Numbering, Chapter Typography, and Footnote Settings are stored in the style sheet. Settings created with the other commands in the Chapter menu are stored with the chapter.

NOTE

In earlier releases of Xerox Ventura Publisher, this menu was called the Page menu. In Version 2.0, the menu's name was changed to Chapter menu.

APPLICATIONS

The documents created in Xerox Ventura Publisher require a certain format. You establish or change this format with the commands available in the Chapter menu. For example, if you are planning to publish a document that is in Landscape, rather than Portrait orientation, the setting for that page orientation is set in the Page Size & Layout command, available in the Chapter menu.

TYPICAL OPERATION

In this example, you open the Chapter menu and review the commands. The example begins with SCOOP.CHP already open. If you do not have this chapter open, use the Open Chapter command in the File menu to retrieve and open SCOOP.CHP.

1. Point to **Chapter** menu. The Chapter menu drops down.
2. Review the various commands available in the menu.
3. Click outside the menu to close it.
4. Turn to Module 46 to continue the learning sequence.

Module 14

CHAPTER TYPOGRAPHY

DESCRIPTION

The Chapter Typography command controls the character and line format for the entire Xerox Ventura Publisher chapter. Any settings made in the Chapter Typography command may be overridden in a frame by using the Frame Typography command (see Module 28), or in a paragraph by using the Paragraph Typography command (see Module 51).

The Chapter Typography command is accessed in the Chapter menu. When accessed, the Chapter Typography Settings dialog box appears.

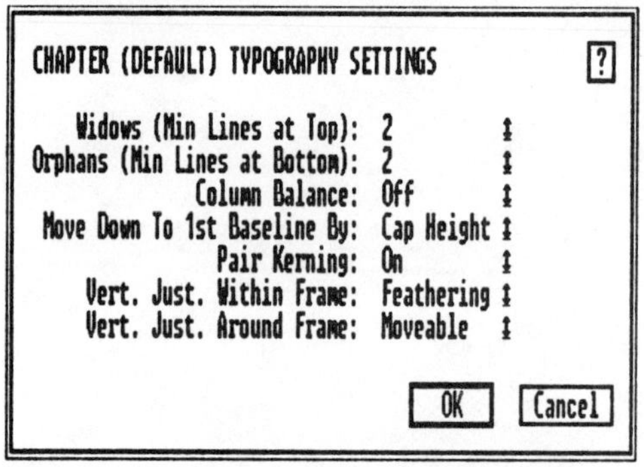

The following options are available in the Chapter Typography Settings dialog box:

Widows	A widow is a single line of text at the top of a page or column which has been separated from the rest of the paragraph on the previous page or in the previous column. The Widows option increases or decreases the number of lines that can be widowed within the frame.
Orphans	An orphan is a single line of text at the bottom of a page or column which has been separated from the rest of the paragraph on the following page or in the following column. The Orphans option increases or decreases the number of lines that can be orphaned within the frame.

NOTE

The default setting for both Widows and Orphans is two. This setting is standard and is sufficient for most applications. This setting requires at least two lines of text be left on the previous page or column or forced to the next page or column.

Column Balance	Set Column Balance On if you want the columns within the frame to balance. This would create columns of the same length. A setting of Column Balance Off allows uneven columns within the frame.
Move Down To 1st Baseline By	Xerox Ventura Publisher provides different settings to determine where the first line of text begins within a frame. Select Move Down To 1st Baseline By Cap Height if you want the top of the column to align with the top of the tallest capital letter in the font you have chosen. Select Move Down To 1st Baseline by Inter-Line if you want the first line of text to start down from the top margin the same amount as the inter-line spacing set with the Spacing command (see Module 67).
Pair Kerning	Select either Pair Kerning Off or On for the frame.
Vert. Just Within Frame	Turns on vertical justification, which spreads text to fill the column. Vertical Justification is only available in the Professional Extension to Xerox Ventura Publisher.
Vert. Just Around Frame	Lets you choose whether to allow frame movement to achieve vertical justification. (Available in the Professional Extension to Xerox Ventura Publisher.)

APPLICATIONS

The Chapter Typography command is used to define the typography of text within a chapter. This permits total control of the placement of text from column to column and from page to page. Being able to control the typography of your entire Xerox Ventura Publisher chapter permits you to change the style of documents to match your needs.

For example, you may want to use the Column Balance option in your Xerox Ventura Publisher document. By turning on the Column Balance in the Chapter Typography menu, all columns are balanced by Xerox Ventura Publisher within your chapter.

TYPICAL OPERATION

In this example, you turn off the Frame Typography and adjust the Chapter Typography for the Xerox Ventura Publisher sample chapter &LSTG-P2.CHP. This example begins with &LSTG-P2.CHP already open. To open &LSTG-P2.CHP, use the Open Chapter command in the File menu.

So your view matches the screen depicted in this module, press Ctrl-R. Your screen should resemble this illustration:

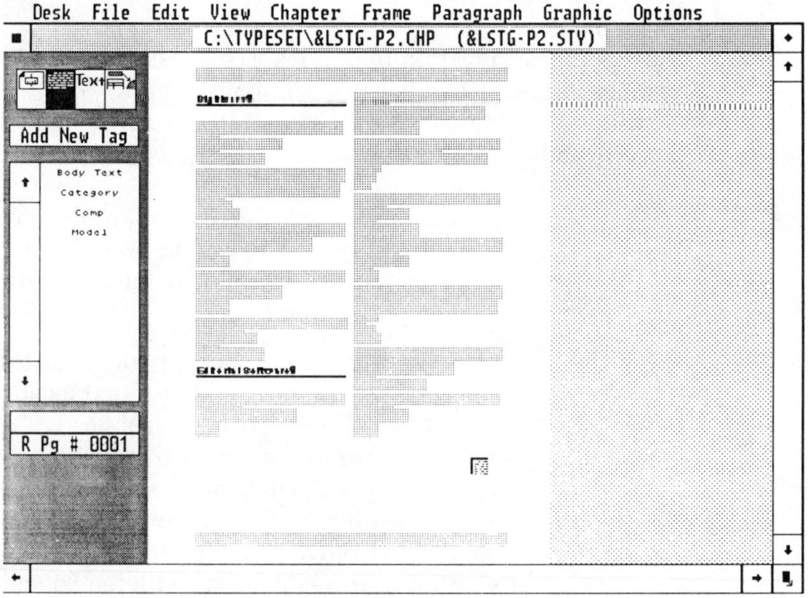

1. Press **Ctrl-U** to select Frame mode and click in the center of the page to select the underlying page frame.
2. Point to the **Frame** menu and click on **Frame Typography** to display the Frame Typography Settings dialog box.
3. Click on **Column Balance** and select **Default** in the pop-up menu. Your screen should resemble the following illustration:

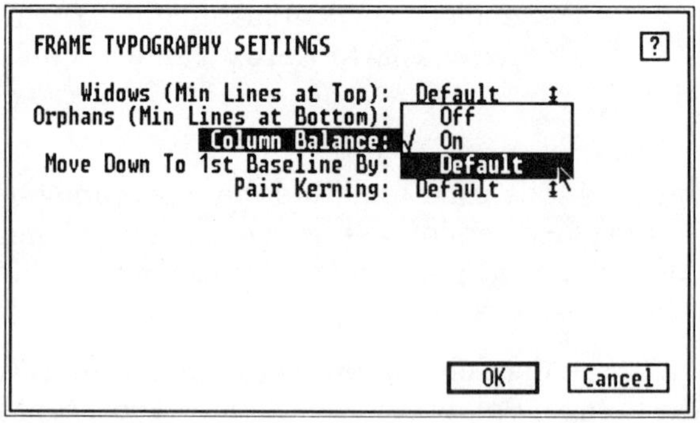

4. Click on **OK**.
5. Point to the **Chapter** menu and click on **Chapter Typography** to display the Chapter (Default) Typography Settings dialog box.
6. Click on **Column Balance** to make the pop-up menu appear.
7. Select **Off** to turn the Column Balance off. Your screen should resemble the following illustration:

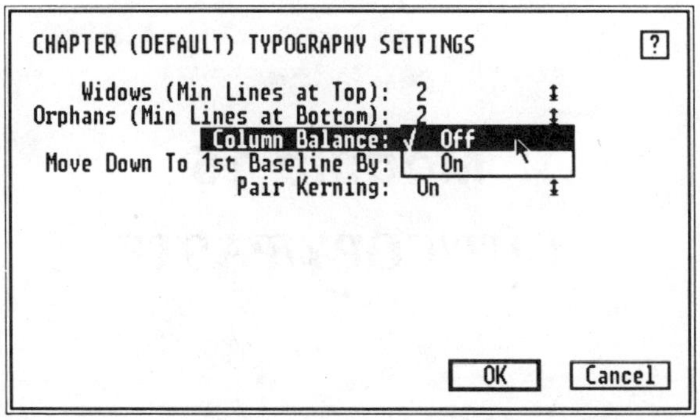

8. Click **OK** and notice the way the columns align on the page.
9. Point to the **Chapter** menu and click on **Chapter Typography** to display the Chapter (Default) Typography Settings dialog box.
10. Click on **Column Balance** to make the pop-up menu appear.
11. Select **On** to turn the Column Balance on. Click on **OK**. Your screen should resemble the following illustration:

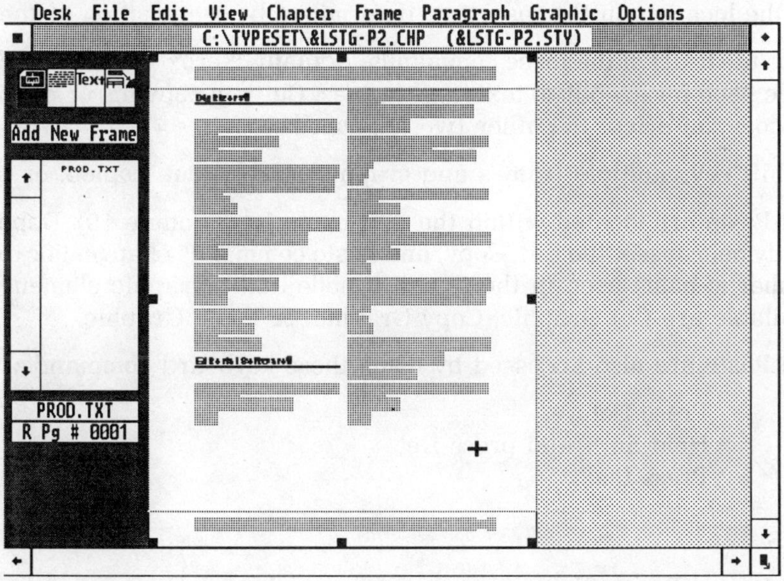

Notice the difference between Column Balance On and Column Balance Off.

12. Point to the **File** menu and click on **Abandon**. Click on **OK** when prompted to revert back to the last saved version.
13. Turn to Module 62 to continue the learning sequence.

Module 15

CUT/COPY/PASTE

DESCRIPTION

The Cut, Copy, and Paste commands allow the deletion and duplication of text, frames, and graphics.

Cut deletes an item that has been selected and places it into a temporary holding area called a clipboard. Copy duplicates an item that has been selected and places it into the clipboard.

Paste retrieves the item from the Clipboard and places it on the page. Paste places the graphics and frames on the page in the same position they were when they were cut or copied. Paste places text at the location on the insertion, determined by the position of the mouse cursor.

The Clipboard is the heart of the three commands. Actually, Xerox Ventura Publisher uses three clipboards—one each for graphics, text, and frames. Cutting, copying, or pasting objects from one clipboard does not affect the other two clipboards.

By using the Shift key, multiple frames and graphics can be cut, copied, or pasted.

Cut, Copy, and Paste are located within the Edit menu (see Module 19). Depending on which mode is currently being used, the Cut, Copy, and Paste commands change. For example, if Xerox Ventura Publisher is being used in the Graphic mode and a graphic element is selected, the commands available are Cut Graphic, Copy Graphic, or Paste Graphic.

Cut, Copy, and Paste are also accessed by using these keyboard commands:

Cut	Press Del
Copy	Hold Shift and press Del
Paste	Press Ins

APPLICATIONS

Cut, Copy, and Paste allows any item on the screen to be deleted, copied, or moved.

Depending on which mode is being used, these three commands assist in the manipulation of text, frames, or graphics. For example, if you are working in the Text mode, these commands can be used to move a block of text, just as Block commands are used in most word processors.

When working with graphics or frames, you might want to repeat a graphic or a frame on several pages throughout the document. By using Copy and Paste, you could reproduce the exact copy of your frame or graphic on other pages.

TYPICAL OPERATION

In this example, you use the cut and paste commands. The example begins with SCOOP.CHP already open and in use. If you do not have this chapter open, use the Open Chapter command in the File menu to retrieve and open SCOOP.CHP. So your view matches the screen depicted in this book, press Ctrl-R.

1. Press **Ctrl-U** and select the frame located in the middle of the page.
2. Point to the **Edit** menu and select **Cut Frame.** Your screen should look like this:

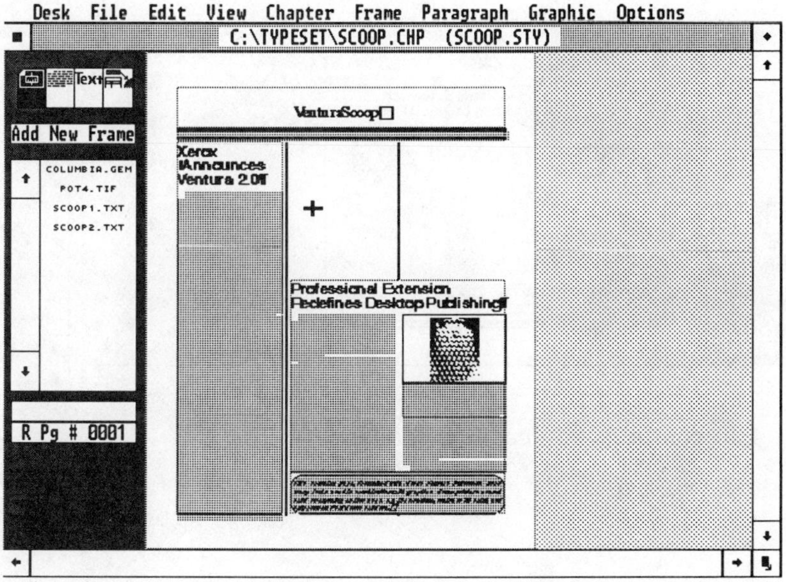

3. Retrieve the frame from the clipboard by pressing **Ins**. Your screen should now resemble this illustration:

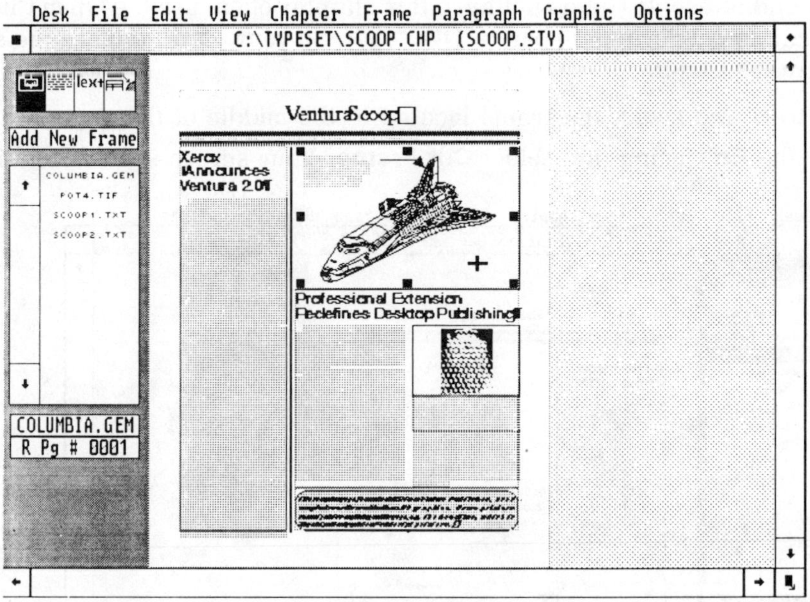

4. Turn to Module 4 to continue the learning sequence.

Module 16
DEFINE COLORS

DESCRIPTION

The Define Colors command defines colors and shades of gray. These colors can then be assigned to text, ruling lines, and graphics.

NOTE
Xerox Ventura Publisher does not determine colors of the final printed page of your document. The printer's ink is what determines the final color of the document.

The colors and shades of gray established with the Define Colors command only determines the colors and shades displayed on your computer screen. Depending on your computer equipment, you may see actual colors, or just shades of gray.

In some cases, you may be using a color PostScript printer, such as the QMS ColorScript 100. If so, your page prints in full color. Others may use a printer that converts the colors to shades of gray.

In most cases, however, you print each page to a black and white laser printer and Select Color Overlays in the To Print option. When this is done, a separate page is printed for each color defined and enabled. Colors are not converted to shades of gray. The printer takes a picture of the different pages and uses them to print the different colors.

To access the Define Colors command, Xerox Ventura Publisher must be in Paragraph Tagging mode. The Define Colors command is located within the Paragraph menu. When selected, the Define Colors dialog box appears:

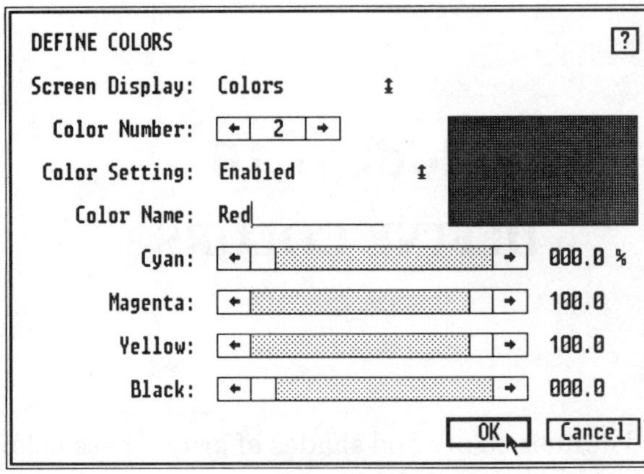

The following options are available within the Define Colors dialog box:

Screen Display	Select either Colors if you are printing to a color printer, or Shades of Gray if you are printing to a black and white printer.
Color Number	Select the color number. Color numbers range from 2 to 7. White is 0, and Black is 1. These numbers are preset and cannot be changed.
Color Setting	Select either Enable if you want to print a color separation for this color, or select Disable if you do not want to print a color separation for this color.
Color Name	Type in a color name. The Color Name defined is printed at the top of each page printed for that color when Spot Color Overlays is on in the To Print dialog box.
Cyan, Magenta, Yellow, Black	Define a color by mixing the colors using the scroll bars. As the color is mixed, you see the new changes in the box with the Define Colors dialog box.

For most applications, during the printing process, different printing plates are made for the colors being printed on your final published document. The black and white pages being printed from the laser printer are photographed, and the people running the printing press determine the final color of your documents.

APPLICATIONS

The main purpose of the Define Color command is to define a color name that can be assigned to fonts, rules, and background patterns. A different black and white page can then be printed for each color. Different printing plates can then easily be made by a printer to allow easy creation of the color document.

If you are using a color laser printer, you can also create the desired color for your document. Over 125 million colors are possible from the settings available in the Xerox Ventura Publisher Define Colors command.

TYPICAL OPERATION

In this operation, you define the color of a paragraph tag. The Xerox Ventura Publisher sample chapter &NEWS-P2.CHP is used. The example begins with &NEWS-P2.CHP already in use. Use the Open Chapter command in the File menu to retrieve and open &NEWS-P2.CHP.

1. Press **Ctrl-I** to select Paragraph Tagging mode.
2. Click on "Widget World News" to select the Masthead paragraph tag.
3. Point to the **Paragraph** menu and select **Define Colors** to display the Define Colors dialog box.
4. Select **Colors** for Screen Display.

NOTE

If you are printing to a black and white printer, select Shades of Gray for Screen Display.

5. Select **5** for Color Number. Select **OK**. Depending on your installation and computer equipment configuration, you may see the color assigned to the paragraph tag on your screen.
6. Turn to Module 34 to continue the learning sequence.

Module 17
DESK MENU

DESCRIPTION

The Desk menu provides Publisher Information which gives the product name, version number, and serial number of your copy of Xerox Ventura Publisher. If you ever need to call the Customer Applications Support Center, operated by Xerox Corporation, you will be asked to provide this information to the customer service representative.

TIP: The phone number of the Xerox Corporation's Customer Applications Support Center is: (214) 436-2616.

To access the Publisher Information from the Desk menu, simply point the mouse cursor to Desk and select Publisher Info. To exit, select OK.

TIP: Located within the Publisher Info dialog box is a dialog box called Ventura Publisher Diagnostics. To access this diagnostic dialog box, position the mouse on the word "Ventura" in the box that says, "Ventura Software, Inc." The information displayed pertains to Ventura's memory limits. Since this book was prepared for the beginning user of Xerox Ventura Publisher, the author has decided not to provide a detailed explanation of the various diagnostic reports. As your knowledge of Xerox Ventura Publisher increases, you will learn more about its operation, and this hidden feature may help you during complex document operations.

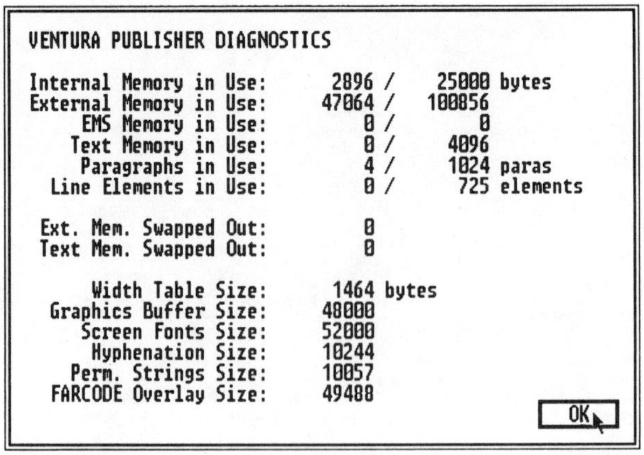

APPLICATIONS

The Desk menu provides the information needed when you call the Xerox Corporation's Customer Application Support Center. In addition, diagnostic information is also available, which requires a higher level of usage skill to understand.

TYPICAL OPERATION

In this example, you access the Publisher Info dialog box from the Desk menu and record the serial number of your copy of Xerox Ventura Publisher. The Xerox Ventura Publisher sample chapter document SCOOP.CHP is used. The example begins with SCOOP.CHP already open. Use the command Open Chapter in the File menu to retrieve and open SCOOP.CHP.

1. Point to the **Desk** menu.
2. Access the Publisher Info and record the serial number of your copy of Xerox Ventura Publisher.
3. Click **OK** to make the dialog box disappear.
4. Turn to Module 13 to continue the learning sequence.

Module 18

DOS FILE OPS

DESCRIPTION

The DOS File Op(eration)s command removes files and creates and removes directories from your disk. These standard DOS operations can be performed on both hard drives and floppy disks.

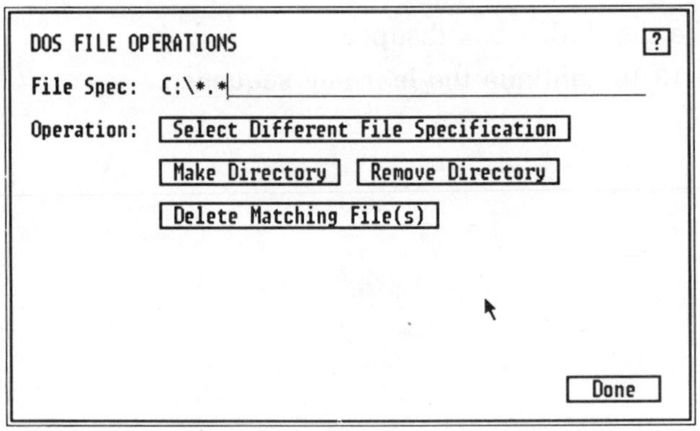

The DOS File Ops dialog box offers these options:

File Spec — Type the directory path, filename, and extension of the file to delete. DOS wild cards can be used for the filename and extension. For example, type C:\GEORGE*.* to access all files in the GEORGE directory. You can also create or delete directories by typing the name of the directory. For example, type C:\GEORGE to create or delete the GEORGE directory.

Operation — Select the function needed to process your files or directories.

Use Select Different File Specification to display a list of the files to delete. Xerox Ventura Publisher displays the Item Selector dialog box when a file is selected. When OK is clicked in the Item Selector box, Xerox Ventura Publisher places the directory path, filename, and extension in the File Spec entry area. If you already know the name of the file you are seeking, you can type its name in the File Spec area as an alternative to choosing Select Different File Specification.

Select Make Directory to create a directory with the name typed in the File Spec entry area.

Select Remove Directory to delete the directory with the name typed in the File Spec entry area.

Select Delete Matching Files to delete the file or files specified in the File Spec entry area.

NOTE

Before a directory can be deleted, all files and subdirectories in the directory must first be deleted.

To use the DOS File Op(eration)s command, select DOS File Ops from the File menu.

NOTE

No DOS file operation is performed if the file is write-protected or if the selected directory or file does not exist.

APPLICATIONS

The DOS File Op(eration)s command deletes files before quitting Xerox Ventura Publisher. Should you run out of room on your hard disk while saving a chapter or a style sheet, you can try to remove old, no-longer-needed files, so there is room to save the chapter or style sheet. To free additional disk space, the DOS File Ops command also removes subdirectories.

The DOS File Op(eration)s command also creates a subdirectory, should you decide to save style sheets or a chapter in a new DOS subdirectory.

You can also create a directory and, using the Copy All command in the Multi-Chapter command (see Module 44), copy all files of a chapter or publication into the new directory.

TYPICAL OPERATION

In this operation, you create a new directory and copy files into the new directory using the Copy All command in Multi-Chapter. The instructions begin with Xerox Ventura Publisher running and the screen blank.

1. Point to the **File** menu and click on **DOS File Ops** to display the Dos File Operations dialog box.
2. Type **C:\SCOOP** for File Spec. Your screen should resemble the following illustration:

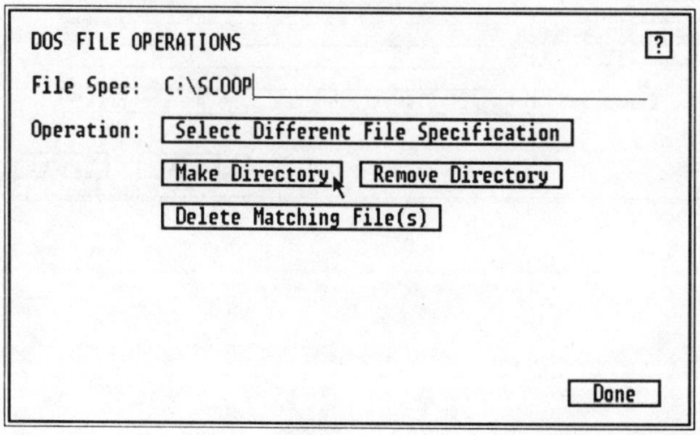

3. Select **Make Directory** for Operation to create the directory.
4. Click **Done** to exit from this command.
5. Point to the **Options** menu and click on **Multi-Chapter** to display the Multi-Chapter dialog box.
6. Select **New** to clear any files that might be displayed.
7. Select **Add Chapter** to display the Item Selector dialog box.
8. Type **SCOOP.CHP** and press **Enter**.

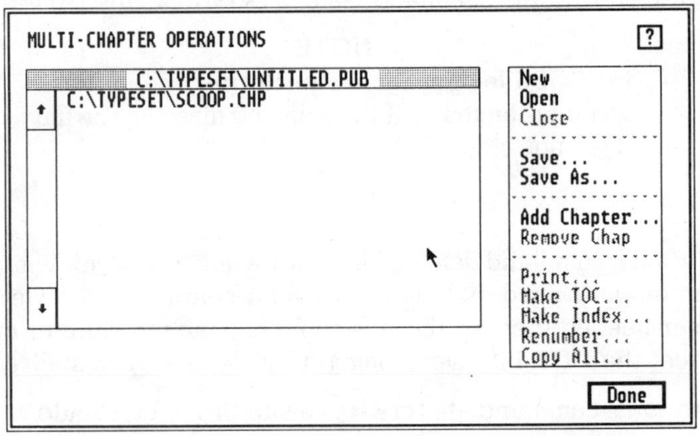

9. Select **Save As** and type **SCOOP.PUB** as Selection to save as a Xerox Ventura Publisher publication.
10. Select **Copy All** to display the Copy All dialog box. Notice the SOURCE PUB or CHP entry area contains the directory path, filename, and extension of the SCOOP publication file.

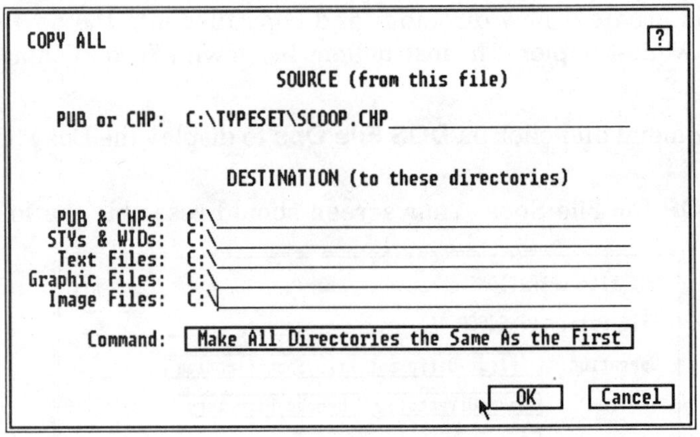

11. Type **C:\SCOOP** in the DESTINATION PUB & CHPS entry area and click on **Make All Directories the Same As the First.**

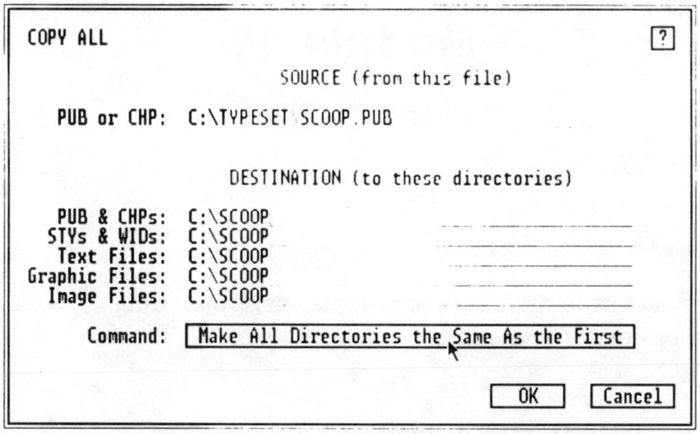

Notice that all destination directories are now the same.

12. Click **Cancel** to return to the Multi-Chapter dialog box.
13. Click **Done** to exit from the command. This ends the learning sequence.

Module 19
EDIT MENU

DESCRIPTION

The Edit menu offers access to a variety of commands. Depending on which mode of operation you are using, these options are available for your use:

In Frame mode:

- Cut, Copy, and Paste frames as well as their contents.
- Remove files from the currently selected frame, or remove a file from the Assignment List so they are no longer a part of the Xerox Ventura Publisher chapter.
- Rename files in the currently selected frame.
- Change a text file in the currently selected frame to another word processor's format.

In Text Editing mode:

- Cut, Copy, and Paste selected text.
- Insert and edit box characters, footnote and index references, fractions, and the frame anchors at the current text cursor location.

In Graphic mode:

- Cut, Copy, and Paste graphics and their contents.
- Remove files from the currently selected frame, or remove a file from the Assignment List so they are no longer a part of the Xerox Ventura Publisher chapter.
- Rename files in the currently selected frame.

In Paragraph Tagging mode:

- No options are available in the Edit menu.

APPLICATIONS

The Edit Menu offers a variety of commands that are useful when working in the Frame, Text Editing, or Graphic mode. Being able to edit—cutting, copying, or pasting—frames, text, or graphics, your use of Xerox Ventura Publisher is easier and takes less time.

TYPICAL OPERATION

In this example, you access and review the Edit menu when Xerox Ventura Publisher is in both Frame and Text Editing mode. The Xerox Ventura Publisher sample chapter SCOOP.CHP is used. The example begins with SCOOP.CHP already open and in use. Use the command Open Chapter in the File menu to retrieve and open SCOOP.CHP.

1. Press **Ctrl-U**. Point to the **Edit** menu and notice the available options.
2. Press **Ctrl-O**. Point to the **Edit** menu and notice the available options. The options are different than those available in step 1. If necessary, repeat step 1 to see the difference.
3. Turn to Module 70 to continue the learning sequence.

Module 20

FILE MENU

DESCRIPTION

The File menu controls the flow of information and files into and out of Xerox Ventura Publisher. In addition, the File menu provides the commands to save your documents and to leave the program.

The options available in the File menu are:

New	Load Diff. Style
Open Chapter	Save As New Style
Save	To Print
Save As	DOS File Ops
Abandon	Quit
Load Text/Picture	

The File menu contains the commands you need to open and close a Xerox Ventura Publisher document, to print it, to load style sheets and files, and to quit the program.

APPLICATIONS

The File menu provides many basic functions. When you need to print a Xerox Ventura Publisher document, the command to begin the printing process is located within this menu.

The File menu offers six basic commands. They are:

- Open or Save a Xerox Ventura Publisher document, or start a new one.
- Load text, line art, or image files into your current Xerox Ventura Publisher chapter file.
- Use a different style sheet than the one currently in use, or save a newly created style sheet.
- Print the Xerox Ventura Publisher chapter.
- Execute some DOS commands.
- Exit Xerox Ventura Publisher by using the Quit command.

TYPICAL OPERATION

In this example, you access the File menu and review the various commands available. The Xerox Ventura Publisher sample chapter document SCOOP.CHP is used. The example begins with SCOOP.CHP already in use. Use the command Open Chapter in the File menu to retrieve and open SCOOP.CHP.

1. Point to the **File** menu. Notice the various options available within this menu.
2. Turn to Module 30 to continue the learning sequence.

Module 21

FILE TYPE/RENAME

DESCRIPTION

The File Type/Rename command changes the word processor format of an existing file. The File Type/Rename command can also be used to create a new text file.

This command is accessed by first selecting either the underlying page frame or the frame holding the text file. The File/Type Rename command is accessed from the Edit menu.

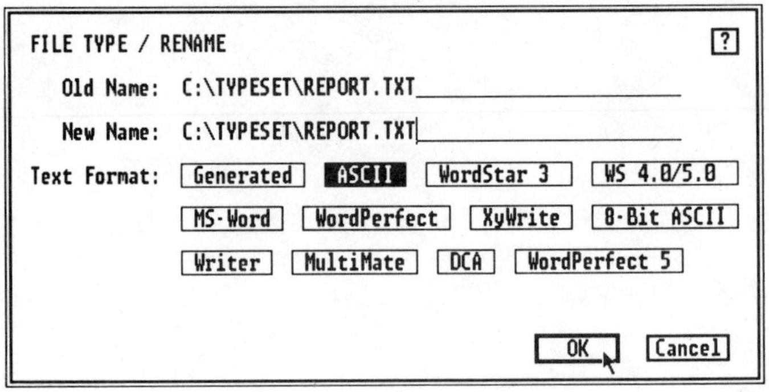

The File Type/Rename dialog box offers the following options:

Old Name	Type the current DOS directory path and filename that you need Xerox Ventura Publisher to process. Xerox Ventura Publisher will automatically enter the directory path and filename of the file in the selected frame or the underlying page. If desired, you can type the name of any other text file loaded into the Xerox Ventura Publisher chapter file.
New Name	Type the new directory path and the filename. Always type the file extension Xerox Ventura Publisher expects for the word processing format. For example, if the text file is XyWrite, use the .TXT extension.
Text Format	Select the type of text file you are creating. The type of file format chosen should be based upon the word processor you are using.

When the File Type/Rename command is executed, Xerox Ventura Publisher adds the name of the new text file in the Assignment List. If the text file you are processing was a caption file, the new entry will be displayed in the Assignment List. If the file was previously loaded into Xerox Ventura Publisher with the Load Text/Picture command (see Module 42), the old filename is replaced with the new filename in the Assignment List.

TIP: You cannot convert captions into separate text files if the captions are attached to frames or box text.

Xerox Ventura Publisher does not create and save the new text file until the current chapter is saved.

APPLICATIONS

File Type/Rename is used to rename an existing text file. It is also used to create a new text file.

This command can also be used to convert text from one word processor format to another. This option allows you to use text files from several different word processors and save them in a common file format, making it easier for you to work with the text files.

The command can also be used to convert caption files to text files. This can be useful if you want to bring the caption text into a word processor for editing.

TYPICAL OPERATION

In this example, you change the ASCII text file format to WordStar format. The Xerox Ventura Publisher sample chapter document &PRPT-P1.CHP is used. The example begins with &PRPT-P1.CHP already open and in use. Use the Open Chapter command in the File menu to retrieve and open &PRPT-P1.CHP. So your view matches the screen depicted in this book, press Ctrl-R.

1. Press **Ctrl-U** to select the Frame mode.
2. Click on the underlying page frame to select it.

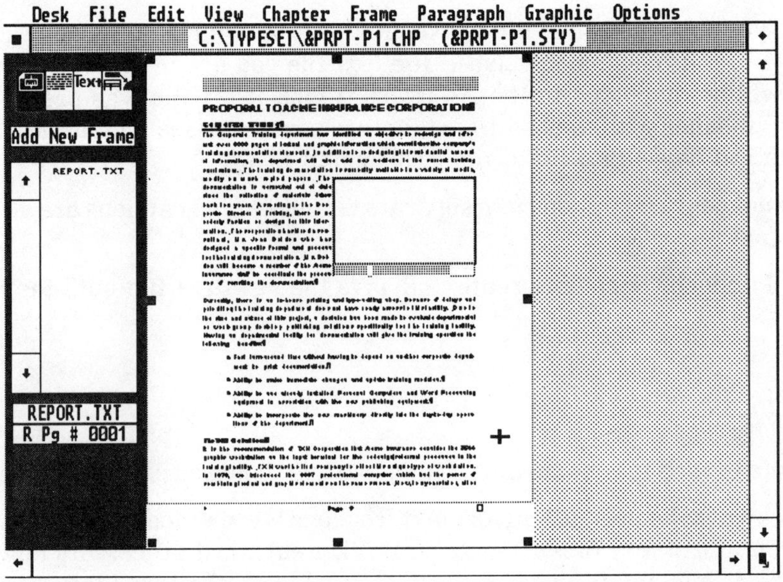

Notice that the name of the text file in the frame is being displayed by Xerox Ventura Publisher in the Current Selection box within the Side Bar. Also, note the filename is being displayed in the Assignment List.

3. Point to the **Edit** menu and click on **File Type/Rename** to display the File Type/Rename dialog box. Your screen should resemble this illustration:

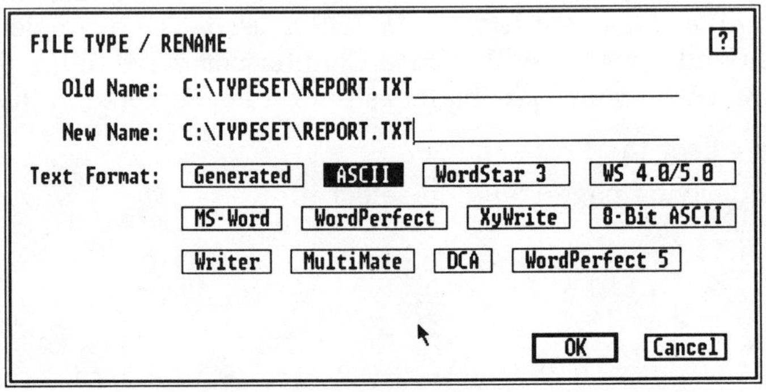

4. Click on the **New Name** line, and press **Backspace** enough times to delete the .TXT extension. Type **.WS** to save the file in WordStar format.

5. Click on **WordStar 4.0/5.0**, and press **Enter**.

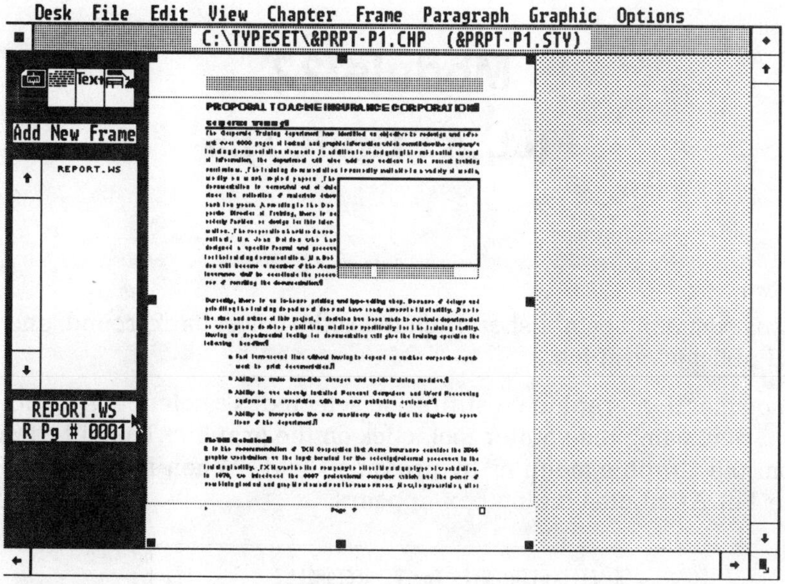

Notice that the new name of the text file in the frame is displayed in the Current Selection box and in the Assignment List. The old name is no longer in the Assignment List.

6. Point to the **File** menu and select **Abandon**. Click on **OK** when prompted to revert back to the last saved version.
7. Turn to Module 69 to continue the learning sequence.

Module 22

FILL ATTRIBUTES

DESCRIPTION

The Fill Attributes command establishes or changes the color, background, and pattern of each Xerox Ventura Publisher graphic.

To access this command, a graphic must first be selected. To select a graphic, first access the Graphics mode. Then, using the pointer tool, click on the graphic. The Fill Attributes command is accessed from the Graphic menu or by pressing Ctrl-F. When the Fill Attributes command is accessed, the Fill Attributes dialog box appears.

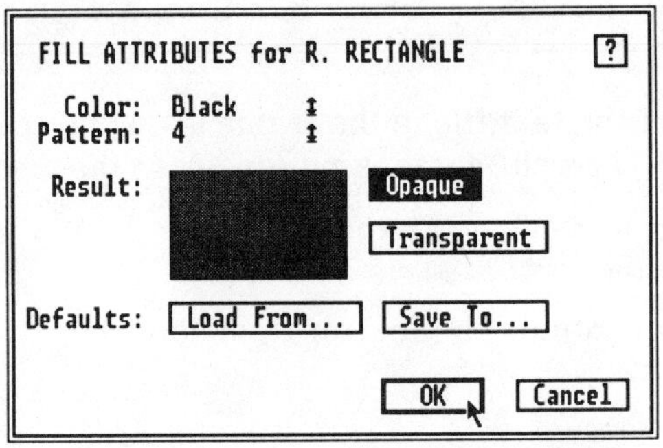

The Fill Attributes dialog box offers these options:

Color	Select a color that was previously defined.
Pattern	Select a number to represent the pattern desired. Select Hollow if no pattern or shade is to be used, or select Solid if a continuous fill pattern is desired.
Result	This area will display how the Fill Attributes selected will appear. Select Opaque to block all graphics underneath the selected graphic, or select Transparent for the graphic on the top if you want the underlying graphics to show through the top one.

TIP: Not all laser printers can print transparent graphics. To determine if your laser printer can print these types of graphics, print CAPABILI.CHP located in the /TYPESET directory to determine the capabilities of your printer.

Defaults — Select Load From to use the settings selected for another graphic, or select the Save To option to make the current settings the default for other graphics of the same type.

APPLICATIONS

Fill Attributes determine the background of Xerox Ventura Publisher graphics that have been created. This is an effective tool to help make more dynamic graphics. By adding a fill color or pattern, graphics can be more outstanding or more easily interpreted by the reader.

TYPICAL OPERATION

In this operation, a graphic is created and filled. The operation begins with Xerox Ventura Publisher running and a blank screen. Use the New command in File to get the blank screen. Use the DEFAULT.STY style sheet.

1. Press **Ctrl-U** to select Frame mode.
2. Move the mouse cursor to the middle of the page and click once.
3. Press **Ctrl-P** to select Graphic Drawing function.
4. Click on the Rounded Box tool, and move to the middle of the page. Click and drag, and create a rounded corner box. Your screen should resemble the following illustration:

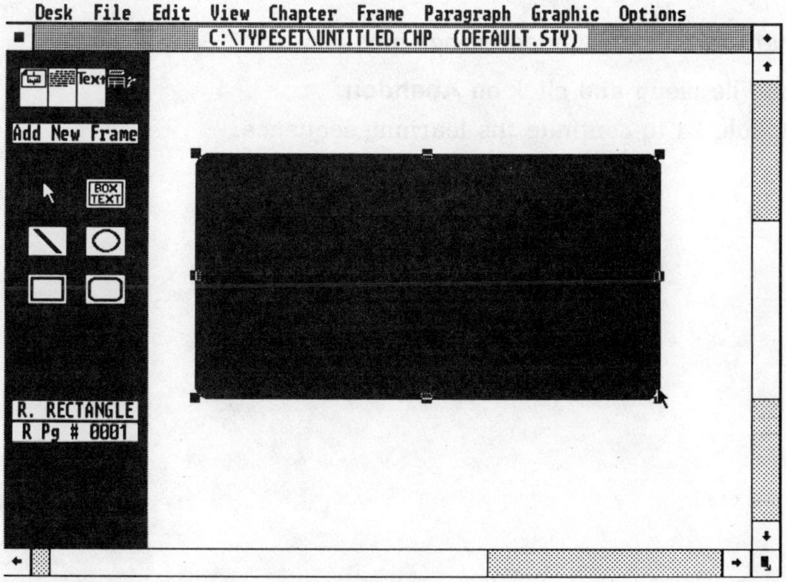

5. Point to the **Graphic** menu and click on **Fill Attributes** to display the Fill Attributes dialog box.

6. Click on **1** for Pattern, click on **Opaque**, and click **OK**. Your screen should resemble the following illustration:

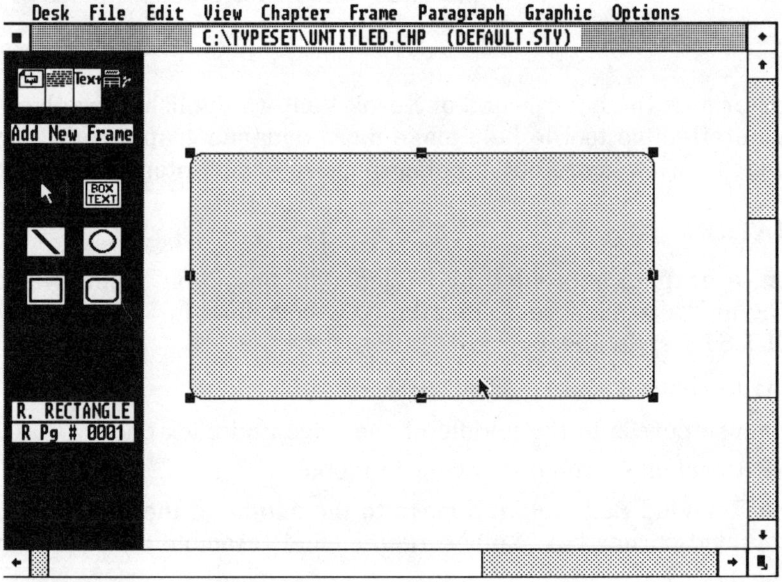

Notice the fill pattern of the rounded corner box.

7. Point to the **File** menu and click on **Abandon**.
8. Turn to Module 24 to continue the learning sequence.

Module 23
FONT

DESCRIPTION

The Font command sets the typeface, size, style, and color of the type for each paragraph tag. The command also allows you to assign underlines and strike-outs to your paragraph text. This command is accessed by selecting a paragraph with the tagging tool and then selecting the Font command from the Paragraph menu.

After the Font dialog box appears, select the face, size, style, and color from lists. These lists can be scrolled through to see more entries than can appear on the screen at one time.

Any changes made with this command affect the paragraph tag associated with the selected text. When a change is made to a paragraph tag, it affects all text marked with that paragraph tag in your document as well as in other documents that use the same style sheet.

A Xerox Ventura Publisher font is a type face of a particular size and style.

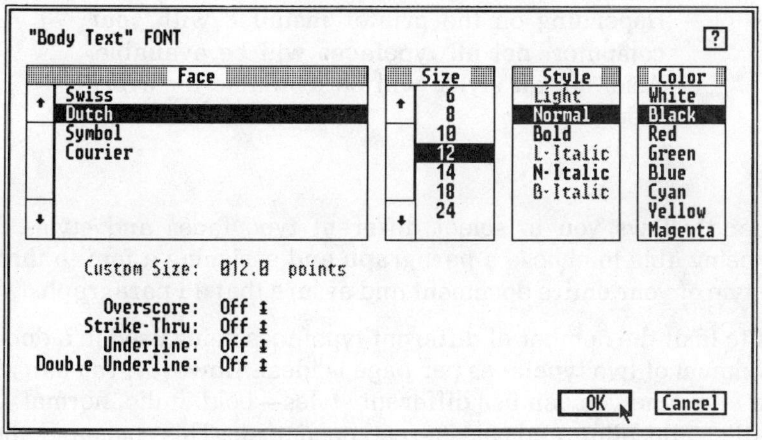

The Font dialog box contains these options:

Face — Select the type face desired for the paragraph tag. Scroll through this list by clicking on the up and down scroll arrows. Not all type faces are available for all printers. When a type face is available, its name is shown in black in the Face list. If it is not available, it will be displayed in gray in the Face list.

Size	Select the size of font desired. For many printers, select from a list of available type sizes. Scroll through this list by clicking on the up and down scroll arrows. Available sizes of fonts are shown in black. Sizes not available are shown in gray. If you are using a PostScript printer, select a custom size by typing the size of the font in the Custom Size entry area.
Style	Select the appearance attributes desired for the font. The style list includes light, normal, bold, bold italic, normal, normal italic, and light italic. If a particular style is not available on your printer, it is displayed in gray.
Color	Select the color desired to be assigned to the font.
Custom Size	Enter the size of type desired (if you are using a PostScript printer). Any size between 1 and 254 points is available.
Overscore	Turn on if overscored type is desired.
Strike-Thru	Turn on if strike-thru (sometimes called overstrike) type is desired.
Underline	Turn on if underlined text is desired.
Double Underline	Turn on if double underlined text is desired.

NOTE

Depending on the printer installed with your computer, not all typefaces will be available. Also, not all styles will be available for every typeface.

APPLICATIONS

The Font command allows you to select different type faces and styles for your various paragraphs. By being able to choose a paragraph and assigning a font to that paragraph, you can control the style of your entire document and assure that all paragraphs will look the same.

It is usually best to limit the number of different typefaces being used in a document. Designers tell us that a maximum of two typefaces per page is ideal. However, you can use different sizes of the same type face, and you can use different styles—bold, italic, normal—of the same font to create stimulating, appealing, and easy-to-read documents. This command allows you to assign fonts and styles to your paragraphs.

Use normal text for your body text, and use the italics and bold attributes for subheadlines and headlines within your Xerox Ventura Publisher documents. Simple designs often work best. Use care not to create documents with every possible attribute used in some form on each page.

TYPICAL OPERATION

In this example, you change the font assigned to a paragraph tag. This example uses the Xerox Ventura Publisher sample chapter &PRPT-P1.CHP. The example begins with &PRPT-P1.CHP already open. Use the Open Chapter command in the File menu to retrieve and open &PRPT-P1.CHP. So your view matches the screen depicted in this book, press Ctrl-N. You may need to adjust your screen using the scroll bars to make your computer look like the illustrations.

1. Press **Ctrl-I** to select the Paragraph Tag mode.
2. Click on the second paragraph.
3. Point to the **Paragraph** menu and click on **Font** to display the Font dialog box.
4. Click on either **Times Roman** or **Dutch** for Face, select **Bold** for Style, **Black** for color. Enter or select **14** point for size.
5. Click on **OK**. Your screen should resemble this illustration:

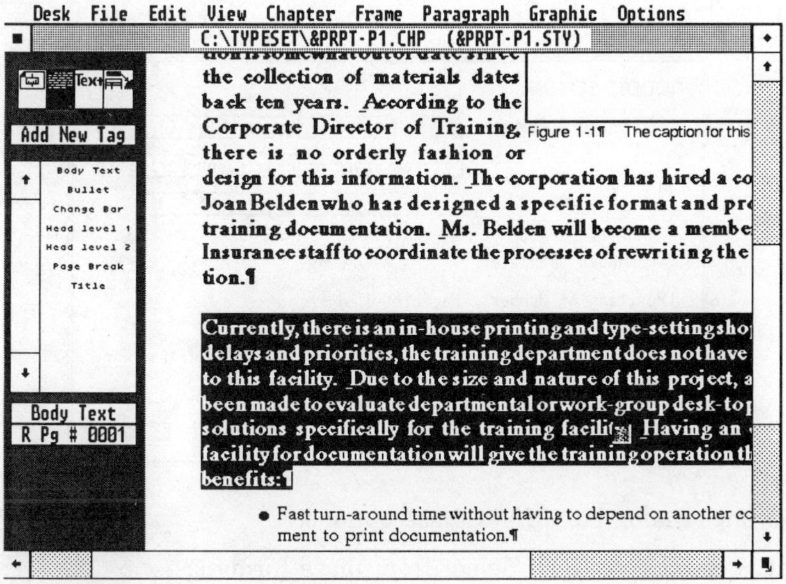

Notice the difference in appearance of the body text.

6. Point to the **File** menu and click on **Abandon**, then click on **OK** when the message box appears asking if you want to abandon changes.
7. Turn to Module 63 to continue the learning sequence.

Module 24
FOOTNOTES

DESCRIPTION

The Footnote Settings command controls the chapter's footnote formatting, the numbering, and positioning of the footnotes. Footnotes are actually created with the Insert Footnote command in the Edit menu. Xerox Ventura Publisher automatically adjusts the space required to place the footnotes at the bottom of the page.

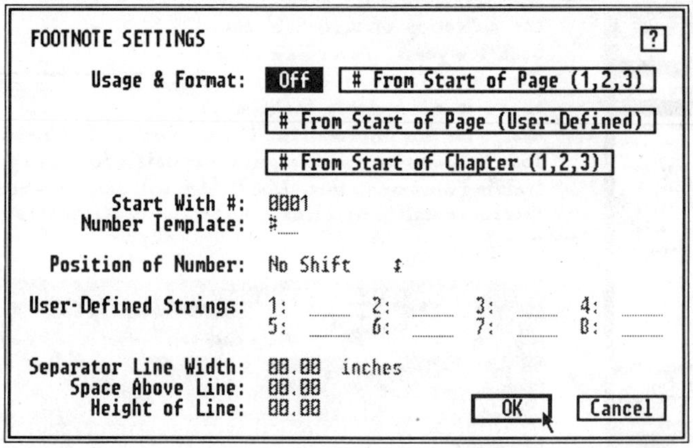

The Footnote Settings dialog box offers these options:

Usage & Format

Select from three formats:

Number (#) From Start of Page (1, 2, 3) — Arabic numbering restarts at the top of each page;

Number (#) From Start of Page (User-Defined) — User-defined designations restart at the top of each page (see User-Defined Strings below);

Number (#) From Start of Chapter (1, 2, 3) — Arabic numbering starts at the beginning of the chapter and continues sequentially through the end of the chapter.

Start With #

Enter the beginning number to use when Arabic numbering is selected for the footnotes.

Number Template	Enter the style desired for printing the footnote numbers at the bottom of the page. For example, enter -#- to make the numbers begin and end with a dash such as: -1-, -2-, and -3-. The pound character (#) indicates the position of the number itself.
Position of Number	Designate where the footnote numbers are to appear: on the same level (No Shift), above (Superscript), or below (Subscript) the regular text.
User-Defined Strings	If # From Start of Page (User-Defined) for Usage & Format is selected, enter the characters to use for up to eight footnotes on a page.
Separator Line Width	Enter the length of the line desired to separate the body text from the footnote text. Enter 00.00 if no line is desired.
Space Above Line	If separator line is used, enter the amount of space between the line and the text above.
Height of Line	If a separator line is used, enter the thickness of the line.

Xerox Ventura Publisher also creates a paragraph tag of your footnotes. You can use the automatically generated paragraph tag to add other attributes to your footnotes. (For more information see the Paragraph Tagging command.) The footnote number at the bottom of the page is automatically assigned a paragraph tag called Z_FNOT#, and the footnote itself is automatically assigned a tag called Z_FNOT ENTRY.

The footnote information is stored in the chapter file.

The Footnote Setting command is located in the Chapter menu.

NOTE

Footnote references must be placed in the underlying page. Xerox Ventura Publisher ignores footnotes in frames or in box text.

APPLICATIONS

The Footnote Settings command offers the capability of adding footnotes to your Xerox Ventura Publisher documents. The common use of footnotes is to provide quick, easy references to other information.

The Footnote itself is created in the Insert Footnote option within the Insert Special Item command located in the Edit menu. The Footnote Settings command controls the format of the footnote after it has been created.

TYPICAL OPERATION

This operation selects the format to be used of a footnote. The Xerox Ventura Publisher sample chapter &LTR1-P1.CHP is used. The instructions begin with the chapter open.

1. Point to the **Chapter** menu and click on **Footnote Settings** to display the Footnote Settings dialog box.
2. Select **# From Start of Page (1,2,3)**, type **0100** for Start With #, and click **OK**.
3. Press **Ctrl-O** to select Text Editing mode.
4. Move the cursor to the word widget in the first sentence. Click the mouse button once.
5. Press **Ctrl-C**. The Special Item box appears. Point to the Footnote. Your screen should resemble this illustration:

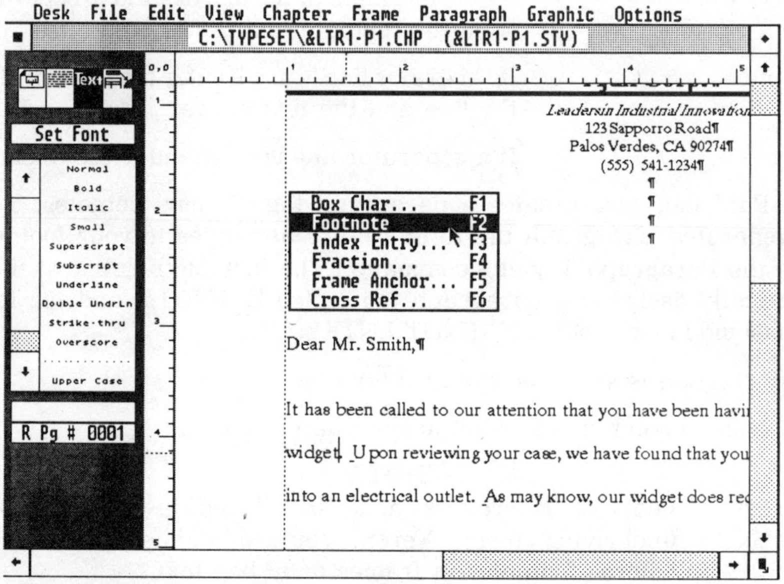

6. Click the mouse button once.
7. Use the scroll bars to move to the bottom of the page.
8. Click and hold the mouse button to select **Text of Footnote**. Press **Del**.

9. Type **Our Special A-199 Widgets**. Your screen should resemble this illustration:

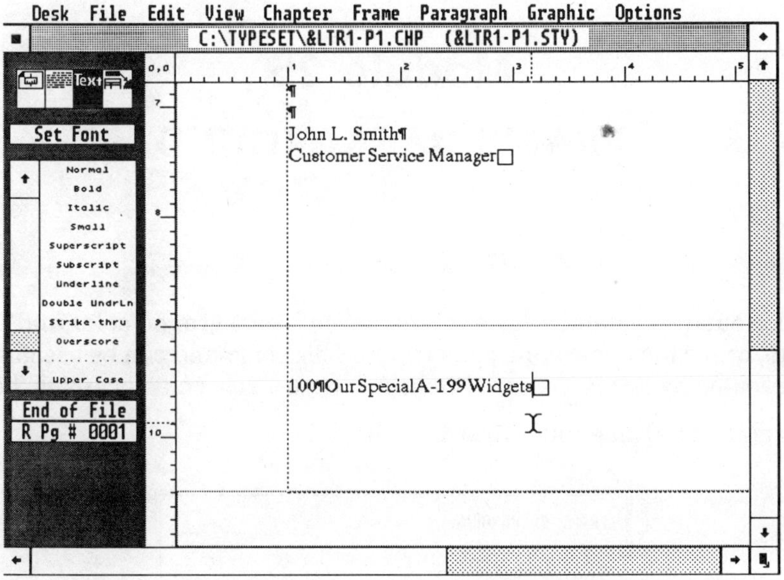

10. Abandon the chapter without saving any changes.
11. Turn to Module 10 to continue the learning sequence.

Module 25

FRAME BACKGROUND

DESCRIPTION

The Frame Background command allows you to create a background color and texture for each frame you create, or for the underlying page frame. This command can be assigned to any frame, including those created by Xerox Ventura Publisher when you specify a caption, header, or footer.

To use this command, a frame must first be selected.

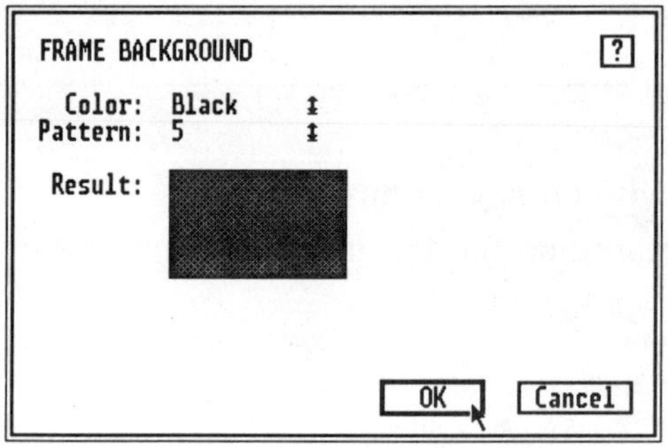

The Frame Background dialog box contains this information:

Color	A pop-up menu is available to choose the color you want to assign to a frame's background.
Pattern	Select a pattern for the color of the Frame's background. If you want no color, choose hollow (most frames are hollow so you can read the text or see the graphic). Solid will cause the Frame's background to be printed in a solid pattern. Choosing a number from 1 to 7 allows you to select different textures of color between hollow and solid.

Result	This square box allows you to see what the background you have selected will look like in your frame. If you do not like the appearance of your frame background, you can change it before leaving the Frame Background dialog box.

The Frame Background command is located in the Frame menu.

APPLICATIONS

Background colors and patterns are an effective tool for highlighting or calling attention to articles or sidebars. As an example, you can create a light gray screen in a frame to call attention to it.

TIP: Be careful not to choose a heavy screen (or high number for the pattern in the Frame Background dialog box) when text is going to be placed in the frame. Choosing too dark a frame background can make your text difficult, if not impossible, to read.

You can also use color to create reverse type in your document. By choosing a solid background and white as the color of your text, you can create reverse type. (Some laser printers are not capable of printing white text on a black background.)

Remember that when you choose a color for a background, your laser printer will create only a black or gray color background. Printer's ink, and not your laser printer, determines the color of your published document. The color selection is useful in creating a color separation (see Module 18 for more information about Color).

TYPICAL OPERATION

In this example, you add a frame and assign a background color and pattern to the frame. The Xerox Ventura Publisher sample chapter document &PRPT-P1.CHP is used. The example begins with &PRPT-P1.CHP already in use. Use the Open Chapter command in the File menu to retrieve and open &PRPT-P1.CHP if necessary. So your view matches the screen depicted in this module, press Ctrl-R. You may need to adjust your screen using the scroll bars to make your computer look like the illustrations.

1. Select the Frame Setting mode if necessary by pointing to the **View** menu and clicking on **Frame Setting**.
2. Click on the **Add New Frame** button. Pull the mouse cursor, which has changed shape to a corner of a box with the letters FR in the corner, to the upper left corner of the &PRPT-P1.CHP document.
3. Click and hold the mouse button. The cursor changes to the shape of a hand.

4. Drag the pointer (you should still be holding the mouse button as directed in step 3) and create a frame as illustrated:

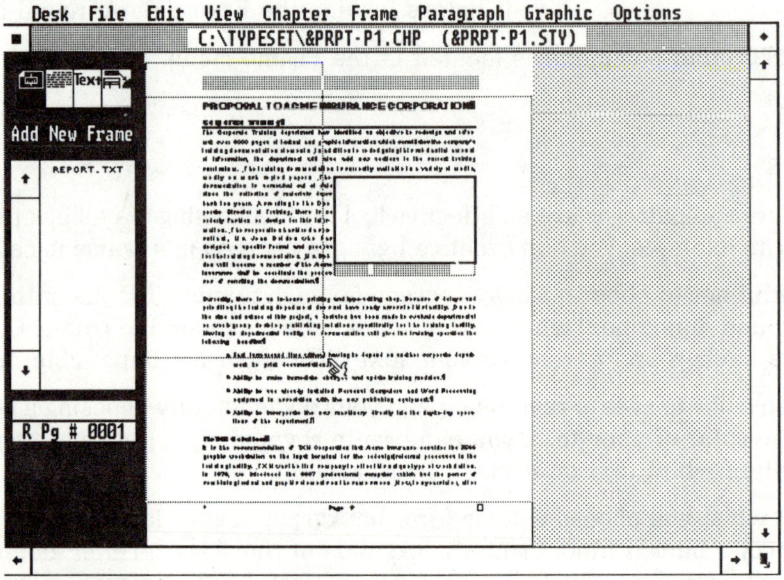

Let go of the mouse button to finish drawing the frame.

5. Move the mouse cursor to the **Frame** menu and click on **Frame Background**. Change the color to **Red** by accessing the pop-up Color menu, and change the Pattern to **5** by accessing the pop-up Pattern menu. Notice the pattern in the Result window.

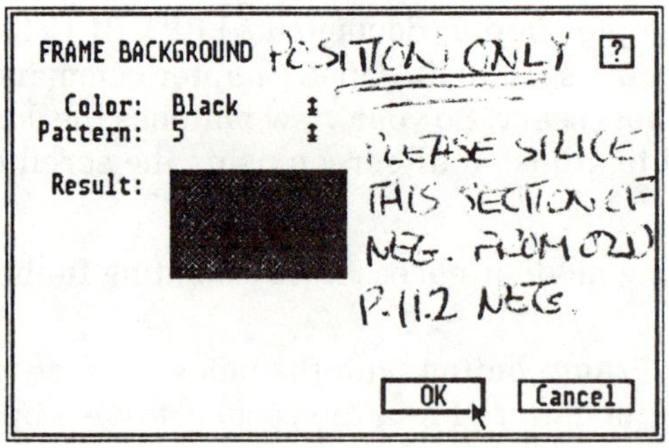

6. Click **OK**. The Frame Background of the frame created in steps 2 through 4 will now have the new background.

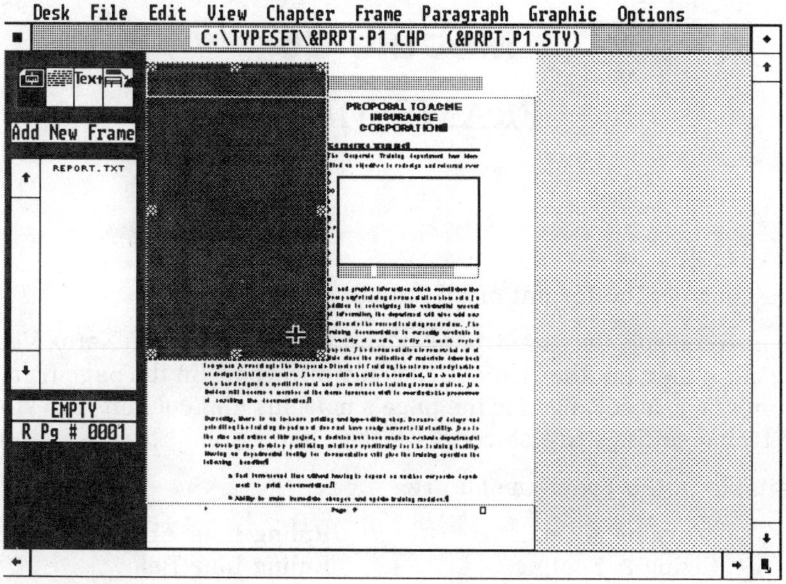

7. Press **Del** to delete the frame.
8. Point to the **File** menu and click on **Abandon** to abandon the changes to the chapter and revert to the previous version of the chapter.
9. Turn to Module 49 to continue the learning sequence.

Module 26

FRAME MENU

DESCRIPTION

The Frame menu controls the format of all frames.

The Frame menu also controls the format of all pages. Remember that in Xerox Ventura Publisher, a page is nothing more than another frame. The only difference in the page frame is the Margin and Column settings. Those settings for the page's margins and columns are stored in the style sheet. All other frame settings are stored with the chapter.

The options available in the Frame menu are:

Margins & Columns	Ruling Line Above
Sizing & Scaling	Ruling Line Below
Frame Typography	Ruling Box Around
Anchors & Captions	Frame Background
Repeating Frame	Image Settings
Vertical Rules	

Changes made to any page affect all non-inserted pages (see Module 41, Insert Page/Remove Page). Changes to each page you insert or to each frame you draw affect only that page or frame.

APPLICATIONS

Xerox Ventura Publisher Frame's menu provides you with the commands needed to maintain extensive control over all the frames that are used in a Ventura chapter.

Each frame can have its own set of formatting attributes, including its own margins and columns, captions, anchors, background, and ruling lines above, below, or around.

When producing documents with simple layouts, such as business reports, memos, or sales letters, the text is normally placed on the underlying page frame. For these types of documents, use the Frame menu to control the format of the underlying page frame.

When creating magazines, newsletters, books, manuals, and other types of publications that might include illustrations or multiple text files on the same page (just like a newspaper has more than one story on a page), you will need to use the Frame menu much more to define the settings for each frame you are placing within the Xerox Ventura Publisher document.

Remember also that frames can be layered, or stacked on top of each other. Each frame is controlled, and its attributes are defined, in the Frame menu.

TYPICAL OPERATION

In this example, you access the Frame menu, after selecting Frame Setting mode, and review the various commands available within the menu. The Xerox Ventura Publisher sample chapter document SCOOP.CHP is used. The example begins with SCOOP.CHP already open and in use. If you do not have this chapter open, use the Open Chapter command in the File menu to retrieve and open SCOOP.CHP.

1. Point to the **View** menu and click on **Frame Setting**. Press **Ctrl-R** if necessary to see the page in reduced view.
2. Click on the **Add New Frame** button in the Side Bar.
3. Move the pointer to the middle of the working area of your screen, then click and drag the mouse cursor to make a new frame. Your screen should resemble this illustration:

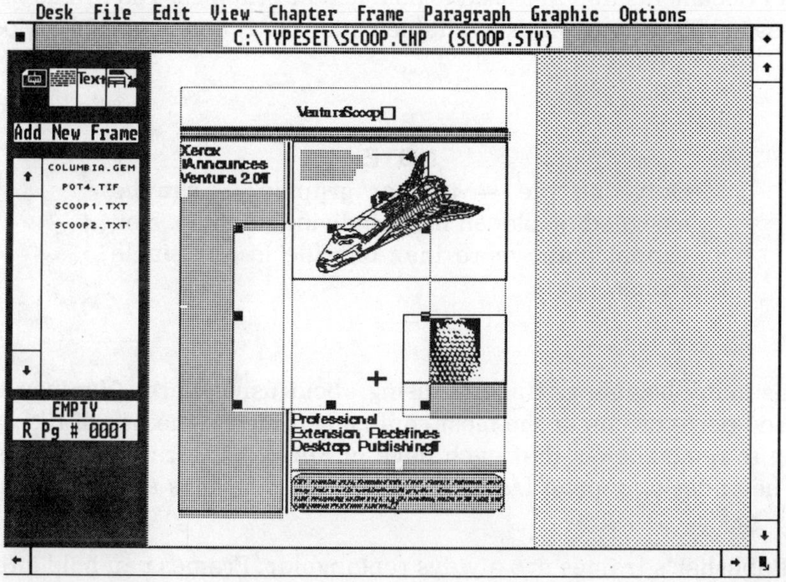

4. Point to the **Frame** menu and notice that all but the last selections are available. The new frame just created could have any of these commands assigned to it.
5. Move the mouse anywhere out of the Frame menu, and click once. The Frame menu disappears.
6. Move the mouse to the frame drawn in step 3, and click once to select it if it is not still selected.
7. Press **Del** to delete the frame drawn in step 3.
8. Point to the **File** menu and click on **Abandon** to abandon the changes to the chapter and revert to the previous version.
9. Turn to Module 27 to continue the learning sequence.

Module 27

FRAME SETTINGS

DESCRIPTION

The Frame Setting mode allows you to create, change, or design the areas within your Xerox Ventura Publisher documents that are used to hold text or graphics. The Frame Setting command also allows access to all the commands available under the Frame menu (see Module 26, Frame Menu).

NOTE

Only one file — text or graphic — can be assigned or placed in an individual frame. You cannot place more than one file in any single frame.

One of the things many beginners find confusing about using Xerox Ventura Publisher is its use of frames. And perhaps one of the most confusing issues is the use of the underlying page frame. The thing to remember is that each page in Xerox Ventura Publisher is nothing more than a frame. The underlying page frame is common to *all* pages and is a permanent part of the style sheet.

Xerox Ventura Publisher's frames are always rectangular. Frames can hold either graphics or text, but only one type of a file at one time. The text placed in a frame is most often imported from a file created with a word processor, but text created directly in Ventura can also be placed in a frame. Graphics must come from an external graphics program, such as AutoCad or PC PaintBrush. Either the underlying page frame, or frames you create can contain either text or graphics files, but once again, not both at the same time.

The underlying page frame and the frame you create are different in several ways. Consider this table:

Underlying Page Frame	*Created Frame*
The underlying page frame cannot be moved.	The frame can be moved with the mouse.
The underlying page frame cannot be deleted.	The frame can be deleted.
The underlying page frame creates the same basic layout for each page with the Xerox Ventura Publisher document.	Frames permit each page to have a different basic layout or design.
The underlying page frame is standard to all pages.	Frames are unique to each page.
The underlying page frame cannot be sized with the mouse.	Frames can be resized with a mouse.
There is only one underlying page frame to a Xerox Ventura Publisher document page.	Multiple frames per page are permitted.

Each time you create a new frame, Xerox Ventura Publisher places it "on top" of any other frame. Of course, you must physically position or place the frame on the page.

Frames can be made to "push away" text included in the underlying page frame or in another frame. In this illustration, notice how the new frame causes the text to be pushed away from the margin:

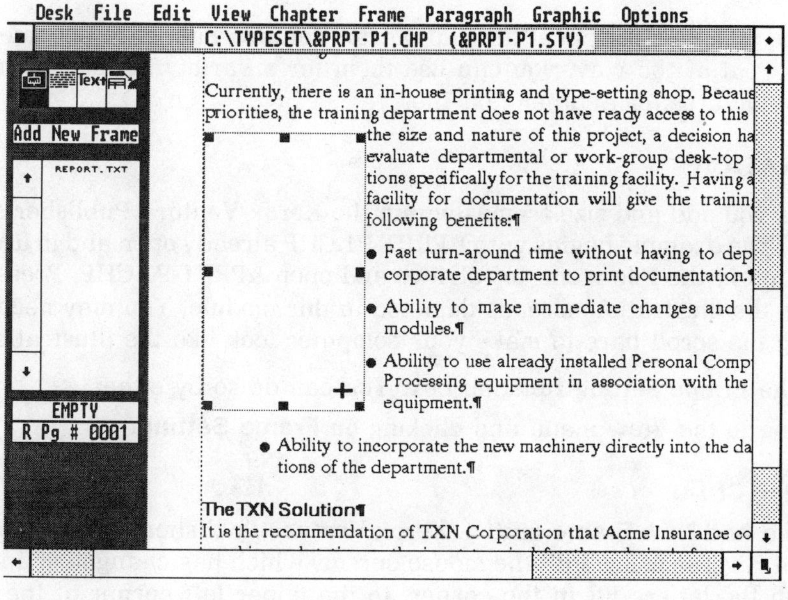

As you can see, this causes the text in one frame (in this case, the underlying page frame) to wrap around the added frame.

Text can also be flowed from one frame to another. This is an important concept when working with newspaper-type columns often found in newsletters. You can, for example, place three frames on a page, and Xerox Ventura Publisher will flow the text from the first frame you added, or the bottom one, to the top frame. The frame's order can be changed in the bottom-to-top sequence by cutting and pasting. When cut and pasted, the frame moves to the top of the sequence. The underlying page frame sequence, however, cannot be changed.

Frames can be sized, changed, or moved.

NOTE

Frames cannot be dragged from one page to another. To move a frame from one page to another, use Cut/Copy/Paste (see Module 15).

Frame Setting is located in the View menu. It can also be accessed by pressing Ctrl-U.

APPLICATIONS

The Frame Setting mode allows you access to the Frame menu. Frames—both the underlying page frame and the frames you draw—establish the overall design and appearance of your Xerox Ventura Publisher publications. The underlying page frame forces a consistent design on each page of your document. Frames you draw can be moved, sized, or deleted, allowing unique designs to your documents. Frames you draw can enhance the appearance of your Xerox Ventura Publisher documents by allowing you to add charts, tables, pictures, line-art, or computer created images.

Frames can also add "white space" to your Xerox Ventura Publisher documents. Since they can "push" text out of the way, you can use them for a variety of reasons, such as adding advertisements, pictures, or another text file.

TYPICAL OPERATION

In this example, you add and size frames within the Xerox Ventura Publisher sample chapter &PRPT-P1.CHP. The example begins with &PRPT-P1.CHP already open and in use. Use the Open Chapter command in the File menu to retrieve and open &PRPT-P1.CHP. Press Ctrl-R so your screen matches the illustration screens depicted in this module. You may need to adjust your screen by using the scroll bars to make your computer look like the illustrations.

1. Click on the Frame Setting function box. You can do so by either:

   a. Pointing to the **View** menu and clicking on **Frame Setting.**

   or

   b. Pressing **Ctrl-U**.

2. Click on the **Add New Frame** button. Xerox Ventura Publisher automatically changed the button to a reverse color. Pull the mouse cursor, which has changed shape to a corner of a box with the letters FR in the corner, to the upper left corner of the &PRPT-P1.CHP document. Your screen should resemble this illustration:

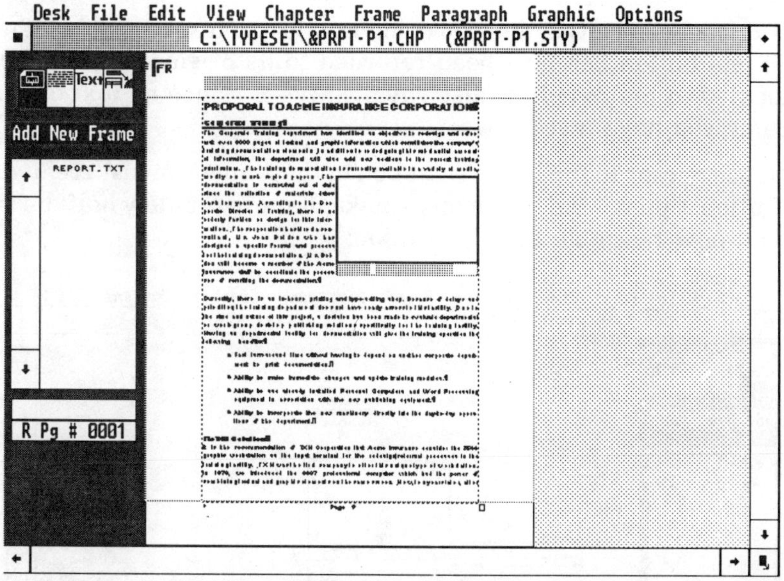

3. Click and hold the mouse button. The cursor changes to the shape of a hand.

TIP: Always drag the mouse down and to the right to create a new frame.

4. Drag the pointer (you should still be holding the mouse button as directed in step 3) and create a frame as illustrated:

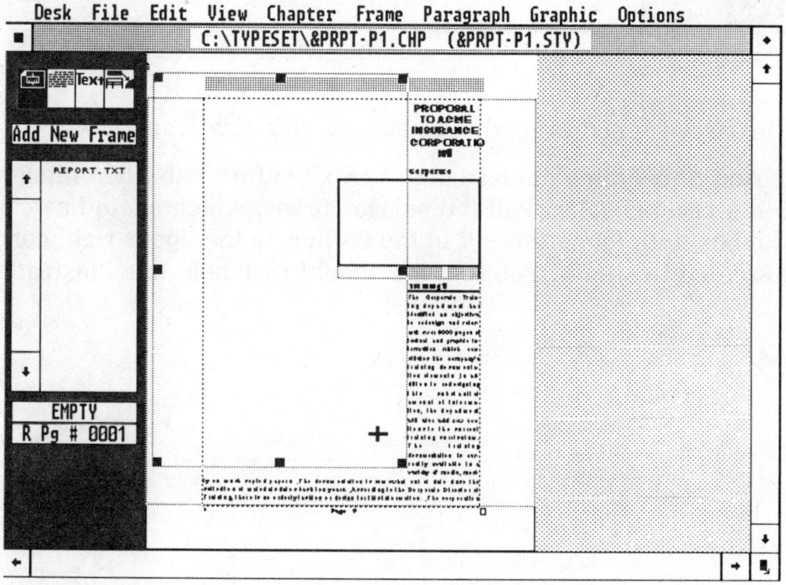

Notice that the text has been moved, and you could now load a text or graphic file into this frame. The Add New Frame button has now been returned to its original appearance. The Current Selection Box, located in the Side Bar, also says "EMPTY" since no text or graphic has been placed in the frame you have just drawn.

5. Move the mouse cursor to the lower right box in the frame you just created. Click and hold the mouse button, "push" the frame up to make it approximately half the size it was. Your screen should now resemble this illustration:

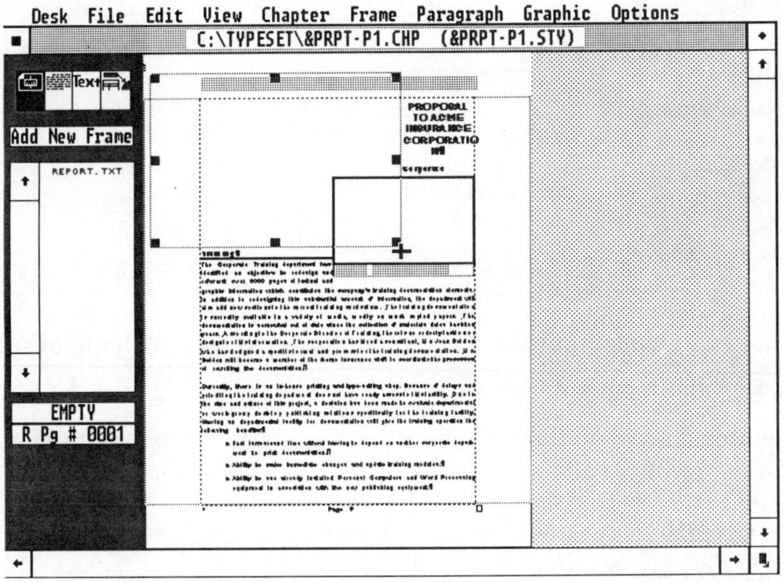

Notice how the text rewrapped around the new, smaller size frame.

6. Click on the **Add New Frame** button again. Xerox Ventura Publisher automatically changes the button to a reverse color. Pull the mouse cursor, which again has changed shape to a corner of a box with the letters FR in the corner, to the upper right corner of the other frame you created in step 4. Your screen should resemble this illustration:

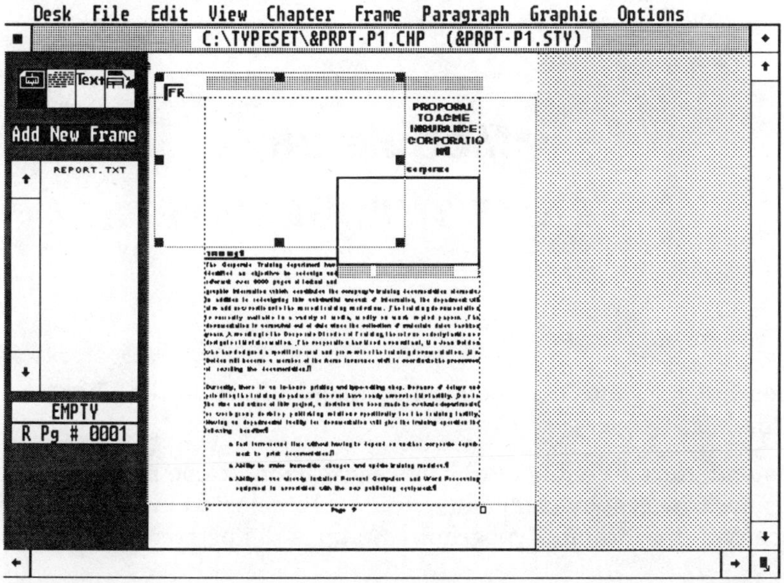

7. Click and hold the mouse button and create another frame. Create an oblong-type frame, as illustrated:

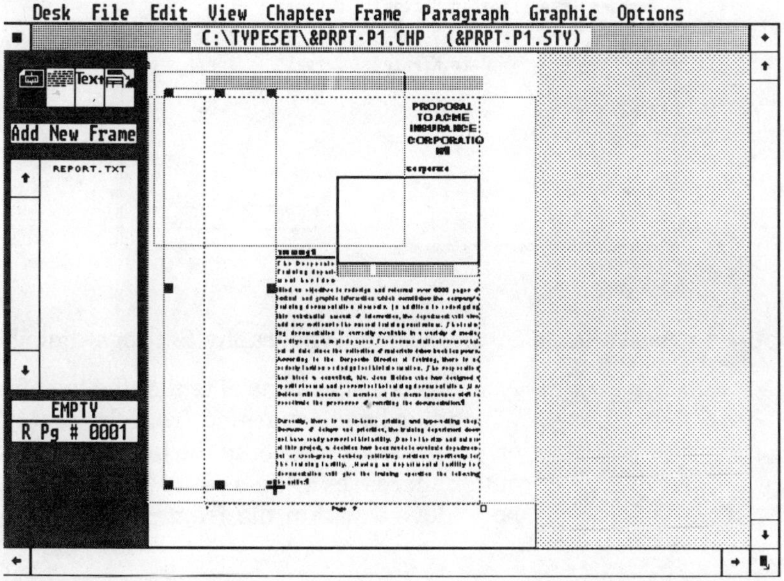

Once again, notice how the text has been pushed away by the new frame.

8. Press **Del** to delete the frame.
9. Point and click at the remaining frame. After it has been selected, press **Del** to delete that frame.
10. Turn to Module 25 to continue the learning sequence.

Module 28

FRAME TYPOGRAPHY

DESCRIPTION

The Frame Typography settings override the settings defined in the Chapter Typography (see Module 14) dialog box.

To use this command, Xerox Ventura Publisher must be in Frame mode. A frame must then be selected. The Frame Typography command can then be selected in the Frame menu. When the command is accessed, the Frame Typography Settings dialog box appears.

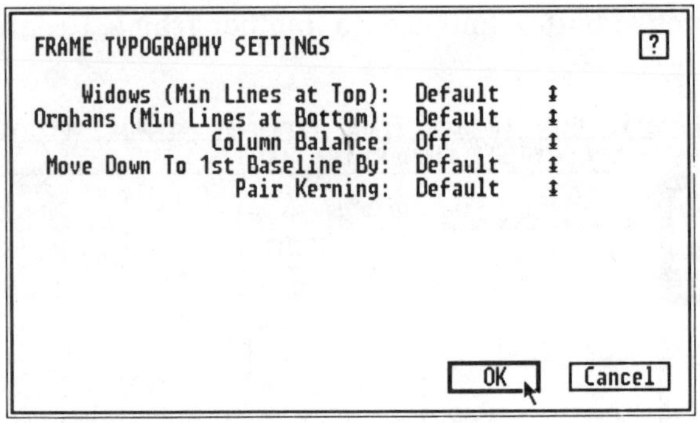

The following options are available in the Frame Typography Settings dialog box:

Widows — A widow is a single line of text at the top of a page or column which has been separated from the rest of the paragraph on the previous page or in the previous column. The Widows option increases or decreases the number of lines that can be widowed within the frame.

Orphans

An orphan is a single line of text at the bottom of a page or column which has been separated from the rest of the paragraph on the following page or in the following column. The Orphans option increases or decreases the number of lines than can be orphaned within the frame.

NOTE

The default setting for both Widows and Orphans is two. This setting is standard and is sufficient for most applications. This setting requires at least two lines of text be left on the previous page or column or forced to the next page or column.

Column Balance

Set the Column Balance on if you want the columns within the frame to balance. This would create columns of the same length. A setting of Column Balance Off will allow uneven columns within the frame.

Move Down To 1st Baseline By

Xerox Ventura Publisher provides two different settings to determine where the first line of text will begin within a frame. Select Move Down To 1st Baseline By Cap Height if you want the top of a column to align with the top of the tallest capital letter in the font you have chosen. Select Move Down To 1st Baseline by Inter-Line if you want the first line of text to start down from the top margin the same amount as the inter-line spacing set in the Spacing command (see Module 67).

Pair Kerning

Select either Pair Kerning Off or On for the frame. To override or accept the Automatic Pair kerning setting in the Paragraph menu. (See Module 49, Paragraph Menu.)

Selecting Default for any of these options forces Xerox Ventura Publisher to use the settings selected in the Chapter Typography menu (see Module 14). Selecting any other setting will override the values chosen in the Chapter Typography menu.

APPLICATIONS

The Frame Typography command is used to fine-tune the typography of text within a frame. This permits a more sophisticated layout and provides a set of different typographical controls in a given frame from the typography used in the rest of the document.

For example, you may not want to use the Column Balance option in your Xerox Ventura Publisher document, but you may want to use it in a specific frame. By using the Frame Typography command, you can opt to use column balancing in a specific frame.

TYPICAL OPERATION

In this example, a new frame is created, and the typography of the frame is set by using the Frame Typography command. The Xerox Ventura Publisher sample chapter &PRPT-P1.CHP is used. The example begins with &PRPT-P1.CHP already open. Use the Open Chapter command in the File menu to retrieve and open &PRPT-P1.CHP.

1. Press **Ctrl-U** to select Frame mode.
2. Select **Add New Frame** from the Side Bar.
3. Draw a new frame in the middle of your page.
4. Point to the **Frame** menu and click on **Frame Typography** to display the Frame Typography Settings dialog box.
5. Change the Widows setting to **4** by accessing the pop-up menu.
6. Press **Enter**. The Frame typography for your new frame has been changed.
7. Press **Del** to remove the frame from your document.
8. Abandon the changes to the chapter.
9. Turn to Module 32 to continue the learning sequence.

Module 29

GO TO PAGE

DESCRIPTION

The Go to Page command allows you to move quickly to any specific page in your document.

The Go to Page command is accessed in the Page menu or by pressing Ctrl-G.

When you access the Go to Page command, the Go to Page dialog box appears. Your screen will look like this illustration:

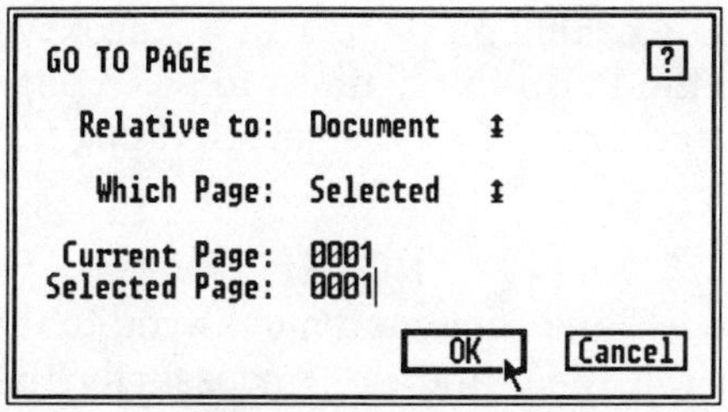

The Go to Page dialog box provides these choices:

Relative To

You can select either document or file. If you choose Document, the Go to Page command takes you page by page regardless of the content of each page. If you first select a frame, then access the Go to Page command, and finally select File, the Go to Page command will only access and move you to those pages with the frames containing the text file.

Which Page

Select first, previous, selected, next, or last. First will move you to the first page of your document or to the first page of your text file. Previous will move you back one page (for example, from page 7 to page 6). Selected moves you to the page you typed in at the bottom of Go to Page dialog box. Next moves you forward one page (for example, from page 7 to page 8). Last moves you to the last page of the document or the last page of a text file.

Current Page

This simply displays the current page of the Xerox Ventura Publisher chapter file.

Selected Page — This displays the page being selected and shows you where Xerox Ventura Publisher will be going. You can type in a specific page number here.

Keyboard Shortcuts There are several keyboard shortcuts to help you move around within a Xerox Ventura Publisher document. They are:

Go to:	*Use This Key:*
First	Home
Previous	PgUp
Next	PgDn
Last	End

APPLICATIONS

The Go to Page command is used to quickly move through your chapter file. This is helpful during the editing, revising, or changing of your document. You can easily go to any specified page by using this command. If you are working on page 1 in a Xerox Ventura Publisher chapter that has 50 pages, you could press the PgDn thirty times to go to page 31, or you could more easily use the Go to Page command, and type 31 as the selected page. By doing so, you will save time and make your work easier.

NOTE

The Go to Page command moves you to the page within the files, and not necessarily the page number within a document. To go to a specific page for a text file, select a frame holding the text file, select File for Relative to:, and then make your selection in the Which Page section of the Go to Page dialog box.

TIP: To halt a Go to command, press Esc.

TYPICAL OPERATION

In this example, you use the Go to Page command. The &PRPT-P1.CHP sample chapter is used. The example begins with &PRPT-P1.CHP already open and in use. If you do not have this chapter open, use the Open Chapter command in the File menu to retrieve and open &PRPT-P1.CHP.

1. Point to **Chapter Menu** and click on **Go to Page**. When the Go to Page dialog box appears, click on the pop-up menu button for Which Page.
2. Select **Last** within the pop-up menu. Select **OK**.
3. Turn to Module 39 to continue the learning sequence.

Module 30

GRAPHIC MENU

DESCRIPTION

The Graphic menu allows access to Xerox Ventura Publisher's commands that control selected graphics that have been created within a Ventura document. These commands affect the graphics drawn and created in the Graphics mode.

The commands available in the Graphic menu are:

Show On All Pages	Fill Attributes
Send to Back	Select All
Bring to Front	Grid Settings
Line Attributes	

To access the various commands available in the Graphic menu, select the Graphic mode.

APPLICATIONS

The Graphic menu provides commands to make working with the graphics created within a Xerox Ventura Publisher easier. The major functions of the commands are:

- Repeat the graphic on each page of a document.
- Move the graphic in front of or behind another graphic.
- Change and set the line and shading attributes.
- Create a grid so the graphics will snap to it, making positioning easier.

There are keyboard shortcuts available for some of the commands located within the Graphic menu. They are:

Ctrl-Z	Send to Back
Ctrl-A	Bring to Front
Ctrl-L	Line Attributes
Ctrl-F	Fill attributes
Ctrl-Q	Select All

TYPICAL OPERATION

In this example, you access the Graphic menu and review the various commands available. The Xerox Ventura Publisher sample chapter SCOOP.CHP is used. The example begins with SCOOP.CHP already in use. If you do not have this chapter open, use the Open Chapter command in the File menu to retrieve and open SCOOP.CHP.

1. Press **Ctrl-P**.
2. Point to the **Graphic** menu and notice the various options available. Only Select All & Grid Settings are currently available since no particular graphic is selected.
3. Turn to Module 47 to continue the learning sequence.

Module 31

GRID SETTINGS

DESCRIPTION

The Grid Settings command defines the settings of a grid used during the sizing and shaping of Ventura Publisher graphics. You can turn the grid either on or off.

When the grid is on, the graphics you create or size will automatically align or "snap" to horizontal and vertical lines of the grid.

The grid lines are invisible and cannot be seen on your computer screen. The following illustration depicts the function of the Grid settings feature in Ventura Publisher:

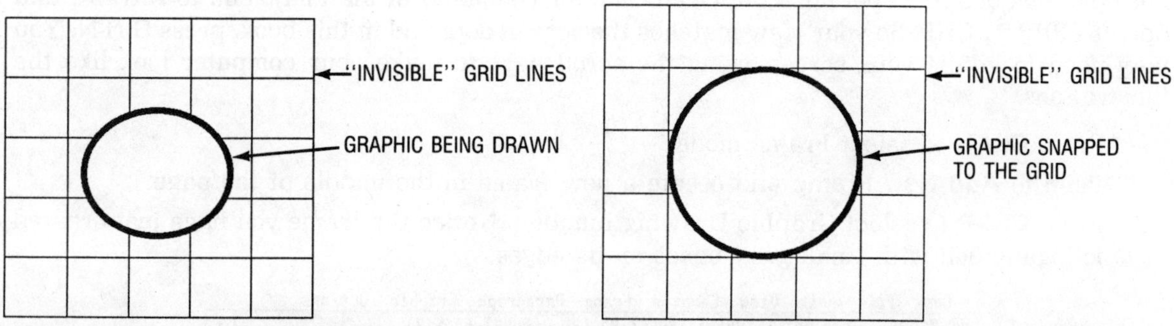

The Grid Settings command is accessed in the Graphic menu. When accessed, the Grid Settings dialog box appears. Your screen will resemble this illustration:

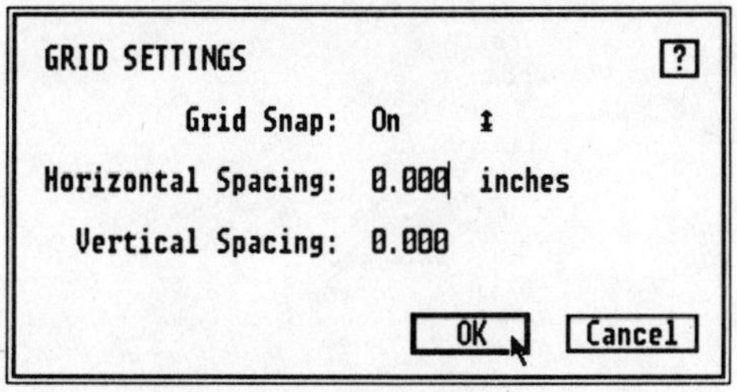

The Grid Settings dialog box provides these choices:

Grid Snap	Select either on or off to make the grid active or not active.
Horizontal Spacing	Type the amount of space desired between the horizontal lines of the grid.

Vertical Spacing — Type the amount of space desired between the vertical lines of the grid.

NOTE

The grid settings affect only the graphics associated with the selected frame. Grid settings apply only to that particular frame, not to all the graphics or frames in your document.

APPLICATIONS

The Grid Settings command allows precise creation of graphics within Xerox Ventura Publisher documents. The grid settings assure perfect vertical and horizontal alignment.

When creating forms or tables, where adjacent boxes must line up exactly, the Grid Settings command allows the precision placement to take place so precise alignment is achieved.

TYPICAL OPERATION

In this operation, you define a grid, turn it on, and draw and resize graphics. The instructions begin with the Xerox Ventura Publisher sample chapter &PRPT-P1.CHP being used. If you do not have this chapter open, use the Open Chapter command in the File menu to retrieve and open &PRPT-P1.CHP. So your view matches the screen depicted in this book, press Ctrl-N. You may need to adjust your screen using the scroll bars to make your computer look like the illustrations.

1. Press **Ctrl-U** to select Frame mode.
2. Point to **Add New Frame** and create a new frame in the middle of the page.
3. Press **Ctrl-P** to select Graphic Drawing function. Notice the frame you have just created is highlighted with small gray boxes on its edges.

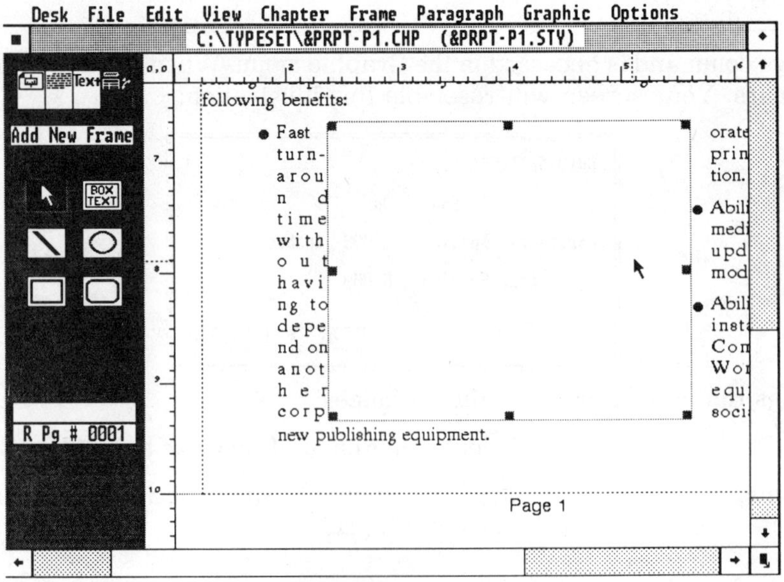

4. Point to the **Graphics** menu and click on **Grid Settings** to display the Grid Settings dialog box.
5. Select **On** for Grid Snap, type **36.00** fractional points for Horizontal Spacing and **24.00** fractional points for Vertical Spacing.
6. Press **Enter**. The Grid has been set.
7. Point and click on the **Box** drawing tool in the Side Bar.
8. Move the mouse cursor to the frame, and click and hold the mouse button. Drag the mouse to draw a box. Release the mouse button.
9. Click on the graphic box just drawn in step 8. Click and hold on the box in the lower right corner, and drag the mouse pointer down and to the right. Your screen should resemble this illustration:

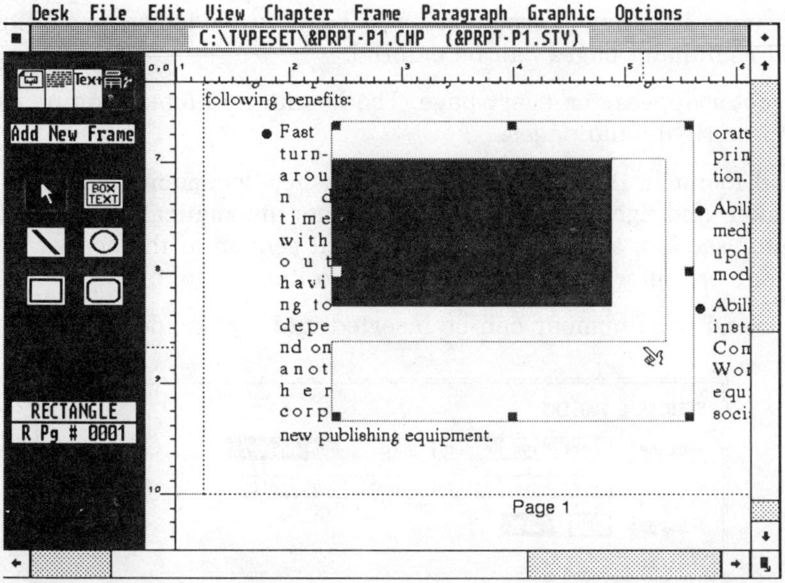

10. Release the mouse button. Notice how the resized graphic snaps to the invisible grid lines.
11. Point to the **File** menu and click on **Abandon**.
12. Turn to Module 72 to continue the learning sequence.

Module 32
HEADERS & FOOTERS

DESCRIPTION

The Headers & Footers command creates the text that is to appear at the top (headers) and bottom (footers) of every page. Different information for the headers and footers and different information for the left- and right-hand pages can be entered.

The header or footer appears on every page. The header and footer can be turned on and off for the left-hand or right-hand pages.

Each header and footer in the Xerox Ventura Publisher document consists of three separate sections: left, center, and right. Xerox Ventura Publisher automatically aligns left the left section, centers the center section, and aligns right the right section of the header and footer on the page. Each header or footer can include one or two lines of text.

Chapter number and page number can be inserted into any header or footer.

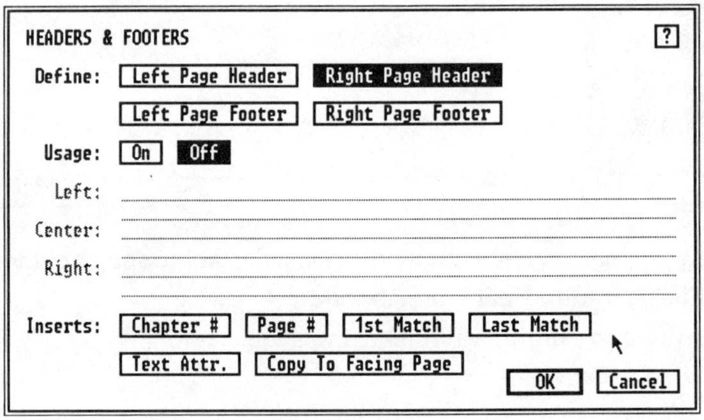

The Header & Footers dialog box offers these options:

Define — Select either the Left Page Header, Right Page Header, Left Page Footer, or the Right Page Footer.

Usage
: Select On to display the header or footer text that is entered. Select Off to hide the information. When the information is hidden by selecting off, it remains in the Xerox Ventura Publisher file but is not displayed on the pages. (The headers and footers on individual pages can be displayed or hidden by using the Turn Footer On/Off and the Turn Header On/Off commands from the Chapter menu. See Module 73 for more information.)

Left
: Enter the text information for the left part of the header or footer.

Center
: Enter the text information for the center part of the header or footer.

Right
: Enter the text information for the right part of the header or footer.

Inserts
: Select either Chapter #, Page #, 1st Match, Last Match, Text Attr., or Copy to Facing Page. Select one of these options so Xerox Ventura Publisher can place automatically the variable information into the header or footer, define the appearance of the text, or copy the information you entered for the header or footer to the facing page.

The variable information includes the Chapter #, Page #, 1st match, and Last Match selections.

Selecting Chapter # in the Header & Footer dialog box inserts the characters [C#] in the header or footer. Each time Xerox Ventura Publisher reads these characters in the header or the footer, it substitutes the current chapter number.

Selecting 1st Match inserts [< tag name] and selecting Last Match inserts [> tag name] in the header or footer. You must substitute for the name of a paragraph tag the "tag name." For example, [> tag name] might become [> Headline 1]. In this case, each time Xerox Ventura Publisher reads these characters, it substitutes the first text marked with the Headline 1 tag on the current page. For Last Match, Xerox Ventura Publisher substitutes the last occurrence of text marked with the paragraph tag on the current page.

The appearance of the header and footer is defined by selecting Text Attribute. Selecting Text Attribute places the characters <D> in the header or footer. Other text attribute codes can be substituted for <D> character. For more information, see Appendix B.

Select Copy to Facing Page to copy the information entered for the header or footer to the facing page.

TIP: Header information cannot be copied to a footer, and footer information cannot be copied to a header.

The options selected in the Page Layout command affect how headers and footers are used in the final printout of your publication. If Single for Sides and Right Side for Start On is selected, Xerox Ventura Publisher uses only the Right Page Header and Right Page Footer. If Single for Sides and Left Side for Start On is selected, Xerox Ventura Publisher utilizes only the Left Page Header and Left Page Footer. If Double for Sides is selected, Xerox Ventura Publisher will utilize both the left and right headers and footers.

Xerox Ventura Publisher also creates two paragraph tags automatically for your headers and footers. These tags can be accessed to add other attributes (such as font, size, color) to your headers and footers.

The header and footer information is stored in the chapter file. The Header & Footer command is accessed in the Chapter menu.

APPLICATIONS

Headers and footers make your publication easier to read. Think how difficult this book would be to use if it had no page numbers. The layout of this book is such that a footer is used on each page. The footer for this book only contains the page number.

In some books, the left page header is often used to name the book, and the right page is used to list the chapter. In this book, the left page header states the module number, and the right page contains the name of the module.

One important feature of this command is that you can have two different headers or footers. This is important to make your pages easier to read. By placing the page number in the outer corner of the pages of the book, it is easier for this book's readers to find a specific page.

TYPICAL OPERATION

In this example, you add a header to the Xerox Ventura Publisher sample chapter SCOOP.CHP. This example begins with SCOOP.CHP already open and in use. If you do not have this chapter open, use the Open Chapter command in the File menu to retrieve and open SCOOP.CHP. You may need to adjust your screen using the scroll bars to make your computer look like the illustrations.

1. Point to the **Chapter** menu and click on **Headers & Footers** to display the Headers & Footers dialog box.
2. Click on the **Right Page Footer** for Define and **On** for Usage. Notice the position of the text cursor at the Left: text insertion point.
3. Type **Scoop News**.

4. Move the cursor to **Right** and then point and click on **Page #** for Inserts. Your screen should resemble this illustration:

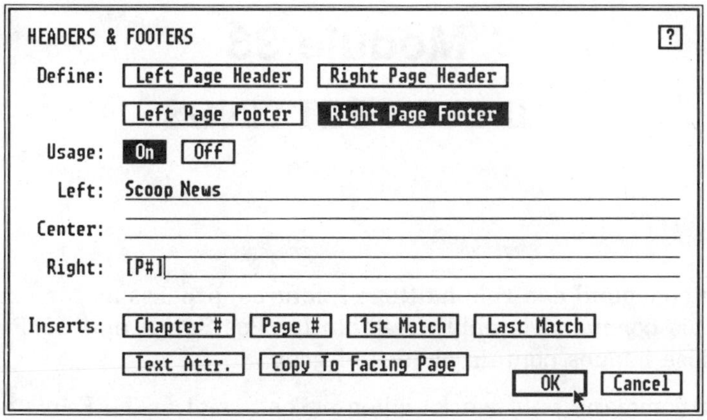

5. Click **OK**.
6. Press **Ctrl-N**. Your screen should resemble this illustration:

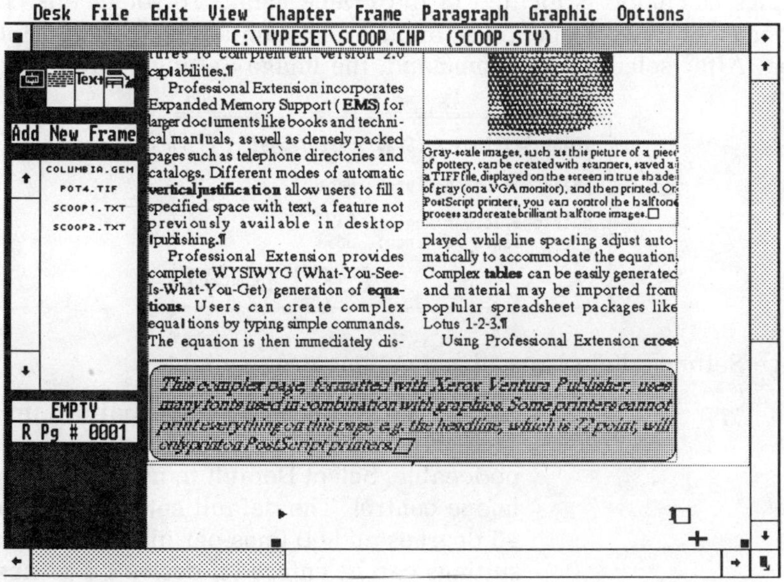

Notice the addition of the footer.

7. Press **Ctrl-S** to save the Xerox Ventura Publisher document.
8. Turn to Module 73 to continue the learning sequence.

Module 33
IMAGE SETTINGS

DESCRIPTION

The Image Setting command controls halftone (pictures) processing for images which contain shades of gray. This command is only available for PostScript and TIFF images and is only available when those images contain shades of gray.

The Image Setting command only works when a PostScript or TIFF image is being sent to a PostScript printer. TIFF files that contain shades of gray will print to non-PostScript-driven printers, such as the Hewlett-Packard LaserJet Series II, but the Image Setting command will have no affect on the image.

The Image Settings command is located in the Frame menu. To select this command, Xerox Ventura Publisher must be in frame mode, and a frame containing a PostScript or TIFF image must be selected. After selecting the command, the Image Settings dialog box will appear:

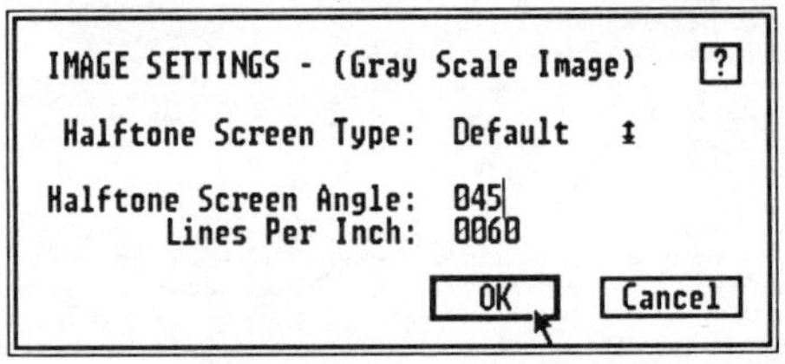

Within the Image Settings dialog box, these options are available:

Halftone Screen Type — The screen produces a regular pattern through the image. This pattern is often rotated, to make the screen less noticeable. Select Default to use the standard settings for image control. The default settings are a screen angle of 45 degrees and 60 lines per inch for laser printers. Other settings can be entered if desired. For most images, these default settings will work.

Halftone Screen Angle — Select an angle of the Halftone Screen. Halftoning is the process of modifying the gray scale image into a form that can be printed by a device that can only produce black dots. A screen is placed on the image and usually rotated to make the dots less noticeable. A 45-degree screen is standard, but for some images, a special effect can be achieved by using a different screen angle.

Lines Per Inch — Select the number of lines per inch that is to be assigned to the image. Most laser printers are only capable of printing at 60 lines per inch. The lines-per-inch setting determines how many dots per inch are placed on the page.

To use this command, a PostScript or TIFF image must be available, and these are generally created with a scanner. In most cases, the image is a photograph, which is a gray scale image. A gray scale image is a scanned image where every dot in the picture is a shade of gray, rather than just black. The Image Settings control is only one part of a series of operations required to print a scanned image.

APPLICATIONS

The Image Settings command is used to enhance the appearance of a PostScript or TIFF image within the Xerox Ventura Publisher chapter, when printed. By making adjustments to the image, a special effect or enhancement to the printed picture can be realized.

TYPICAL OPERATION

In this example, you use the Image Settings command to adjust the gray scale image. This example uses the Xerox Ventura Publisher sample chapter SCOOP.CHP. The example begins with SCOOP.CHP already open and in use. If you do not have this chapter open, point to the File menu and use the Open Chapter command to retrieve and open SCOOP.CHP. So your view matches the screen depicted in this book, press Ctrl-N. You may need to adjust your screen using the scroll bars to make your computer look like the illustrations.

1. Press **Ctrl-U** to select Frame mode.
2. Click in the middle of the frame holding the jar to select the frame.
3. Point to the **Frame** menu and click on **Image Settings** to display the Image Settings dialog box.
4. Type **090** for Halftone Screen Angle and **0100** for Lines Per Inch.

5. Click **OK**. Your screen should resemble this illustration:

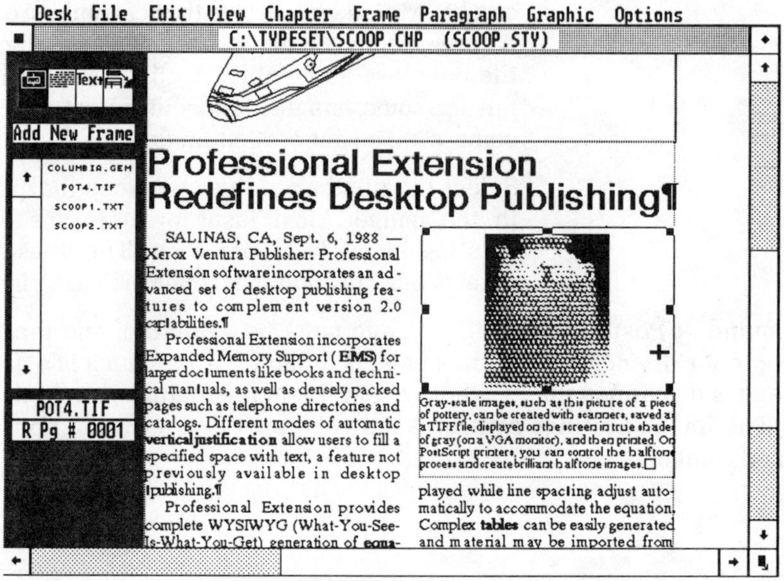

NOTE

Depending on your computer equipment, you may not notice any difference in the changes made on your screen image. You may want to print this document to a laser printer to see the changes. The amount of change you see will be determined by the capability of the printer you are using.

6. Abandon the changes to the chapter.
7. Turn to Module 40 to continue the learning sequence.

Module 34

INSERT CROSS REFERENCE

DESCRIPTION

The Insert Cross Reference option inserts the current page or chapter number anywhere on a page, including the captions, frames, or box text.

To insert a cross reference of the current page number or chapter number, Xerox Ventura Publisher must be in Text Editing mode, and the cursor must be positioned in the text where the reference is to be placed. Then select the Insert Special Item command from the Edit menu. Select Insert Cross Reference or press F6. The following message box appears:

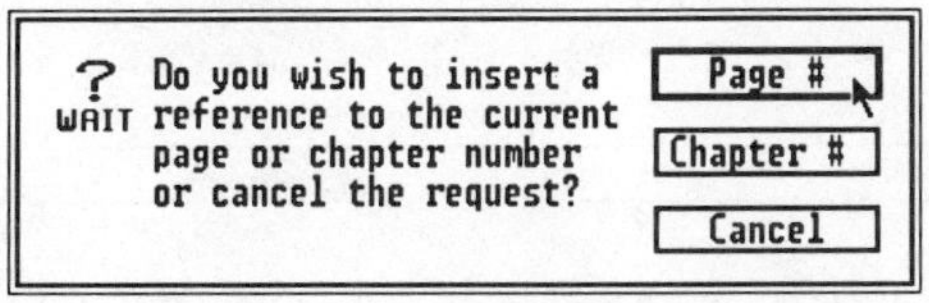

Select either Page # or Chapter # to insert a reference to the current page number or the current chapter number within the text. Select Cancel to cancel the request.

APPLICATIONS

The Insert Cross Reference provides even more flexibility to Xerox Ventura Publisher by allowing the option of inserting chapter numbers or page numbers anywhere within the text. For example, you could create thumb tabs (those blocks placed at the edge of the page to make it easier to locate pages). By placing a reference of the Chapter Number within the thumb tab, each page would be easily marked as to which chapter it is.

TYPICAL OPERATION

In this operation, you insert a cross reference in the Xerox Ventura Publisher sample chapter &MAG-P3.CHP. This operation begins with &MAG-P3.CHP already open and in use. If you do not have this chapter open, use the Open Chapter command in the File menu to retrieve and open &MAG-P3.CHP.

1. Press **Ctrl-O** to select Text Editing mode.
2. Move the cursor to the "s" in the word "Laser" located in the top line. Click the mouse once.
3. Point to the **Edit** menu and click on **Insert Special Item**.

4. Press **F6** to select Cross Ref from the Insert Special Items dialog box.
5. Click on **Page #** when the message box appears. Your screen should resemble the following illustration:

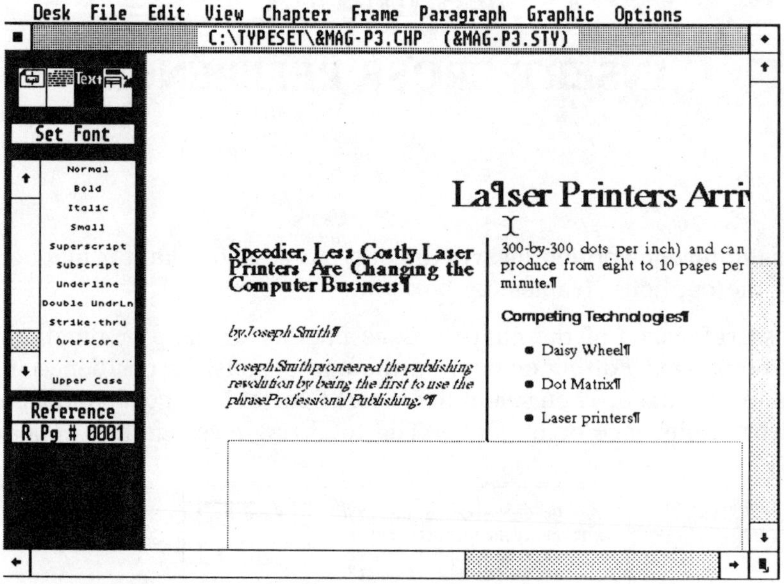

6. Point to the **File** menu and click on **Abandon**. Click on **OK** when prompted to revert back to the last saved version.
7. Turn to Module 8 to continue the learning sequence.

Module 35

INSERT/EDIT ANCHOR

DESCRIPTION

The Insert/Edit Anchor command places a frame anchor into text. The Insert/Edit Anchor command links a specific frame to an anchor's location within the text of a Xerox Ventura Publisher document. The frame then moves whenever this specified location in the text moves.

To insert a frame anchor within the text of a page, Xerox Ventura Publisher must be in text mode. The next step is to position the cursor where you want to insert an anchor point and click the mouse once. Select Insert Special Items in the Edit menu and then select Frame Anchor from the Insert Special Items dialog box. The Insert/Edit Anchor dialog box appears.

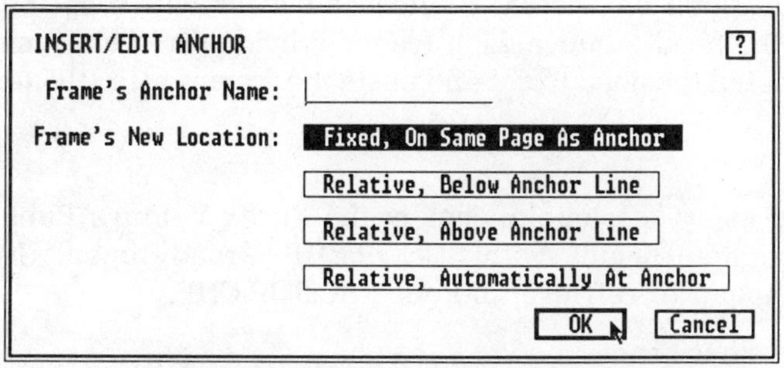

Within the Insert/Edit Anchor dialog box, the following options are available:

Frame's Anchor Name — Type the name of the Frame Anchor desired. The name typed in this section of Insert/Edit Anchor dialog box *must* match the name entered for the chosen frame in the Anchors & Captions dialog box (see Module 7). It does not matter if the information is in upper or lower case. If the name typed in this section does not match the name typed into the Anchors & Captions dialog box, Xerox Ventura Publisher will display an error message.

Frame's New Location — Select either Fixed, On Same Page As Anchor; Relative, Below Anchor Line; Relative, Above Anchor Line; or Relative, Automatically At Anchor.

If Relative, Above Anchor Line is selected, the bottom of the frame is moved to the line above the text line containing the anchor. If Relative, Below Anchor Line is selected, the top of the frame is moved to the line below the text line containing the anchor.

If Fixed, On Same Page As Anchor is selected, the frame's position on a new page is exactly the way it was on the old page.

If Relative, Automatically At Anchor is selected, the frame automatically moves as the text moves.

TIP: Always check each page after the Re-Anchor Frames command has been executed to make sure that the frames are properly positioned, are not pushed off the edge of the page, and do not overlap other frames.

APPLICATIONS

The purpose of Insert/Edit Anchor is to place an anchor within the text so that the illustrations placed within a frame automatically move with the text. If the text is edited, changed, or deleted, or if different attributes are assigned to the text, the text can drastically change. Illustrations intended to complement the text will no longer be positioned at the correct point. Xerox Ventura Publisher can automatically move the illustration as the text is re-aligned with this command.

By using Insert/Edit Anchor, the exact point in the text when a frame is to be anchored is determined. From that point on, Xerox Ventura Publisher will keep the frame in its correct position, eliminating the need to move each frame individually. This command can save hours of work, having eliminated the need to cut and paste the frames after the text has been realigned.

TYPICAL OPERATION

In this operation, you insert a frame anchor in the Xerox Ventura Publisher sample chapter SCOOP.CHP. This example begins with SCOOP.CHP already open. Use the Open Chapter command in the File menu to retrieve and open SCOOP.CHP.

1. Press **Ctrl-U** to select Frame mode.
2. Point to the frame containing COLUMBIA.GEM and click once.
3. Point to the **Frame** menu and click on **Anchors & Captions**. The Anchors & Captions dialog box appears.
4. Type **1** for Anchor. Press **Enter**.
5. Press **Ctrl-O** to select the Text Editing mode.
6. Move the mouse to the "t" in the word three, located in the first sentence in the third paragraph in the left column. Click once.
7. Point to the **Edit** menu and select **Ins Special Item**. Your screen should resemble this illustration:

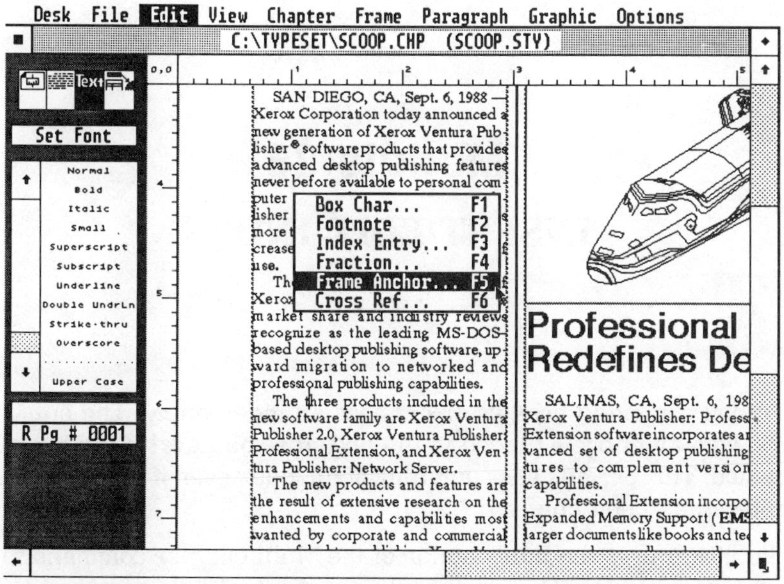

8. Press **F5** to display the Insert/Edit Anchor dialog box.
9. Type **1** for Frame's Anchor Name.
10. Select **Relative, Automatically At Anchor** for Frames New Location, and click **OK**. Your screen should resemble this illustration:

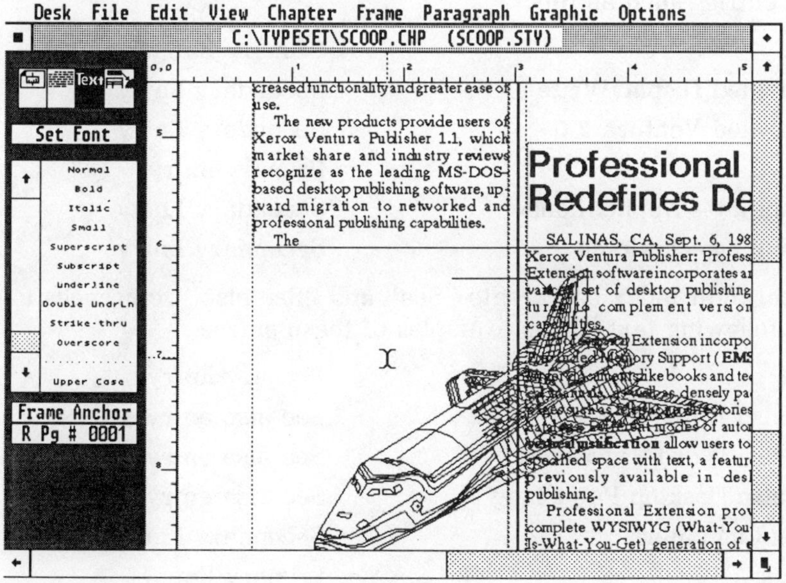

11. Point to the **File** menu and select **Abandon**. Confirm the Abandon when the message box appears.
12. Turn to Module 53 to continue the learning sequence.

Module 36

INSERT/EDIT INDEX

DESCRIPTION

The Insert/Edit Index command creates or changes an index entry. The entry is attached to a point in the text. Once an entry is placed in the text, it remains with the same text, even if the text is cut and pasted. This permits easy updating of an index even if the sequence of paragraphs, pages, and chapters has been changed.

Xerox Ventura Publisher uses the Index option of the Multi-chapter command to create an index from the various index entries. During processing, the Multi-chapter command extracts the entries, along with their page numbers, sorts the entries in alphabetical order, and finally places the entries in a text file. This text file can then be loaded and formatted as any other Xerox Ventura Publisher file.

The Insert/Edit Index command creates a two-level index. This allows an index to have primary and secondary entries such as this:

Books	Primary Entry
Illustrated DisplayWrite 4	Secondary Entry
Illustrated Ventura 2.0	Secondary Entry
Services	Primary Entry
Consulting—Applications	Secondary Entry
Consulting—Training	Secondary Entry

In addition, Insert/Edit Index can create "See" and "See also" references to other entries in the index. The following text shows examples of these entries:

Books	Primary Entry
See also Authors	See also entry
See also Word Processing	See also entry
See also Desktop Publishing	See also entry
Using Computers	Secondary Entry
Consultants	Primary Entry
See Sheldon, George	See Entry

Insert/Edit Index also permits the insertion of a word or phrase with one type of spelling and a sort with another type. For example, if "The Illustrated Ventura 2.0 Book" were being indexed, it would naturally sort with the T's. Obviously, it should be sorted with the I's. To do so, enter Illustrated Ventura 2.0 Book as the sort key. There can be sort keys for both primary and secondary entries.

The Insert/Edit Index command is used by inserting the text entry point at the desired position for the entry and then selecting the Index Entry option from the Insert/Special Item command in the Edit menu. This command then inserts a mark at the location of the text entry point. The mark can be seen if the Show Tabs & Returns command in the Options menu has been set.

Always make sure that index entries are part of the paragraph and not in separate paragraphs of their own. If the index entry is not a part of a paragraph, your Xerox Ventura Publisher document will not format correctly.

Xerox Ventura Publisher must be in the Text mode to use this command. After selecting Insert Special Item from the Edit menu, press F3 or use the mouse to select Index Entry to make the Insert/Edit Index Entry dialog box appear.

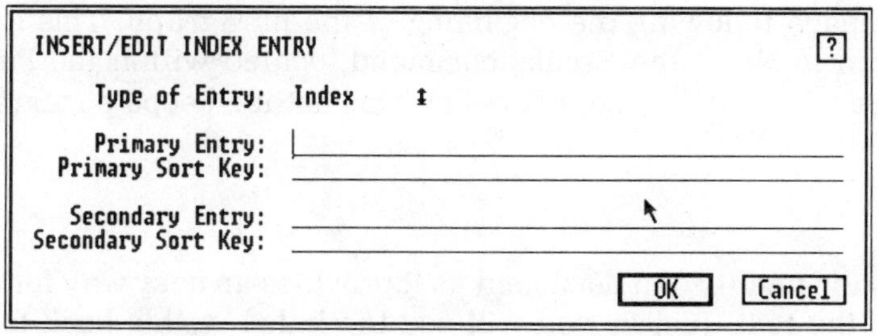

The options available within the Insert/Edit Index Entry dialog box are:

Type of Entry	Select the type of entry desired. The options are Index, See, and See Also.
Primary/Secondary Entry	Type the primary or secondary entry. For a "See" or "See also" entry, type the reference in the Secondary Entry area.
Primary/Secondary Sort Key	Type the content of the sort key.

When entries are being typed, make certain that words are spelled exactly the same each time an entry is made for the same subject. If spelling errors occur, Xerox Ventura Publisher sorts the entries differently and presents multiple entries because of the misspelling. For example, if you type "consultant" for one primary entry and "consultants" for another, Xerox Ventura Publisher will provide two entries within the index because one ends with an "s."

Xerox Ventura Publisher permits the edit of an index entry by selecting its mark in the text and selecting the Edit Special Item command from the Edit menu.

However, another way to edit and, sometimes, enter index entries, is to use a word processor. Consider these examples:

<$IPrimary Entry[Sort Key]; Secondary Entry[Sort Key]>.

For a "See" entry, type: <$SPrimary Entry[Sort Key];See Reference[Sort Key]>.

For a "See Also" entry, type: <$APrimary Entry[Sort Key];See Also Reference[Sort Key]>.

TIP: Placing these entries anywhere in a paragraph makes the text file nearly impossible to use. One solution to this problem is to place the index entries after the last sentence of the paragraph, but included as part of the paragraph, as shown in this example.

The Insert/Edit Index command creates or changes an index entry. The entry is attached to a point in the text. Once an entry is placed in the text, it remains with the same text, even if the text is cut and pasted. This permits easy updating of an index even if the sequence of paragraphs, pages, and chapters have been changed. <$IInsert/Edit Index command;description> <$AInsert/Edit Index command;Multi-Chapter command>.

If a paragraph breaks to a second page in the Xerox Ventura Publisher chapter, the index entries are for the page following the beginning of the paragraph. This can be prevented by setting Allow Within to No in the Breaks command located within the Paragraph menu (see Module 11 for more information about Breaks). This setting keeps paragraphs from breaking across the pages.

APPLICATIONS

An index enhances the quality of a document as it provides an easy way for the reader to locate information within the text. Just as you will use the index in this book to locate information about various commands, functions, and features of Xerox Ventura Publisher, readers of your documents will find them easier to use if an index is included.

Xerox Ventura Publisher will create the index automatically for you with the Make Index command after the index entries have been made.

Perhaps the most difficult thing about creating an index for your publications is the fact that you must think like a reader; and you must remember that a reader using an index is trying to find something, because that is why they are using the index. The bigger the index, the more entries, the better. And remember that all people do not think the same. For example, if your document had a section in it about the care and treatment of a lawn, some people would look under lawn to find the information, while others would look under grass, and still others would look under yard. The index should have references under grass and yard to see lawn.

Another point to consider when creating an index is that the index should contain as much information as possible. For example:

Lawn

Care, 9

Cutting, 12

Diseases, 11

Fertilizing, 19

Insect Damage, 21

Replacing, 14

With this type of index, the reader could easily find information about fertilizing a lawn.

TYPICAL OPERATION

In this operation, you insert two index entries into the Xerox Ventura Publisher sample chapter &LSTG-P2.CHP. This operation begins with &LSTG-P2.CHP already open. Use the command Open Chapter in the File menu to retrieve and open &LSTG-P2.CHP.

1. Press **Ctrl-O** to select the Text Editing mode.
2. Move the cursor to the "C" in Chorus Data Systems.
3. Point to the **Edit** menu and click on **Ins Special Item**. Press **F3** to access the Insert/Edit Index Entry dialog box.
4. Type **Chorus Data Systems** for Primary Entry and type **PC-Eye** for Secondary Entry.

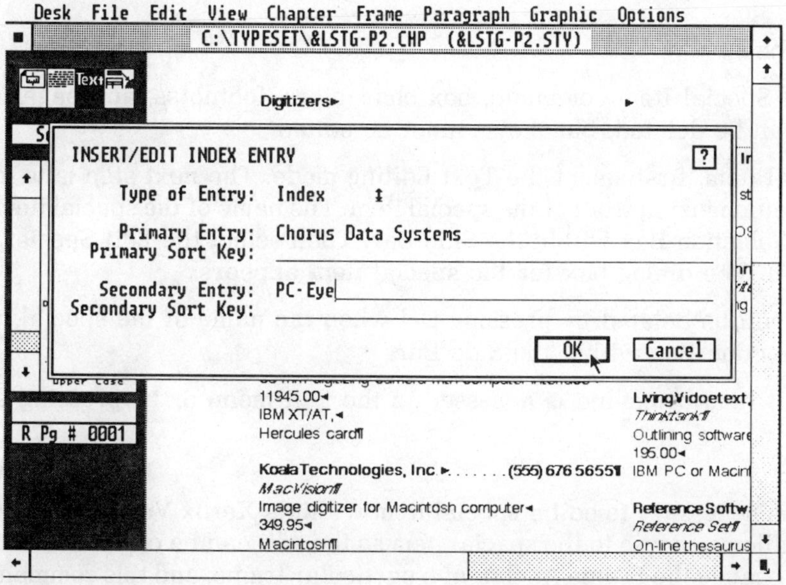

5. Press **Enter**.
6. Point to the **File** menu and click on **Abandon**. Click on **OK** when prompted to revert back to the last saved version.
7. Turn to Module 7 to continue the learning sequence.

Module 37

INSERT/EDIT SPECIAL ITEM

DESCRIPTION

The Edit Special Item command permits easy access to edit these special codes:

Index Entries
Fractions
Frame Anchors

Within the Edit Special Item command, box characters, footnotes, and page/chapter number special codes can be deleted, but they cannot be edited.

To edit a special item, first select the Text Editing mode. The next step is to move the mouse cursor to the position just in front of the special item. The name of the special item should appear in the Current Selection Box within the Side Bar. Then select the Edit Special Item command in the Edit menu. The dialog box for the special item appears.

A special item can be deleted by pressing Del when the name of the special item appears in the Current Selection Box within the Side Bar.

The Edit Special Item command is accessed in the Edit menu or by pressing Ctrl-C.

APPLICATIONS

Many times, it is necessary to edit a special item within a Xerox Ventura Publisher document. This command allows access to the special item so the edit can be completed. For example, you might decide to change the Frame Anchor of a particular frame, and this command permits those changes to be made.

TYPICAL OPERATION

In this example, you access the Insert Special Item dialog box and review the various commands. The Xerox Ventura Publisher sample chapter SCOOP.CHP is used. The example begins with SCOOP.CHP already open and in use.

1. Press **Ctrl-O** to access the Text Editing mode.
2. Move the text cursor to an area in the text and click the mouse button once.
3. Press **Ctrl-C**. Review the various options available to select.
4. Move the mouse outside the box and click once.
5. Turn to Module 35 to continue the learning sequence.

Module 38

INSERT FRACTION

DESCRIPTION

The Insert Fraction command allows the creation of true typographic fractions. True fractions look like this:

¼ or ¾ and not like this: 1/4 or 3/4

True typographic fractions use smaller type which is shifted up and down, and are numbers separated by a special fraction bar available in the symbol font.

To insert a fraction within the text, Xerox Ventura Publisher must be in the Text Editing mode. Place the cursor at the location of the text where a fraction is to be created. Select Insert Special Item from the Edit menu, or press Ctrl-C. Then select Fraction from the Insert Special Item dialog box, or press F4. The Fraction Editing screen appears:

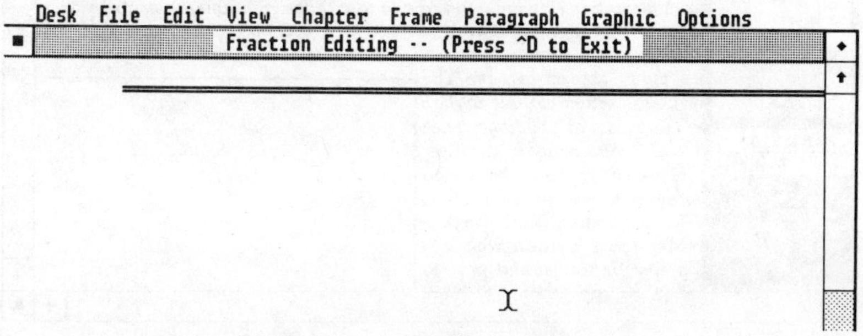

Press Ctrl-C and then press F4 to insert a fraction like this: ¼ or $\frac{1}{4}$. Within a moment, the results will appear below the fraction editing line. Now type the fraction.

Type 1/4 to create a ¼ fraction. Or type 1 over 4 to create a $\frac{1}{4}$ fraction. Then press Ctrl-D to return to the main screen.

TIP: Be sure to leave a space on either side of the word over.

APPLICATIONS

The Insert Fraction option allows the creation of typographically correct fractions without spending the time to change fonts, shift text, and insert fraction bars.

TYPICAL OPERATION

In this example, you insert a fraction in the text of the Xerox Ventura Publisher sample chapter &PRPT-P1.CHP. The example begins with &PRPT-P1.CHP already open.

1. Press **Ctrl-O** to access the Text Editing mode.
2. Move the cursor to the middle of the third line of text. Click once.
3. Point to the **Edit** menu and click on **Insert Special Item**.
4. Press **F4** to select Fraction from the Insert Special Item dialog box.
5. Press **F2**. Type **3/4**.
6. Press **Ctrl-D** to return to the main screen. Your screen should resemble the following illustration:

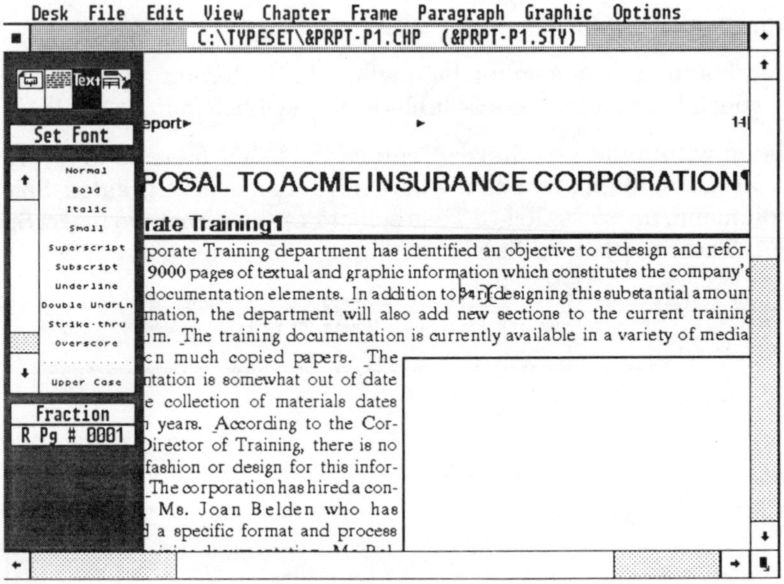

7. Abandon the changes to the chapter.
8. Turn to Module 68 to continue the learning sequence.

Module 39

INSERT/REMOVE PAGE

DESCRIPTION

The Insert/Remove Page command allows the addition or deletion of pages to a Xerox Ventura Publisher chapter file. Adding a new page creates a new underlying page. Xerox Ventura Publisher will not delete a page that contains any information in the underlying page. Xerox Ventura Publisher will delete a page that contains information in other frames, but not in the underlying page frame.

The underlying page frame is part of the actual page structure. Other frames can be positioned on top of the underlying page frame. The underlying page frame contains the information for the margin settings and number of columns. This underlying page frame information is a part of the style sheet being used with each document. If the underlying page contains any other information, it cannot be deleted.

Xerox Ventura Publisher allows you to have more than one underlying page. Additional underlying pages can be added anywhere within a document. Since each underlying page operates separately from any other underlying page, additional underlying pages can be inserted in the middle of an existing group of pages. Xerox Ventura Publisher will not flow text from one underlying page to another. Text being placed onto different underlying pages must be maintained in separate text files.

The Insert/Remove Page command is accessed in the Chapter menu. When accessed, the Insert/Remove Page dialog box will appear, and your computer screen will resemble the following illustration:

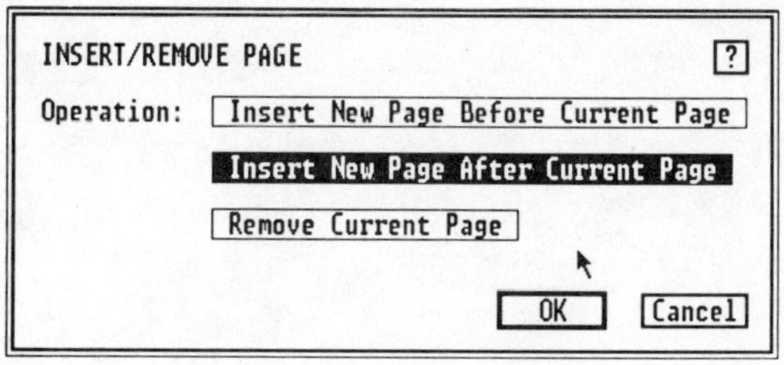

The Insert/Remove page dialog box provides these choices:

- Insert new page before current page.
- Insert new page after current page.
- Remove current page.

APPLICATIONS

Xerox Ventura Publisher automatically creates and inserts new pages when a text file placed in the underlying page requires more than one page because of its length. Xerox Ventura Publisher removes those pages if portions of the text file are deleted.

There are times when you may want to insert a new page. For example, you might decide to add a graph, chart, or text table within a document — if so, the Insert/Remove Page command permits the addition of these types of items.

NOTE

Xerox Ventura Publisher does not limit the number of pages that can be added. When a page is added, Xerox Ventura Publisher automatically moves to that new inserted page. When a page is removed, Xerox Ventura Publisher automatically moves to the previous page.

TYPICAL OPERATION

In this example, you insert a new page after the current page. The Xerox Ventura Publisher sample chapter &MAG-P3.CHP is used. The example begins with &MAG-P3.CHP already open. Use the Open Chapter command in the File menu to retrieve and open &MAG-P3.CHP.

1. Point to the **Chapter** menu and click on **Insert/Remove Page**.
2. Select **Insert New Page After Current Page** in the Insert/Remove Page dialog box.
3. Select **OK**. Within a moment, you see the new page inserted by Xerox Ventura Publisher.
4. Point to the **Chapter** menu and click on **Insert/Remove Page**.
5. Select **Remove Current Page** in the Insert/Remove Page dialog box. Select **OK**.
6. Turn to Module 43 to continue the learning sequence.

Module 40
LINE ATTRIBUTES

DESCRIPTION

The Line Attributes command allows the selection of different types of lines created with the Graphics Drawing function. The lines created when drawing circle, box, rectangle, rounded corner rectangle, as well as straight lines, can have different thicknesses and colors. A straight line can also have a different end style, such as an arrow.

LINE THICKNESSES AND COLORS

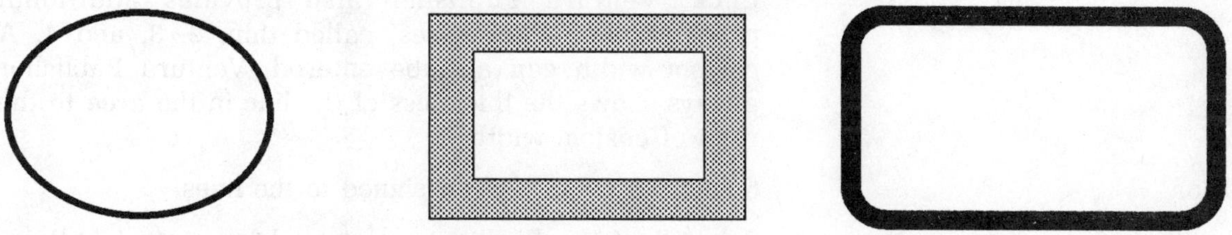

END STYLES AND LINE THICKNESS

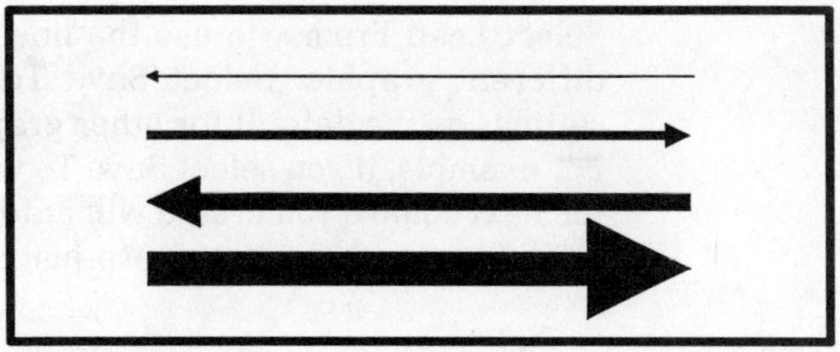

The Line Attributes command is accessed from the Graphic Menu or by pressing Ctrl-L.

NOTE

Select a Graphic with the Graphics Drawing tool before accessing Line Attributes command.

After selecting the Line Attributes command, the Line Attributes dialog box appears. Your screen should resemble this illustration:

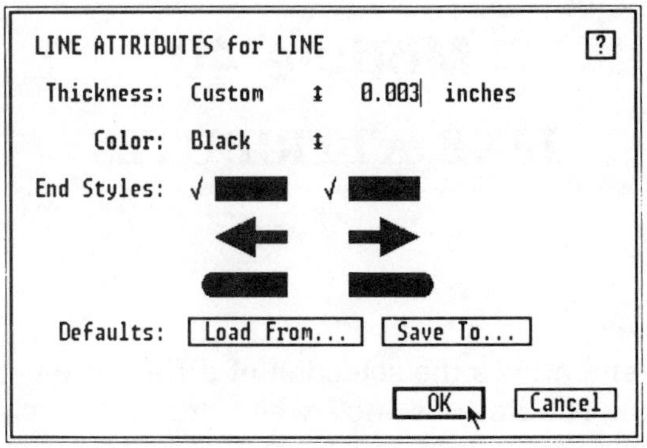

The Line Attributes dialog box provides these choices:

Thickness	Select the thickness of the line. The thickness can be none (for those boxes or circles where no border is desired) to thick. Ventura Publisher also provides additional predetermined thicknesses, called thin, 2, 3, and 4. A custom width can also be entered. Ventura Publisher always shows the thickness of the line in the area to the right of custom width.
Color	Select the color being assigned to the lines.
End Styles	Select the type of ends you want to place on straight lines. Ventura Publisher permits the choice of square ends, arrowhead ends, or round ends. Each end of a line can have a different end style assigned to it.
Defaults	Select Load From... to use the line attributes saved for a different graphic. Select Save To... to use the current settings as the default for other graphics of the same kind. For example, if you select Save To while creating a square, the next square you create will automatically use the same attributes as those that were just saved.

APPLICATIONS

Varying the thickness of lines offers versatility when creating graphics. By using different line sizes, many different effects can be created. For example, you might want to draw a line and use an arrowhead line end style to point to a special place on your document. You can also assign a color to a line within a document, allowing a more interesting graphic effect when reproduced.

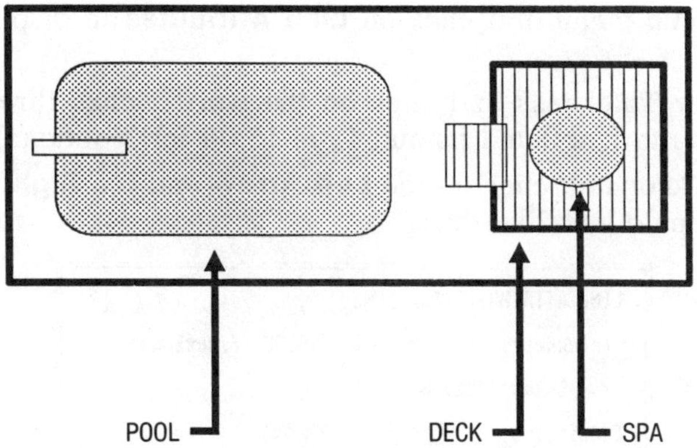

TYPICAL OPERATION

In this operation, you draw a line and change the thickness of it. The instructions begin with Xerox Ventura Publisher running and &BOOK-P1.CHP open. Press Ctrl-R to Reduce View.

1. Press **Ctrl-U** to select the Frame mode.
2. Point and click on **Add New Frame** in the Side Bar.
3. Draw a new frame in the middle of the page.
4. Press **Ctrl-P** to select the Graphic Drawing function.
5. Click on the **Line** tool in the Side Bar and then draw a line. Your screen should resemble this illustration:

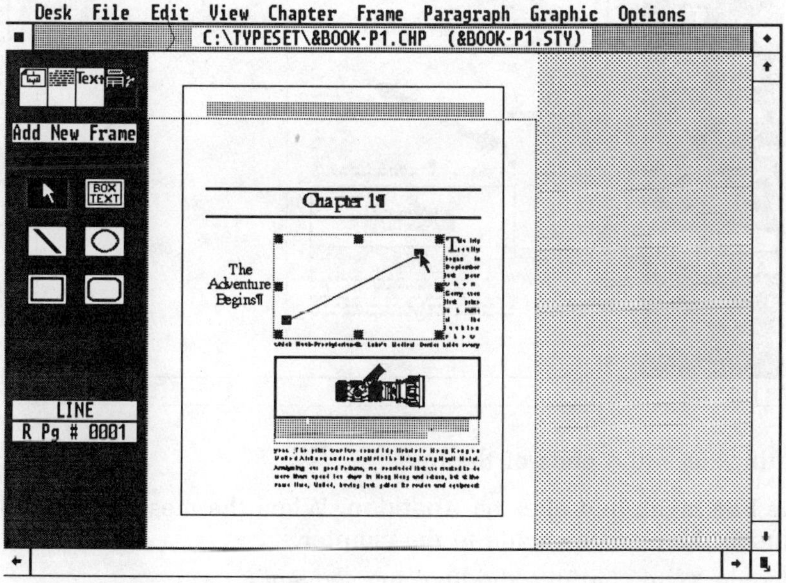

6. Point to the **Graphic** menu and click on **Line Attributes** to display the Line Attributes dialog box.
7. Select **Custom** for Thickness and click on the word inches three times to change the measurement units to fractional points. Type **15.00** for fractional points.
8. Select **Black** for Color and click on the **Left Arrow** and the **Right Arrow** for End Styles. The dialog box should look like this:

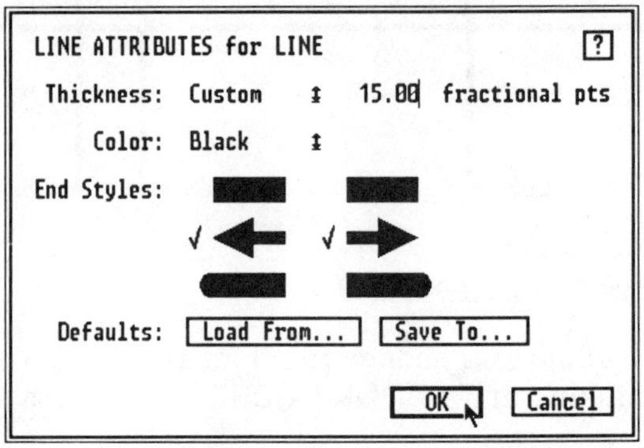

9. Click **OK**.

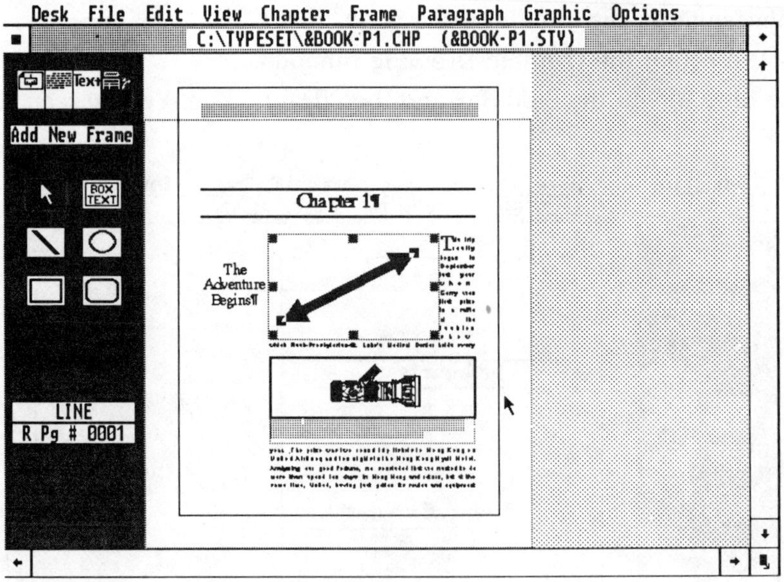

Notice the new thickness and ends of the line.

10. Point to the **File** menu and click on **Abandon**. When the message box appears, click on **OK** to abandon the changes made to the chapter.
11. Turn to Module 37 to continue the learning sequence.

Module 41

LOAD DIFFERENT STYLE

DESCRIPTION

The Load Diff.(erent) Style command applies a different style sheet to the chapter currently being displayed on the screen. If the chapter is then saved, Xerox Ventura Publisher ignores the old style sheet and replaces it with the new style sheet. In Xerox Ventura Publisher, a style sheet is a separate file used to control the style and appearance of your final document. This style sheet is only associated with the Xerox Ventura Publisher chapter file.

NOTE

When the Open Chapter command is executed, Xerox Ventura Publisher automatically loads the style sheet assigned to that chapter.

APPLICATIONS

The Load Diff.(erent) Style command is used to retrieve an existing style sheet. It is often easier to modify an existing style sheet than to create a new one from the beginning. Loading a different style sheet, making the necessary changes, and saving it under a new name (see Module 60) is the best way to create your own set of new style sheets.

TYPICAL OPERATION

In this example, you load a new style sheet after a chapter has been opened. The Xerox Ventura Publisher sample chapter SCOOP.CHP is used. This operation begins with SCOOP.CHP already open and in use. If you do not have this chapter open, use Open Chapter in the File menu to retrieve SCOOP.CHP. So your view matches the screen depicted in this module, press Ctrl-R.

Your screen should resemble this illustration:

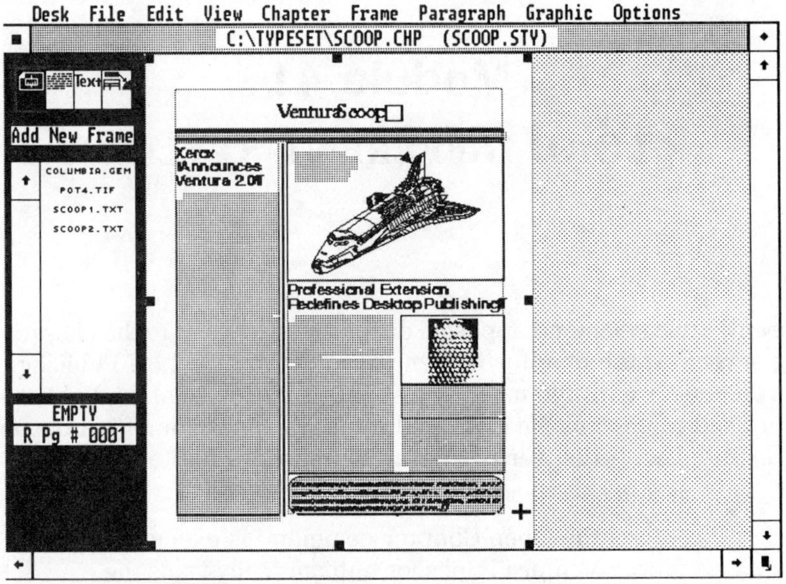

1. Point to the **File** menu and click on **Load Diff. Style** to display the Item Selector dialog box. Your screen should resemble this illustration:

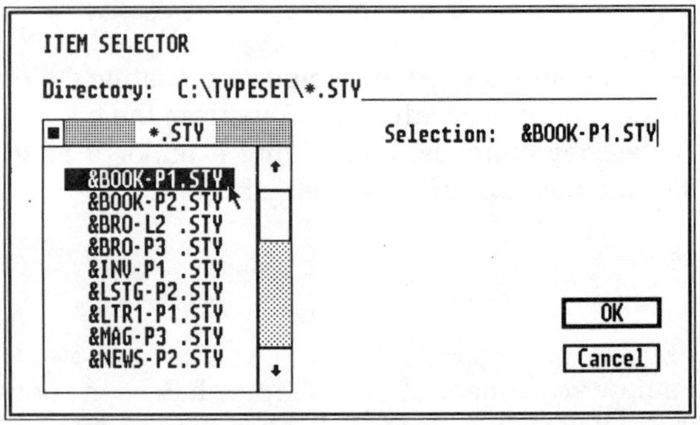

2. Double click on **&BOOK-P1.STY** to select it as the new style sheet. (Use the scroll bars to find it in the window.) Your screen should now resemble this illustration:

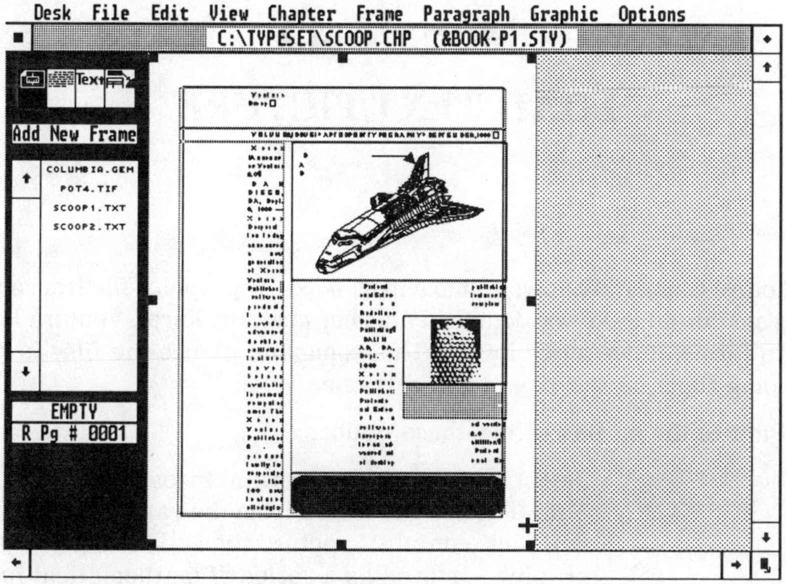

3. Point to the **File** menu and click on **Abandon** to revert back to the original SCOOP.CHP.
4. Turn to Module 6 to continue the learning sequence.

Module 42

LOAD TEXT/PICTURE

DESCRIPTION

The Load Text/Picture command allows you to import a text or graphics file from a word processor or graphics program into your Xerox Ventura Publisher chapter. Xerox Ventura Publisher divides graphics into two forms: Line-Art or Image. This command places the files in the Assignment List prior to placing them on the page or in a frame.

The Load Text/Picture dialog box offers these options:

Type of File	Select the type of file you want to load: Text, Line-Art, or Image. Text files are generated from the various word processors. Line art files contain "vector" type drawings, which means the graphic is stored as a series of mathematical formulas. Vector drawings are common for business or scientific graphics, maps, and mechanical-type drawings. Image files contain bit-map graphics. Usually more of an artistic type drawing, the image is stored as a series of on and off bits of information.
Text Format	Select the type of text file you are loading, which is determined by which word processor you are using.
# of Files	Select Several if you want to load several files of the same type at one time.
Destination	If the file(s) to be loaded are text files, you may select one of the destination options, select List of Files to load the file into the Assignment List. To load the file into an existing text file, select Text Clipboard and then paste the file at the desired location. To load the file into an existing file automatically, move the text cursor to the desired location and select Text Cursor.

If you select Line-Art or Image, the dialog box changes to show you the available Line-Art or Image file formats available for importing into Xerox Ventura Publisher. When you select Line-Art, a list of possible file types is displayed. Select the type of Line-Art file format you are loading, which depends on the type of Line-Art program you are using. As long as your graphics program produces files compatible with any of the following, you should be able to import the graphic into Xerox Ventura Publisher.

Here is the list of Line-Art and Image programs/files that can be imported into Xerox Ventura Publisher:

GEM	Macintosh Paint
CGM	PC Paintbrush (PCX)
DXF	PostScript
HALO	TIFF
HPGL	Video Show
Lotus 1-2-3 (PIC)	Windows
Macintosh PICT	

NOTE

Use PC Paintbrush, PostScript, or TIFF formats to load files created by a scanner.

When you select Image, a list of possible file types is displayed. Select the type of Image file format you are loading, which depends on the type of Image program you are using. As long as your graphics program produces files compatible with any of the previous, you should be able to import the graphic into Xerox Ventura Publisher.

After selecting the type of file you wish to load, Xerox Ventura Publisher then displays the Item Selector, with the appropriate subdirectory and file extension already chosen. Finally select the filename, and choose OK.

The Load Text/Picture command is located in the File menu.

APPLICATIONS

The Load Text/Picture command is used to build a list of text and graphics files you want to use within a Xerox Ventura Publisher document.

When a text file is loaded into Xerox Ventura Publisher, the file will be updated by Ventura if you make any changes to the text. You should make a backup of a text file *before* you load the text file into Xerox Ventura Publisher.

Graphic files—both Line-Art and Image—cannot be altered or changed at anytime within Xerox Ventura Publisher. If you want to change the file, you must do so before the file is loaded into Ventura.

This command is used to import the text, line-art, and image files that were created in other programs.

TYPICAL OPERATION

In this operation, you load a picture file in the Assignment List, then place the picture on the underlying page.

1. Type **VP** from the DOS prompt. Within a few moments, Xerox Ventura Publisher will start, and a blank opening screen will appear. Press **Ctrl-U** to access the Frame mode.

2. Point to the **File** menu and pull the mouse to **Load Text/Picture**. Your screen will resemble this illustration:

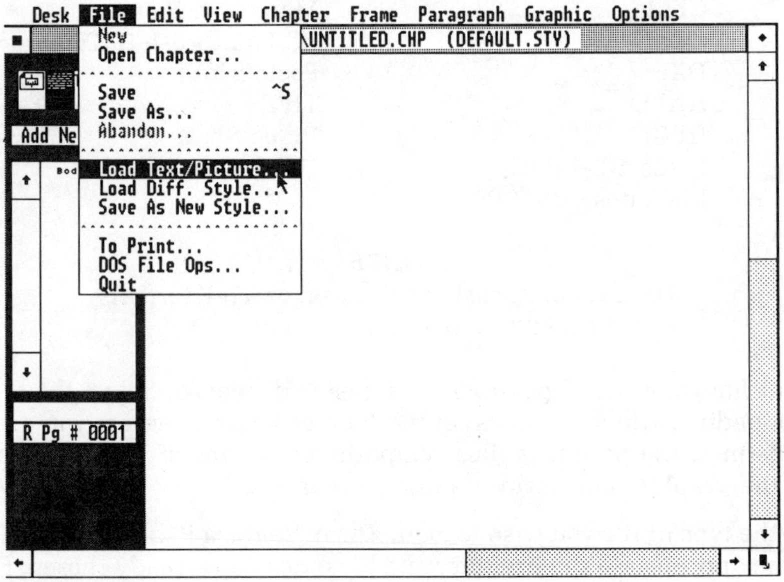

3. Click on **Load Text/Picture**. Within a moment, the Load Text/Picture dialog box will appear, and your screen will resemble this illustration:

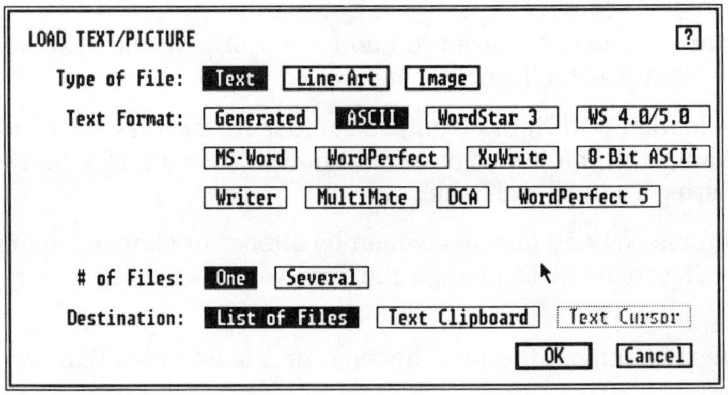

4. Click on **Line-Art** for Type of File, and select **GEM** as Line-Art Format. Select **One** as the # of Files. Your screen should resemble this illustration:

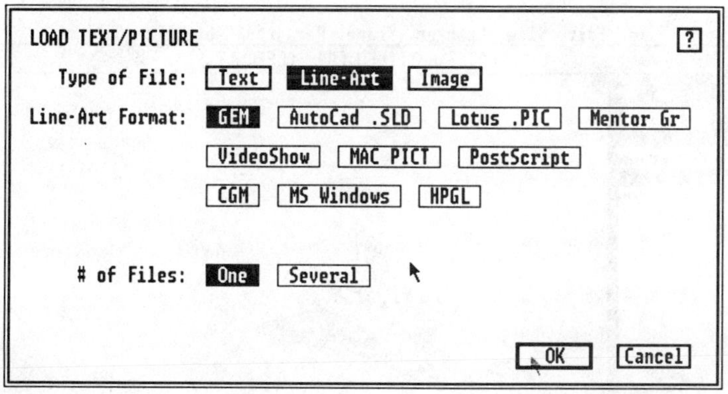

5. Click **OK** to display the Item Selector dialog box. Your screen should resemble this illustration:

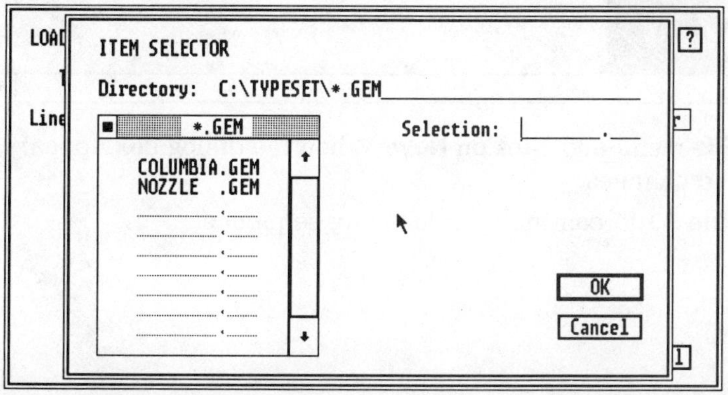

6. Double click on the **COLUMBIA.GEM** file to load the file. Within a few moments, Xerox Ventura Publisher will return to the opening screen, and the file COLUMBIA.GEM will be listed in the Assignment List.

7. Click in the page area and double click on **COLUMBIA.GEM** in the Assignment List. Press **Ctrl-R** to see a reduced view of the page. Within a moment, your screen should resemble this illustration:

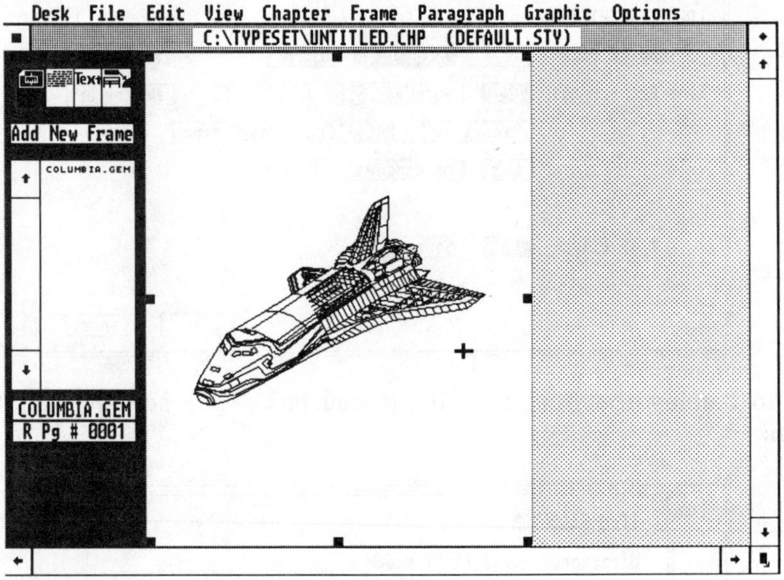

8. Point to the **File** menu and click on **New**. When the dialog box appears, click on **Abandon** to not save the changes.
9. Turn to Module 58 to continue the learning sequence.

Module 43

MARGINS & COLUMNS

DESCRIPTION

The Margins & Columns command establishes the number and sizes of the columns in each frame or in the underlying page frame. This command also sets the margins and columns in those frames that are automatically generated by Xerox Ventura Publisher, such as those used to establish the headers, footers, and captions.

For the underlying page frame or any other frame, the Margins & Columns command sets:

- The top, bottom, left, and right margins
- The number of columns (The maximum number of columns permitted in any frame is 8.)
- The width of each column and the amount of spacing between each column

All underlying pages will have the same margins and same number of columns. Of course, the left page and the right page can have a different number of columns and a different margin setting. But *all* right pages will have the same margins and the same number of columns. And all left pages will also have the same margin and column settings. To create different margins and columns for the left and right pages, you must be working within a double-sided publication.

The Margins & Columns command is available in the Frame menu. To access this command, you must be in Frame mode. After selecting the command, a Margins & Columns dialog box appears.

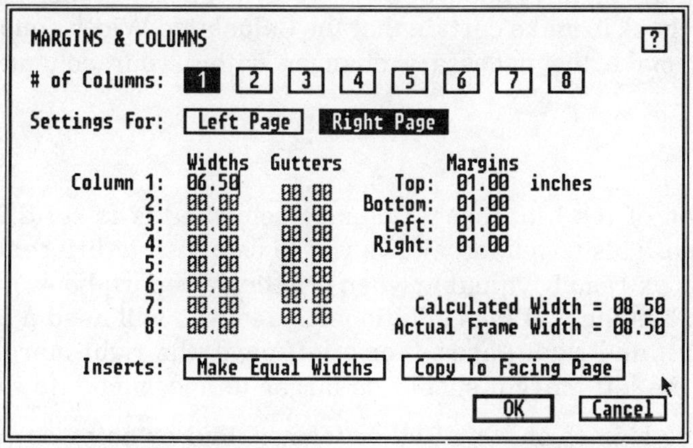

The Margins & Columns dialog box contains these options:

# of Columns	Select the number of columns needed for the frame or the underlying page.
Settings For	Select either the left or right page.
Column Widths & Gutters	Type the width and gutter for each column selected in the # of columns.
Margins	Type the margin for the Top, Bottom, Left, and Right side of the frame or underlying page.
Inserts	Select Make Equal Widths if you want all the columns to have the same width. Xerox Ventura Publisher will automatically compute the width for you. Select Copy To Facing Page if you want the information entered in the dialog box copied to the other page. Of course, this command only works if you are preparing a two-sided document as established in the Page Size & Layout command.
Calculated Width	This shows you the amount of space you have selected and used. This data is used to compare against the Actual Frame Width, which Xerox Ventura Publisher displays for comparison. Since you have control over the width of your columns, Xerox Ventura Publisher will not readjust your settings for you.
Actual Frame Width	This shows you the actual width of the frame. Before selecting OK, always make sure the Calculated Width is less than or equal to the amount shown in the Actual Frame Width.

TIP: If the margin and column appearance on your computer screen does not match what you specified, check to make certain that the Calculated Width equals the Actual Frame Width. If not, make the necessary changes within your column widths and gutter dimensions.

APPLICATIONS

The obvious application of the Margins & Columns command is to set different margins and columns for each frame. This command allows you to establish a different margin for the left and right pages. This is extremely valuable when creating a report, book, or magazine that will be bound. Because the binding will take additional space, you will need a larger margin on the inside portion of the left and right pages. (For a left page, the right margin should be larger, and for a right page, the left margin should be larger to accommodate the binding.)

You may also be adding frames on top of other frames, and by doing so you may want to add columns within that new frame. This is often effective in newsletter or newspaper-type documents.

This allows a three-column newsletter, for example, to have another frame added and have additional columns inserted for a complementary text article.

Finally, this command is also used to add "white space" around a graphic placed in a frame. By doing so, the graphic will not run tight against text, which would make the text difficult to read.

TYPICAL OPERATION

In this example, you add a new frame and assign margins and columns to that frame. The example begins with a blank screen and the DEFAULT.STY style sheet being used.

1. Press **Ctrl-R** to see a reduced view of the page. Press **Ctrl-U** to select Frame mode.
2. Point to the **Options** menu and click on **Show Column Guides** to turn on the column guides if they are not already on. If they are on, ignore this step.
3. Move the mouse cursor somewhere in the middle of the page and click once.
4. Point to the **Frame** menu and click on **Margins & Columns**. The Margins & Columns dialog box will appear.
5. Select **3** for **# of Columns**.
6. Type the following values:

	Widths	**Gutters**
Column 1:	**1.00**	
Column 2:	**2.25**	**.50**
Column 3:	**2.00**	**.50**

Your screen should resemble this illustration:

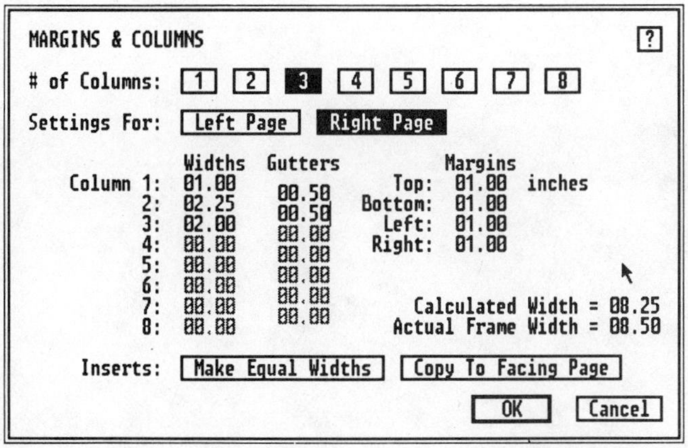

Notice that the calculated width is 8.25 inches. The actual frame width should be 8.5 inches.

7. Readjust the settings to match the actual width. You can make the margins and columns any width to make the Actual Frame Width and Calculated Width match. (This may take several adjustments.)

8. Select **OK**. Your screen should now resemble this illustration:

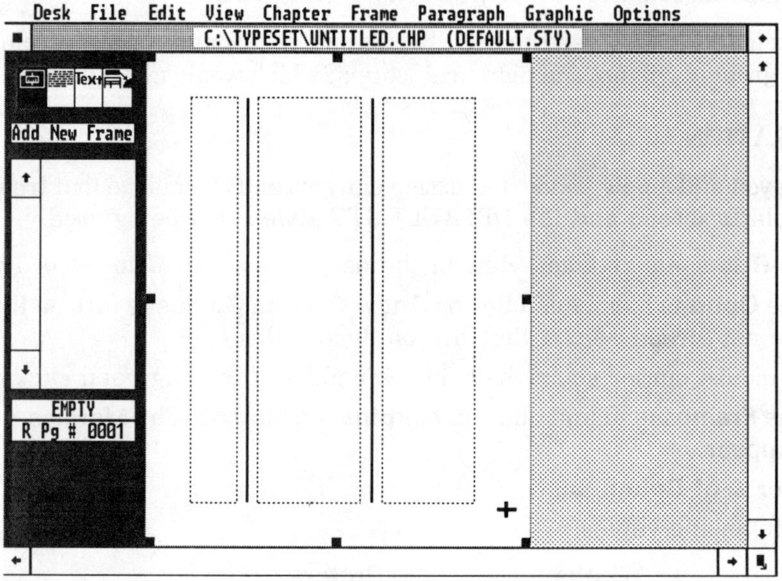

Notice the columns created within the frame.

9. Turn to Module 51 to continue the learning sequence.

Module 44

MULTI-CHAPTER

DESCRIPTION

The Xerox Ventura Publisher Multi-Chapter command links multiple chapter files together into a single publication. Once all the chapters are grouped, a PUB file is created which contains the list of chapter files making up the publication. Several functions can be executed on the PUB file, including the generation of a table of contents, creation of an index, renumbering of the pages within all chapters that make up the publication, and finally, printing the document.

Multi-Chapter also contains a file management utility option that copies the multiple files associated with a Xerox Ventura Publisher document from one location to another.

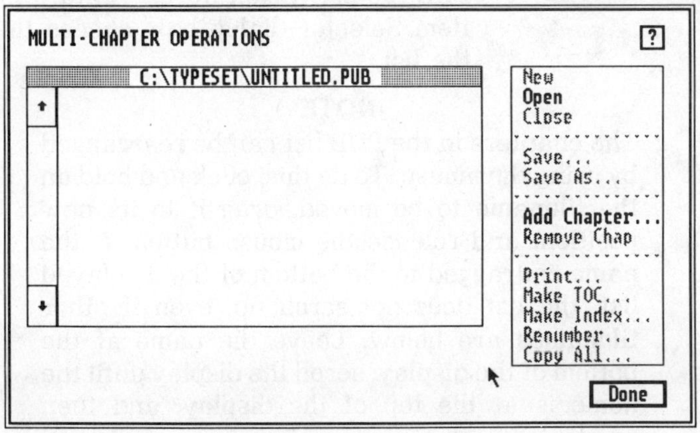

The Multi-Chapter dialog box offers these options:

New	Select this option to create a new PUB file. When Xerox Ventura Publisher displays the Item Selector dialog box, type the name of the new PUB file.
Open	Select this option to open an existing PUB file. When Xerox Ventura Publisher displays the Item Selector dialog box, type the PUB file to open.
Close	Select this option to close an open PUB file.

Save

Select this option to save a PUB file that has been created or changed. If a chapter file is open when the Multi-Chapter command is selected, the Save option creates a PUB file containing the current chapter plus any others added to the list. When Xerox Ventura Publisher displays the Item Selector dialog box, type the name of the PUB file to create. In this instance, do not use the New option to create the PUB file.

NOTE

The PUB file must be created and *saved* before an index or table of contents can be created with the Multi-Chapter options.

Save As

Select this option within the Multi-chapter dialog box to save an existing PUB file under a new name. Xerox Ventura Publisher displays the Item Selector dialog box. Type the name of the new PUB file to create.

Add Chapter

Select this option to add another chapter file to the current PUB file list. When Xerox Ventura Publisher displays the Item Selector dialog box, choose the CHP file to add to the list.

NOTE

The chapters in the PUB list can be rearranged by using the mouse. To do this, click and hold on the filename to be moved, drag it to its new position, and release the mouse button. If the name is dragged to the bottom of the displayed list, the list does not scroll up, even if other filenames are below. Leave the name at the bottom of the display, scroll the display until the name is at the top of the display, and then reselect it and drag it again.

Remove Chapter

Select a chapter file in the list, then choose this option to remove the selected file from the list.

Print

Select this option to print the PUB file. Xerox Ventura Publisher then displays the To Print dialog box. All options in the Print dialog box are the same except for Multi-Chapter. Multi-Chapter applies when files are being printed to disk. Select Combined to send all output of the various chapter files to one print file, or select Separate to route the output of each chapter file to a new print file.

Make TOC

Select this option to create a publication-wide table of contents from the selected chapters. When selected, Xerox Ventura Publisher displays the Generate Table of Contents dialog box.

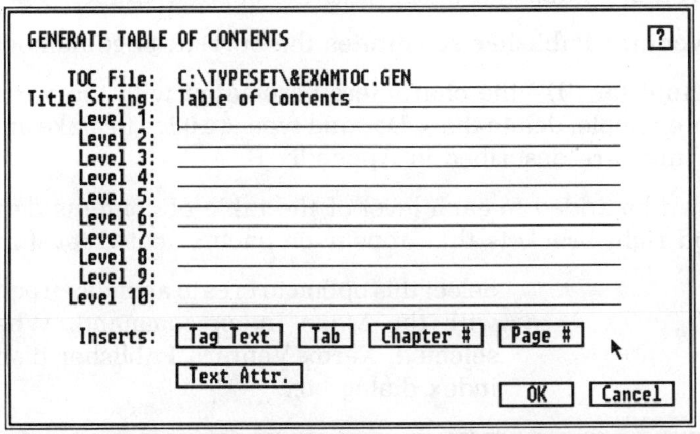

The Generate Table of Contents dialog box offers these options:

TOC File

Type the directory path, filename, and extension of the file to hold the table of contents information. Use the .GEN extension since Xerox Ventura Publisher is generating the file. After the file has been created, it can be loaded into a chapter file just as any other text file can be.

Title String

Type the title name desired at the top of the table of contents.

Level 1 through 10

Type the names of the paragraph tags to be used for each level of the table of contents. For example, Level 1 might be tag Headline 1 and Level 2 might be tag Subheadline.

Inserts

Select the type of information Xerox Ventura Publisher is to add on each level of the table of contents. Also, within this option, the appearance of the entries is defined. The information Xerox Ventura Publisher inserts into the table of contents definition is:

Item	*Inserted Characters*
Tag Text	[*tag name]
Tab	tab character (➔)
Chapter #	[C#]
Page #	[P#]
Text Attr	<D>

For the [*tag name], replace "tag name" with the name of the paragraph tag being associated with the table of contents level.

For the tab character, Xerox Ventura Publisher enters a tab character.

For the [C#], Xerox Ventura Publisher substitutes the current chapter number.

For the [P#], Xerox Ventura Publisher substitutes the current page number.

For the <D>, substitute for "D" the characters associated with the various text attributes Ventura supports. For example, delete the <D> and type <193> to make an ellipse (...) appear. The letters and attributes are described in Appendix B.

Any additional text can be added to each level of the table of contents definition by typing it outside of the left and right brackets that appear on each selected level line.

Make Index — Select this option to create an index from the entries created with the Make Index command. When Make Index is selected, Xerox Ventura Publisher displays the Generate Index dialog box.

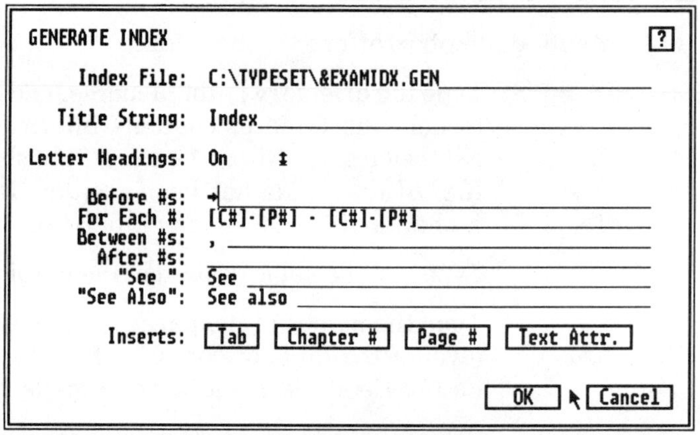

The options available in the Generate Index dialog box are:

Index File — Type the directory path, filename, and extension of the file to hold the table of contents information. Use the .GEN extension since Xerox Ventura Publisher is generating the file. After the file has been created, it can be loaded into a chapter file just as any other text file can be. If desired, use the default path and name Xerox Ventura Publisher supplies.

Title String — Type the title desired at the top of the index.

Letter Heading — Select whether or not Xerox Ventura Publisher is to place letters of the alphabet automatically at the beginning of each grouping in the index. For example, the A's listing would automatically begin with a single letter A.

Before #s	Type the character to appear after the index text and before the page number. The default is a tab. A comma followed by a space can be substituted if desired. If used, the comma and space option would produce index entries that look like this: Books Illustrated DisplayWrite 4, 32 Illustrated Ventura 2.0, 13
For Each #	Type the format desired for the same index entries that appear on multiple sequential pages. For example, the index can include both the chapter and the page number. [C#]-[P#] generates page numbers like this: Multi-Chapter, 5-18
Between #s	Type the punctuation desired between each chapter and page number. The default is a comma followed by a space. Typical output would look like this: Multi-Chapter, 5-18, 25, 76
After #s	Type the punctuation desired for use after the last page number. The default is none, but a period or other punctuation could be added. If added, typical output would look like this: Multi-Chapter, 5-18, 25, 76.
See	Type the text desired for the "see" entries. The default is See.
See Also	Type the text desired for "see also" entries. The default is See also.
Inserts	Select the formatting information desired for the index entries. The information Xerox Ventura Publisher inserts into each entry each time you click on the item is:

Item	*Inserted Characters*
Tab	tab character (→)
Chapter #	[C#]
Page Number	[P#]
Text Attr.	<D>

For Tab, Xerox Ventura Publisher enters a tab character.

For the [C#], Xerox Ventura Publisher substitutes the current chapter number.

For the [P#], Xerox Ventura Publisher substitutes the current page number.

For the <D>, substitute for "D" the characters associated with the various text attributes Ventura supports. For example, delete the <D> and type <193> to make an ellipse (...) appear. The letters and attributes are described in Appendix B.

Renumber — Select this option to automatically renumber the chapters, page, table, and figure numbers across chapter boundaries.

TIP: To make this feature work, use the Update Counters feature to set the initial chapter, page, table, and figure counter for each chapter to Previous Number + 1.

Copy All — Select this option to automatically copy all files associated with a chapter or publication. Each type of file—style sheet, picture, text, graphics—can be copied to a different disk. Xerox Ventura Publisher will also automatically update the references and pointers in the chapter and publication files to the new drives and directories. When this option is selected, the Copy All dialog box appears.

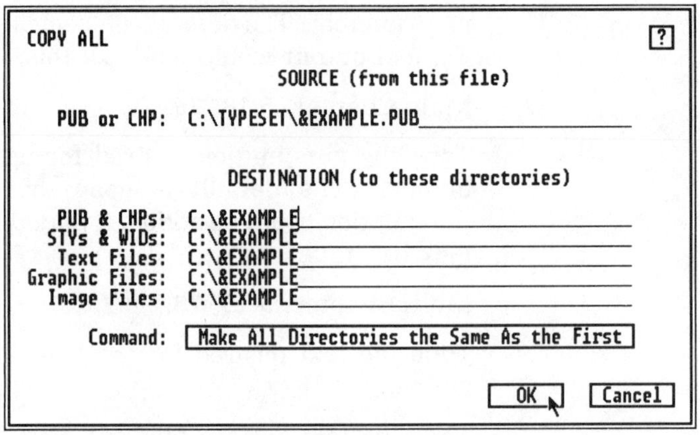

The options available in the Copy All dialog box are:

SOURCE — Type the directory path and filename and extension of the chapter file [CHP] or publication file [PUB] to be copied. If a publication is open and no chapters are selected in the Multi-Chapter dialog box, Xerox Ventura Publisher automatically inserts the publication file. If a chapter is selected, this entry is automatically the chapter file.

DESTINATION — Type the directory path where the files are to be copied. PUB & CHP, STY & WIDS, Text Files, Graphic File, and Image Files can be copied to different locations or the same location.

Command — Select Make All Directories the Same as the First option to copy all files to the same directory path as the first entry.

NOTE

In the Copy All dialog box, you must click on OK. Pressing Enter does not work. This is to eliminate starting the copying process by accidentally pressing Enter.

The Multi-chapter command is accessed from the Options menu.

APPLICATIONS

The primary purpose for using the Multi-chapter command is to produce extremely long documents. Xerox Ventura Publisher can easily produce documents of 1000 pages or more. Rather than trying to work with a very long document, it only makes sense to create several smaller documents and then, using Multi-chapter, make them into one publication, and finally print the publication. A good example is a book where each module would be created as its own Xerox Ventura Publisher chapter and then, finally, all the chapters would be printed in one publication.

Multi-chapter also allows you to see every file associated with a chapter.

One of the other prime functions of the Multi-chapter command is the ability to create the "front matter" and "back matter " of a book automatically. What could be a laborious job—creating an index and table of contents—Xerox Ventura Publisher does quickly with the options located within the Multi-chapter command.

The Multi-chapter command also permits page numbering across the boundaries of a chapter.

And Multi-chapter also offers the ability to copy the entire Xerox Ventura Publisher chapter or publication to another disk or directory. This is the best way to make backup copies of your Xerox Ventura Publisher chapters or publications. Trying to do so with the DOS commands can create problems. The reason is that the Xerox Ventura Publisher chapter file tells the program where to look for different files. If you do not place the files exactly where Xerox Ventura Publisher expects to find them, the chapter or publication will not open as expected.

TYPICAL OPERATION

In this operation, you create a publication file, make an index, and print the file. The instructions begin with Xerox Ventura Publisher running and the screen blank. The DEFAULT.STY stylesheet is loaded.

1. Point to the **Options** menu and click on **Multi-Chapter** to display the Multi-Chapter dialog box. Select **New** to remove any titles from the list.

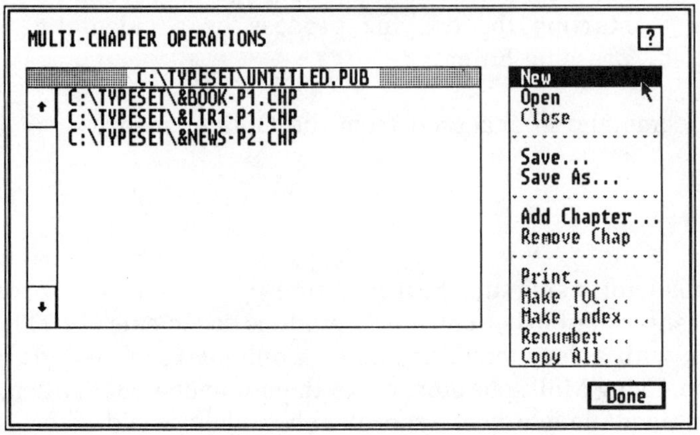

2. Click on **Add Chapter** to display the Item Selector dialog box.
3. Select **&BOOK-P1.CHP** and click **OK**.

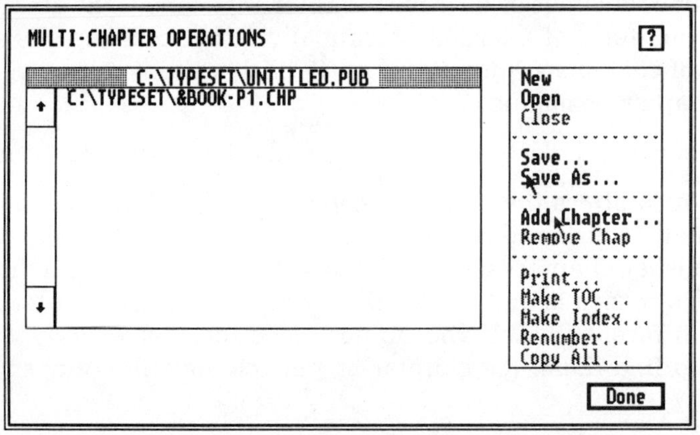

4. Click on **Add Chapter** to display the Item Selector dialog box.
5. Select **&BOOK-P2.CHP** and click **OK**.
6. Click on **Add Chapter** to display the Item Selector dialog box.
7. Select **&LSTG-P2.CHP** and click **OK**.
8. Click on **Save As** to display the Item Selector dialog box. Type **MYPUB1** for selection and press **Enter**.

9. Click **Make Index** to display the Generate Index dialog box.

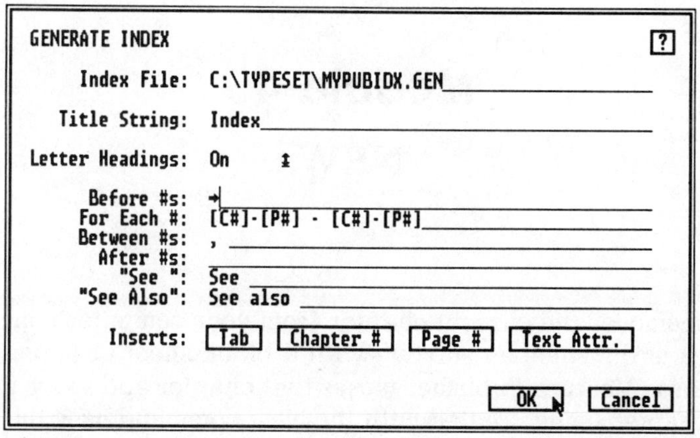

10. Click **OK**.
11. Click **Print** to display the To Print dialog box. Press **Enter**. Within a few moments, the various chapters print as a publication.
12. Click **Done**.
13. Turn to Module 21 to continue the learning sequence.

Module 45

NEW

DESCRIPTION

The New command removes the current chapter from your computer's memory and creates a blank chapter file. It is the same as starting with a blank sheet of paper. If another chapter is currently open, Xerox Ventura Publisher closes that chapter and saves it before creating the new file. The new chapter being created with the New command uses the last style sheet and defaults. New is accessed without specifying the name of a new file. When a filename is not specified, Xerox Ventura Publisher creates a new blank file.

New is located in the File menu.

APPLICATIONS

New provides a quick, easy way of creating a new file with Xerox Ventura Publisher. The obvious application for this command is to simply start composing a brand new chapter.

The New command can also be used to create various smaller chapters that can later be joined into one larger publication (see Module 44).

Finally, this command can also be used to simply start over when everything seems to have gone wrong from the very beginning. (This happens not only to beginners, but sometimes to even experienced users!) Using New provides you with a fresh start.

TYPICAL OPERATION

In this example, you use New to start another chapter. The Xerox Ventura Publisher sample chapter document SCOOP.CHP is used. The example begins with SCOOP.CHP already open and in use. If you do not have this chapter open, use Open Chapter in the File menu to retrieve and open SCOOP.CHP.

1. Point to the **File** menu and click on the **New** command.
2. Respond to the dialog box asking if you want to save or abandon the changes.

NOTE

This dialog box will appear only if you have made changes in the current chapter. If you have not made any changes, the dialog box will not appear.

3. Turn to Module 48 to continue the learning sequence.

Module 46

OPEN CHAPTER

DESCRIPTION

The Open Chapter command retrieves a previously stored chapter, as well as its related files, including the style sheet, text files, and graphic files.

Only one chapter can be open at a time in Xerox Ventura Publisher. If another chapter is currently open, Xerox Ventura Publisher will prompt you to save the existing open chapter. Select either Save to save your changes, or Abandon to throw away your changes.

To open a Xerox Ventura Publisher chapter, the filename *must* have the extension CHP. Xerox Ventura Publisher will not open a chapter unless the filename extension is CHP.

While Xerox Ventura Publisher is opening a chapter file, different messages may appear on your screen. This is a normal operation. Xerox Ventura Publisher places all possible hyphenation points in the text to increase the reformatting speed each time you make any change within the text.

The Open Chapter command is located in the File menu.

APPLICATIONS

The Open Chapter command opens a previously saved chapter file. The reason for opening a previously created and saved chapter file is to edit it in some way.

You could also use a previously saved chapter file as a template for another similar document. By opening a chapter and then using the Save As command (see Module 59) to create a new version of the publication, you can use the previously saved chapter as a template or guide for the next version of a document.

TYPICAL OPERATION

In this example, you open a previously saved chapter. If a chapter is open on your computer screen, select Quit from the File menu. After Ventura prompts you to save the current chapter, you will return to the DOS prompt. Restart Xerox Ventura Publisher in the normal manner, and you will return to a blank screen, ready to continue with these steps:

1. Point to the **File** menu. Select **Open Chapter**. The Item Selector dialog box appears. Your screen should resemble this illustration:

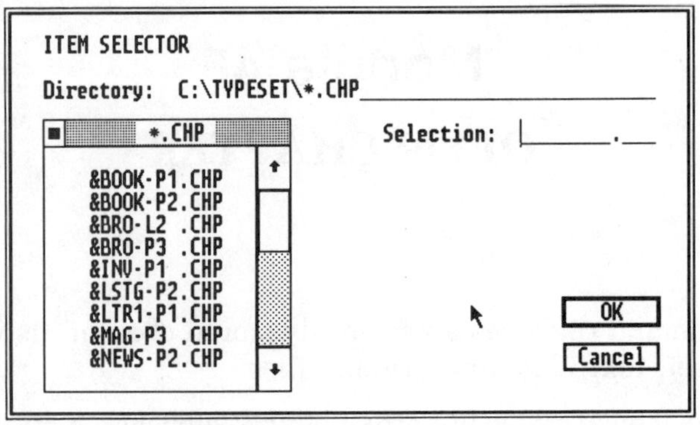

2. Type **\TYPESET*.CHP** for directory.
3. Type **SCOOP** for selection and press **Enter**. The new chapter SCOOP.CHP will appear on your screen within a few moments.

4. Turn to Module 59 to continue the learning sequence.

Module 47
OPTIONS MENU

DESCRIPTION

The Options menu provides a variety of different commands for your use when working with Xerox Ventura Publisher. The commands available within the Options menu are:

Set Preferences	Show/Hide All Pictures
Set Ruler	Show/Hide Tabs & Returns
Set Printer Info	Show/Hide Loose Lines
Add/Remove Fonts	Turn Column Snap Off/On
Show/Hide Side Bar	Turn Line Snap Off/On
Show/Hide Rulers	Multi-Chapter
Show/Hide Column Guides	

The commands available in the Options menu are available regardless of which mode of operation is currently being used in Xerox Ventura Publisher.

Some of the commands in the Options menu are switches. For example, Show Rulers switches between Show Rulers and Hide Rulers. If the Rulers are shown in the working area, when the Options menu is accessed, the command available would be Hide Rulers. If the Rulers were not displayed in the working area when the Options menu was accessed, the command would be Show Rulers.

APPLICATIONS

The Options menu offers access to a variety of miscellaneous commands within Xerox Ventura Publisher. The commands include:

- Setting preferences throughout the entire Xerox Ventura Publisher document
- Setting screen and printer options
- Adding or Removing fonts
- Performing Multi-chapter operations, including copying all Xerox Ventura Publisher chapters and all associated files

TYPICAL OPERATION

In this example, you display the Options menu and review its various commands. The Xerox Ventura Publisher sample chapter SCOOP.CHP is used. The example begins with SCOOP.CHP open. Use the Open Chapter command in the File menu to retrieve and open SCOOP.CHP.

1. Point to the **Options** menu and review the commands available within the menu.
2. Turn to Module 15 to continue the learning sequence.

Module 48

PAGE SIZE & LAYOUT

DESCRIPTION

The Page Size & Layout command assigns the physical size of the paper used in the printing, the printing orientation, and the selection of either single- or double-sided formatting.

TIP: Only one set of sizes and layout specifications is permitted per Xerox Ventura Publisher chapter.

The Page Size & Layout dialog box provides you with these options:

Orientation
Paper Type & Dimension
Sides
Start On

Each of these options provides a pop-up menu to permit additional selections. The selections available are:

Orientation — Select either Landscape or Portrait printing. The difference is:

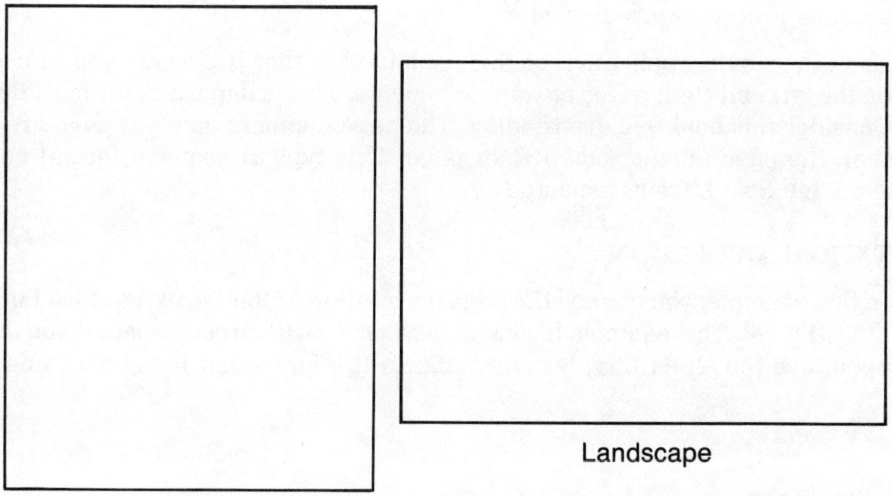

Landscape

Portrait

Paper Type & Dimension	Select the physical size of the paper on which your chapter is to be printed. Remember that smaller page sizes can be printed on printers that handle only one size of paper if you decrease the page's height and width in the frame Sizing and Scaling menu.
Sides	Select either Single-sided or Double-sided formatting. The Facing pages option in the View menu only works when you have selected the Double-sided option.
Start On	Select either Right or Left side.

NOTE

You must select Sides: Double to allow different headers & footers, margins, column widths, vertical rules, and tag spacing setting for left and right pages.

The settings selected with the Page Size & Layout command are stored in the style sheet.

The Page Size & Layout command is located in the Chapter menu.

APPLICATIONS

The Page Size & Layout command is used to change between portrait and landscape printing. This command allows you to decide the appearance of your finished printed page.

For most of your documents, you use the standard 8½" x 11" paper size. However, you might need to use a larger size piece of paper, such as 11" x 17" or Broadsheet. These options allow you to print in a shrink or overlap mode and can be used to create larger, oversized documents, such as a newspaper or poster.

The other main application of this command is that it permits you to use different formatting on the left and right pages of your documents. This is important for most double-sided documents. Consider this book you are reading. The page numbers on a left page are in a different position than the page numbers on a right page. This type of common format can be established with the Page Size Layout command.

TYPICAL OPERATION

In this example, you change the page orientation of the Xerox Ventura Publisher sample chapter SCOOP.CHP. This example begins with SCOOP.CHP already open. If you do not have this chapter open, use the Open Chapter command in the File menu to retrieve and open SCOOP.CHP.

1. Press **Ctrl-R** to reduce the view of the page. Your screen should resemble this illustration:

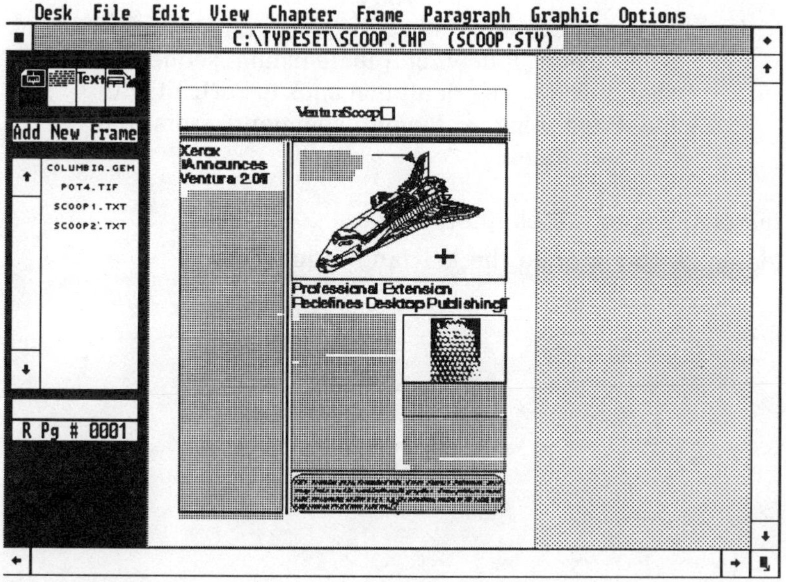

2. Point to the **Chapter** menu and click on **Page Size & Layout** to display the Page Layout dialog box.
3. Click on the **Orientation** pop-up menu and select **Landscape**.
4. Click on **OK**. Your screen should now resemble this illustration:

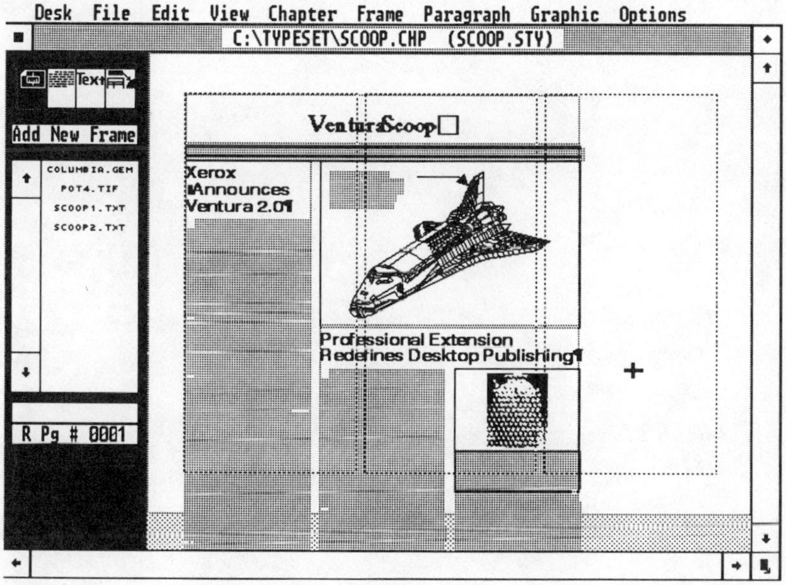

Notice the new layout of the page.

NOTE

So your screen matches the illustrations in this book when following the learning sequence, change the page orientation back to Portrait with the Page Size & Layout command from the Chapter menu.

5. Abandon the changes to the chapter.
6. Turn to Module 29 to continue the learning sequence.

Module 49

PARAGRAPH MENU

DESCRIPTION

The Paragraph menu defines the individual Paragraph Tags (the format assigned to the paragraphs within your Xerox Ventura Publisher document) contained in the style sheet. These tags are used to change the text format for each paragraph in a Ventura chapter.

The options available in the Paragraph menu are:

- Font
- Alignment
- Spacing
- Breaks
- Tab Settings
- Special Effects
- Attribute Overrides
- Paragraph Typography
- Ruling Line Above
- Ruling Line Below
- Ruling Box Around
- Define Colors
- Update Tag List

Before any option in the Paragraph menu can be selected, the Paragraph mode must be selected. The Paragraph mode can be selected by accessing the View menu and selecting Paragraph, or by pressing Ctrl-I.

Although you will not need to use all of the commands in the Paragraph menu for each Xerox Ventura Publisher document you produce, you will be using the first three commands—Font, Alignment, and Spacing—many times to control the appearance of your paragraphs.

APPLICATIONS

As a desktop publisher, your most important task and goal is to convey a written message to a reader by communicating with the printed word. Although Xerox Ventura Publisher provides you with many tools to meet that goal, perhaps none are as important as the commands found in the Paragraph menu. These commands provide the control over the computer-generated typesetting process.

TYPICAL OPERATION

In this operation, you access the Paragraph menu and review the various commands located within the menu. The Xerox Ventura Publisher sample chapter document SCOOP.CHP is used. The example begins with SCOOP.CHP already in use. Use the command Open Chapter in the File menu to retrieve and open SCOOP.CHP.

1. Press **Ctrl-I** to change to the Paragraph mode.
2. Point at the **Paragraph** menu, and notice the various commands available within the menu.
3. Move the mouse to any area outside of the Paragraph menu and click once. The Paragraph menu disappears.
4. Turn to Module 50 to continue the learning sequence.

Module 50

PARAGRAPH TAGGING

DESCRIPTION

Xerox Ventura Publisher's Paragraph Tagging function allows you to design, create, change, and assign attributes to the paragraphs within your document. When in the Paragraph Tagging mode, you can assign a Tag from the style sheet. Those tags available are selected from the Assignment List in the Side Bar. The tag attributes are changed by using the options or commands available in the Paragraph menu.

Xerox Ventura Publisher contains two types of tags. They are user-defined tags, which you create, and Ventura-generated tags, which Xerox Ventura Publisher automatically creates when you use certain commands, such as Headers & Footers, or Auto-Numbering.

Tags can be changed, assigned, or even deleted. By using tags, you can create special styled paragraphs, such as those with bullets, or large first letters, or with an unique indent or outdent. The real power of using a tag is that whatever attribute is assigned to a tag, then all paragraphs within the Xerox Ventura Publisher document that have the same tag will have the same attributes. For example, if you set the tag called Headline to be centered, 24-point Dutch, then all paragraphs in your document tagged as Headline—whether they are on page 1, 19, or 99—would be set in 24-point Dutch type, and they would be centered.

NOTE

Body Text is located in each style sheet, and although you can change the attributes of this tag, it cannot be deleted.

Xerox Ventura Publisher tags can be assigned to any paragraph, but not to an individual word or sentence within a paragraph. To Xerox Ventura Publisher, a paragraph is any group of characters, words, or sentences that end with a Required Carriage Return. A paragraph can be as short as a word, or can run many pages long.

Xerox Ventura Publisher tags are saved in a Ventura file called a style sheet.

The Paragraph Tagging mode is enabled by pressing Ctrl-I or by accessing the View menu and selecting the Paragraph option.

APPLICATIONS

Xerox Ventura Publisher makes setting text easier by using the Paragraph Tagging feature. Because each tag can be set to assign a different style to a paragraph, you are able to take advantage of design freedom. And since more than one paragraph can be assigned with the same tag, you assure a uniform appearance throughout the document.

For example, you can assign attributes to each level of headline, subheading, and captions throughout the Xerox Ventura Publisher document. Then, whatever text is chosen as the headline, it will be set with the correct attributes and will always be the same throughout the entire document.

All text not assigned a tag will automatically be assigned Body Text by Xerox Ventura Publisher. Whatever the attributes for Body Text, all body text paragraphs throughout the document will look alike.

Xerox Ventura Publisher Paragraph Tags enforce a consistent appearance of text throughout the entire document. Because the paragraph tags are saved in a style sheet, you can use the same style sheet with other text document, and by assigning paragraph tags, each publication will look the same.

TYPICAL OPERATION

In this example, you use the Paragraph mode and select a paragraph. Then you assign another paragraph tag to the paragraph. The Xerox Ventura Publisher sample chapter &NEWS-P2.CHP is used. The example begins with &NEWS-P2.CHP already open and in use. Use the command Open Chapter in the File menu to retrieve and open &NEWS-P2.CHP. So your view matches the screen depicted in this book, press Ctrl-N. You may need to adjust your screen using the scroll bars to make your computer look like the illustrations.

1. Press **Ctrl-I** to select Paragraph mode. The mouse cursor changes shape. It looks like the corner of a box with lines of text inside of it.
2. Click on the words "Software Salaries: How do you stack up?" Notice that Xerox Ventura Publisher reverses the color of the selected paragraph text.

3. Point and click on **Body Text** in the Assignment List. Notice that the words "Software Salaries: How do you stack up?" now appear on your screen with the same attributes and appearance as the other body text. Your screen should resemble this illustration:

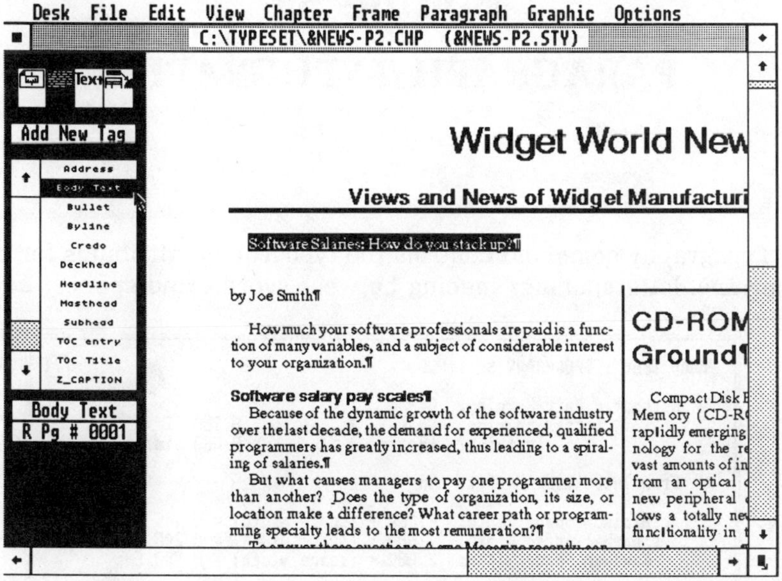

Also notice that the Current Selection Box shows the name of the tag (Body Text) assigned to this paragraph.

4. Point and click on **Headline** in the Assignment List. The words "Software Salaries: How do you stack up?" once again revert to their normal size.
5. Abandon the changes to the chapter.
6. Turn to Module 77 to continue the learning sequence.

Module 51
PARAGRAPH TYPOGRAPHY

DESCRIPTION

The Paragraph Typography command controls the typographic attributes for each paragraph tag, including kerning, letterspacing, spacing between words, and spacing between lines.

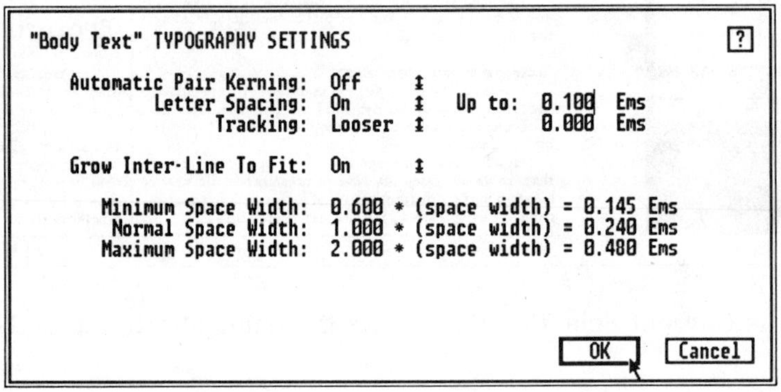

The options available within the Paragraph Typography settings dialog box are:

- Automatic Pair Kerning
- Letter Spacing
- Tracking
- Grow Inter-Line to Fit
- Minimum Space Width
- Normal Space Width
- Maximum Space Width

Within each option, different settings are available, offering an array of powerful typographic controls to your individual paragraph tags.

For example, in automatic kerning, Xerox Ventura Publisher will automatically kern letter pairs. There are over 30,000 possible pairs of characters, but only 100 to 500 (depending on the style of your font) need to be kerned. Kerning permits the characters to be squeezed together, making the type characters easier to read. A classic example is the combination of A and W. Xerox Ventura Publisher will automatically kern these letters for you when used in combination.

Automatic kerning is turned on or off for the entire chapter in the Chapter Typography (see Module 14) option. If it is turned on for the entire chapter, kerning can be turned on or off for any specific paragraph tag within the Paragraph Typography Settings dialog box.

To turn Automatic Pair Kerning for a particular paragraph tag on or off, simply access the Paragraph Typography Settings dialog box and, using the pop-up menu, select either on or off. Xerox Ventura Publisher takes care of the kerning for you automatically, and for most cases, that will be sufficient.

TIP: To see the effect of the automatic kerning on your computer screen, you must turn on On-Screen Kerning in the Set Preferences command in the Options menu.

One of the other options available within the Paragraph Typography Settings dialog box includes Letter Spacing. When Xerox Ventura Publisher justifies a line of text, space is added and subtracted between each word until the last character on a line reaches the right column. Letterspacing attempts to control the appearance of a line of text by adding additional space between the characters of each word. By doing so, not as much white space is required between the words. If letterspacing is turned on, additional spaces are added between letters until the space between words is equal to or less than the amount specified in the Maximum Space Width.

To use Letter Spacing, you must first set the horizontal alignment to justified in the Alignment dialog box, turn Letter Spacing on in the Paragraph Typography Settings dialog box, and set the Minimum Space Width to less than the Normal Space Width. A typical number would be 0.700 (70% of the Normal Space Width). Remember that values above the normal space width would have no effect. The Minimum Space Width is the smallest amount of space that can appear between words in a justified line. Set the Normal Space Width to 1.000, and set the Maximum Space Width to the largest space allowable between words during justification. A typical value is 2.000 (double the Normal Space Width). Finally, set the maximum space allowed between letters during letterspacing in the Up to area. A typical amount is 0.100 Ems.

Xerox Ventura Publisher calculates the space character's width and shows it in Ems, a typographic measurement equal to the width of the capital M in the current font and point size being used and assigned to the paragraph tag.

Tracking increases or decreases the space between every letter in a paragraph. To use the Tracking control, select Looser to increase the space, and select Tighter to decrease the amount of space. Then enter on the Tracking line the amount of space to add or subtract between individual letters. The amount of tracking is also set in Ems.

Grow Inter-Line To Fit allows larger type sizes to fit within a line. For example, you might want to use a large size typeface for one or two words within a paragraph of text. If the Grow Inter-Line is turned off, the words with the bigger size text, assigned in the Set Font function within the Text Editing mode, will overlap the previous line of text. If Grow Inter-Line is turned on, the amount of spacing between lines of the paragraph will be increased so as to prevent the larger text overlapping the previous line of text.

NOTE

These controls available to set the Paragraph typography are powerful tools. However, they can easily be abused. It is recommended that a conservative approach be taken when making adjustments within this dialog box. Be careful not to use too much or too little spacing, because either can make your text impossible to read.

The Paragraph Typography Settings dialog box is located within the Paragraph menu. The Paragraph tagging mode must be enabled and a paragraph selected to access this command.

APPLICATIONS

Automatic pair kerning makes headlines easier to read and more attractive by placing individual letters closer together. Kerning also reduces the amount of space needed for some text.

The Grow Inter-Line To Fit option automatically increases the space between lines. This command is also available for creating local overrides to the Paragraph font settings when needing to create a new tag. For example, if you wish to change a paragraph's font, but do not need to change the alignment or space between paragraphs, you should select the entire paragraph in text mode, and then change the font with the Set Font command in the Side Bar. The inter-line spacing will automatically adjust if Grow Inter-Line To Fit is turned on. This procedure eliminates the need for another paragraph tag.

Letter Spacing reduces the number of lines that would have too much white space (called loose lines) between words by adding space between the letters in the words on the line.

Tracking is used to expand or contract headlines to fit a given space, or, if used in the body text, the entire document can be expanded or reduced in size with only a minor, subtle change in the overall appearance.

TYPICAL OPERATION

In this example, you adjust the Paragraph Typography of a paragraph in a chapter. The Xerox Ventura Publisher sample chapter SCOOP.CHP is used. The example begins with SCOOP.CHP already open and in use. If you do not have this chapter open, use the Open Chapter command in the File menu to retrieve and open SCOOP.CHP. Change the view size to Normal view.

1. Press **Ctrl-I** to enable the Paragraph Tagging mode.
2. Point to and select the first paragraph of text in the left column of your screen.
3. Point to the **Paragraph** menu and click on the **Paragraph Typography** option.
4. Type **0.500** to change the Tracking. Your screen should resemble the following illustration:

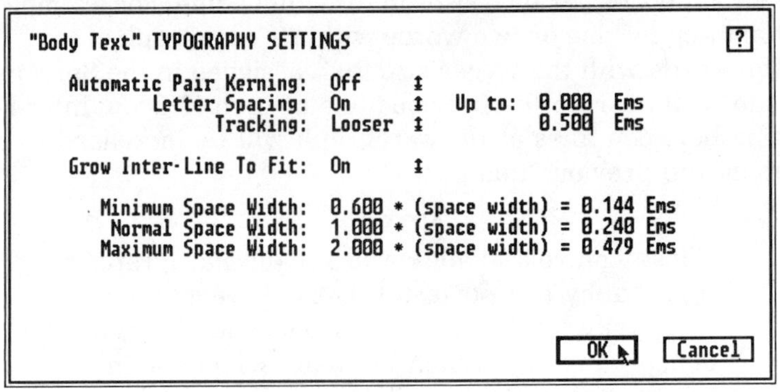

5. Select **OK**. Your screen should resemble this illustration:

Notice the exaggerated word spacing now being shown.

6. Abandon the changes by pointing to the **Edit** menu and clicking on **Abandon**. Confirm the abandon command in the dialog box.
7. Turn to Module 71 to continue the learning sequence.

Module 52
QUIT

DESCRIPTION

The Quit command ends the current Xerox Ventura Publisher session and returns you to DOS. Quit closes all open files. If you have made any changes to any of the various Ventura documents, the program asks if you want to save the changes before quitting.

Quit also creates the VP.INF file in the VENTURA directory. The next time you start Xerox Ventura Publisher, the program uses the VP.INF file to set the defaults to the way they were when you last used Xerox Ventura Publisher. The VP.INF file does not reopen the last chapter file you were using.

Quit is located in the File menu.

APPLICATIONS

Quit is the command used to end a session in Xerox Ventura Publisher. You might use the command in another program, such as your word processor.

You should always use the Quit command rather than simply turning the computer power off. Quit closes all open Xerox Ventura Publisher files and provides dialog boxes to save any changes that have been made since the last time the chapter was saved.

TYPICAL OPERATION

In this example, you quit and abandon the Xerox Ventura Publisher sample chapter document SCOOP.CHP. The example begins with SCOOP.CHP already open and in use. If you do not have this chapter open, use the command Open Chapter in the File menu to retrieve and open SCOOP.CHP.

1. Point to the **View** menu and click on **Text Editing**. Press **Ctrl-N** to see the page in normal view.
2. Click after the word "Ventura" in the headline, and type **Latest**.

3. Point to the **File** menu and click on **Quit**. Your screen should resemble this illustration:

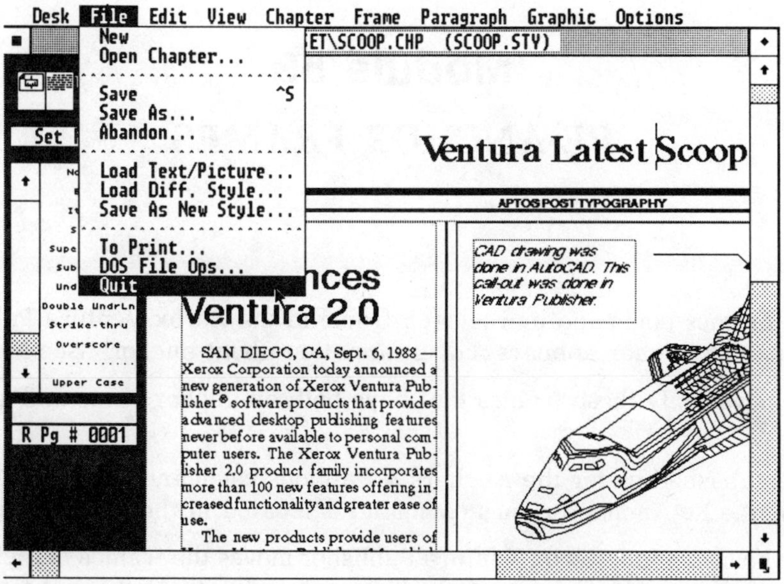

Within a moment, another dialog box appears asking if you want to save or abandon the changes you have made to the chapter, or if you want to cancel the Quit command. Your screen should resemble this illustration:

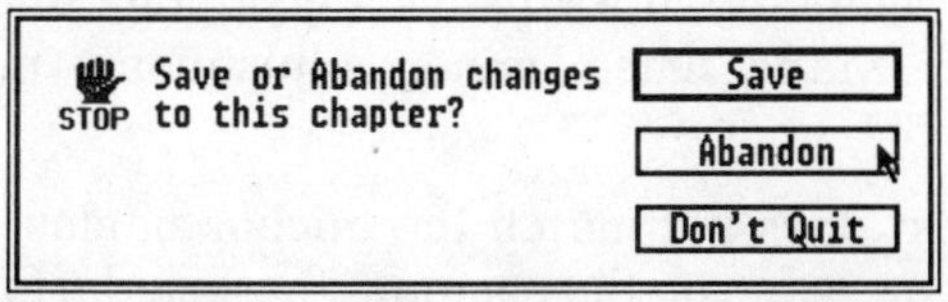

4. Click on **Abandon**. Ventura returns you to the DOS prompt.
5. Turn to Module 26 to continue the recommended learning sequence.

Module 53

RE-ANCHOR FRAMES

DESCRIPTION

The Re-Anchor Frames command moves each frame in the Xerox Ventura Publisher chapter to the page where its anchor appears. For information about anchors, see Module 35.

This command moves only those frames that have both an anchor name and a text anchor in the same page.

The anchor is established under the Anchors & Captions command, located within the Frame menu. However, the Re-Anchor Frames command is located in the Chapter menu.

After selecting the command, Xerox Ventura Publisher moves the frames to their anchor points within the text. If the anchored frames are at a point in the text where the text is currently at the top or bottom of a page, the Re-Anchor command moves those frames to the upper and lower margins. Those frames must then be relocated manually by selecting the Frame mode and then moving them with the mouse.

TIP: Whenever using the command, it is always a good idea to check each anchored frame within your chapter. Many times, minor adjustments must be made for optimum appearance.

If the anchor name in the text does not match the anchor names assigned to a frame, Xerox Ventura Publisher displays a message on the computer screen during the Re-Anchor command's execution. You may then correct the name of the anchor in the text before the re-anchor process continues.

APPLICATIONS

This command is used to move frames to anchor points within your text. Frames that contain charts, diagrams, or pictures associated with certain text need to be kept with the text. During the editing and moving text processes, the frames could be no longer near the associated text. By using the Re-Anchor Frames command, the frames are moved to that text.

TYPICAL OPERATION

In this example, you re-anchor the frames within the Xerox Ventura Publisher sample chapter &BOOK-P1.CHP. The example begins with &BOOK-P1.CHP already in use. If you do not have this chapter open, use the Open Chapter command in the File menu to retrieve and open &BOOK-P1.CHP.

1. Press **Ctrl-I** to select the Paragraph tagging mode.
2. Click on the first paragraph of text. Its tag name is Firstpar.
3. Select **Spacing** from the Paragraph menu.
4. To move the frame anchor, change the line spacing by typing **18.00** fractional points for Inter-Line and click **OK**.
5. Notice the changes to the spacing of the paragraph. The frame anchor at the end of the paragraph is now below the illustration.
6. Point to the **Chapter** menu and select **Re-Anchor Frames**. A message box appears asking if you wish to re-anchor this page's frames, all frames, or cancel.
7. Select **All Pages** in the chapter to be re-anchored.

NOTE

After using this command, you should check each page within the chapter to fine-tune or adjust any frame.

8. Select **Abandon** from the File menu and click on **OK**. Confirm the abandon when asked if you want to save or abandon the changes.
9. Turn to Module 36 to continue the learning sequence.

Module 54

REMOVE TEXT/FILE

DESCRIPTION

The Remove Text/File command completely deletes a file and its content from a frame or underlying page frame or from the Assignment List.

The file is *not* deleted from the disk. To delete a file from the disk, use the DOS Files Operation (see Module 18 for more information).

To access the Remove Text/File command, the frame or underlying page frame must be selected. Xerox Ventura Publisher must be in Frame mode before the frame can be selected. The Remove Text/File command can then be accessed from the Edit menu. When selected, the Remove File dialog box appears.

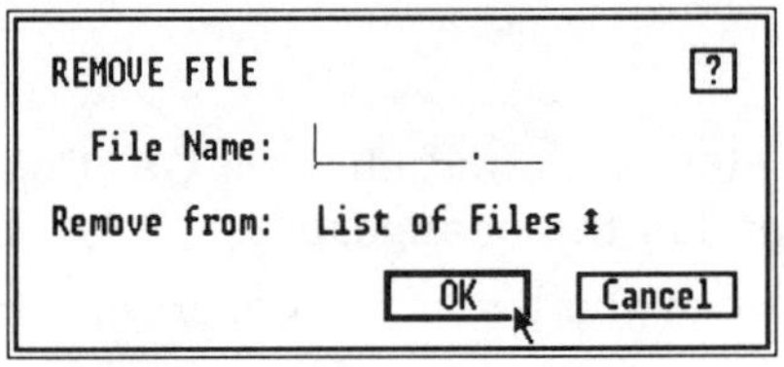

The Remove Text/File dialog box offers these options:

File Name	Type the name of the file as it appears in the Assignment List. Xerox Ventura Publisher will automatically enter the name of the file in the selected frame or underlying page frame.
Remove from	Select either List of Files or Frame. If you select Frame, the file will be removed from the frame, but will remain in the Assignment List. If you select List of Files, the file will be removed from the frame and the Assignment List.

TIP: Any unused file should be removed from the Assignment List. By doing so, you speed up the operation of Xerox Ventura Publisher. All text files included in the Assignment List are loaded into memory, whether or not they are placed anywhere in the chapter. Removing unnecessary files eliminates this use of the computer memory.

APPLICATIONS

The Remove Text/File command is used to remove files from a frame or from the Assignment List. Removing unwanted files from the Assignment List will speed the amount of time it takes for Xerox Ventura Publisher to open a chapter file for you. Removing a file from a frame is useful when a frame has been copied for its attributes, such as rules, margins, columns, background pattern, but the text file within the frame is not wanted.

TYPICAL OPERATION

In this operation, you draw a frame, load a text file in the frame, delete the frame, and finally, remove the text file from the assignment list. The Xerox Ventura Publisher sample chapter document &PRPT-P1.CHP is used. The example begins with &PRPT-P1.CHP already open and in use. If you do not have this chapter open, use the Open Chapter command in the File menu to retrieve and open &PRPT-P1.CHP. Press Ctrl-R to change to reduced view.

1. Press **Ctrl-U** to change to the Frame mode.
2. Click on **Add New Frame** in the Side Bar, move to the middle of the page, and draw a new frame. Your screen should resemble this illustration:

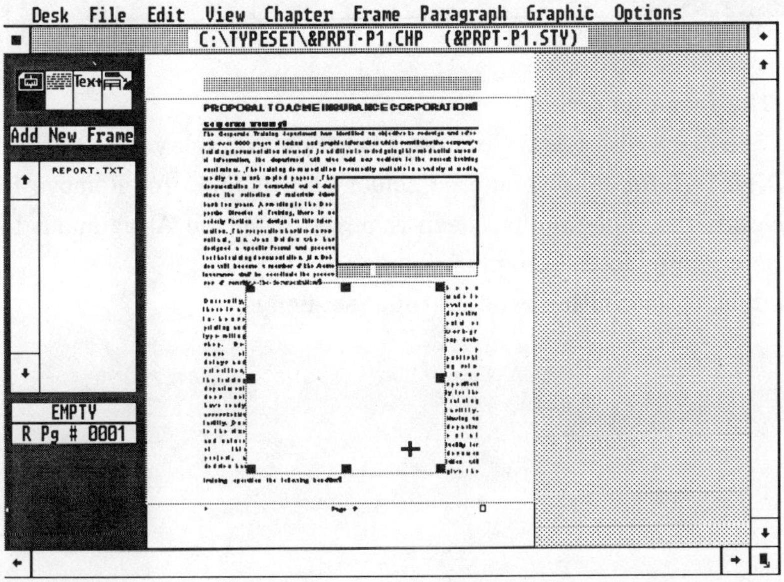

3. Point to the **File** menu and click on **Load Text/Picture**. Select **Text** for type of file and **ASCII** for Text Format. Click on **OK**. The Item Selector appears.

4. Double click on **REPORT.TXT**. Your screen should resemble this illustration:

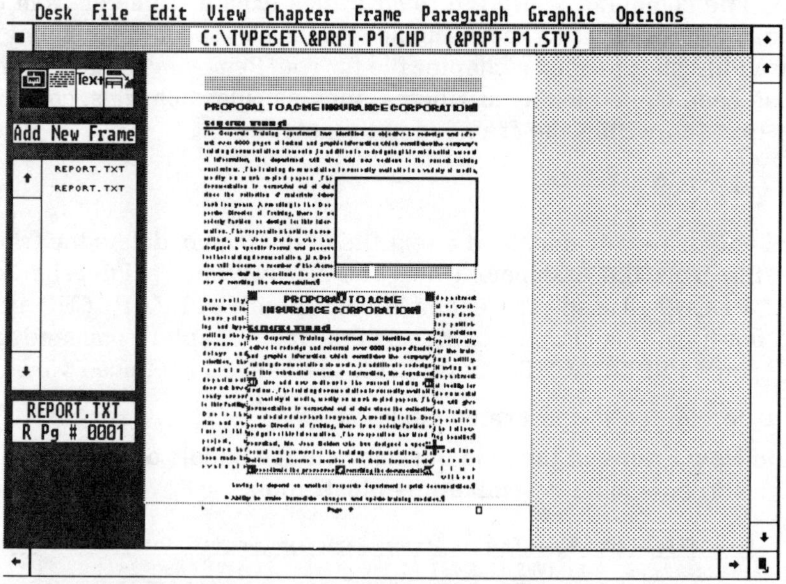

5. Press **Del**. The frame is deleted.
6. Point to the **File** menu and select **Remove Text/File** to display the Remove File dialog box.
7. Type **REPORT.TXT** for File Name and select **List of Files** for Remove from.
8. Click **OK**. Notice the filename has been removed from the Assignment List.
9. Abandon the changes to the chapter.
10. Turn to Module 11 to continue the learning sequence.

Module 55
RENUMBER CHAPTER

DESCRIPTION

The Renumber Chapter command updates the numbering of paragraphs defined in the Auto-Numbering option. Paragraphs can be automatically numbered by Xerox Ventura Publisher with the Auto-Numbering command (see Module 9 for more information about Auto-Numbering).

The Renumber Chapter command is located in the Chapter menu.

APPLICATIONS

The Auto-Numbering command does not change the paragraph numbers automatically each time a paragraph is added or deleted. When paragraphs are edited, changed, moved, deleted, or added, the Renumber Chapter command must be accessed to renumber the paragraphs.

TYPICAL OPERATION

In this example, you renumber the Xerox Ventura Publisher sample chapter &BOOK-P1.CHP. The example begins with &BOOK-P1.CHP already open and in use. If you do not have this chapter open, use the Open Chapter command in the File menu to retrieve and open &BOOK-P1.CHP.

1. Press **Ctrl-O** to access the Text Editing mode, place the text cursor to the left of The Adventure Begins, and press **Return** to add a new paragraph.
2. Type **Fun & Excitement**
3. Point to the **Chapter** menu and click on **Renumber Chapter**. The entire chapter has been renumbered.
4. Press **Ctrl-S** to save the changes.
5. Turn to Module 22 to continue the learning sequence.

Module 56

REPEATING FRAME

DESCRIPTION

The Repeating Frame command duplicates a frame on every page of your Xerox Ventura Publisher chapter. All attributes assigned to the frame—its ruling lines, background, and contents—are also copied onto each chapter page.

A repeating frame can also be hidden on selected pages within your Xerox Ventura Publisher chapter. For example, you could have a repeating frame and its contents appear on all pages within your document except the first page.

NOTE

Repeating Frames cannot have captions.

Repeating Frames can be sized and positioned on a page, but they cannot be cut, copied, or pasted. Any change made to a repeating frame *changes* all reoccurrences of the repeating frames on each page. In other words, the Repeating Frame will be *exactly* the same throughout the entire Xerox Ventura Publisher chapter.

When a Repeating Frame is selected, it is displayed in gray, rather than black, to alert you that the frame is a repeating frame, and not a regular frame.

To use the Repeating Frame command, first create the frame that you wish repeated on each page within your Xerox Ventura Publisher document. Then, while in the Frame mode, access the Frame menu and select the Repeating Frame command.

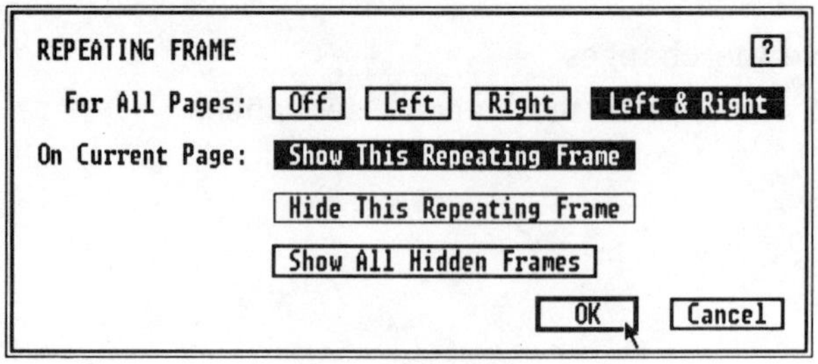

When the Repeating Frame dialog box appears, the following commands are available:

For All Pages: Select Off, Left, Right, or Left & Right. Select Left if you want the Repeating Frame to appear only on the left pages; select Right if you want the Repeating Frame to appear only on the right pages; select Left & Right if you want the Repeating Frame to appear on both left and right pages. Select Off if you want to remove the Repeating Frame from all other pages within the Xerox Ventura Publisher chapter.

On Current Page: Select Show This Repeating Frame, Hide This Repeating Frame, or Show All Hidden Frames. Select Hide This Repeating Frame to remove a repeating frame from a page. To restore a hidden frame, select Show This Repeating Frame. If you have selected another frame, and then return to the hidden, repeating frame, select Show All Hidden Frames.

APPLICATIONS

This command is used to place text or graphics on every page within your document. For example, you might want to produce a document that has a company letterhead or logo on each page. The Repeating Frame command allows you to position the text or graphics on each page automatically. This eliminates the necessity to position the text and logo on each page. Rather, the Repeating Frame command will routinely repeat on each page for you.

This command can also be used to create headers and footers larger than those generated by Xerox Ventura Publisher.

TYPICAL OPERATION

In this operation, a repeating frame is created. The Xerox Ventura Publisher sample chapter document &PRPT-P1.CHP is used. The example begins with &PRPT-P1.CHP already open. Use the Open Chapter command in the File menu to retrieve and open &PRPT-P1.CHP.

1. Select the Frame mode by pressing **Ctrl-U**. Select Reduced View by pressing **Ctrl-R**.
2. Select **Add New Frame** from the Side Bar and move to the center of the page. Click and hold the mouse, and draw a medium size frame.

3. Point to the **Frame** menu and click on **Frame Background**. Select **Solid** for pattern and click on **OK**. Your screen should resemble this illustration:

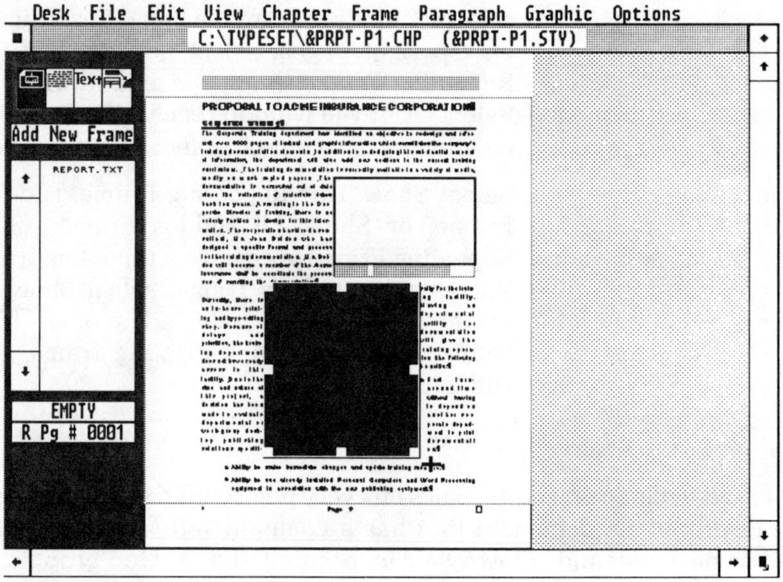

4. Point to the **Frame** menu and click on **Repeating Frame**. Click on **Left & Right** and click on **OK**.
5. Point to **Chapter** menu and click on **Insert/Remove** page. Click on **Insert New Page After Current Page**. Select **OK.**

6. Press **PgDn**. Your screen should resemble this illustration:

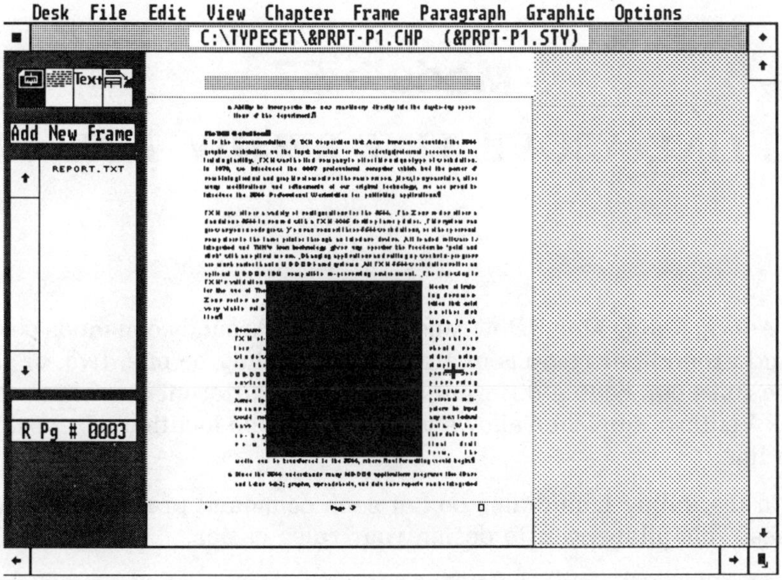

Notice the repeating frame.

7. Point to the **File** menu and select **Abandon**. Confirm the Abandon in the confirmation block.
8. Turn to Module 57 to continue the learning sequence.

Module 57

RULING LINE ABOVE, LINE BELOW, BOX AROUND

DESCRIPTION

The Ruling Line Above, Ruling Line Below, and Ruling Box Around commands position ruler lines above, below, and around paragraphs or frames. There may be one, two, or three rule lines. Each of the three rules can have a different height and a different amount of spacing between each rule. Xerox Ventura Publisher allows you to define the location, size, color, texture, and spacing of each line.

A display area in the Ruling Line dialog box of each command previews the size and spacing of the ruling lines. This allows you to design your rules easier.

When a ruling line is desired above, below, or around a paragraph, the commands are selected with the paragraph tag. After selecting the paragraph mode, then select the command from the Paragraph menu. The changes made with these commands affect the paragraph tag associated with the selected text. When a change is made to a paragraph tag, it affects all text marked with that paragraph tag in your current Xerox Ventura Publisher document as well as in other Xerox Ventura Publisher documents that use the same style sheet.

When a ruling line is desired above, below, or around a frame, the commands are selected with the frame tool. After selecting the Frame mode, then select the command from the Frame menu. A Ruling Box Above, Below, or Around command can be assigned to any frame, including the underlying page frame.

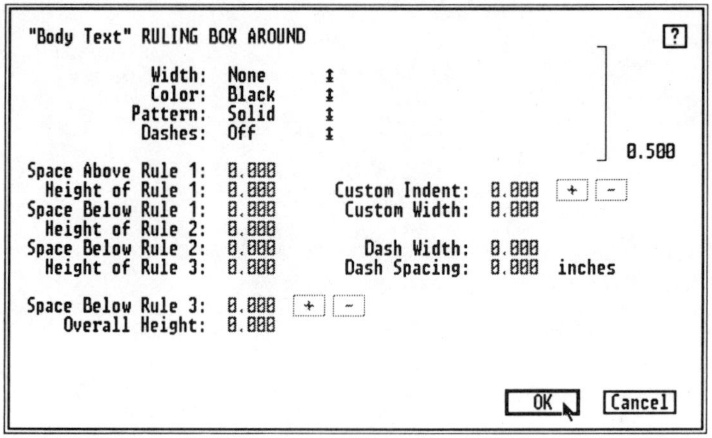

The dialog boxes for all three commands contain these options:

Width	Select the overall width of the rule or box. The available options are the width of the paragraph's text, the frame's margins, the current column in the frame, or the width of the frame itself. A custom width can also be specified by selecting Custom, then typing the width in points in the Custom Width entry area.
Color	Assign a color to the ruling line if desired.
Pattern	Select the pattern of the ruling lines. Use Solid for a continuous black line. The same pattern will be used for all lines in the ruling.
Dashes On/Off	Choose either solid or dashed lines. If a dashed line is chosen, type the dash length and space between dashes in the Dash Width and Dash Spacing entry areas.
Space Above Rule 1	Type the white space needed above the first line of the ruling.
Height of Rule 1/2/3	Type the width or thickness of each line in the ruling.
Space Below Rule 1/2/3	Type the white space needed below each line in the ruling.
Overall Height	Xerox Ventura Publisher calculates the height of the rules and displays it in this area for you.
Dash Width	If dashed lines were selected, type the width of the dashes.
Dash Spacing	If dashed lines were selected, type the length of the space between the dashes.
Custom Indent	If a Custom Width was specified, type the amount of offset desired for the line length. If adding to the length, select + (plus). If subtracting from the length, select – (minus).

TIP: Some laser printers cannot support extremely thin ruling lines, often referred to as hairlines. If your printer does not print a thin ruling line, enlarge the width of the ruling line.

APPLICATIONS

Ruling Lines Above, Below, or Around Text or Frames are used to emphasize or isolate text or pictures. The reason for doing so will depend on your publication. For example, you might be creating an advertisement that contains a discount coupon. You may want to use a Ruling Box Around—with dashes—to emphasize the coupon, and for the consumer to use a guide to cut out the coupon from the rest of the advertisement.

Adding rules above or below text usually adds design and style to a document. What would first appear as bland or dull is often a bright and dazzling document when these simple rules are added.

Perhaps one of the best ways to learn how to affectively use ruling lines is to look through and study magazines, books, and newspapers. Notice the way other graphic designers use these simple techniques to make their layout more interesting and to attract your attention.

TYPICAL OPERATION

In this example, you add a new frame and use the Ruling Box Around command. The Xerox Ventura Publisher sample chapter document &PRPT-P1.CHP is used. The example begins with &PRPT-P1.CHP already open. Use the Open Chapter command in the File menu to retrieve and open &PRPT-P1.CHP.

1. Press **Ctrl-U** to select the Frame mode and press **Ctrl-N** to view page in Normal View.
2. Select **Add New Frame** from the Side Bar.
3. Move the cursor to the middle of the page, and draw a new frame. Your screen should resemble this illustration:

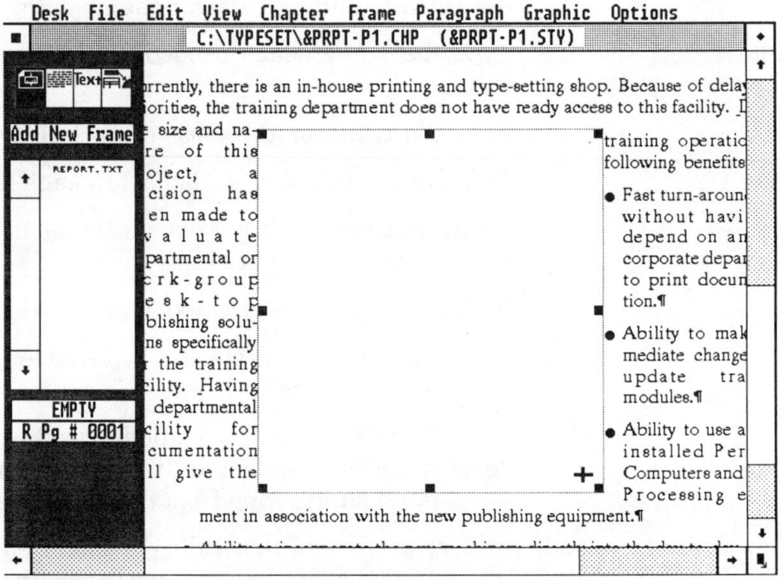

4. Point to the **Frame** menu and click on **Ruling Box Around** to display the Ruling Box Around dialog box.
5. Select **Frame** for Width, **Black** for Color, and **Solid** for Pattern.
6. Type **0.200** for Space Above Rule 1, **0.100** for Height of Rule 1, **0.150** for Space Below Rule 1, **0.130** for Height of Rule 2.

NOTE

All of these settings are in inches.

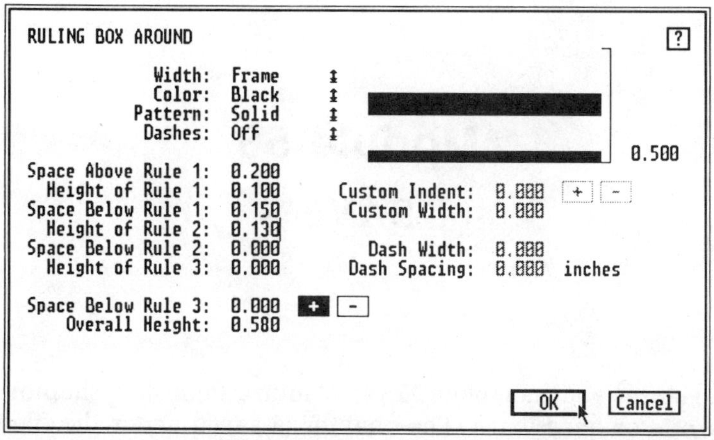

Notice the lines and spacing are displayed in the area to the right of where you typed these numbers.

7. Press **Enter**. Your screen should resemble this illustration:

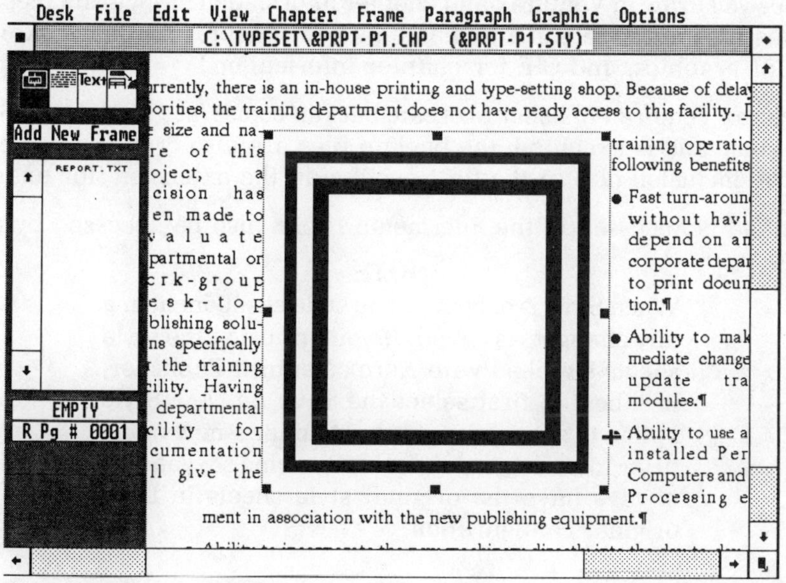

8. Press **Del** to delete this new frame.
9. Abandon the changes to the chapter.
10. Turn to Module 67 to continue the learning sequence.

Module 58

SAVE

DESCRIPTION

The Save command stores your complete Xerox Ventura Publisher chapter document in a file on your floppy diskette or hard drive. The chapter is saved under the filename shown in the Title Bar on your computer screen. The style sheet and each text file are also saved if they have been changed.

When the Save command is executed, Xerox Ventura Publisher also saves all captions, internal graphics (the ones you draw in Ventura), and chapter information in separate files. Xerox Ventura Publisher creates files with the same filename as your chapter, but uses extensions CAP for captions, VGR for graphics, and CIF for chapter information.

If you have set Xerox Ventura Publisher to create backup copies (see Module 62, Set Preferences), when the Save command is executed, the backup files are also created. The backup files are recognized by the inclusion of $ in the first position in the extension (for example, .$HP).

The Save command is accessed in the File menu. It can also be accessed by pressing Ctrl-S.

NOTE

When Save is executed, the style sheet, including any changes, is saved. If you are using the style sheets supplied with Xerox Ventura Publisher, it is best to first select the Save As New Style option to save the style sheet under a new name prior to saving the chapter. By doing so, you will always have the original style sheets in their original configuration.

Save should not be confused with Save As (see Module 59). Save As allows you to save the Xerox Ventura Publisher document under a new name, where Save retains the document under the name displayed in the Title Bar.

APPLICATIONS

The Save command protects you against losing your work. You should get into the habit of using this command often. By saving your changes under an existing filename, you can always retrieve your work. This protects you should your computer lose power and an accidental erasure occur. It also protects you against a major mistake.

Should the power to your computer go off, you can restart the computer and reopen your document. If you should make a major mistake, you can use Abandon (see Module 4) to automatically revert to a previously saved version of the Xerox Ventura Publisher chapter.

TIP: You cannot overuse Save. Although it is not necessary to keep an alarm clock at your computer, you should use Save every 10 to 20 minutes and before you attempt any major revisions. The more you use Save, the more likely you can recover from any unexpected problem that might occur with your work in Xerox Ventura Publisher.

TYPICAL OPERATION

In this operation, you use Save to save the chapter.

1. Point to the **File** menu and click on **Open Chapter**. When the Item Selector dialog box appears, use the scroll bars to locate **SCOOP.CHP**. Your screen should resemble this illustration:

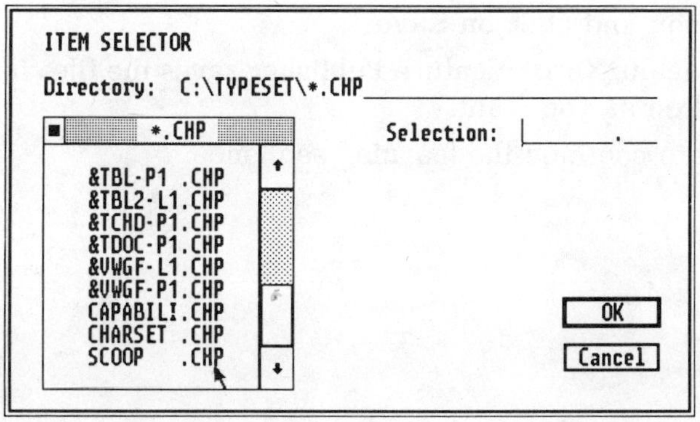

2. Double click on **SCOOP.CHP**. Your screen should resemble this illustration:

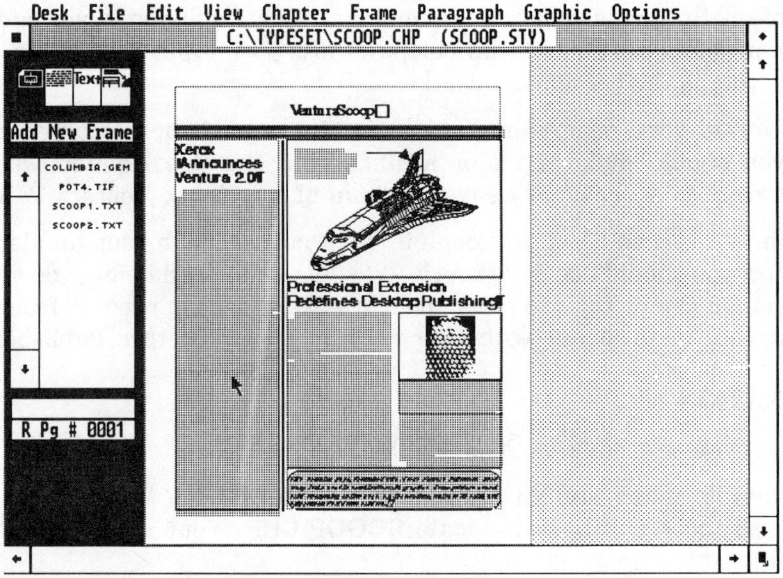

3. Point to the **File** menu and click on **Save**.
4. Press **Ctrl-S**. Once again, Xerox Ventura Publisher saves the files for you. As you can see, you can Save as often as you want.
5. Turn to Module 52 to continue the learning sequence.

Module 59

SAVE AS

DESCRIPTION

The Save As command allows you to save your Xerox Ventura Publisher document under a new name. This actually creates a duplicate copy of your document. You can use the Save As command to make the duplicate copy by using another filename or another DOS path or both.

The style sheet and each associated text file are also saved—under their original filenames—if they have been changed in any way. Save As creates only a copy of the Xerox Ventura Publisher files. This command does not create new copies of the text file or style sheet.

The Save As command is located in the File menu.

APPLICATIONS

Save As is used to create a duplicate copy of a Xerox Ventura Publisher document. This is used when you want to keep the original document intact, but require changes. For example, suppose you had to change a business report proposal. Rather than alter the original proposal, you would simply copy it by using Save As, then make changes to the new copy. By doing so, you could still publish the first proposal, even though you have altered it to produce the second draft or proposal.

NOTE

Do *not* use Save As for making a backup copy of your documents to a floppy diskette. When you use the Save As command, Xerox Ventura Publisher only creates a copy of the Ventura chapter file, but not your text and graphics files. To make a backup copy of your complete Xerox Ventura Publisher documents, use the Copy All command (see Module 44, Multi-Chapter, for more information).

TYPICAL OPERATION

In this operation, you use the Save As command. The Xerox Ventura Publisher sample chapter SCOOP.CHP is used. The example begins with SCOOP.CHP already open and in use. If you do not have this chapter open, use the Open Chapter command in the File menu to retrieve and open SCOOP.CHP.

1. Point to the **File** menu and click on **Save As** to display the Item Selector dialog box.

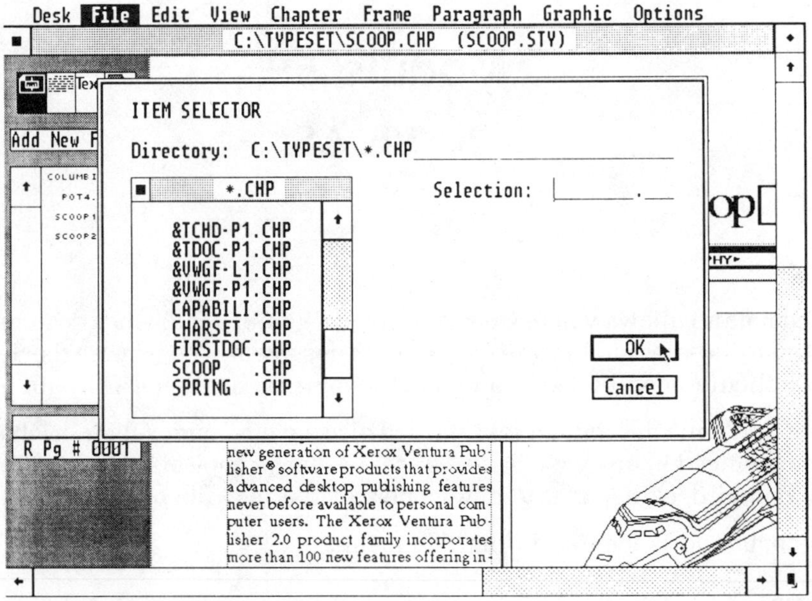

The Item Selector should be set to the TYPESET directory on the C drive and files with the .CHP extension.

2. Type **SCOOP2.CHP** in the Selection entry area and press **Enter**. Within a moment, Xerox Ventura Publisher displays a message that the chapter is being saved, and you are returned to the regular screen area. Notice the Title Bar. The document has been renamed to SCOOP2.CHP.
3. Turn to Module 45 to continue the learning sequence.

Module 60

SAVE AS NEW STYLE

DESCRIPTION

The Save As New Style command saves the current style sheet under a new name. The Xerox Ventura Publisher style sheet contains information used to control the final appearance of your document. Xerox Ventura Publisher uses a separate computer file, called a style sheet, to contain the information that controls the style of your document. These files are identified by the .STY extension. Each Xerox Ventura Publisher chapter uses a style sheet.

The Save As New Style command not only saves the current style sheet under a new name, but it also modifies an existing style sheet.

NOTE

Saving a Xerox Ventura Publisher chapter after modifying a style sheet or saving a modified style sheet under its original name changes the appearance and style of other chapters using that same style sheet. *Always save modifications to current style sheets under a new name with this command.* If you don't, your modifications will affect the other chapters.

The Save As New Style command is located in the File menu.

APPLICATIONS

The main purpose of this command is to create new style sheets. It is generally a good idea to create a new style sheet for each kind of document. Remember that style sheets are separate files and control the general appearance and style of your final Xerox Ventura Publisher document. One style sheet can be associated with many different Xerox Ventura Publisher chapters. If you were to change the style sheet that has been associated with many different Xerox Ventura Publisher chapters, then all chapters would reflect those changes.

This is a powerful feature: all documents using the style sheet will look the same. Of course, if you don't want all documents to look the same, you need to create a new style sheet with the Save As New Style command.

TYPICAL OPERATION

In this example, you save the &NEWS-P2 style sheet as a new style sheet. The Xerox Ventura Publisher sample chapter &NEWS-P2.CHP is used. The example begins with &NEWS-P2.CHP already open and in use. Use the command Open Chapter in the File menu to retrieve and open &NEWS-P2.CHP.

1. Point to the **File** menu and click on **Save As New Style** to display the Item Selector dialog box.
2. Type **C:\TYPESET*.STY** for Directory (if that is not the current directory).
3. Type **TESTSAVE** for Selection and press **Enter** to save the new style sheet. Notice that the style sheet name in the Title Bar has changed to (TESTSAVE.STY).
4. Point to the **File** menu, click on **Load Diff. Style**, and click on **&NEWS-P2.STY** to eliminate using this new style sheet.
5. Point to the **File** menu and click on **Abandon**. When the message box appears, click on **OK** to abandon the changes made to the chapter.
6. Turn to Module 41 to continue the learning sequence.

Module 61

SELECT ALL

DESCRIPTION

The Select All command selects every graphic associated with the currently selected frame.

After all the graphics have been selected, all the graphics can be moved, copied, cut and pasted, or deleted.

To access the Select All command, Xerox Ventura Publisher must first be in Graphic Drawing mode, and then a frame must be selected. The Select All command can then be accessed in the Graphic menu, or by pressing Ctrl-Q.

TIP: A graphic can be unselected from the Select All command by holding the Shift key and pointing at the graphic.

APPLICATIONS

The Select All command can be used to move every graphic associated with a specific frame to a new location. The Select All command can also be used to change the attributes of all graphics. For example, the line thickness of all graphics can be changed by first selecting all the graphics, and then assigning a different line attribute.

This command also shows which graphics are associated with a specific frame.

TYPICAL OPERATION

In this example, you use Select All to select all the graphics, and then assign a common line thickness. Finally, you delete all the selected graphics. The Xerox Ventura Publisher sample chapter document SCOOP.CHP is used. The operation begins with SCOOP.CHP already open and in use. If you do not have this chapter open, use the command Open Chapter in the File menu to retrieve and open SCOOP.CHP.

1. Point to the **Chapter** menu and select **Insert/Remove Page** to display the Insert/Remove Page dialog box. Select **Insert New Page After Current Page** and press **OK**.
2. Press **Ctrl-P** to select Graphic Drawing mode.
3. Point to the middle of the page and click once.

4. Select the square box tool and draw three boxes within the middle of the page. When completed, your screen should look like this illustration:

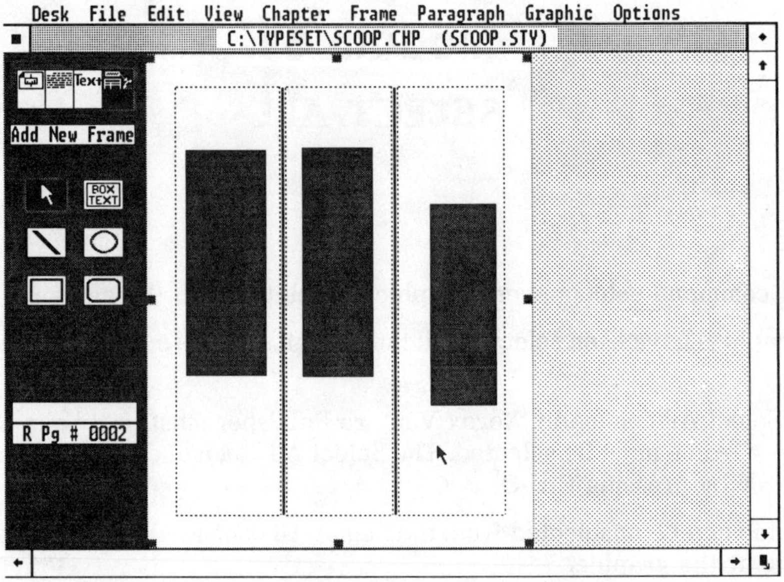

5. Press **Ctrl-Q** to activate Select All. Notice that the three boxes are now selected.
6. Point to the **Graphic** menu and click on **Line Attributes** to display the Line Attributes dialog box.

7. Select **Custom Width** for Thickness and type **12.00** for fractional points. Click **OK**.

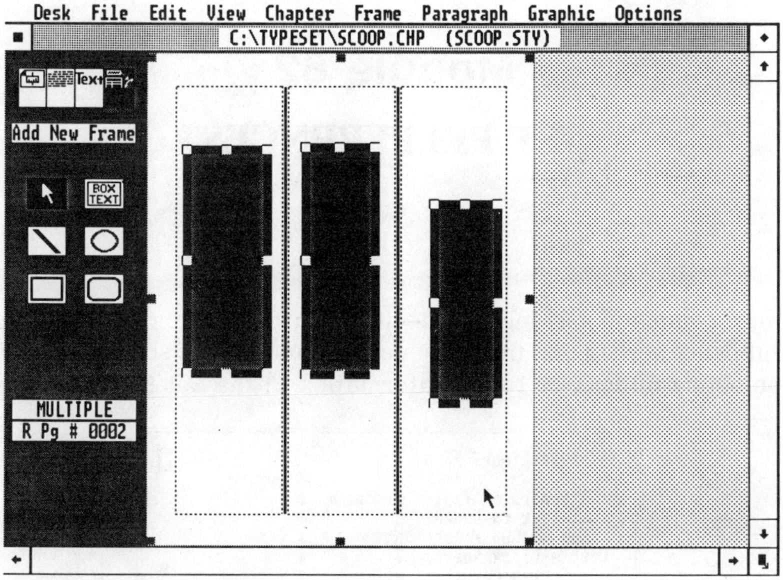

Notice the new line thickness for all the boxes.

8. Press **Del**. Notice that all the boxes disappeared.
9. Point to the **File** menu and click on **Abandon**. Click on **OK** when prompted to revert back to the last saved version.
10. Turn to Module 12 to continue the learning sequence.

Module 62

SET PREFERENCES

DESCRIPTION

The Set Preferences command sets miscellaneous features which affect the appearance of the Xerox Ventura Publisher screen and the basic performance of the software. All the preferences are entered by selecting options or typing information in the Set Preferences dialog box.

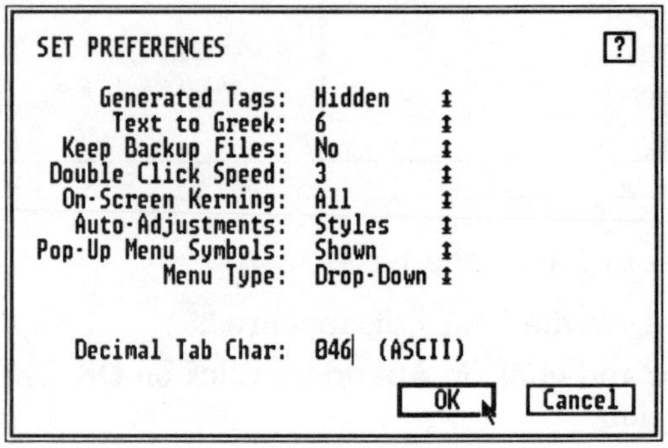

The options in the Set Preferences dialog box are:

Generated Tags

Select whether you want Xerox Ventura Publisher to show or hide the generated paragraph tags. Xerox Ventura Publisher automatically generates these tags when you use commands to create headers, footers, footnotes, and auto-numbering schemes.

Text to Greek

Select the amount of greeking you want Xerox Ventura Publisher to use with the Reduced View or Facing Pages View commands. Greeking speeds up the performance of Xerox Ventura Publisher. With greeking, Xerox Ventura Publisher changes the text of specified sizes to a series of lines. Greeked text displays the general appearance of the page. Select All to greek all of the text. Select None to prevent any text from being greeked. The numbers between all and none specify the type size to be greeked when you are looking at the screen with the Reduced View or Facing Pages View.

Keep Backup Files	Select Yes to create backup files each time the current files are saved. If you select Yes, Xerox Ventura Publisher saves copies of the chapter, caption, text, and style sheet files when you use the Save or Save As commands. Xerox Ventura Publisher designates the backup files by changing the first letter of the file extension to $. The backup file for TESTDOC.CHP is TESTDOC.$HP. Select No if you do not want to create backup files.
Double Click Speed	Select the amount of time between clicks before Xerox Ventura Publisher recognizes a double click from the mouse. The selections are Slow, 2, 3, 4, and Fast. If you select Slow, you must allow more time between the first and second clicks. If you select Fast, you allow less time between clicks.
On-Screen Kerning	Select the smallest type size to show kerning on the screen. Select All if you want to kern all text on screen. Select None if you do not want to kern any text. The numbers between All and None specify the type size in points where Xerox Ventura Publisher begins on-screen kerning. For example, if you select 18, Xerox Ventura Publisher kerns all the text that is 18 points in size or larger. Xerox Ventura Publisher runs faster when it displays a screen without kerning than one with all of the characters kerned.
Auto-Adjustments	Select styles to adjust automatically the space between lines when you change point sizes in the Font dialog box. Select None to keep the line spacing the same no matter what the point size. Select " and -- to allow Xerox Ventura Publisher to convert typewriter style quotes and dashes to typeset styles. Select Both if you want both the typographic and style conversions.
Pop-Up Menu Symbols	To remove the Pop-Up menu symbol (¦) from the many dialog boxes where pop-up menus are used, select Hidden for the Pop-Up menu symbols.
Menu Type	This option allows you to select whether you want drop down menus (when the mouse touches the menu name, the menu drops down) or if you want pull down menus (you must press and hold the mouse button on the menu name). Select whichever option you prefer to use.
Decimal Tab Char	Type the decimal value of the ASCII character used for decimal points. The default is 046 for a period. Xerox Ventura Publisher uses this ASCII character for aligning the decimal point column of decimal tabs. (See the Tab Setting command for more information on decimal tabs.)

The Set Preferences command is located in the Options menu.

APPLICATIONS

Preferences are nothing more than your choices of how you want to run Xerox Ventura Publisher. They have little effect on the final appearance of your printed document. Preferences do affect the way Xerox Ventura Publisher is used and the way the program is operated.

The number of tag names in the Assignment List can be smaller by hiding the generated tag names.

Maximum speed performance is available from Xerox Ventura Publisher by selecting All for Text to Greek and None for On-Screen Kerning. Both of these preferences reduce the amount of time Xerox Ventura Publisher requires to create an image on your screen.

It is a good work habit to create a backup copy of your Xerox Ventura Publisher files. The backup files can save a lot of time if you make a major mistake. Simply rename the backup files to those of the working files and continue working.

You might want to increase the speed Xerox Ventura Publisher recognizes double clicks from the mouse.

If a character other than a period is used for a decimal point (sometimes a , is used in other parts of the world), type the decimal value of the character in Decimal Tab Character.

Auto-Adjustment affects the appearance of the printed page. Normally, Xerox Ventura Publisher automatically adjusts the space between lines when point sizes of the text are changed. The fonts are normally designed with the correct amount of space above and below the characters to provide an appealing appearance. You may want to overrule automatic line adjustment if you are using different type sizes but need all lines spaced the same, regardless of the type size. Being able to convert typewriter style quotes and dashes to true typesetting symbols improves the professional appearance of your finished documents.

TYPICAL OPERATION

In this operation, you change the preference for greeking text, and you observe how it effects the performance of Xerox Ventura Publisher. The instructions begin with the Xerox Ventura Publisher SCOOP.CHP open.

1. Press **Ctrl-R**. Notice the appearance of your page.
2. Point to the **Options** menu and click on **Set Preferences** to display the Set Preferences dialog box.
3. Select **None** for Text to Greek. Press **Enter**. Notice that none of the words are greeked, and watch how long it takes Xerox Ventura Publisher to draw the screen.

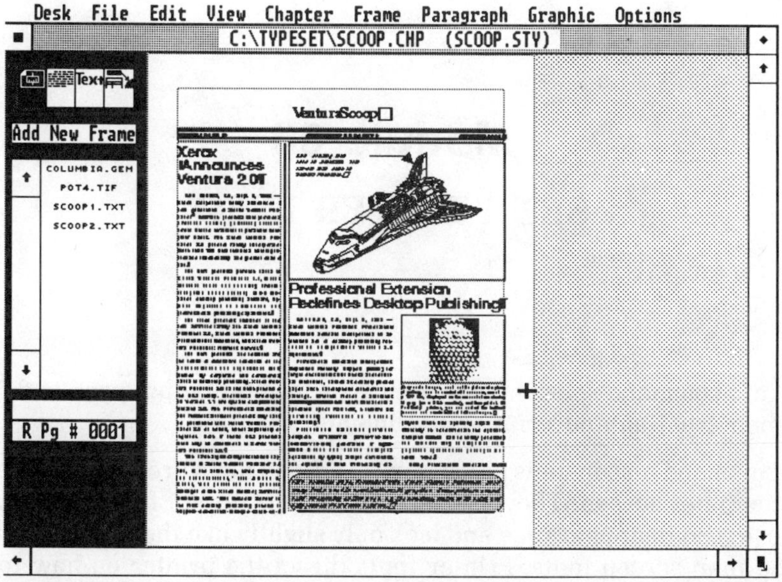

4. Point to the **Options** menu and click on **Set Preferences** to display the Set Preferences dialog box.
5. Select **All** for Text to Greek. Press **Enter**. Notice that all the words are greeked, and watch how much faster Xerox Ventura Publisher draws the screen.

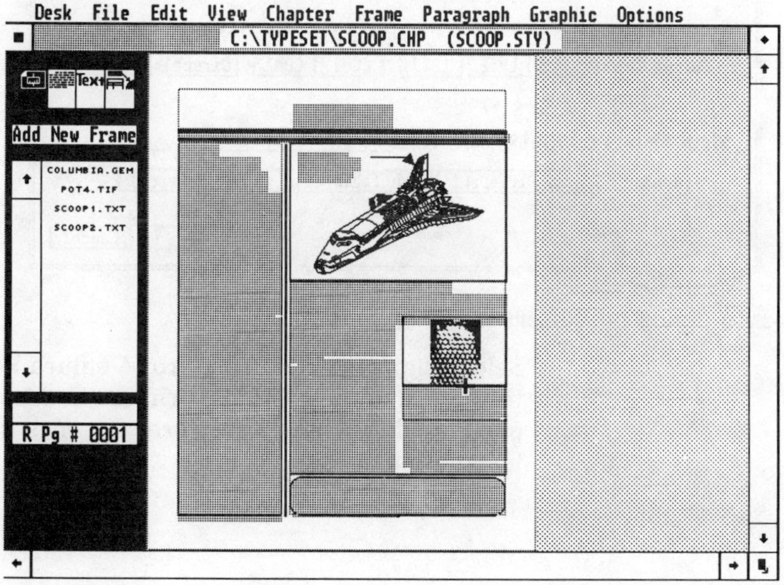

6. Abandon the changes to the chapter.
7. Turn to Module 33 to continue the learning sequence.

Module 63

SET PRINTER INFO

DESCRIPTION

The Set Printer Info command selects the printer type, printer output port, and fonts file (Width Table) to use when creating and printing documents.

The Set Printer command also installs screen fonts. Screen fonts are what create the characters you see on the computer screen. They are separate and different fonts from the printer fonts. Screen fonts are jagged in appearance and look only slightly like the printer fonts. Printer fonts are more precise than screen fonts. Printer fonts direct the printer on how to generate each character it prints.

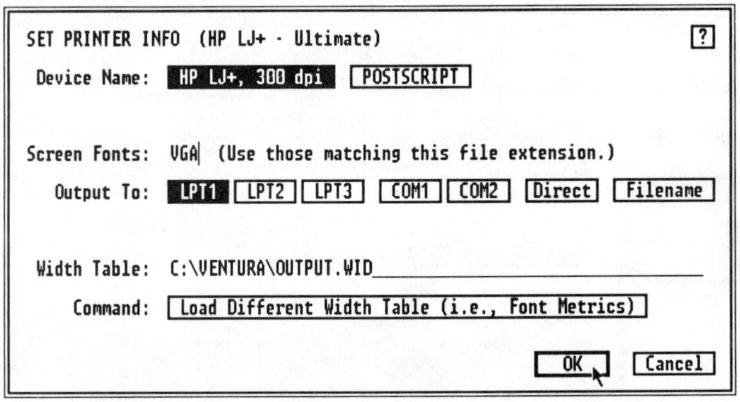

The Set Printer Info dialog box offers these options:

Device Name — Select the printer to use. Xerox Ventura Publisher places the names of the available printers in this dialog box. The printers displayed here were the ones selected during installation.

Screen Fonts

Type the file extension for the screen font files Xerox Ventura Publisher is to use. For example, type VGA if you want Xerox Ventura Publisher to use screen fonts designed for a VGA monitor (screen). Before screen fonts can be used, they must be loaded on your hard disk. Xerox Ventura Publisher automatically loads the screen fonts for your system during installation based on the type of monitor being used (CGA, EGA, VGA, etc.).

NOTE

If you ever change computer monitors, rerun the installation to add the screen fonts. If you are adding more fonts for your current monitor, copy them to the Ventura directory for screen fonts by using the DOS Copy command. All screen font files for a particular type of monitor must have the same DOS file extension.

Output To

Select the output port of the printer. To print to disk, select Filename. When the To Print or Multi-Chapter Print commands are used, Xerox Ventura Publisher displays a dialog box, allowing you to enter a filename to contain the printed output.

Width Table

Type the name of the directory path, the filename, and extension of the fonts file (Width Table) desired to use for printing the document. Each fonts file is used for a specific printer. Xerox Ventura Publisher automatically places the name of the fonts file for your default printer.

NOTE

If you ever change printers, enter the name of the new fonts file in the Width Table section. Before printer fonts (often called soft fonts) can be used, they must be loaded on your hard disk. Xerox Ventura Publisher automatically loads the printer fonts for your system during the installation, after you specify the type or types of printers. If you ever add a new printer, rerun installation to add the printer fonts. If you are adding more printer fonts for a currently installed printer, copy them to the directory for fonts by using the DOS Copy command. You can use Xerox Ventura Publisher's Add/Remove Fonts command (see Module 5 for more information) to add the fonts to the existing font file for your printer.

The fonts available in the width table determine what type faces, sizes, and styles are available in the fonts dialog box.

Command — Select Load Different Width Table if you want Xerox Ventura Publisher to list all the available fonts files. If this option is selected, Xerox Ventura Publisher displays the Item Selector dialog box with a list of fonts files.

The Set Printer Info command is accessed from the Options menu.

APPLICATIONS

The Set Printer Info command permits selection between different printers as well as prints a file to a disk.

By being able to select between printers, you can have more than one printer installed for your use. This permits you to use Printer Command Language-based laser printers (such as Hewlett-Packard) and PostScript-based laser printers. You can also use this command to use both a draft and a high-quality output printer. For example, you might want to install a dot matrix printer for drafts and use a laser printer for the final output.

The second application, printing to a disk, is a useful command. It will save you time, as it is always faster to print to a disk. You can also later take the disk to another computer for printing. To do this, first print the file to the disk. Then transfer the disk to the next computer and type:

COPY THEFILE.EXT LPT1:

where THEFILE.EXT is the name of the file and its extension, and LPT1: is the name of the parallel port. This command works only for parallel printer ports, and you should be using a parallel port to drive a laser printer.

If you are using a PostScript-based printer, copy the file DTR.TXT from the PostScript directory on the Xerox Ventura Publisher utilities disk. Before copying the print file to the printer, first copy DTR.TXT by entering this command at the DOS prompt:

COPY DTR.TXT LPT1:

where LPT1 is the name of the parallel port.

This command prepares the PostScript-driven printer for the printed file.

NOTE

Not all PostScript-driven printers will support this command from a printed file on a disk. Check your printer's manual for more information.

TYPICAL OPERATION

In this operation, you output the SCOOP.CHP to a file rather than a printer. The example begins with SCOOP.CHP already open and in use. If you do not have this chapter open, use the Open Chapter command in the File menu to retrieve and open SCOOP.CHP.

1. Point to the **Options** menu and select **Set Printer Info** to display the Set Printer Info dialog box.
2. Select **Filename** from the **Output To:** area.
3. Select **OK**.
4. Point to the **File** menu and select **To Print** to display the Print dialog box.
5. Select **OK**.
6. Type **TESTFILE.EXT** when prompted by Xerox Ventura Publisher to enter a filename.
7. Point to the **Options** menu and select **Set Printer Info** to display the Set Printer Info dialog box.
8. Select **Printer** from the **Output To:** area.
9. Select **OK**.
10. Turn to Module 74 to continue the learning sequence.

NOTE

This operation creates a fairly large file on your hard disk. To save disk space, you may want to delete the file with the DEL command at the DOS prompt.

Module 64

SET RULER

DESCRIPTION

The Set Ruler command establishes the measurement units and zero points of the horizontal and vertical rulers displayed on your computer screen. The Show/Hide Rulers command also displays or hides the Xerox Ventura Publisher rulers.

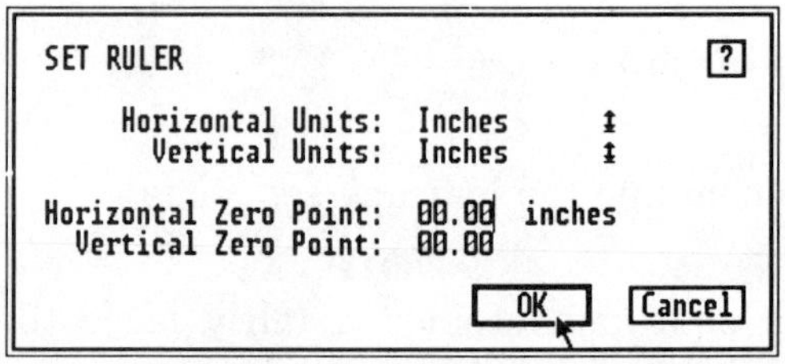

The measurement units available on the Xerox Ventura Publisher rulers are inches, centimeters, and picas.

Inches and centimeters are common units of measure found on rulers. Picas are a standard measurement unit used by printers and in the typesetting industry. A pica is approximately one-sixth of an inch, so there are six picas to an inch. Each pica contains 12 smaller units, called points. Points are standard measurement units used to measure type sizes.

The Set Ruler command also establishes the zero point for the horizontal and vertical rulers displayed on the Xerox Ventura Publisher screen. When the zero point is set to something other than the upper left corner of the page, the ruler displays measurement units for both before and after zero.

The zero point can be positioned by typing the Horizontal Zero Point and the Vertical Zero Point within the Set Ruler dialog box. The zero point can also be set by simply using the mouse. A zero point is nothing more or less than picking up the ruler and moving where the zero of the ruler begins. To move the zero point, click and hold on the 0,0 box, located in the Xerox Ventura Publisher screen where the horizontal and vertical rulers intersect. Drag the pointer to the new position of the zero points and release the mouse button. (Xerox Ventura Publisher generates cross-hairs while resetting the zero point to help make the placement more accurate.) To reset the zero points to the upper left corner of the page, click the mouse once inside the 0,0 box.

The Set Ruler command is accessed in the Options menu.

APPLICATIONS

The Set Ruler command allows you to use any standard unit of measurement while working with your Xerox Ventura Publisher documents. In the beginning, you will probably work with inches, only because that will be the most comfortable for you. However, it is suggested that you work with picas and points. The reason is clear: by doing so, you are using the same measurement used to determine the size of the type. At first, working with points and picas may be uncomfortable, but when you master working with this measurement system, you will find working with measurements in your Xerox Ventura Publisher documents much easier.

Remember these values:

6 picas to an inch
12 points to a pica
72 points to an inch

Being able to move the zero point is similar to picking up a ruler and repositioning it as you work on your desk. By being able to reposition the zero point, you are doing nothing more than moving the ruler, even though Xerox Ventura Publisher will continue to display it in the same position on the computer screen.

TYPICAL OPERATION

In this example, you set the ruler and move the zero point of the rulers. The Xerox Ventura Publisher sample chapter SCOOP.CHP is used. The example begins with SCOOP.CHP already open. Use the command Open Chapter in the File menu to retrieve and open SCOOP.CHP. Change view to Normal by pressing Ctrl-N and, if not already on, select Show Rulers from the Options menu.

1. Point to the **Options** menu and select **Set Ruler** to display the Set Ruler dialog box.
2. Click on **Picas** for both the Horizontal Units and Vertical Units.
3. Click **OK**. Notice the rulers are now displayed in picas, and what was a one-inch mark is now a six-pica mark.
4. Click and hold on the **0,0** box where the horizontal and vertical rulers intersect.

5. Drag the mouse cursor to 12 picas vertical and 12 picas horizontal. Your screen should resemble this illustration:

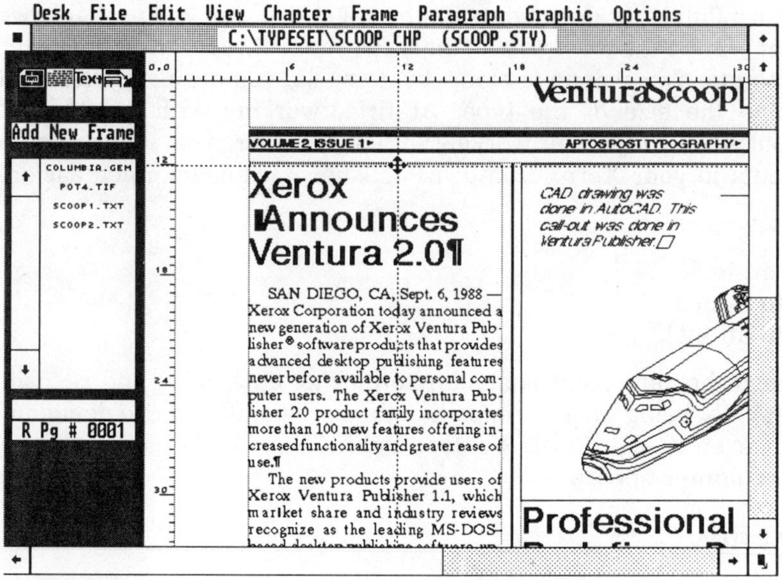

Release the mouse button. Notice the new zero points for the vertical and horizontal rulers.

6. Abandon the changes to the chapter.
7. Turn to Module 23 to continue the learning sequence.

Module 65

SHOW/HIDE SIDE BAR, RULERS, COLUMN GUIDES, ALL PICTURES, TABS & RETURNS, LOOSE LINES

DESCRIPTION

The various Show/Hide commands set how the Xerox Ventura Publisher screen looks. Some of these commands also offer tools to increase the speed of the program. Some of the other commands assists in locating formatting errors.

All the Show/Hide commands are located in the Options menu. They are:

Show/Hide Side Bar	This command displays and removes the left part of the Xerox Ventura Publisher screen which contains the Mode Selector, Assignment List, Current Selection Indicator, and Page Counter. The Hide Side Bar command removes the entire Side Bar from the screen, and allows you to see more of the Xerox Ventura Publisher document page. This command can be accessed within the Options menu or by pressing Ctrl-W.
Show/Hide Rulers	This command displays and hides both the vertical and horizontal rulers on the Xerox Ventura Publisher screen.
Show/Hide Column Guides	This command displays and removes the dotted lines that show the position of columns on the underlying page in the Xerox Ventura Publisher chapter.
Show/Hide All Pictures	This command displays pictures in the frames or replaces the pictures with a shaded, gray box the size of the frame.
Show/Hide Tabs & Returns	This command displays and removes those special text characters that show the position of tabs, carriage returns, non-break spaces, line breaks, index marks, frame anchors, discretionary hyphens, and end of file markers. This command can be accessed within the Options menu or by pressing Ctrl-T.
Show/Hide Loose Lines	This command displays and removes the highlighting of lines that contain more space between words than the Maximum Space width settings in the paragraph typography dialog box.

The Xerox Ventura Publisher default settings for the show/hide commands are:

Hide Side Bar	Hide All Pictures
Show Rulers	Hide Tabs & Returns
Show Column Guides	Show Loose Lines

When any of the commands have been selected, their names change within the Options menu. For example, if you select Show Rulers, the command in the menu changes to Hide Rulers. Whether you are hiding or showing an option when you access the menu determines what the command will be when you access the Options menu.

APPLICATIONS

Showing the Side Bar offers you easy access to all of the tools, lists, and information displayed in it. Hiding the Side Bar allows you to see more of your page. Before hiding the Side Bar, select the tools you need. Remember that Ctrl-W shows/hides the Side Bar. Other keyboard shortcuts (see Appendix D) offer access to some of the commands within the Side Bar.

Showing the rulers gives you an excellent guideline for drawing and placing Xerox Ventura Publisher frames and graphics. A moving dotted line in each ruler displays the exact location of the mouse. Hiding the rulers provides a slightly larger area to see your document on your screen.

Showing the column guides provides a guideline for drawing and placing Xerox Ventura Publisher frames and graphics in relation to the columns on the underlying page. Hiding the column guides removes the dotted lines, making the page look more like it will appear when actually printed.

Showing the pictures allows you to see how each picture will look on the page. By seeing the pictures that will appear in your document, you can better design the overall appearance of your Xerox Ventura Publisher documents. Showing the pictures, however, dramatically slows down the speed of Xerox Ventura Publisher. This is because Xerox Ventura Publisher must redraw or repaint the picture each time the screen is adjusted. Hiding the pictures replaces the actual picture with a gray box, and Xerox Ventura Publisher can redraw the screen much faster. When the pictures are hidden, they are still printed in the normal manner. The gray box is never printed. Because of how much this command speeds up Xerox Ventura Publisher, it is suggested that the pictures be hidden except when you are actually working with them.

Showing the Tabs and Returns allows you to see the positions of important hidden characters with the Xerox Ventura Publisher text. This is helpful when editing a document because you can make sure the special control characters are in the correct places. For example, if you are creating a columnar table with tabs, but it is not aligning correctly, by seeing the tabs, you can determine what position they are in and how and where they can be moved. Hiding the Tabs and Returns eliminates the display of all the special control characters (similar to codes in word processors), making the document easier to read and review.

Showing the Loose Lines allows you to see the lines in which the word spacing is too wide. This permits you to fix these lines by using a discretionary hyphen in the first word below the loose line. Hiding the loose lines prevents reverse video lines on your computer screen.

TYPICAL OPERATION

In this example, you hide and show the Side Bar, Tabs & Returns, the Rulers, and the Pictures. The Xerox Ventura Publisher sample chapter document SCOOP.CHP is used. The operation begins with SCOOP.CHP already open. Use the Open Chapter command in the File menu to retrieve and open SCOOP.CHP. So your view matches the screen depicted in this book, press Ctrl-N. You may need to adjust your screen using the scroll bars to make your computer look like the illustrations.

1. Press **Ctrl-W** to Hide the Side Bar.

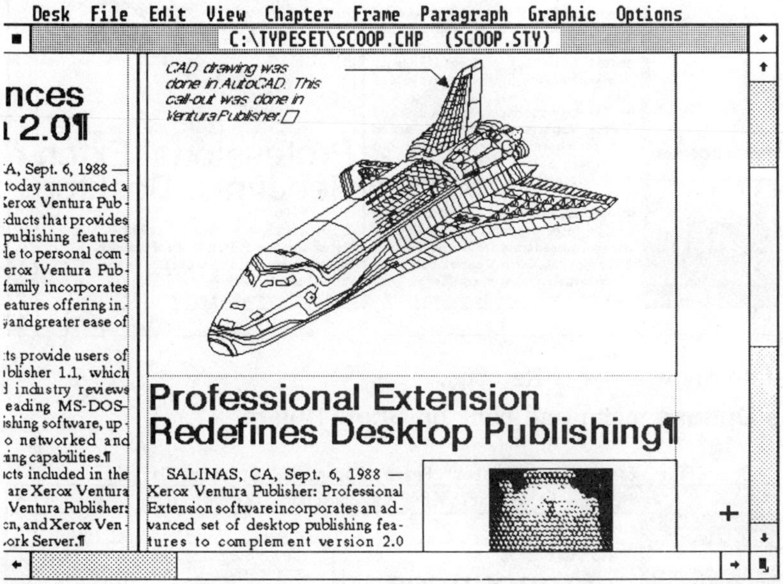

2. Press **Ctrl-W** again to Show the Side Bar.

3. Press **Ctrl-T** to Hide Tabs & Returns.

4. Press **Ctrl-T** to Show Tabs & Returns.
5. Point to the **Options** menu and click on **Show Rulers**.

6. Point to the **Options** menu and click on **Hide Rulers**.

7. Point to the **Options** menu and click on **Hide All Pictures.**

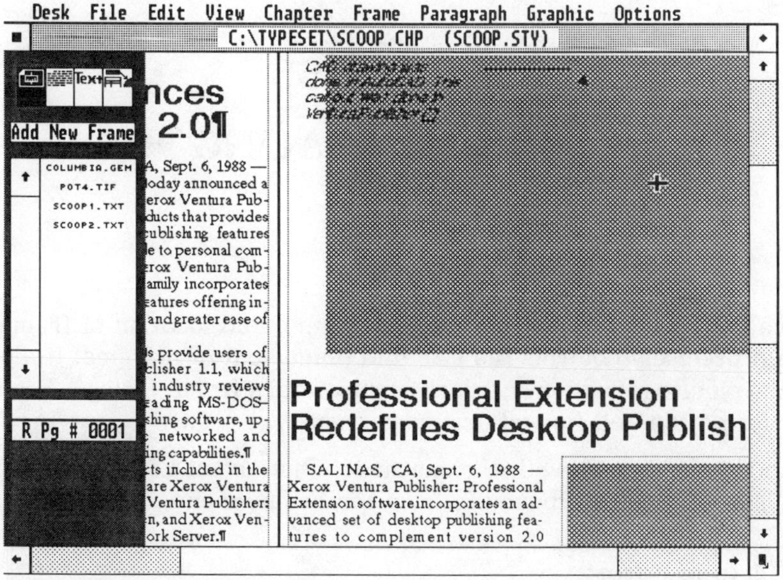

8. Point to the **Options** menu and click on **Show All Pictures.**
9. Abandon the changes to the chapter.
10. Turn to Module 75 to continue the learning sequence.

Module 66

SIZING & SCALING

DESCRIPTION

The Sizing & Scaling command controls the size, shape, and location of frames. The Sizing & Scaling command precisely controls the size and placement of a frame. It also allows you to exactly control the picture reduction or enlargement within a frame. Sizing & Scaling also controls the way text is formatted and flowed around a frame.

Use this command by first selecting the Frame mode. Then select a frame with the mouse cursor and select the Sizing & Scaling command from the Frame menu.

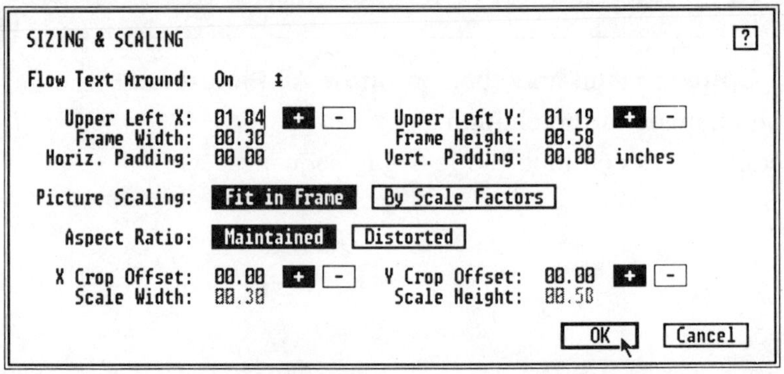

The options in the Sizing & Scaling dialog box are:

Flow Text Around	Select whether or not the text is to flow around the frame. Selecting Off allows the text to flow through the frame.
Upper Left X	Type the distance desired from the left edge of the page to the upper left corner of the frame.
Frame Width	Type the desired width of the frame.
Horizontal Padding	Type the distance between the left and right edges of the frame and the text that flows around the frame.
Upper Left Y	Type the distance from the top edge of the page to the upper left corner of the frame.
Frame Height	Type the height of the frame.

Vertical Padding — Type the distance between the top and bottom edges of the frame and any text that flows around the frame.

Picture Scaling — Select Fit in Frame to alter the graphic both horizontally and vertically so it fits within the borders of the frame. If the frame proportions are different from those of the picture and if Aspect Ratio is set to Distorted, using this option distorts the picture to fill the frame, both on screen and when printed. If Aspect Ratio is set to Maintained, the picture fills the frame as much as possible without changing its vertical or horizontal proportions. Select By Scale Factors to precisely control the vertical and horizontal proportions of the graphic. Set the size of the picture by using Scale Width and Scale Height (see the illustration in the Typical Operation section). If the picture is scaled by factors, you can crop the picture by moving the graphic within the frame with the X Crop Offset and Y Crop Offset options.

NOTE

Use the mouse for cropping a picture with By Scale Factors for Picture Scaling. To do this, press and hold Alt, click and hold on the picture, move the picture within the frame to the desired cropping location, and release both the Alt and the mouse button.

Aspect Ratio — Select Maintained to keep the horizontal and vertical proportions of an imported graphic equal to those of the original graphic. Select Distorted to fill the frame with the picture, regardless of how this distorts the proportions of the graphic.

X Crop Offset — Type the distance to move the graphic horizontally within the frame. Select + to move the graphic to the right. Select – to move the graphic to the left. This option works only if By Scale Factors for Picture Scaling has been selected.

Scale Width — Type the exact width desired for the graphic if By Scale Factors for Picture Scaling has been selected.

Y Crop Offset — Type the distance to move the graphic vertically within the frame. Select + to move the graphic up. Select – to move the graphic down. This option works only if By Scale Factors for Picture Scaling has been selected.

Scale Height — Type the exact height for the graphic if By Scale Factors for Picture Scaling has been selected.

NOTE

To be sure that your scanned images are always scaled correctly, select Picture Scaling: By Scale Factors and Aspect Ratio: Maintained. Select OK, and your picture will print exactly as scanned.

APPLICATIONS

The Sizing & Scaling command is used to place frames and pictures in precise locations within your document. You specify in inches or picas and points the exact location of the frame on your page.

This command also allows you to superimpose text on pictures. This is a design technique that will allow the text to flow on top of your pictures.

The Sizing & Scaling command also allows you to crop pictures as well as scale them, either in a maintained or distorted format.

The Sizing & Scaling command may also be used when you need to create a document with a non-standard page size. The Page Size & Layout command allows several standard page sizes. If your page size is different, select the closest *larger* page size, then adjust the underlying page with the Sizing & Scaling command. To allow for crop marks, you may want to adjust the location of the page by setting the X and Y coordinates of the top left corner of the page.

TYPICAL OPERATION

In this operation, you adjust the sizing and scaling of a graphic picture and use your mouse to crop the picture. You work with maintaining and distorting its original size. The instructions begin with SCOOP.CHP open.

1. Press **Ctrl-U** to select Frame mode.

2. Click on the frame on the page that contains the COLUMBIA.GEM drawing. Your screen should resemble the following illustration:

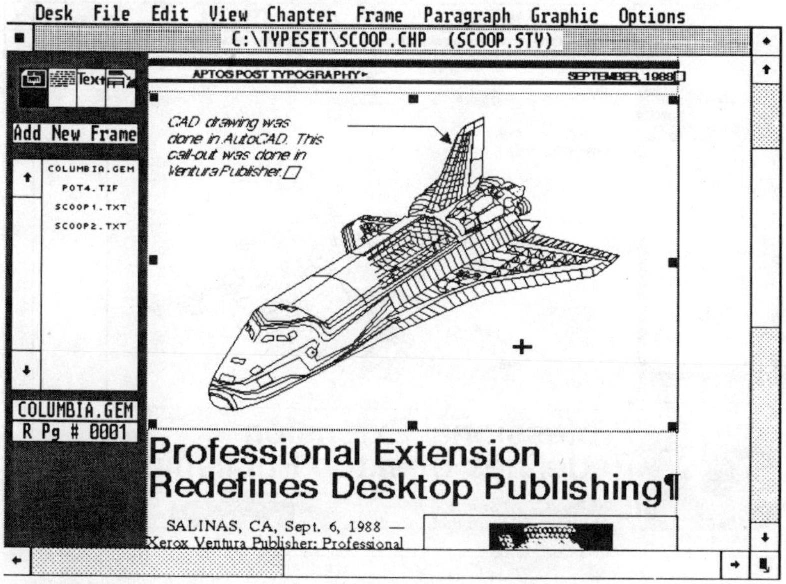

3. Point to the **Frame** menu and click on **Sizing & Scaling** to display the Sizing & Scaling dialog box.
4. Select **By Scale Factors** for Picture Scaling and **Maintained** for Aspect Ratio. Your screen should resemble this illustration:

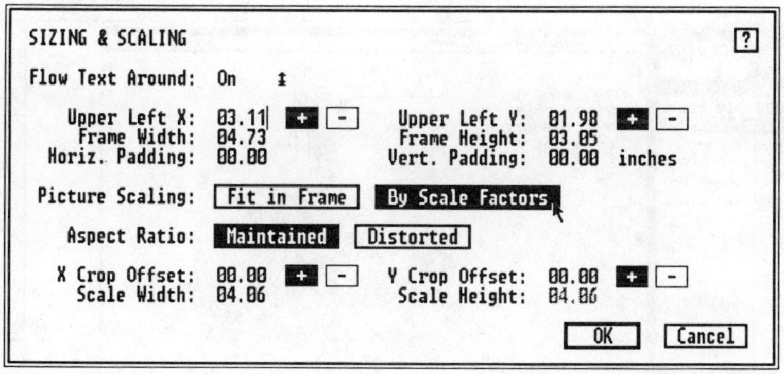

5. Click **OK**. Your screen should resemble the following illustration:

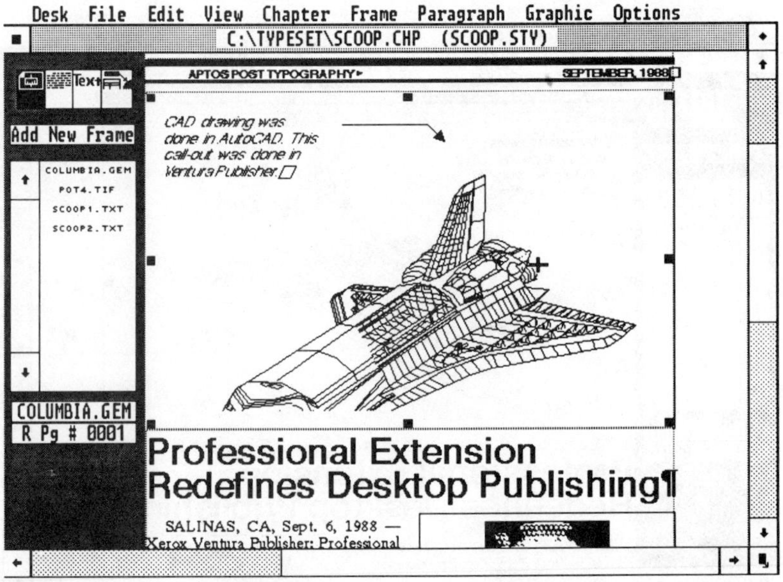

6. Point to the **Frame** menu and click on **Sizing & Scaling** to display the Sizing & Scaling dialog box.
7. Select **By Scale Factors** for Picture Scaling and **Distorted** for Aspect Ratio. Click **OK.** Your screen should resemble this illustration:

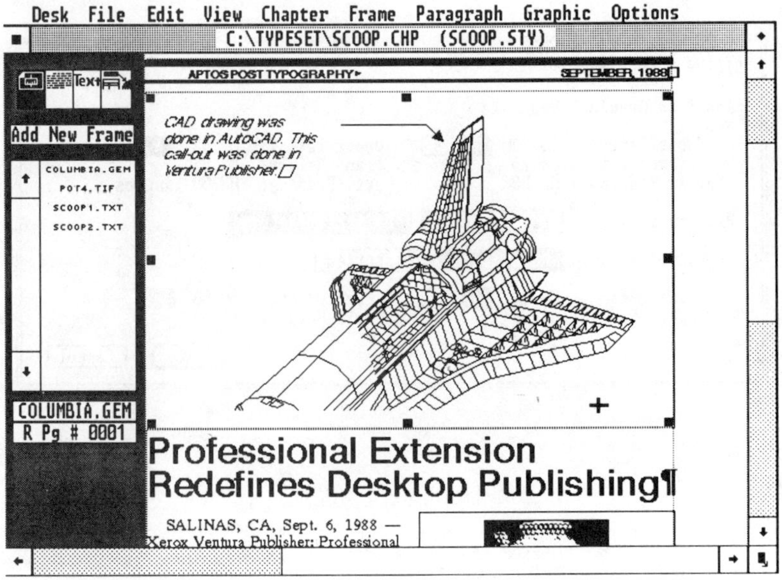

8. Point to the middle of the frame. Press and hold **Alt** and click on the left mouse button. The mouse pointer changes shape. Move the picture to crop it. Your screen should resemble the following illustration:

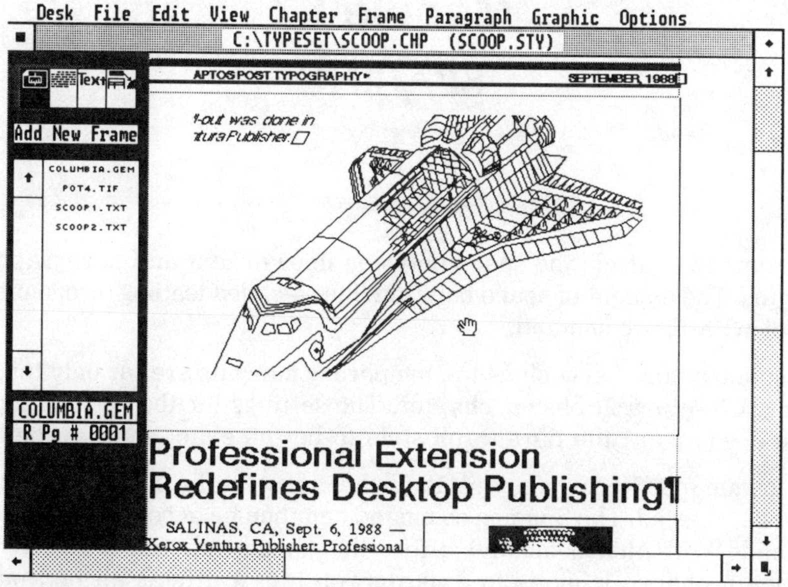

9. Release **Alt** and the mouse button.
10. Point to the **File** menu and select **Abandon** to ignore the changes.
11. Turn to Module 56 to continue the learning sequence.

Module 67

SPACING

DESCRIPTION

The Spacing command controls the space between lines of text and paragraphs and also sets temporary margins. The amount of space between lines—called leading (pronounced led-ding)—is adjusted and set with this command.

The amount of space entered as well as the temporary margins are for only the left or the right pages in the Xerox Ventura Publisher chapter. The settings for the spacing must be copied to the facing page if you want the paragraph style to be the exact same on both pages.

To access this command, Xerox Ventura Publisher must be in the Paragraph mode. Then a paragraph must be selected. The Spacing command can then be accessed in the Paragraph menu. The changes made with this command affect the paragraph tag assigned to the selected paragraph. When a change is made to a paragraph tag, it affects all text marked with that paragraph tag in the Xerox Ventura Publisher document as well as in other documents that use the same Xerox Ventura Publisher style sheet.

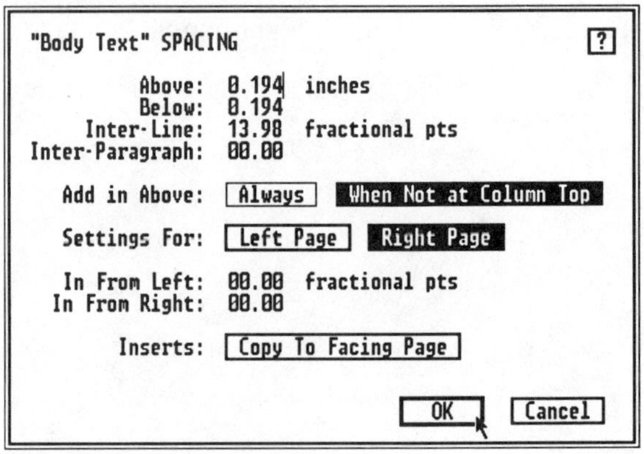

The Spacing dialog box offers these options:

Above — Enter the amount of space Xerox Ventura Publisher is to insert above a paragraph.

Below — Enter the amount of space Xerox Ventura Publisher is to insert below a paragraph.

TIP: The Above and Below commands only insert the space you specify between different paragraphs. For example, if your entire document were nothing but Body Text, the amounts entered in Above and Below would have no effect. But the space would be added between two different paragraph tags, such as Body Text and Headline.

Inter-Line — Enter the amount of space required between the baseline of the characters on one line and the baseline of the characters on the next line (this is the leading).

TIP: Typography experts agree that the correct line spacing should be the amount of the type size and approximately 20% additional space. For example, for 10-point type, set the line spacing (Inter-Line) to 12 point.

NOTE

Xerox Ventura Publisher automatically creates adequate and proper inter-line spacing based on the size of the type chosen. For most publications, this inter-line spacing inserted by Xerox Ventura Publisher will be adequate.

Inter-Paragraph — Enter the amount of space desired between paragraphs, that have identical Inter-Paragraph space settings.

NOTE

The Inter-Paragraph option is useful for creating varying spaces between different paragraphs. For example, add inter-paragraph spacing to the body text tag when you want additional space between body text and headlines.

Add In Above — Select either Always or When Not at Column Top. Xerox Ventura Publisher will either add the space specified at all times, or only when the paragraph is not at the top of a column or frame.

Settings For — Select Left Page or Right Page and enter the In from Left/Right (margin) settings desired for that page.

In From Left — A temporary margin can be created by entering the amount of offset desired in this area. Enter the amount of offset desired for the left paragraph margin here.

In From Right — Just like the In From Left option, In From Right sets a temporary right margin for a paragraph. Enter the amount of offset desired for the right paragraph margin.

Inserts — Select Copy to Facing Page to copy the specifications to the facing page.

The Spacing command provides a lot of typographical control. Do not overlead or underlead your paragraphs. Too much or too little space between paragraphs can make your text very difficult to read.

APPLICATIONS

Paragraph spacing is important to make your documents easy to read. Too little space between lines can make the text impossible to read, especially with computer generated type on a laser printer.

Adding space between paragraphs is an important design tool. For some documents, you will want additional space between paragraphs, while in other documents, you will not want much space between paragraphs. With the Spacing command, you are able to precisely determine how much space is desired or required between your text lines and paragraphs.

TYPICAL OPERATION

In this operation, you adjust the spacing in the Body Text. The Xerox Ventura Publisher sample chapter &NEWS-P2.CHP is used. The example begins with &NEWS-P2.CHP already open. Use the Open Chapter command in the File menu to open &NEWS-P2.CHP. So your view matches the screen depicted in this book, press Ctrl-N. You may need to adjust your screen using the scroll bars to make your computer look like the illustrations.

1. Press **Ctrl-I** to select the Paragraph Tag mode.
2. Click on the third paragraph in the left column.
3. Point to the **Paragraph** menu and click on **Spacing** to display the Spacing dialog box.
4. Type **22.00** fractional points for Inter-Line and press **Enter**. Your screen should resemble this illustration:

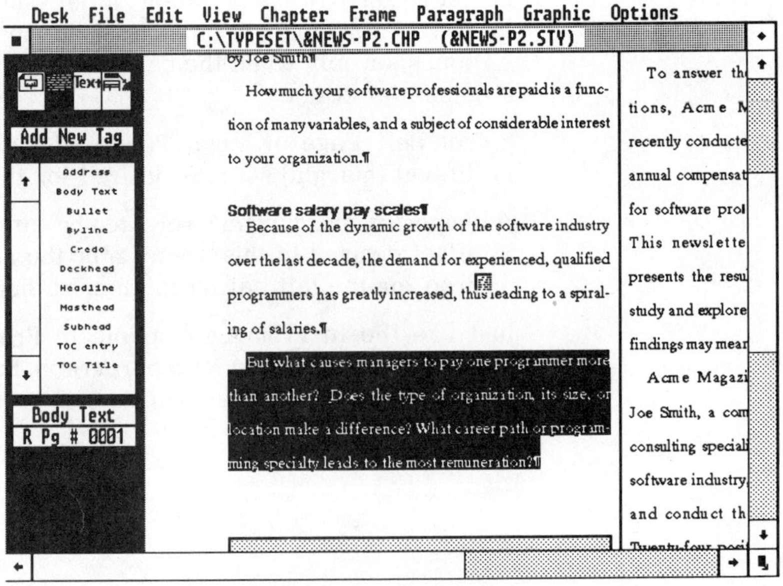

Notice how difficult this text would be to read with the excessive inter-line spacing added (leading).

5. Point to the **Paragraph** menu and click on **Spacing** to display the Spacing dialog box.
6. Type **07.00** points for Inter-Line and press **Enter**. Your screen should resemble this illustration:

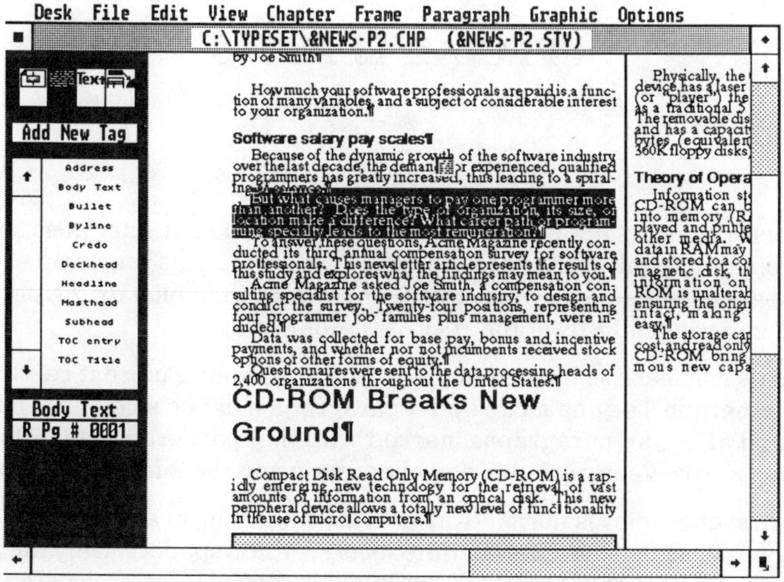

Notice how it is nearly impossible to read the text due to insufficient leading.

7. Point to the **File** menu and click on **Abandon** and click on **OK** when prompted to revert back to the last saved version.
8. Turn to Module 28 to continue the learning sequence.

Module 68

SPECIAL EFFECTS

DESCRIPTION

The Special Effects command allows the addition of a big first character (also sometimes called a drop cap or dropped capital) at the beginning of a paragraph. This command can also establish a bullet at the beginning of a paragraph. The font used for the bullet or the big first character can be selected independently from the rest of the paragraph.

The Special Effects command is located in the Paragraph menu. Before it can be accessed, you must be in the Paragraph Tagging mode and a paragraph must be selected. The changes made with this command affect all paragraphs marked with that paragraph tag in the document, as well as any other Xerox Ventura Publisher chapters using the same style sheet.

TIP: The big first character is normally used at the beginning of an article or chapter in such publications as magazines, newsletters, books, or newspapers. Only the first paragraph contains the large first character. To create this special effect, select the first paragraph (normally Body Text) and then select Add New Tag from the Side Bar. Then call the new tag First Paragraph and, finally, add the special effects to the new tag.

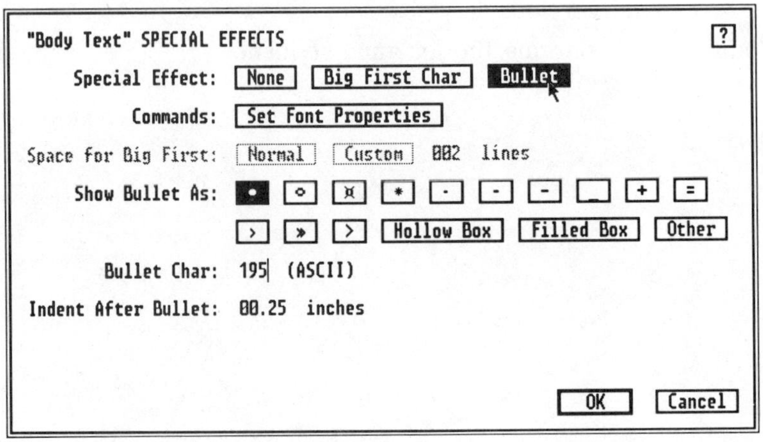

The Special Effects dialog box offers these options:

- Special Effect
- Commands
- Space For Big First
- Show Bullet As
- Bullet Char
- Indent After Bullet

Each of these options provides the following settings:

Special Effect	Select either None, Big First Char, or Bullet. Select Big First Char to add a big first character or drop capital to the front on your paragraph. Select Bullet to add a bullet to the front of the paragraph. Select None to remove an existing special effect from a paragraph tag.
Commands	Select Set Font Properties to display the Fonts Settings dialog box. The fonts selection available will depend on the equipment you are using. Select the typeface, size, style, color, and shift up or down (Zero Shift usually works best).
Space for Big First	Select either Normal or Custom. This command determines how many lines of text the first character will occupy. Normal allows Xerox Ventura Publisher to create the number of lines automatically. Custom allows you to select the number of lines the Big First Character will occupy.
Show Bullet As	Select the character to be used as your bullet from those displayed. If you want to use your own special character, select other.
Bullet Char	If you chose Other in the Show Bullet As selection, you can specify a number for the ASCII character you want to use as your bullet. For a list of the ASCII characters and their decimal number equivalents, see Appendix E.
Indent After Bullet	Enter the amount of space between the bullet and the text following the bullet. If you do not specify some space, the bullet will overlap the first word in your paragraph.

APPLICATIONS

Drop Caps and Bullets draw attention to the beginning of a paragraph. They are used to enhance the appearance of a Xerox Ventura Publisher document.

Bullets are used to help make items on lists stand out. By using Xerox Ventura Publisher special effects command, you do not need to use "typewriter style" bullets, such as *. Being able to use real typographic bullets adds impact to your documents.

TYPICAL OPERATION

In this example, you create a new paragraph tag and assign a Special Effect to the paragraph. The Xerox Ventura Publisher sample chapter &NEWS-P2.CHP is used. The example begins with &NEWS-P2.CHP already open. Use the Open Chapter command in the File menu to retrieve and open &NEWS-P2.CHP. So your view matches the screen depicted in this book, press Ctrl-N.

You may need to adjust your screen using the scroll bars to make your computer look like the illustrations.

1. Press **Ctrl-I** to select Paragraph Tagging mode.
2. Click on **Add New Tag** in the Side Bar to display the Add New Tag dialog box.
3. Type **First Paragr** for Tag Name to Add and press **Enter**.
4. Click on the first paragraph. Click on the **First Paragr** in the Assignment List to assign this tag to the selected paragraph.
5. Point to the **Paragraph** menu and click on **Special Effects** to display the Special Effects dialog box.
6. Select **Big First Char** for the Special Effect.
7. Select **Set Font Properties** for Commands to display the Font dialog box.
8. Click on **Swiss** for Face, **18** for Size, **Bold** for Style, and **Black** for Color. (Depending on your printer, you may need to select a different typeface.)
9. Press **Enter** to return to the Special Effects dialog box. Then press **Enter** to see the page. Your screen should resemble this illustration:

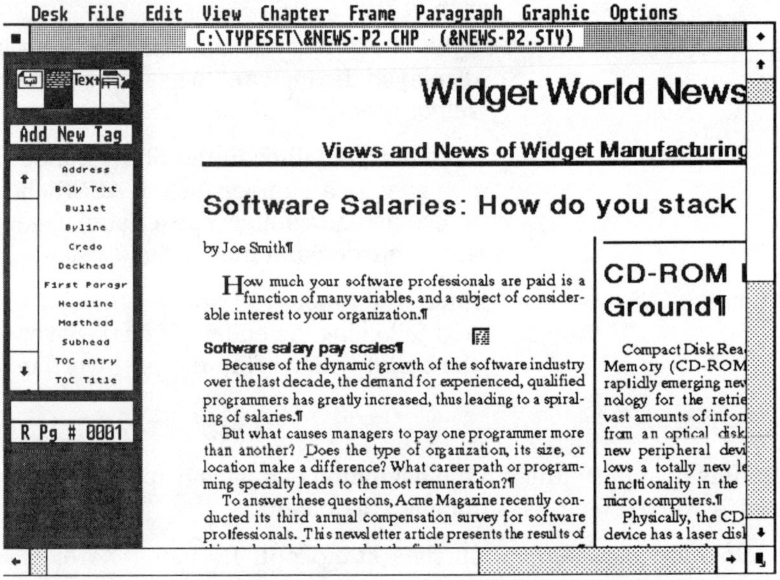

10. Point to the **File** menu and select **Abandon**. Then click on **OK** when the message box appears asking in you want to save or abandon the changes.
11. Turn to Module 61 to continue the learning sequence.

Module 69

TAB SETTINGS

DESCRIPTION

The Tabs Setting command establishes the position, type, and number of horizontal tabs for a paragraph tag. A total of 16 tabs can be set for one tag. Tabs can be left-aligned, centered, right-aligned, or decimal.

The Tab Settings command is employed by first selecting a paragraph and then selecting the Tabs Settings command from the Paragraph menu. Xerox Ventura Publisher must be in Paragraph mode before a paragraph can be selected. The changes made with this command affect the paragraph tag associated with the selected text. When a change is made to a paragraph tag, it affects all text marked with that paragraph tag in the document, as well as in other documents that use the same style sheet.

TIP: A line of tabs must end with a carriage return or line break (press Ctrl-Enter for a line break).

A leader character can also be assigned to fill the blank space created in the front of each tab. After selecting the Tabs Settings command, the Tab Settings dialog box appears.

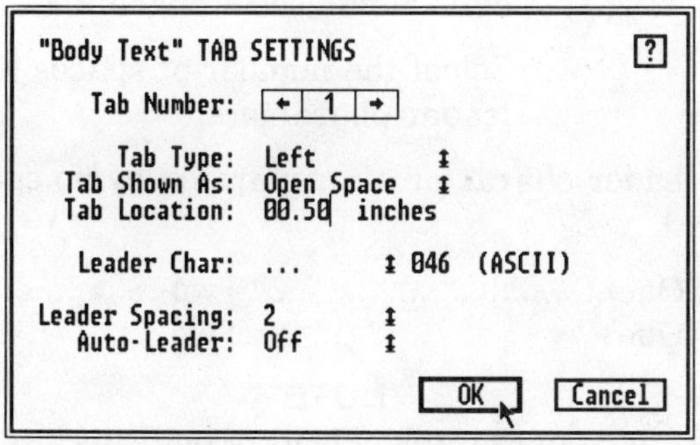

The Tabs Settings dialog box provides these options:

Tab Number — Select the number of the tab to be set. Use the arrows to scroll through the number of tabs. Up to 16 tabs can be operative at one time. Each tab can be selectively turned on or off. For example, tabs 1, 3, 4 could be on and tabs 2 and 8 through 16 could be off.

Tab Type	Select the alignment of the current tab being set to either Left, Center, Right, or Decimal. Left, Center, and Right align the tabbed text at the left, center, and right of the current tab. Decimal aligns numbers at the decimal character in the number. The default decimal character is a period. To change the character use the Set Preferences Command in the Options menu.

TIP: Justification overrides tab settings. Therefore, tabs do not work when the paragraph has been tagged with justification alignment. To change the alignment of a justified paragraph so a tab can be set, use the Alignment command located in the Paragraph menu.

Tab Shown As	Choose if a leader character should be shown in the tab space.

This text demonstrates tabs without leader characters and tabs with leader characters.

Without Leaders One Two Three
With Leaders . . . . .One . . . . .Two . . . . .Three

Tab Location	Enter the distance from the left-hand margin to the position of current tab. This is not the distance between tabs, but always the distance from the left margin to the tab.
Leader Char	Select a leader character or define one of your own. The Xerox Ventura Publisher options are spaces, periods (....) or underlines (______). Define your own leaders by selecting Other and typing the decimal value for the ASCII character to use. For a list of ASCII characters and their decimal equivalents see Appendix E.
Leader Spacing	Select the number of spaces (0 to 8) desired between the leader characters.

This text demonstrates a leader character of . separated by no spaces and separated by two spaces.

No Spaces ....One ....Two ....Three
Two Spaces. . . . . .One. . . . . .Two. . . . . .Three

NOTE

To create paragraph indents or outdents, use the Alignment command located within the Paragraph menu. Do not use the Tab Setting command to create indents or outdents, because tabs in a paragraph disable the automatic word wrap function of Xerox Ventura Publisher. In addition, a tab line cannot wrap to a second line.

The Tabs Setting command can also be used to format simple equations. To do so, set a center tab for the position on the page where the center of the equation is to appear. Then, press Tab and type the equation. The equation will automatically center itself at the tab stop. The Professional Extension of Xerox Ventura Publisher 2.0 provides a complete Equation program.

APPLICATIONS

Tabs in Xerox Ventura Publisher work much like tabs in a word processor or a typewriter. Tab settings are used to align text or numbers for simple tables. Whenever a horizontal tab character is encountered within the text, Xerox Ventura Publisher positions the next character at the next tab location. By doing so, simple tables can easily be created.

Text in a table can be aligned to the right, left, or center of a tab position. In addition, numbers can be aligned on a decimal.

TYPICAL OPERATION

In this operation, you create a table using tabs and then save the file. The instructions begin with a blank screen. Use the DEFAULT.STY style sheet. If necessary, use both the New command and Load Diff. Style command in the File menu. Change view to Normal.

1. Press **Ctrl-U** to select Frame mode.
2. Click on **Add New Frame** and draw a frame that is the width of the column.
3. Press **Ctrl-O** to select Text Editing mode. Click in the frame, and type the following information. (Press **Tab** each time you see <Tab> and press **Enter** each time you see <Enter>.)

   Seminar<Tab>**Location**<Tab>**# of Participants**<Enter>
   Desktop Publishing Overview<Tab>**Philadelphia**<Tab>**22**<Enter>
   Introduction to Ventura<Tab>**Washington, DC**<Tab>**31**<Enter>
   Advanced Ventura Training<Tab>**New Orleans**<Tab>**19**<Enter>
   The Desktop Publishing Operations<Tab>**San Jose**<Tab>**26**<Enter>

When you are finished, your screen should resemble this illustration:

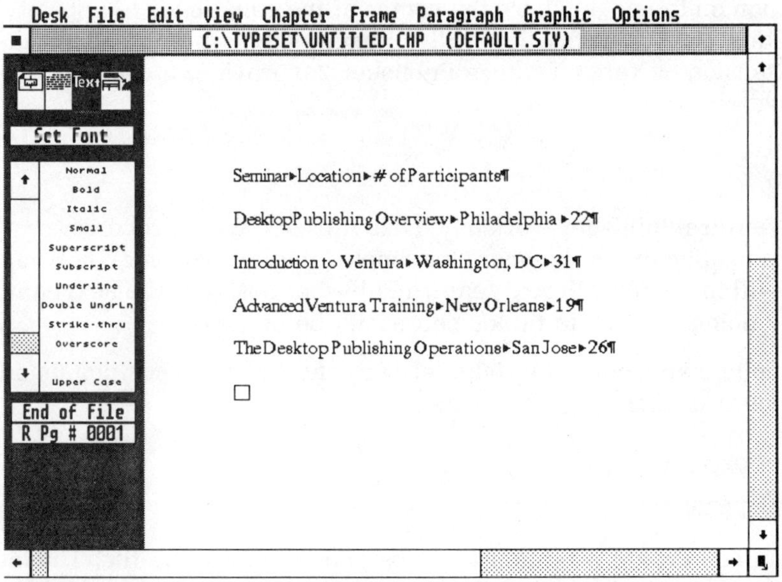

Notice that the tabs are represented by right arrows. If they are not visible, select Show Tabs & Returns in the Options menu.

4. Press **Ctrl-I** to select the Paragraph Tagging mode.
5. Click on **Add New Tag** to display the Add New Tag dialog box.
6. Type **Tabs** for Tag Name to Add and press **Enter**.
7. Press and hold **Shift** and click on each line of text.

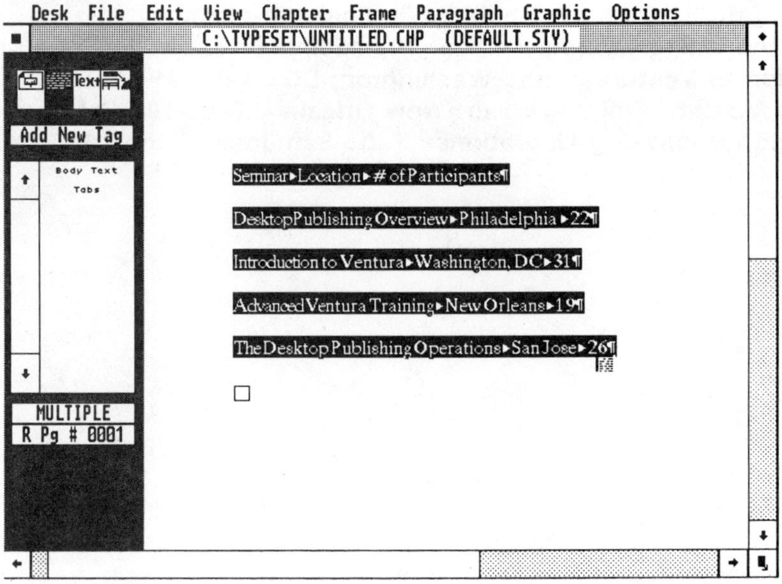

8. Click on **Tabs** in the Assignment List to assign the tag to the selected paragraphs.
9. Point to the **Paragraph** menu and select **Alignment** to display the Alignment dialog box.
10. Select **Left** for Alignment and click **OK**.
11. Point to the **Paragraph** menu and select **Tab Settings** to display the Tab Settings dialog box.
12. Select **1** for Tab Number, **Left** for Tab Type, **Show as Open Space** for Tab Shown As, and **3.50** (inches) for Tab Location.
13. Select **2** for Tab Number, **Left** for Tab Type, **Show as Open Space** for Tab Shown As, and **4.75** (inches) for Tab Location.
14. Press **Enter**. Notice the words have aligned. Your screen should resemble the following illustration:

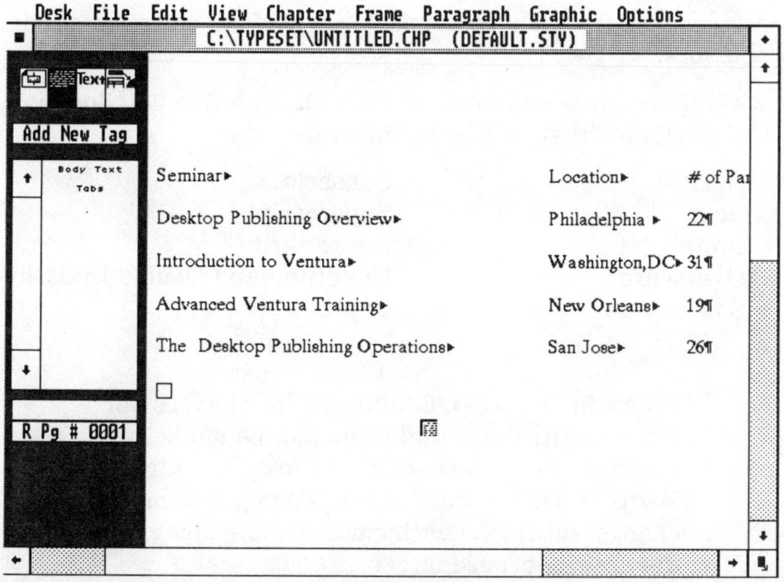

15. Point to the **File** menu and click on **Save As New Style**. Name the new style sheet TAB.STY.
16. Point to the **File** menu and click on **Save**. Type **TAB.CHP** for Selection when the Item Selector appears.
17. Turn to Module 14 to continue the learning sequence.

Module 70
TEXT EDITING

DESCRIPTION

The Text Editing feature in Xerox Ventura Publisher works like a word processor. It is a very limited word processor and does not have the power to perform complicated functions like other regular word processors.

Text Editing allows you to create, edit, and delete text. With this function, you can change the text attributes. The attributes that can be changed include:

Normal	Subscript
Bold	Superscript
Italic	Strike thru
Overscore	Underline and Double Underline
Small Caps	Capitalization

NOTE

When in the Text Editing mode, changes for the text attributes and fonts can be made to a single character or to blocks of text. In contrast, Xerox Ventura Publisher's Paragraph mode changes *all* attributes, including line spacing, for *the entire paragraph*.

In addition to changing the attributes of text, the Text Editing mode allows the kerning of text, inserting index references, frame anchors, and footnotes. Tabs, carriage returns, line breaks, and non-break spaces can also be edited. The Text Editing feature allows you to access most of the commands listed under the Edit menu.

To edit when in the Text Editing mode, simply select the Text Editing function. Then move the mouse cursor to the item you need to edit. Click and hold the mouse button, and drag the mouse to the right. Release the mouse button when the item has been selected. The area selected will be highlighted by Xerox Ventura Publisher. You can then edit or change the selected text.

TIP: To mark a block of text, you can also move the mouse cursor to the beginning of the text you want to select and press and release the mouse button. Move the mouse cursor to the end of the text to be selected, press and hold the Shift key, and then click the mouse button.

When selecting text, you cannot select text across page or frame boundaries.

Although you can create text files directly in Xerox Ventura Publisher with this function, it is advisable to use an external word processor, such as WordPerfect, Microsoft Word, DisplayWrite 4, or WordStar, to create your text files. Such word processors make the preparation of text much easier than using Xerox Ventura Publisher's limited word processing functions. For example, the lack of search and replace, spell checking, and block movement functions in Xerox Ventura Publisher makes it an unlikely choice to prepare text. Remember that Xerox Ventura Publisher is primarily a page composition program, and not a word processor.

The Text Editing function is accessed by selecting it in the Mode Selector in the Side Bar. It can also be accessed in the View menu or by pressing Ctrl-O.

APPLICATIONS

Text editing is used to change the attributes of your prepared text. For example, if you typed a headline in upper and lower case, but now decide it would look better in all upper case, you can select the text and choose upper case to change the text. In the same token, the text could be underlined, bolded, or italicized.

TIP: Selecting Normal in the Side Bar clears all attributes within the selected text and returns the text to the attributes established by the paragraph tag.

Text Editing also permits a font change of text within a paragraph. Sometimes, for emphasis, you may want to change a type font within a sentence. To make the change, Text Editing is used, and Set Font is chosen from the Side Bar.

You can assign as many attributes as you desire to text that has been selected. The list of possible attributes available are displayed in the Assignment List within the Side Bar.

NOTE

When you edit a text file with Xerox Ventura Publisher's Text Editing function, the text file is changed by Ventura. If you were to delete a block of text with Xerox Ventura Publisher in your text file, then Xerox Ventura Publisher would delete the entire block of text. When the text attributes are changed, Xerox Ventura Publisher places markers within the text file. For this reason, you should always make a backup copy of the text file *before* importing it into Xerox Ventura Publisher.

TYPICAL OPERATION

In this operation, you edit text by adding words, deleting, and changing the appearance of the text in the &LTR-P1.CHP chapter. The instructions begin with the chapter open. Use the Open Chapter command located in the File menu to retrieve the &LTR-P1.CHP. Use the scroll bars to adjust your computer screen to match the illustrations.

1. Press **Ctrl-O** to select the Text Editing mode.
2. Move the cursor to the "w" in the word "widget" in the first sentence. Click once.
3. Type **Super-Charged** and press **Spacebar**.
4. Move the cursor to the "f" in the word "found" in the second sentence.
5. Click and drag the mouse to highlight the word "found" and then press **Del**.
6. Type **determined**. Your screen should resemble the following illustration:

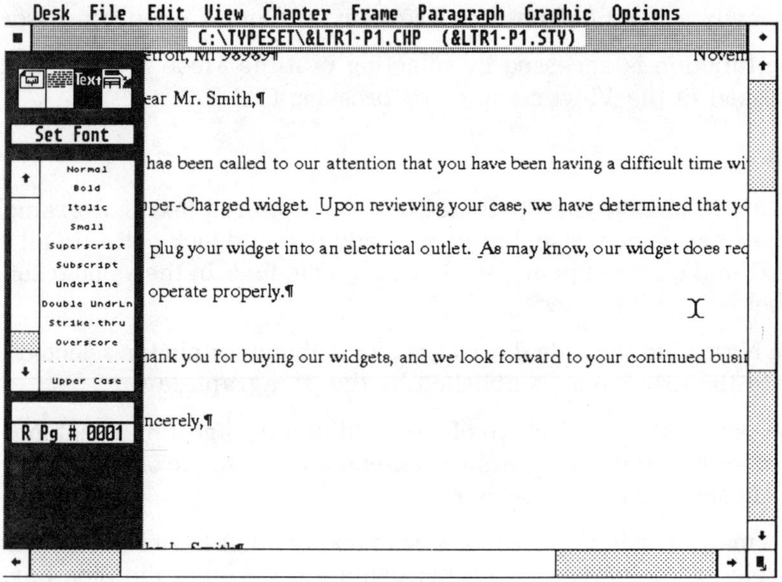

7. Move the cursor to "J" in John, and click once. Move the cursor to "r" in Manager, press and hold **Shift**, and click the mouse button.

8. Click on **Bold** in the Assignment List. Your screen should resemble the following illustration:

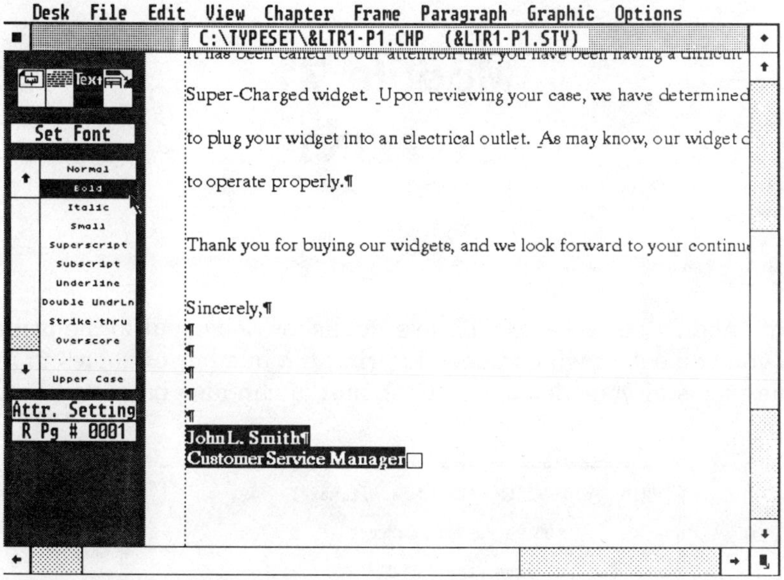

9. Abandon the changes to the chapter.
10. Turn to Module 20 to continue the learning sequence.

Module 71

TO PRINT

DESCRIPTION

The To Print command prints a Xerox Ventura Publisher document to the printer or to a disk. Before printing, you can select which pages to print, the number of copies to print, and which order to print the pages of your document. Crop marks can also be added before the printing process is started.

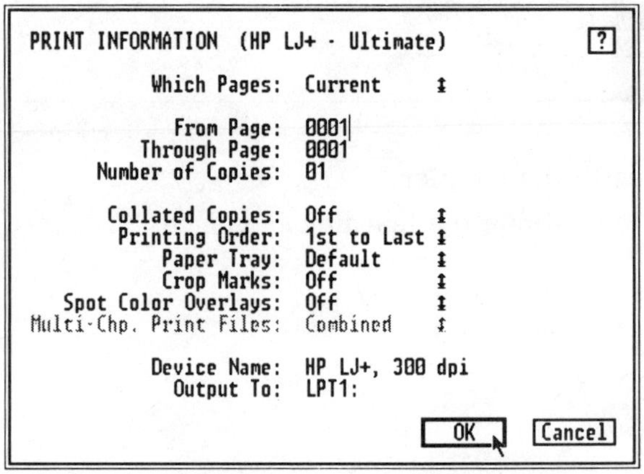

The To Print command presents the Print Information dialog box. The options available are:

Which Pages	Paper Tray
From Page	Crop Marks
Through Page	Spot Color Overlays
Number of Copies	Multi-Chapter Print Files
Collated Copies	Device Name
Printing Order	Output To

Some of the options offer pop-up menus to assist in making your selection.

NOTE

Always select the printer you want to use *before* selecting To Print. You can select your printer, if you have more than one installed, with the Set Printer Info command in the Options menu (see Module 63).

There are many different possible selections available within the Print Information dialog box. These include:

Which Pages	To print only a part of the chapter, use the pop-up menu and choose Selected. Then type the first page to be printed on the From Page line, and type the last page to be printed on the Through Page line. To print only the current page, use the pop-up menu and choose Current. To print the entire chapter, use the pop-up menu and choose All. To print on both sides of the page, use the pop-up menu and select Left or Right. (Some laser printers will smear the toner if a page is reinserted, and for best reproduction, it is wise to print only on one side of a piece of paper.)
Number of Copies	Type the number of copies you need to print.
Collated Copies	Select On if you want all copies to print in page sequence. Select Off if you want all the copies of each page to print together. (This setting greatly increases the speed of your printing process.)
Printing Order	Select to print the first page or last page first.
Paper Tray	There are four choices available: Default, Alt #1, Alt #2, and Manual. Choose Default if you are using a laser printer with only one paper tray, or if you are using a dot matrix printer with an automatic tractor feed that advances the paper. If your laser printer has additional paper trays, use Alt #1 and Alt #2 to use those trays. Select Manual if you want to hand-feed each piece of paper into your printer.
Crop Marks	Select Crop Marks On to place camera crop marks exactly at the edge of a page. (Depending on your laser printer, this feature may not work as many laser printers cannot print to the edge of the paper.)
Spot Color Overlays	Select Spot Color Overlays On to generate a separate page for each color enabled in the Define Colors command (see Module 16).
Multi-Chapter	This Option is only available when working on a Multi-Chapter publication. See Module 44 for more information about Multi-Chapters.

Device Name/Output To — The settings displayed here are based on the printer and printer port that have been selected in the Set Printer Info command. To change, access the Options menu and select Set Printer Info.

To print a document to a file, first select the Set Printer Info command in the Options menu and select Output To: Filename. Then select To Print from the File menu. The Output To line in the Print Information dialog box displays the word "filename." After selecting OK, the Item Selector appears and you can then enter the name of the file you wish to create print to.

If you have selected oversize page dimensions in the Page Layout dialog box, another dialog box appears as soon as you have selected OK in the Print Information dialog box. This dialog box offers three choices:

Shrink
Overlap
Nothing

Choose Shrink if you want to reduce the 11 x 17 page to fit an 8½" x 11" sheet of paper (this option will only work if you are using a PostScript printer). Choose Overlap if you want to print four 8½" x 11" pages which can be pasted together to form one 11 x 17 page. Choose nothing if your printer can actually handle an 11 x 17 sheet of paper.

TIP: If you need to stop the printing when it is in progress, press Esc. The printing will stop *after* the current page is printed. This will not be an instant stop for most laser printers.

To access the To Print command, select the File menu.

APPLICATIONS

The application of this command is obvious: this command generates the printed pages of your document. The command also allows you to tailor your printed output.

For example, suppose you are working on a 30-page document and decide to change only page 22. The document is already printed, but you need just one copy of the new page 22. This command allows you to print just page 22.

This command also allows you to print to a file, so the file can be sent to a commercial typesetter. This is an important function available in Xerox Ventura Publisher for those who need truly professional output. By sending a Xerox Ventura Publisher file to typesetter, your finished output has a higher resolution than that which is available from today's laser printers.

TYPICAL OPERATION

In this example, you print the Xerox Ventura Publisher sample chapter document SCOOP.CHP. The example begins with SCOOP.CHP already open and in use. If you do not have this chapter open, use the Open Chapter command in the File menu to retrieve and open SCOOP.CHP.

1. Point to the **File** menu and click on **To Print**.
2. Select **All** for **Which Pages** and click on **OK**. Within several minutes, the printer generates the pages.
3. Turn to Module 60 to continue the learning sequence.

Module 72

TURN COLUMN/LINE SNAP ON/OFF

DESCRIPTION

The Turn Column Snap On and Turn Line Snap On commands force frames to align with the page's column guides and the Inter-Line spacing in the underlying page. The Turn Column Snap Off and Turn Line Snap Off commands allow frames to be placed anywhere on the page.

When Column Snap is on, any new frame and previous frames that are resized snap to the edge of a column when you move the edge of the frame to approximately 1/10 of an inch from the column edge. All four borders of a new frame snap to the edge if you are close enough to the column border. Frames do not snap to the top or bottom of the column guides. Only the one or two edges snap to the column border when an existing frame is resized. When Line Snap is on, new frames and frames resized snap to the nearest line guide in the underlying page.

Both the Line and Column snap commands are located in the Options menu. When you select either command, its name changes. For example, when Turn Column Snap On is selected, its name in the menu changes to Column Snap Off.

The Inter-Line spacing settings for the Body Text create an invisible grid that is used to snap the frames.

APPLICATIONS

The Turn Column Snap On command forces pictures and text frames placed on the page to align perfectly with other text columns. When resizing, the frames are sized in one-line increments.

Turn Line Snap On ensures that frames in adjacent columns line up exactly and forces the top of one frame to align with the bottom of the frame above it. The Turn Line Snap On command also forces a line of text in a column to move down exactly one line by increasing the height of a frame that has been snapped to the column.

When the Turn Column Snap Off and Turn Line Snap Off commands are used, you can place frames anywhere on the page, without regard to any alignment.

Most Xerox Ventura Publisher users are probably better served by using the Turn Column Snap On and Turn Line Snap On commands. The more precise alignment usually guarantees a cleaner, more professional-looking design.

TYPICAL OPERATION

In this operation, you turn Column and Line Snap off, resize a frame, turn both snaps on, and create another frame. The instructions begin with Xerox Ventura Publisher running and the &NEWS-P2.CHP open. Press Ctrl-R.

1. Press **Ctrl-U** to select Frame mode.
2. Point to the **Options** menu and click on **Turn Column Snap Off**.
3. Point to the **Options** menu and click on **Turn Line Snap Off**.
4. Click on **Add New Frame**, point and click the mouse cursor in the left column, and drag the mouse slowly to the right. Your screen should resemble the following illustration:

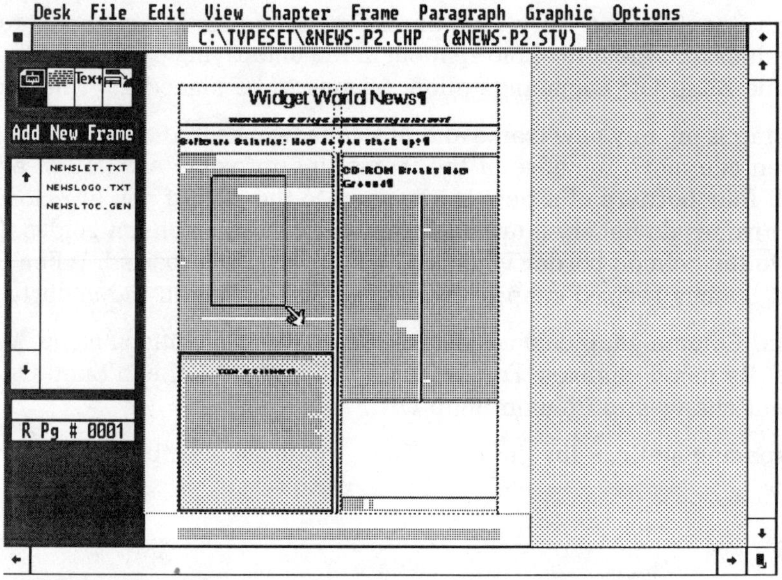

The new frame is created evenly and smoothly. Release the mouse button.

5. Press **Del** to delete the frame.
6. Point to the **Options** menu and click on **Show Column Guides** to turn on the column guides (if they are not already on).
7. Point to the **Options** menu and click on **Turn Line Snap On**.

8. Click on **Add New Frame**, point and click the mouse cursor in the left column, and drag the mouse slowly to the right. Your screen should resemble the following illustration:

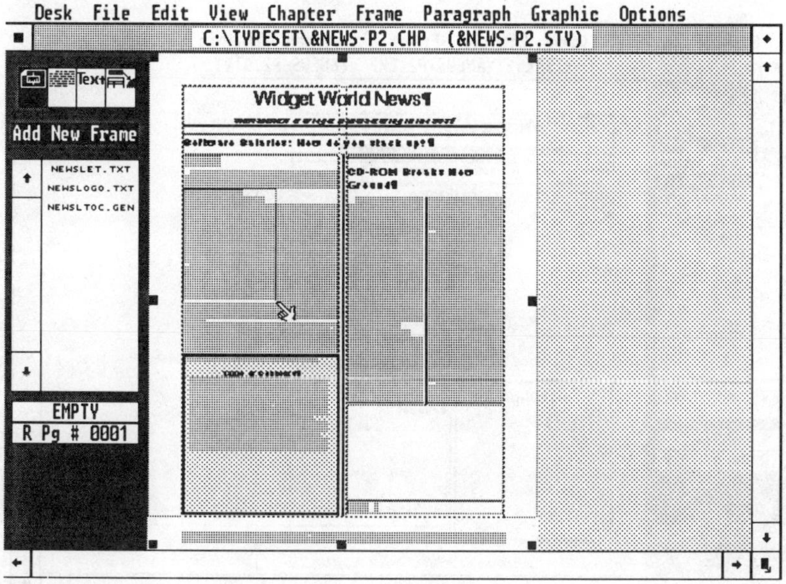

Notice how the bottom edges seem to snap into position as you draw. Release the mouse button.

9. Press **Del** to delete the frame.
10. Point to the **Options** menu and click on **Turn Column Snap On**.

11. Click on **Add New Frame** and slowly draw a box in the left column. Be sure to draw the frame borders within 1/10 of an inch of the column guide to make the frame snap to the column. Your screen should resemble the following illustration:

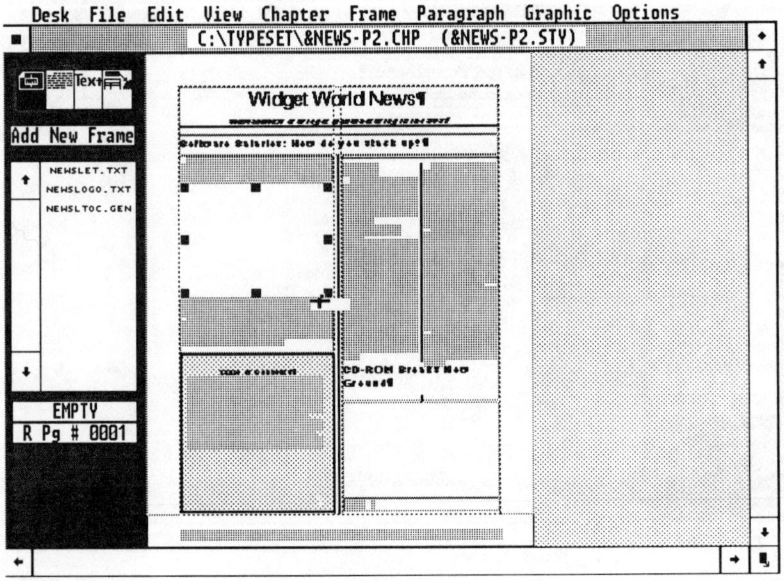

Notice how the new frame snaps to the column guides when the mouse button is released.

12. Point to the **File** menu and click on **Abandon**.
13. Turn to Module 5 to continue the learning sequence.

Module 73

TURN HEADER/FOOTER ON/OFF

DESCRIPTION

The Turn Header On/Off and the Turn Footer On/Off commands show or hide the text placed in the header or the footer. If a Header or Footer is being displayed, the command available is Turn Header Off or Turn Footer Off. If a header or footer is not being displayed, the command available is Turn Header On or Turn Footer On.

These commands display or hide the header or footer text on specific pages.

This information about displaying or hiding the header or footer is stored in the current page within the Xerox Ventura Publisher chapter. When the header or footer is turned off, the header or footer space will remain on your Xerox Ventura Publisher page. The header or footer text will be hidden, and it will not print.

The Turn Header/Footer On/Off commands are accessed in the Chapter menu.

APPLICATIONS

Headers and footers can be turned off or removed from specific pages within your Xerox Ventura Publisher documents. This book is an example of how headers are sometimes turned off. Notice that the header is turned off on the starting page of the modules and appendixes.

Turn off the header or footer in publications where full-page advertisements or illustrations are used (such as magazines).

TYPICAL OPERATION

In this example, you turn off the footer in the Xerox Ventura Publisher sample chapter &NEWS-P2.CHP. The operation begins with &NEWS-P2.CHP already in use. If you do not have this chapter open, use the command Open Chapter in the File menu to retrieve and open &NEWS-P2.CHP.

1. Point to the **Chapter** menu and click on **Turn Footer Off**. Notice that the footer is now hidden.
2. Abandon the changes to the chapter.
3. Turn to Module 65 to continue the learning sequence.

Module 74

UPDATE COUNTERS

DESCRIPTION

This feature resets the figure, page, table, or chapter counters at any point in the chapter. This command allows the automatic linking of page, table, or figure counter across chapter boundaries.

To use this feature of Xerox Ventura Publisher, access the Update Counters command located in the Chapter menu. Not only can the counters be reset, but the numbering style can also be selected. The styles of numbering available are:

1,2	i,ii
A,B	One,Two
a,b	ONE,TWO
I,II	one,two

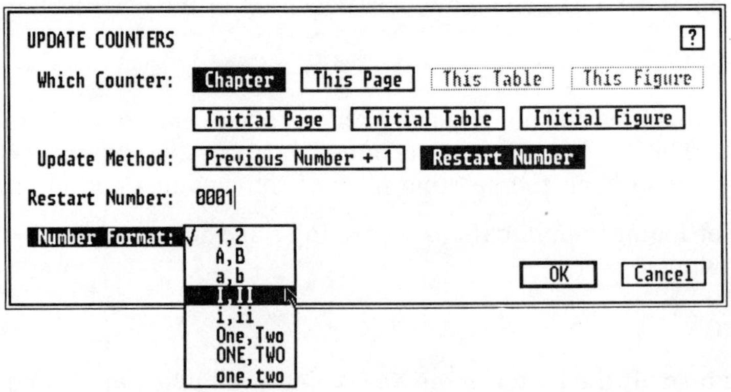

Within the Update Counters dialog box, the following options are available:

Which Counter

Select either Chapter, This Page, This Table, This Figure, Initial Page, Initial Table, or Initial Figure. These options allow you to choose what you want counted within the Xerox Ventura Publisher chapter.

Update Method

Select Either Previous Number + 1 or Restart Number to tell Xerox Ventura Publisher which number to use when counting.

Restart Number	Enter a number if you desire any number other than one to begin the counting.
Number Format	Select one of the numbering format styles available.

TIP: When starting a counter for the first time, the initial default settings are arabic format (1,2) and start at the number 1. If these are your desired settings, you need only select the counter from the Update Counters dialog box.

Counters can be changed two ways. The counter for the chapter, initial page, initial table, or initial figure can be set. This is done to link the chapter with a previous chapter (see Module 44 for more information about Multi-Chapter). The counter for this page, table, or figure can also be reset, and this is done when you need to change the numbering sequence within a chapter.

APPLICATIONS

Being able to number pages, tables, and figures automatically will enhance your publications. It is most important when creating longer reports, books, technical manuals, or business documents that requires extensive use of tables, figures, or even appendices.

The Update Counters dialog box allows the consecutive numbering of paragraphs, pages, figures, or tables across chapters. This allows you to work with smaller chapters and still be able to produce logically numbered pages.

The commands also permit the override of automatically generated numbers for a given page, table, or figure.

Being able to choose which style of counting desired is also another useful benefit of this command.

TYPICAL OPERATION

In this example, you begin counting figures in the Xerox Ventura Publisher sample chapter called &BOOK-P2.CHP. This example begins with &BOOK-P2.CHP already open and in use. If you do not have this chapter open, use the Open Chapter command in the File menu to retrieve and open &BOOK-P2.CHP.

1. Press **Ctrl-U** to select Frame mode.
2. Click in the middle of the frame holding the nozzle picture.
3. Point to the **Chapter** menu and select **Update Counters** to display the Update Counters dialog box.
4. Select **This Figure** in Which Counter, **Restart Number** in Update Method.

5. Type **12** for Restart Number.

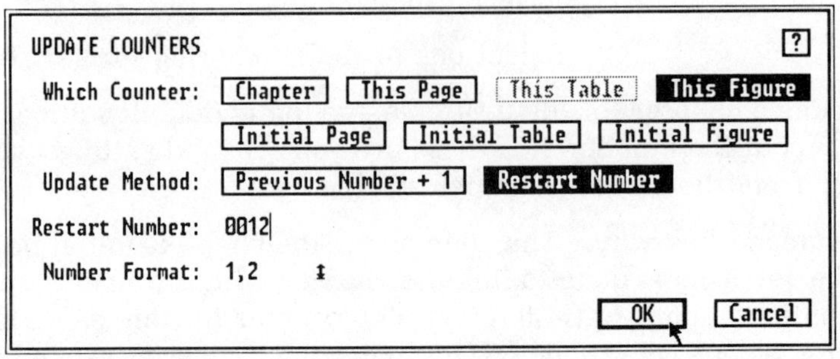

6. Click **OK**.
7. Point to the **File** menu and click on **Abandon** and click on **OK** when prompted to revert back to the last saved version.
8. Turn to Module 44 to continue the learning sequence.

Module 75

UPDATE TAG LIST

DESCRIPTION

The Update Tag List command provides several tools to help manage the paragraph tags that are stored in a style sheet. These tools are:

- Remove Tags
- Rename Tags
- Assign Tag Names to Function Keys
- Print the Style Sheet
- Save the Style Sheet

When the Update Tag List command is accessed from the paragraph menu, the Update Tag List dialog box appears. A list of all the tags associated with the current style sheet is displayed.

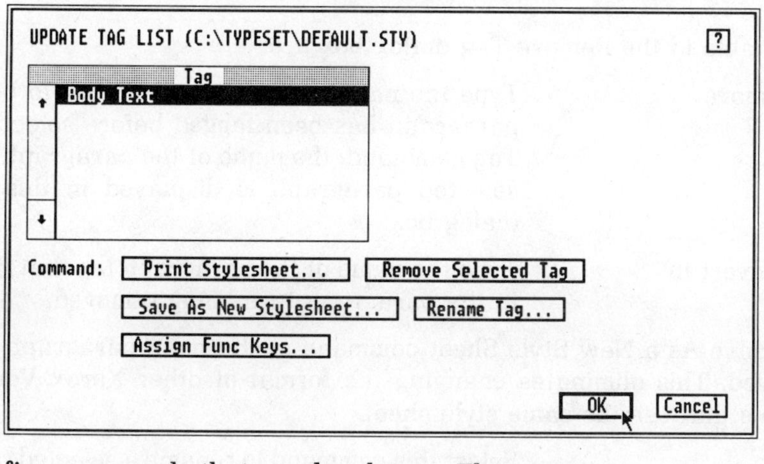

There are then five commands that can be chosen. They are:

Print Stylesheet — Select this command to print the contents of the current style sheet. Xerox Ventura Publisher will copy the file and create a file with the same name as the style sheet, adding a .GEN extension. This file can then be imported into Xerox Ventura Publisher with the Load Text/Picture command, using the Generated Text format. The style sheet can then be printed.

Remove Selected Tag

Select this command to delete an existing tag from the current style sheet. This command can be accessed from the paragraph menu before a paragraph is tagged with the paragraph tagging tool or after a paragraph has been tagged.

After the Remove Selected Tag command has been selected, the Remove Tag dialog box appears. Your screen should resemble this illustration:

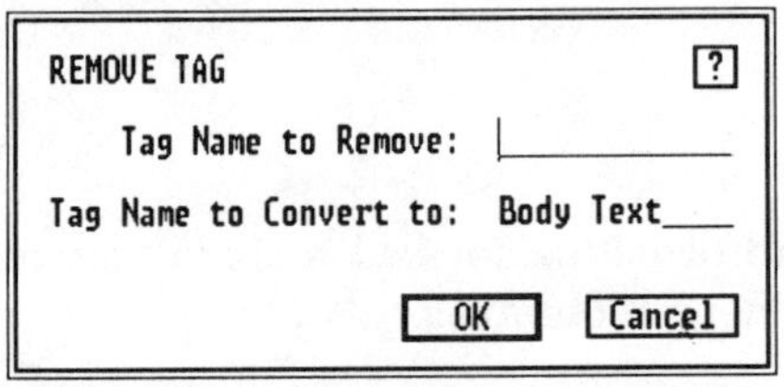

Before a tag is removed, you must assign another tag to take its place. For example, you might decide to remove the paragraph tag called subheadline and reassign all paragraphs tagged as subheadline with the headline paragraph tag. After completing the execution of this command, all the paragraphs tagged as subheadline in your document will now be reassigned and have the headline tag assigned. The paragraphs will also now assume the attributes assigned to the headline tag.

The options available in the Remove Tag dialog box are:

Tag Name to Remove

Type the name of the paragraph tag to be removed. If a paragraph has been tagged before selecting the Remove Tag command, the name of the paragraph assigned to the selected paragraph is displayed in this section of the dialog box.

Tag Name to Convert to

Type the name of the paragraph tag that is to be assigned to the paragraph tags being removed.

TIP: Use the Save As a New Style Sheet command each time a paragraph tag is renamed or removed. This eliminates changing the format of other Xerox Ventura Publisher documents that use the same style sheet.

Rename Tag

Select this command to rename a selected tag. Simply enter the new name of the tag.

Save As New Style Sheet

Select this command to save a style sheet under a new name: the Item Selector dialog box appears, and you can then type the new name in the Selector area.

Assign Function Keys

The Assign Function Keys command allows you to assign your paragraph tags to the first 10 function keys on your computer.

TIP: The Update Tag List command is accessed in the Paragraph menu or by pressing Ctrl-K. When selecting the Assign Function Key option, it is not necessary to select text first.

Assign Function Keys does not change paragraphs or the predefined tags in the style sheet. This command only affects the style sheet. Using this command affects the style sheet for your current document and any other document that uses the current style sheet.

When you select Assign Function Keys from the Update Tag List dialog box or by pressing Ctrl-K, the Assign Function Keys dialog box appears. Your screen should look like this illustration:

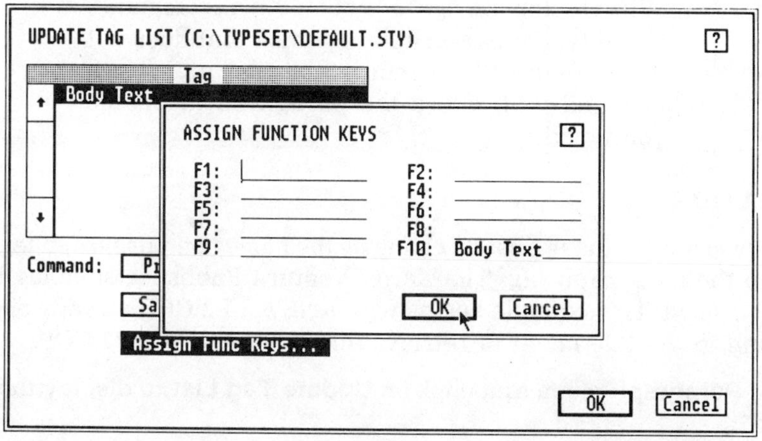

The Assign Function Keys dialog box contains spaces for naming 10 paragraph tags to the function keys on your keyboard F1 through F10. F10 is also the default of the Body Text tag. To assign a paragraph tag to one of the function keys, simply type the name of the paragraph tag beside the function key in the Assign Function Keys dialog box.

APPLICATIONS

This command allows you to remove tags that are no longer being used. By doing so, you will speed up Xerox Ventura Publisher. It is always preferable to eliminate any unused paragraph tags from a style sheet.

This command can also be used to make it easy to find the paragraph tags within the assignment sheet. By eliminating unused or unneeded tags, it will be easier to find the other used paragraph tags.

The command also makes it possible to document any style sheets you have created or changed. By using the Print Stylesheet command, you can document the contents of a style sheet.

When you have assigned paragraph tags to your function keys, you can tag or retag your paragraphs from both the Paragraph Tagging and the Text Editing modes. This is an extremely useful command that increases the speed at which you can tag your paragraphs.

For example, suppose you created a paragraph tag called Italic Body and assigned the F1 key to that tag. Now, as you wade through your text, you can remain in the Text Editing mode. As you select text to edit, delete, or change, you can do so in the normal manner. When you want to assign the Italic Body paragraph tag to your text, simply select the text and press F1.

You can also change the format of any text you are adding to a Ventura Publisher document. For example, if you want to add a new paragraph in the Italic Body format, you position the cursor, press F1, and begin typing. The new text will be formatted in accordance with the attributes you assigned to Italic Body paragraph tag.

NOTE

When using Assign Function Keys command, if you type a paragraph tag name that does not exist, Ventura Publisher will display a message box and will ignore the paragraph tag name you typed.

TYPICAL OPERATION

In this operation, you update the tag list by changing the name of a paragraph tag and by assigning a function key to the paragraph tag. The Xerox Ventura Publisher sample chapter document &NEWS-P2.CHP is used. The example begins with &NEWS-P2.CHP already open. Use the Open Chapter command in the File menu to retrieve and open &NEWS-P2.CHP.

1. Point to the **Paragraph** menu and click on **Update Tag List** to display the Update Tag List dialog box.
2. Click on **Rename Tag** to display the Rename Tag dialog box.
3. Move the cursor to the Old Tag Name line and press **Esc** to delete the tag name **Address**.
4. Type **Subhead** for Old Tag Name, move the cursor to the New Tag Name line, and type **Subhead 1**. Press **Enter**.
5. Click on **OK** in the Update Tag List dialog box. A message box appears asking if you want to Save, Save As, or Abandon changes to the stylesheet.
6. Click on **Save**. Notice the new tag name in the Assignment list.
7. Point to the **Paragraph** menu and click on **Update Tag List** to display the Update Tag List dialog box. Click on **Save** when the message box appears asking if you want to Save or Abandon changes.
8. Click on **Assign Func Keys** to display the Assign Function Keys dialog box.
9. Move the cursor to the F2 line and type **Subhead 1**. Press **Enter**. A message box appears, asking if you want to Save, Save As, or Abandon changes to the stylesheet.
10. Click on **Abandon**.
11. Abandon the changes to the chapter.
12. Turn to Module 64 to continue the learning sequence.

Module 76

VERTICAL RULES

DESCRIPTION

The Vertical Rules command sets rule lines running between the top and bottom of the page in each frame or on the underlying page. A frame or underlying page may have a rule between each of its columns, plus two additional vertical rules. Xerox Ventura Publisher automatically positions the rules between the columns based on the columns defined with the Margins & Columns command.

The positions and widths of the other two vertical rules can be set as needed or desired. This command applies to all underlying pages and frames, even those frames that Xerox Ventura Publisher creates for its headers, footers, captions, and footnotes.

Different vertical rules for the left and right pages can be specified if a double-sided publication is being created. The left and right pages can be complementary to each other, a complete reversal, or they can be totally different from each other.

This command is accessed by selecting a frame or the underlying page with the frame-setting tool and then selecting Vertical Rules from the Frame menu. The Vertical Rules dialog box then appears.

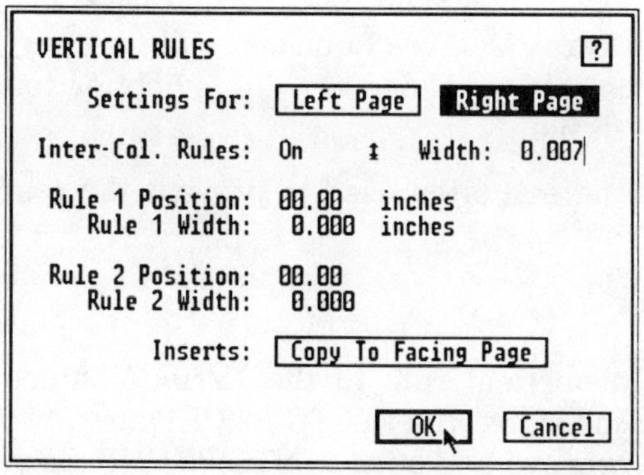

The Vertical Rules dialog box contains this information:

Settings For — Select either the Left Page or Right Page. Whichever page you were on when you selected the Vertical Rules command will automatically be selected.

Inter-Col. Rules	Select Inter-Col. Rules to be on or off. This command will direct Xerox Ventura Publisher to place rules between each column in the frame or underlying page. If On is selected, then type the width of the column in Width area.
Rule 1/Rule 2 Position	Type the distance from the left edge of the page (not the edge of the frame) where each rule is to appear. If no rule is desired, type 00.00.
Rule 1/Rule 2 Width	Type the width of the rule.
Inserts	Select Copy to Facing Page to automatically copy the information in the dialog box to the facing page. Doing this transfers the width of the inter-column rules and reverses the positions of the rules setup in the dialog box. Copy to Facing Page works only if preparing a two-sided document as established in the Page Size & Layout command. If creating complementary pages, enter the information separately for each page.

TIP: If you do not see a vertical rule within a frame, the frame may be in the wrong position relative to the vertical rule set in the Vertical Rules dialog box.

Frame-wide paragraphs will interrupt vertical rules on the Xerox Ventura Publisher page. Column-wide paragraphs do not interrupt the vertical rule. To set the alignment of the paragraph, see Module 6.

APPLICATIONS

The Vertical Rules command places rules between text columns and places rules elsewhere on the page. By adding rules to your document, the overall design is often improved. Adding rules between text columns (what Xerox Ventura Publisher calls gutters) not only enhances the design of the document, but also helps the reader see the article or text. This is commonly used in newsletter and newspaper design.

Rules help create sections and are often used to prevent the reader's eyes flowing from one column to another.

TYPICAL OPERATION

In this example, you add a vertical rule to the Xerox Ventura Publisher sample chapter &LSTG-P2.CHP. The operation begins with &LSTG-P2.CHP already open. Use the command Open Chapter in the File menu to retrieve and open &LSTG-P2.CHP. So your view matches the screen depicted in this book, press Ctrl-N. You may need to adjust your screen using the scroll bars to make your computer look like the illustrations.

1. Press **Ctrl-U** to select Frame mode.
2. Click on the underlying page.
3. Point to the **Options** menu and click on **Hide Tabs & Returns**.

4. Point to the **Frame** menu and click on **Vertical Rules.**
5. Click **On** for Inter-Col. Rules, and type **0.014** inches as the width. Click **OK.** Your screen should resemble this illustration:

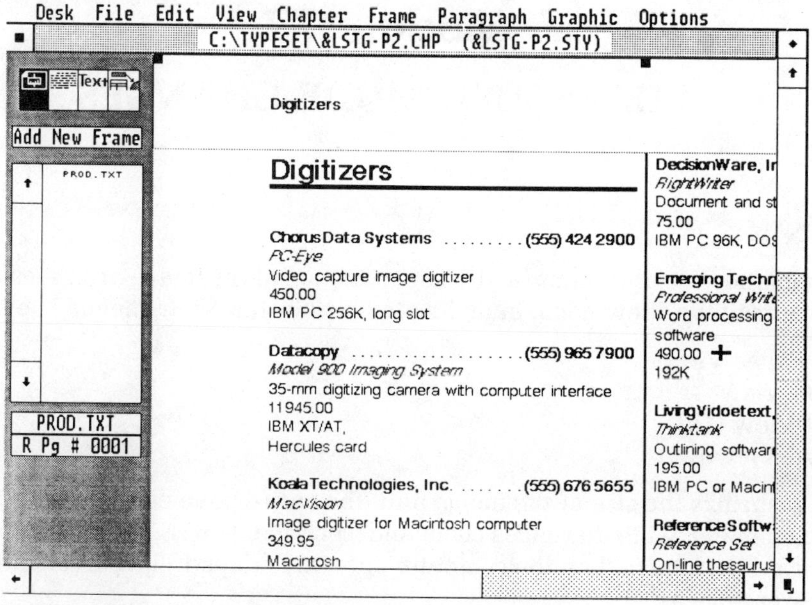

Notice the addition of the Vertical Rule between the columns.

6. Point to the **File** menu and click on **Abandon**. Click on **OK** when prompted to revert back to the last saved version.
7. Turn to Module 31 to continue the learning sequence.

Module 77

VIEWS AND MODE CHANGES

DESCRIPTION

The View commands sets the magnification or reduction of the image area seen on the computer screen. There are four View commands located within the View menu. They are:

Facing Pages View
Reduced View
Normal View (1x)
Enlarged View (2x)

Reduced View shrinks the size of the image until the entire page can be seen. Depending on the options selected in the Set Preferences command (see Module 62), Xerox Ventura Publisher will "greek" all or most of the text on the computer screen. Reduced View is selected from the View menu or by pressing Ctrl-R.

Normal View displays the image to nearly the way it looks when it is printed. When in Normal View, you only see a portion of your document (unless you are creating an extremely small document of only a few inches in size). To see more of your document, use the scroll bars. Normal View is selected from View menu or by pressing Ctrl-N.

Enlarged View doubles the size of the image shown in the Normal View. Once again, only a portion of your document will be seen when in the Enlarged View. Enlarged View is selected from the View menu or by pressing Ctrl-E.

TIP: By placing the pointer at a specific spot on the working part of the screen and pressing Ctrl-E, Xerox Ventura Publisher positions the selected area in the upper left corner of the enlarged screen.

Facing Pages View shrinks the size of the image until both pages, left and right, can be seen on your computer screen. Facing Pages View is accessed in the View menu. There is no keyboard shortcut to use to select this view. When in Facing Pages View, you cannot drag frames across pages.

Mode Changes are also accessed in the View menu. Any one of the four modes of operation within Xerox Ventura Publisher can be selected. They are:

Frame Setting
Paragraph Tagging
Text Editing
Graphic Drawing

In addition to selecting Frame Setting, Paragraph, Text Editing, or Graphic Drawing in the View menu, each of these modes can be selected with the following keyboard commands:

Ctrl-U	Frame Setting
Ctrl-I	Paragraph Tagging
Ctrl-O	Text Editing
Ctrl-P	Graphic Drawing

These modes can be selected with the icons in the Side Bar also.

APPLICATIONS

These commands offer you different ways of working within Xerox Ventura Publisher. For example, when in the Reduced View, you can see the layout of the entire page. You can see where to place frames, graphics, and text and have a good idea how your finished page will look when printed. Normal View allows you to see as close as possible how your printed page will appear. Enlarged View permits precise adjustments and placements within your Xerox Ventura Publisher document. Facing Pages View allows you to see how the document's design compliments each facing page.

The purpose of the Facing Pages View command is to permit you to see and change the general layout of a two-page spread. You will be able to see how your frames, graphics, rules, text, and other page elements will appear when a document is finally published. This command allows you to make adjustments to the overall design of your facing pages to create a complimentary effect.

NOTE

If you have chosen to start your document with a right-hand page, the Facing Page View command will show only one page when you are viewing page 1 of your document.

When the Side Bar is hidden, accessing the View menu permits the selection of the different Xerox Ventura Publisher modes of operation. Of course, accessing the View menu to change a mode of operation is just an alternative way of making the selection.

Each of the keyboard commands offered in this module is just another way of executing a command and often saves time.

TYPICAL OPERATION

In this example, you change the views of the Xerox Ventura Publisher sample chapter SCOOP.CHP. The example begins with SCOOP.CHP already open and in use. If you do not have this chapter open, use the Open Chapter command in the File menu to retrieve and open SCOOP.CHP.

1. Point to the **View** menu and click on **Reduced View**. Notice the full view of the page you can now see on your screen:

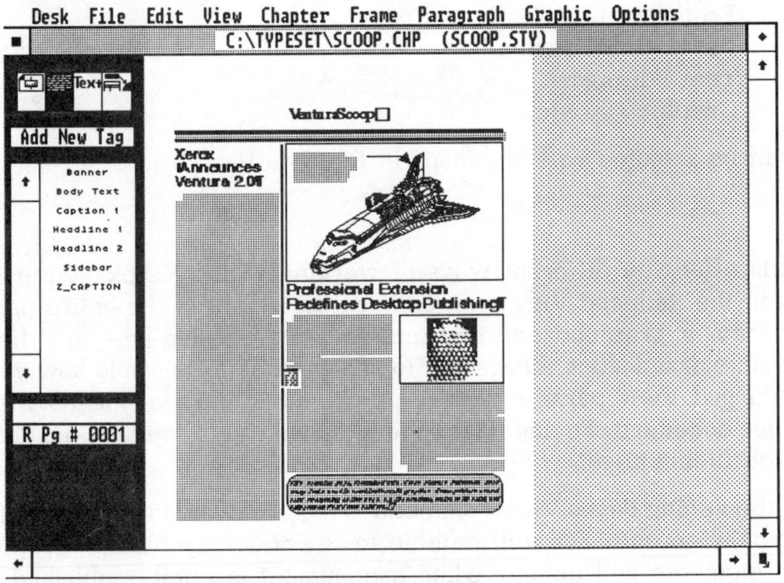

2. Position the mouse cursor in the middle of your computer screen and press **Ctrl-E**. Your screen should now resemble this illustration:

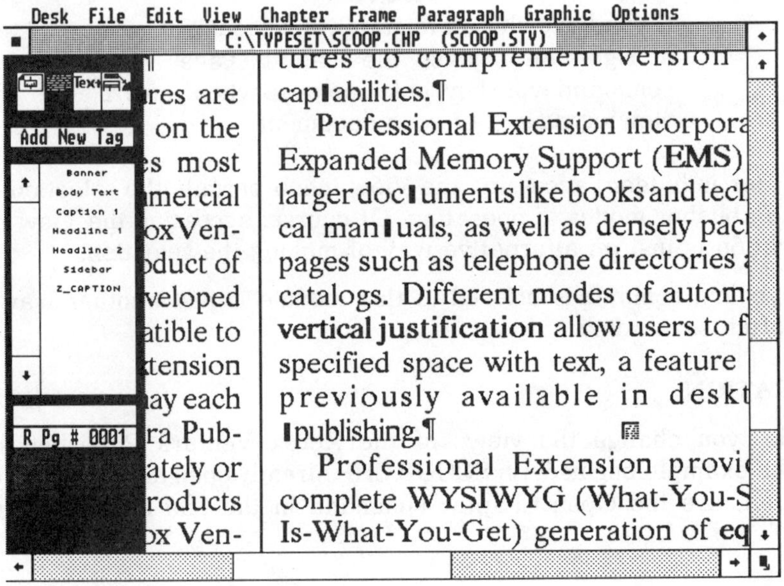

Notice that the enlarged view on your computer screen is in the portion of the page where you placed the mouse cursor before pressing Ctrl-E.

3. Point to the **View** menu and click on **Normal View**. Your screen should resemble the following illustration:

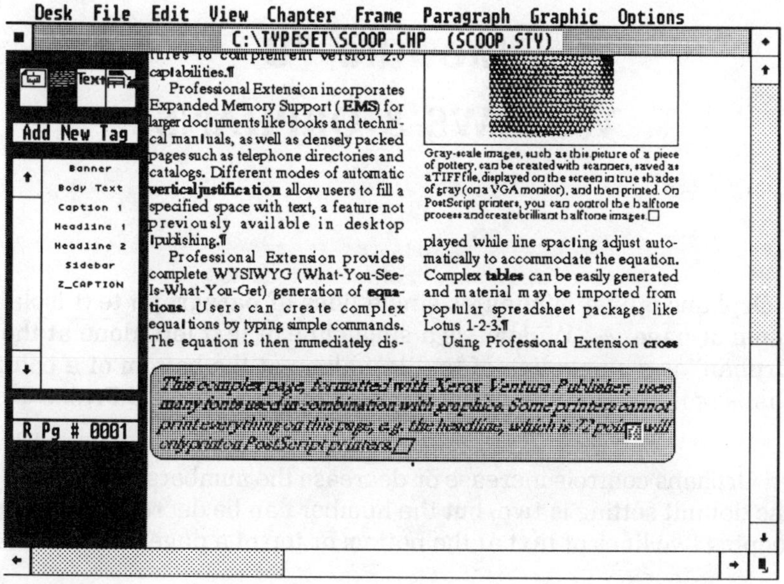

Notice the actual-size view on your computer screen.

4. Press **Ctrl-R** to change to Reduced View.
5. Press **Ctrl-U** to select the Frame mode. Notice the Side Bar.
6. Press **Ctrl-I** to select the Paragraph Tagging mode. Notice the Side Bar.
7. Press **Ctrl-O** to select the Text Editing mode. Notice the Side Bar.
8. Turn to Module 19 to continue the learning sequence.

Module 78
WIDOWS & ORPHANS

DESCRIPTION

The Widows & Orphans option eliminates single lines of paragraph text isolated at the top or bottom of a column or page. A "Widow" is a single line of text left alone at the top of a column or page. An "Orphan" is a single line of text left alone at the bottom of a column or page. The Widows & Orphans option is located in the Chapter Typography and Frame Typography dialog boxes.

The Widows and Orphans controls increase or decrease the numbers of lines that can be widowed or orphaned. The default setting is two, but the number can be decreased or increased. For most applications, keeping two lines of text at the bottom or top of a page or column is most desirable.

APPLICATIONS

On the printed page, widows and orphans create a sloppy, sometimes difficult to read, appearance. Although Xerox Ventura Publisher can easily prevent unsightly widows and orphans, the inclusion of widows and orphans is one of the most common problems when preparing a published page.

With this command, you select the minimum number of lines Xerox Ventura Publisher can leave alone on the top or bottom of a column or page. Xerox Ventura Publisher's default is two lines, and this initial setting eliminates all widows and orphans.

However, because of the extreme flexibility designed in Xerox Ventura Publisher, you can change the minimum number of isolated lines. You can choose a setting of 1 (which permits widows and orphans) to a maximum setting of 5 (which forces Xerox Ventura Publisher to keep five lines of text at the top or bottom of a page or column).

NOTE

If Ventura Publisher cannot break a paragraph in compliance with settings you choose in the Widows & Orphans dialog box, then the entire paragraph will be moved to the next page or column.

TYPICAL OPERATION

In this operation, you set the orphan value to one so Xerox Ventura Publisher will create isolated text lines. You then flow text between two frames and intentionally create an orphan. Finally, you change the Widows & Orphans command to eliminate the orphan. The instructions begin with Xerox Ventura Publisher running and a blank file running. Use the DEFAULT.STY style sheet.

1. Point to the **Chapter** menu and click on **Chapter Typography**.
2. Select **1** for Orphans (Min Lines at Bottom) and click **OK**.
3. Click on **Add New Frame**, click and hold on the working part of the screen, drag to the right, and create a small frame.
4. Press **Shift-Del** to copy the frame to the clipboard.
5. Press **Ins** to paste the copy of the frame to the screen.
6. Click and hold on the second frame, and drag it to the right until the screen looks similar to this illustration:

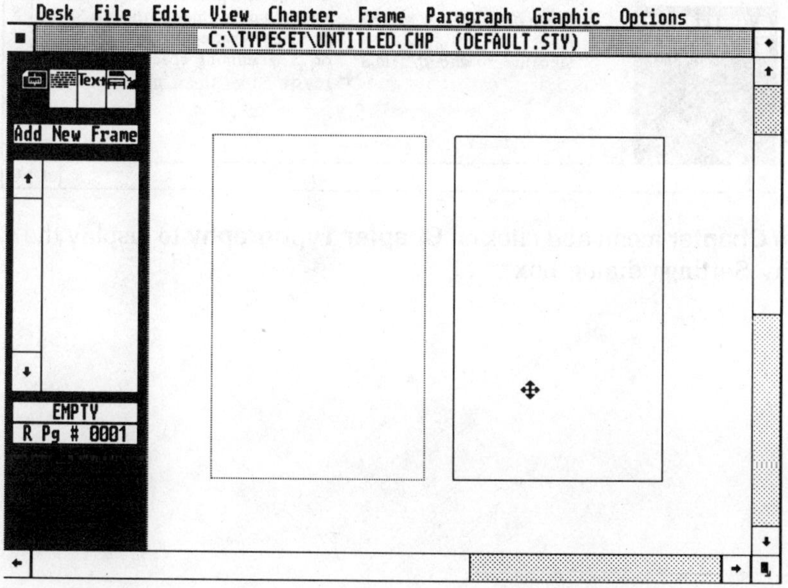

7. Release the mouse button.
8. Click on the frame to the left, point to **File** menu, and click on **Load Text/Picture** to display the Load Text/Picture dialog box.
9. Click on **Text** for Type of File, **ASCII** for Text Format, **One** for # of Files, and **OK** to display the Item Selector dialog box.
10. Double click on **NEWSLET.TXT** from the TYPESET directory to select and load it.
11. Click on the frame to the right to highlight it, and click on **NEWSLET.TEX** in the Assignment List to flow text to the second frame.

12. Click on the left frame, and click and hold on the bottom middle black box. Drag the frame up until only one line of the current paragraph shows at the bottom of the page. (That one line is an Orphan.) Your screen should resemble the following illustration:

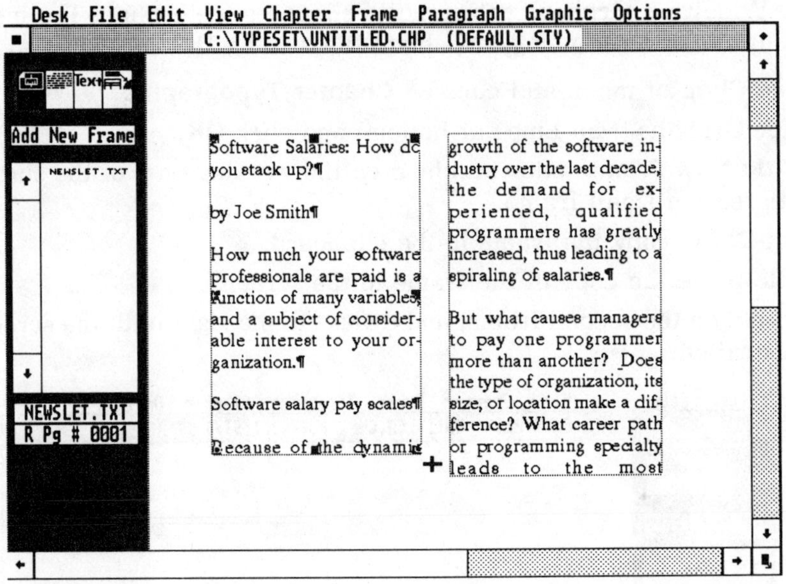

13. Point to the **Chapter** menu and click on **Chapter Typography** to display the Chapter (Default) Typography Settings dialog box.

14. Select **2** for Orphans (Min Lines at Bottom) and press **Enter**.

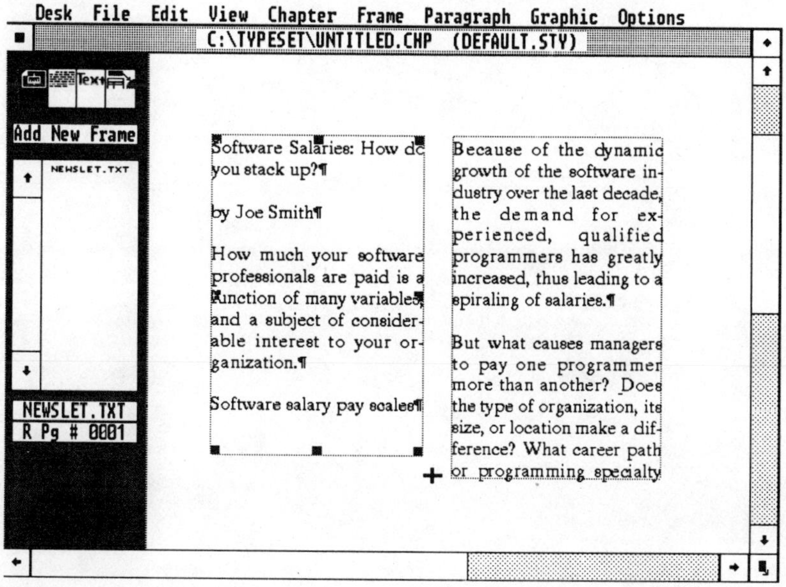

Xerox Ventura Publisher has eliminated the orphan by moving the entire paragraph to the right frame.

15. Point to the **File** menu and click on **Abandon**.
16. Turn to Module 76 to continue the learning sequence.

Appendix A

TERMS AND DEFINITIONS

Term	*Definition*
80286	The microprocessor chip (CPU) used in AT type computers.
8088	The microprocessor chip (CPU) used in PC/XT type computers.
Ascender	The upward stroke of lower case letters, such as the h, k, l, and t.
ASCII	Acronym for AMERICAN STANDARD CODE for INFORMATION INTERCHANGE; 7-bit code that refers to the 256 characters that are used to represent the letters, numbers, control characters, and graphics symbols; the first 128 ASCII are standardized, the upper 128 differ between packages and computer models.
Asynchronous	A term used to describe the way information is sent using a modem.
Baseline	The imaginary line that type sits on.
Baud Rate	The speed of communications handled by the printer or modem, usually measured in bits per second.
Bit Map	The pattern of dots that makes up a digitized image.
Bits/Bytes	BIT: constructed from the words BInary digiT, the term refers to a single digit of a binary number (0/1) BYTE: (8 bits) the number of bits required to encode one character of information in any given computer system.
Bug	An unintentional error in a program.
Button	One of the choices within a dialog box such as OK or Cancel.
CAD	Computer Aided Design/Computer Aided Drafting.
Camera-Ready	Graphic layouts that are ready for mass reproduction.
Case	A choice between normal upper and lower case, all capitals, and small capitals.
CGA	Color Graphics Adapter; the graphics card that controls a color monitor with a resolution of 320 x 200 pixels.
Click	To quickly press and release the mouse button.
Click and Hold	To press and hold the mouse button.
Clipboard	A temporary holding area where items can be cut or copied. Xerox Ventura Publisher has three clipboards: one for graphics, text, and frames.

Term	Definition
Compatible	Having the same characteristics and capabilities of an IBM PC; able to use software written to run on IBM PC.
Computer Configuration	A complete hardware setup, usually consisting of a system unit, disk drives, a monitor, a keyboard, and a printer.
Computer System	Refers to the entire hardware package and would most properly include all software as well.
Computerese	A kind of confused gobbledegook double talk language only computer experts or hackers can understand.
CPU	Central Processing Unit; the part or parts of computer hardware that carry out data manipulation (processing or moving data) and control the sequence of operations performed by the computer; the "brain" of the computer.
Crop	To eliminate unwanted portions of a picture.
Crop Marks	See Register Marks.
Cursor	A visible marker used to represent the current position on the display screen.
Daisywheel	An impact printer mechanism which is usually a 4" diameter metal or plastic wheel with molded characters on the outer perimeter which produces good quality printing.
Database	A collection of related information which is usually filed in a memory area where the data can be easily retrieved.
Desktop Publishing	The use of a personal computer to generate near-typeset-quality documents.
Dialog Box	Some commands, when accessed, require different options to be selected in order to complete the command. In order to make those various selections available within a command, the program displays a dialog box. When a command is listed in a menu followed by an ellipsis (...), a dialog box will appear when the command is selected.
Double Click	To press and hold the mouse button two times very rapidly.
Double-Sided Publication	A publication, that when printed, will be printed on both sides of the paper.
DPI	Dots Per Inch.
Drag	To press and hold the mouse button, and then move the mouse, dragging an object on the computer screen from one location to another.
Drop Capital	A large capital letter used at the beginning of some paragraphs.
DTP	Desktop Publishing.
EGA	Enhanced Graphics Adapter; the graphics card that controls an Enhanced Color Monitor with a resolution of 640 x 350 pixels.
Em	A space the width of the M character in the font.
En	A space the width of the N character in the font. An En is exactly one-half the width of an Em.
Fixed Disk	A hard disk; a sealed disk drive with greater capacity and speed than a floppy disk drive.

Term	*Definition*
Floppy Disk	An oxide-coated, flexible-plastic, magnetic recording medium; access time is slow and capacity is small; it is used to record information in the form of binary digits.
Flush Left	Aligning the text along the left margin, with the right margin of the text jagged.
Flush Right	Aligning the text along the right margin, with the left margin of the text jagged.
Font	A specific typeface including a size and style. For example, Swiss 12-point Italic or Dutch 10-point Bold.
Format	The command used to prepare a disk to accept data: The style of letters such as bold, italic, or underline.
Function Key	The special keys located on the side or top of a computer keyboard; these keys perform special functions or actions when used in different applications.
Greek	A computer function that converts lines of text into a series of unreadable lines. By doing so, the computer runs faster, rather than building each small line of text.
Gutter	The white space between columns of text.
Hacker	A person who is extremely knowledgeable about computers.
Hard Disk	A mechanical device on which a magnetic secondary-storage medium is mounted to make its data accessible to the computer; a drive contains all electrical and mechanical components necessary to read or write data on its medium (same as fixed disk or winchester disk).
Hardware	The physical elements included in a computer system.
Hyphenation	The breaking of a word at the end of a line of text at the word's syllables.
Icons	Pictures or graphical representations of actions or objects.
Image	A picture which is composed of individual dots created with a "paint" program or with a scanner.
Indent	The white space at the beginning of the paragraph, on the first line.
Interface	A device that allows the computer to work with the outside world; a shared boundary between two systems or two devices.
Italic	Slanted type often used to emphasize specific text.
Justified	Text where both the left and right margins are aligned.
K	A Kilobyte; generally used to describe the storage capacity of a computer's RAM memory or disk storage.
Kerning	The reduction of space between letters of a word.
Keyboard	The part of a computer which looks like a typewriter and allows communication between operator and computer.
Kilo Byte	1024 bytes (210); for most purposes "1000" bytes.
LAN	LOCAL AREA NETWORK; a communications system that interconnects computer equipment within a limited geographical area.

Term	Definition
Landscape	Horizontal or wide page orientation.
Laser Printer	A printer that uses technologies similar to photocopiers for printing; fast, quiet, high quality; high price.
Layout	The overall design of a page.
Leading	The amount of space between the lines of text.
Letterspacing	The amount of space between the letters of a word.
Lower Case	The use of small letters, such as g, s, m, and h.
Mainframe	The central control and processor of any large computer complex; the largest type of computer.
MDA	Monochrome Display Adapter; the card that controls a monochrome monitor (one color); usually cannot display graphs.
Megabyte	1024 Kilobytes; a million bytes; usually refers to the storage capacity of a hard disk drive.
Menu Bar	The area of the top of the computer screen where the various menus can be accessed.
Microcomputer	A complete computer system built around a microprocessor CPU; a desktop computer; a personal computer.
Modem	MOdulator/DEModulator; a device for changing serial binary numbers into a signal that can be transmitted over standard telephone lines, or the reverse; device that allows different computers to "talk" to each other.
Monitor	The TV-like set which contains the CRT (screen) for you to look at as you work at the keyboard.
Mouse	An input device that is used to move the cursor around the screen in order to carry out various operations.
MS-DOS	MicroSoft Disk Operating System.
Network	An intercommunicating group of computer systems and/or terminals.
Operating System	The system software that makes the computer system run; an organized collection of techniques and procedures to supervise and control the running of all other programs.
Orphan	A line of text left alone on the bottom of a page or a column.
Paragraph	A character, a word, a group of words, a sentence, or a group of sentences that end with a required carrier return. The required carrier return is placed in the text each time the Enter key is selected.
PC	A personal computer with an 8088 CPU.
PC AT	A personal computer with an 80286 CPU.
PC-DOS	IBM's personal computer disk operating system.
PC XT	A personal computer with an 8088 CPU and usually a hard disk.
Pica	A pica is approximately 1/6 of an inch. There are 12 points in a pica. The pica is a measurement used by printers.

Term	*Definition*
Plotter	An output device similar to a printer, but used mainly for printing graphic images by moving a pen around on the paper.
Point	A point is approximately 1/72 of an inch. The point is a measurement used by printers. There are 12 points in a pica.
Point	To move the mouse until the screen cursor is resting in a position where an item is to be selected.
Port	The connection point in the computer for peripherals, such as the mouse, monitor, and printer.
Portrait	Vertical or tall page orientation.
PostScript	A language used to describe how to print a page which consists of both text and pictures.
Pop-Up Menu	A menu that pops up when selected. These menus are found within a dialog box.
Printer	The hardware which prints the data on paper.
Program	A set of commands or steps that control the actions of the computer.
Programming	A predefined method for using and combining language and a set of instructions or symbols in the writing of a program.
Proportional Spacing	A font where the width of each letter is different. For example, the M is much wider than the i.
PS/2	IBM's Personal System/2 computers, which have replaced the PC line of personal computers.
Pull-Down Menu	A menu that drops down so commands can be accessed. The menu drops down when clicked on with the mouse.
RAM	Random Access Memory; a kind of internal memory whose locations can be accessed and the contents retrieved with the same access time for all locations; the computer memory where calculations and processing take place; data stored in RAM memory is lost when the power is turned off.
Register Marks	Alignment marks which are used by a printer when printing more than one color on a sheet of paper.
ROM	Read Only Memory; memory from which it is possible to read information but onto which data cannot be written; data stored in ROM memory remains when the power is turned off.
Rule	A line used as a divider between text or pictures.
Rulers	A measuring device located on the left and top of the computer screen work area.
Sans Serif	A typeface without serifs, such as Helvetica or Swiss.
Scanner	A device which converts a paper drawing or picture into a computer image.
Scroll Bars	The bars positioned along the right and bottom borders of the screen. Scroll Bars are used to move the portion of the page that is visible. By clicking or dragging the Scroll Bar with the mouse the page can be moved.

Term	Definition
Serif	The short lines at the end of the main strokes of letters. Some typefaces are called serif, such as Times or Dutch.
Software	The programs that cause the computer to perform specific functions.
Spreadsheet	A type of application software used mainly for analysis.
SQL	STRUCTURED QUERY LANGUAGE; an IBM relational database product and query/reporting language.
Style Sheet	A file that contains specific information used to control the format and appearance of a document. Information regarding the format of paragraphs, the page layout, and columns is some of the data stored within a style sheet.
Tag	The format that establishes the appearance of a paragraph.
Terminal	Any device for providing input and/or output to and/or from a computer.
Thin Space	A space half the size of an En space.
Title Bar	The title bar appears at the top of the screen and displays the current chapter file and current style sheet being used.
Type Style	One or more of the following: normal, italics, boldface, underlined, strikethru.
Typeface	A family of fonts where all letters, numbers, and symbols have a uniform appearance. Century Schoolbook is one example of a family of type.
Underlying Page	A special frame common to all pages within a Xerox Ventura Publisher chapter and a permanent part of the style sheet. The underlying page controls the overall appearance of the entire document.
Upper Case	Capital letters such as G, J, B, and M.
User	Someone who uses a computer.
User Friendly	An abused term which refers to software that is supposed to be easy to operate.
VGA	Video Graphics Array, the latest graphic technology being used in the PS/2 computer.
Widow	A line left alone at the top of a page or a column.
Width Table	A table that contains information about the fonts.
Winchester disk	A hard or fixed disk drive.
Word Processing	A type of software application which is used for the creation, changing, and storing of text.
Word Spacing	Adding spacing between words to fill a text line, making it look justified.
WYSIWYG	An acronym meaning What You See Is What You Get. WYSIWYG means the final copy generated from your printer will look like what appears on your computer screen.

Appendix B

TEXT ATTRIBUTE CODES

Xerox Ventura Publisher translates, displays and prints text attributes, such as boldface and underline, from each word processor it supports. For example, any text assigned Bold in WordPerfect 5.0 is automatically assigned Bold when imported into Xerox Ventura Publisher. Any text attributes added using Xerox Ventura Publisher's Text Editing mode are stored in the text file, and it is stored in the word processor's native file format.

Xerox Ventura Publisher can create a much wider range of text attributes than any word processor. Those attributes are also stored in the word processor text file, using the codes shown below.

For example, the beginning of medium italic text is set by inserting <MI> directly before the text to be italicized.

You can insert the text attribute code in your word processor. To do so, simply insert the code between the left and right angle brackets. For example, typing this text in your word processor:

> This is an example of <U>underlined<D> text.

would create text in Xerox Ventura Publisher that looked like this:

> This is an example of underlined text.

The text attribute can be set for any of the basic attributes, typeface, point size, kerning, offset, and color.

Basic Attributes

The basic text attribute codes and attributes are:

Code	*Attribute*
<B>	Bold weight type
<D>	Normal weight type
<I>	Italic type
<L>	Light weight type
<M>	Medium weight type
<O>	Overscore
<S>	Small Type

Code	Attribute
<U>	Underline
<X>	Strikethrough
< = >	Double underline
< ^ >	Superscript
<v>	Subscript

The attributes can be used alone or in combination. For example, <B> can be entered to begin bold, or <BIU> can be entered to begin bold italic underline text.

All attributes are terminated at the end of a paragraph, even if the Resume Normal code <D> is not found.

Also, all previous attributes are terminated any time new attributes are set. For example, consider this sentence:

The man jogged down the street.

To assign bold only to the word "man" type:

The <B>man<D> jogged down the street.

To assign bold only to the word "man" and underline to jogged, type:

The <B>man <U>jogged<D> down the street.

To assign bold to both man and jogged, and underline to the word jogged, type:

The <B>man <BU>jogged<D> down the street.

Of course, if you are using a supported word processor, simply enter the command in your word processor as desired, and Xerox Ventura Publisher will translate the word processor code automatically for you.

Typeface

To set the typeface, type <Fnnn> where nnn is the number of the typeface desired. The numbers and typefaces are:

Number	Typeface
1	Courier
2	Swiss (like Helvetica)
14	Dutch (like Times)
20	New Century Schoolbook
21	Palantino
22	Garamond
23	Bookman
24	Lubalin
25	Souvenir
26	Benguiat
27	Glypha
28	Friz Quadrata

Number	*Typeface*
29	Zapf Chancery
30	Trump Medieval
31	Melior
32	Galliard
33	New Baskerville
34	Goudy
35	Park Avenue
36	Bodoni
37	Bodoni Poster
38	Century Old Style
39	Cheltenham
50	Helvetica Narrow
51	Avant Garde
52	Optima
53	Korinna
54	Helvetica Light
55	Helvetica Black
56	Franklin Gothic
57	Franklin Gothic Heavy
58	Helvetica Condensed Light
59	Helvetica Condensed
60	Helvetica Condensed Black
100	American Typewriter
101	Machine
103	Prestige Elite
104	Orator
105	Letter Gothic
128	Symbol
129	Zapf Dingbats
130	Sonata
255	Reset to typeface for tag

Point Size

To set the point size, type <Pnnn> where nnn is the number of points. The maximum point size available is 254. <P255> resets the point size to that specified in the paragraph tag.

Kerning

To begin the kerning value, type <Knnn> where nnn is any value between – 127 and + 127. Replace n with the amount of left horizontal shift, measured in 1/300th of an inch. The value – 001 resets the kerning to zero.

Use <B%n> to Kern/Track the text, and replace n with the number of ems to add (positive values of n) or subtract (negative number of n) between each character in the selected text. Place <D%0> to mark the end of the text which should be kerned or tracked.

Base Line Jump

To make the base line jump up or down, type <Jnnn> where nnn is the number of points to shift the base line. The n may range from 1 to 256. Use <J0> to reset the Base Line Jump to zero.

Color

To set the color of text, type <Cnnn> where nnn is the number of the color to use. The numbers and colors are:

Number	*Color*
0	White
1	Black
2	Red
3	Green
4	Blue
5	Cyan
6	Yellow
7	Magenta

Use <C255> to reset the color to the color assigned in the tag.

Other Inserted Text

There are some other text codes that can be inserted. They are:

Code	*Text Attribute*
<$B0>	Box (Hollow)
<$B1>	Box (Filled)
<->	Discretionary Hyphen
<_>	Em Space
<~>	En Space
<+>	Figure Space
<R>	Line Break
<N>	Non-Breaking Space
<$R[P#]>	Page Number
<¦>	Thin Space

Appendix C

TAGGING TEXT WITH A WORD PROCESSOR

Xerox Ventura Publisher's Text Editing function was not designed for extensive word processing. It should be used for "fine-tuning" text, making final editions, deletions, and other minor changes.

When you must enter large amounts of text, it is always better to use a regular word processor. You can then import the text that was prepared in the word processor into Xerox Ventura Publisher for formatting.

In the same manner, it is normally better to use a word processor to tag the text, rather than using Xerox Ventura Publisher's Paragraph Tagging function. This is because tagging paragraphs with a word processor is faster than tagging with Ventura.

When a paragraph is tagged with a word processor, the same information is typed that Xerox Ventura Publisher automatically adds to a text file when text is tagged with Xerox Ventura Publisher.

For example, you have two headline tags in your style sheet called H1 and H2 for tagging level one and two headlines. You are working with the following text:

> Desktop Publishing Training
>
> This document contains the four-part plan designed to train our employees in desktop publishing techniques.
>
> Classroom Training
>
> This section contains our plan to establish formal classroom training.
>
> Training Consultant
>
> This section contains our recommendation to use the services of a training consultant to train our employees in the use of Xerox Ventura Publisher.

If you use Xerox Ventura Publisher's paragraph tagging function to format the first headline as a level one headline, Xerox Ventura Publisher adds the paragraph tag's name to the word processing file:

> @H1 =

so the text file appears:

> @H1 = Desktop Publishing Training

Xerox Ventura Publisher adds this text to the word processing file if you are using Paragraph Tagging to format the next two headlines as level two headlines.

> @H1 = Desktop Publishing Training
> This document contains the four-part plan designed to train our employees in desktop publishing techniques.
> @H2 = Classroom Training
> This section contains our plan to establish formal classroom training.
> @H2 = Training Consultant
> This section contains our recommendation to use the services of a training consultant to train our employees in the use of Xerox Ventura Publisher.

You can tag the paragraphs if you simply type the paragraph tag text with your word processor. The tag text must begin in the very left margin.

A paragraph tag always begins with @ and ends with a space, and the = sign, and a space. For example, @Bullet = is a proper tag name for Xerox Ventura Publisher.

NOTE

The @ *must* always be the first character in the line at the beginning of a tagged paragraph.

Typically, it is best if you keep tag names short. This reduces the amount of paragraph tag text that clutters the computer screen as you edit your text file with a word processor. For example, suppose that in the previous example you use the words HEADLINE 1 and HEADLINE 2 for the level one and two headline tags. Your file would now look like this:

> @HEADLINE 1 = Desktop Publishing Training
> This document contains the four-part plan designed to train our employees in desktop publishing techniques.
> @HEADLINE 2 = Classroom Training
> This section contains our plan to establish formal classroom training.
> @HEADLINE 2 = Training Consultant
> This section contains our recommendation to use the services of a training consultant to train our employees in the use of Xerox Ventura Publisher.

The clutter becomes even more obvious and unworkable if your document is heavily tagged with long-named tags. For example, suppose each of the paragraphs under the headline is tagged with SUMMARY 1, for the section summary. The text file now looks like this:

> @HEADLINE 1 = Desktop Publishing Training
> @SUMMARY 1 = This document contains the four-part plan designed to train our employees in desktop publishing techniques.
> @HEADLINE 2 = Classroom Training
> @SUMMARY 1 = This section contains our plan to establish formal classroom training.
> @HEADLINE 2 = Training Consultant
> @SUMMARY 1 = This section contains our recommendation to use the services of a training consultant to train our employees in the use of Xerox Ventura Publisher.

To keep your paragraph tags short, here are some suggested tag names and functions:

Name	Function	Type in Text File
BY	Byline	@BY =
BL	Bullet List Item	@BL =
DC	Drop Capital	@DC =
C#	Chapter Number	@C# =
HO	Chapter Headline	@HO =
H1	Level One Headline	@H1 =
H2	Level Two Headline	@H2 =
H3	Level Three Headline	@H3 =
H4	Level Four Headline	@H4 =
IH	Hanging Indent	@IH =
IN	Normal Indent	@IN =
QL	Long Quote	@QL =
QS	Short Quote	@QS =
SH	Subheadline	@SH =
SS	Section Summary	@SS =
T1	Table Column One*	@T1 =
T2	Table Column Two*	@T2 =
T3	Table Column Three*	@T3 =

* A table where tag items for each column with a different paragraph tag uses the principles of vertical tabs.

Any paragraph not tagged will be assigned the attributes of Body Text within the current style sheet. Accordingly, you do not need to enter the paragraph tag @BODY TEXT = . Xerox Ventura Publisher will automatically assign untagged paragraphs to the body text tag.

If you have three paragraphs in a row with the same tag name, and the text is not body text, you *must* place the tag name on each paragraph. Paragraph tag names do not carry over to the next paragraph. Xerox Ventura Publisher recognizes the end of a paragraph by the carriage return.

You must spell the tag name exactly as it appears in the style sheet. For example, Bullet 1 and Bullet1 are two *different* paragraph tags to Xerox Ventura Publisher. If Xerox Ventura Publisher cannot match a paragraph tag in your text with one in the current style sheet, it will apply the Body Text tag attributes to the paragraph with the unrecognized paragraph tag and add the new name to the Assignment List.

One tip to accurately placing paragraph tags is to use the Macro feature of your word processor. For example, you could create a macro that automatically types @Headline 1 = each time you need it. Not only will the macro save you the time of typing in the paragraph tag, but it will eliminate a typo or spelling error.

THE BLANK LINES PROBLEM

As you work with a word processor, you naturally press Enter twice at the end of a paragraph. Once, to mark the end of the paragraph, and the second time to create a blank line. The blank line between paragraphs makes the finished document more readable. However, Xerox Ventura

Publisher interprets these blank lines—placed between the paragraphs—as paragraphs to be formatted. This creates a real problem when you begin formatting your document in Xerox Ventura Publisher.

Consider this example:

You create a headline tag that forces Xerox Ventura Publisher to always position the headline and first paragraph following the headline on the same page. This prevents a headline from appearing by itself at the bottom of a page.

If the headline appears near the bottom of the page when the document is formatted, the first paragraph of the text actually appears at the top of the next page. This is because Xerox Ventura Publisher interprets the blank line between the paragraphs, and not the subsequent text, as the next paragraph. Xerox Ventura Publisher is actually keeping the next paragraph (the blank line) with the headline as requested. But the result is not expected or desired.

In addition, if paragraph spacing is added using Xerox Ventura Publisher's Spacing command, there may be too much space between paragraphs because of the blank lines.

One approach to this problem is to use Xerox Ventura Publisher's blank line filter. To use the filter, type this as the very first line of your text file:

@PARAFILTER ON =

This filter causes Xerox Ventura Publisher to ignore blank lines when a text file is loaded. However, the filter also removes blank lines if you ever save the text file from within Xerox Ventura Publisher.

The removal of the blank lines, although needed for proper formatting within Xerox Ventura Publisher, makes your editing task more difficult.

As recommended in the beginning of this book, you should be an experienced word processor user. You should be able to use the Search and Replace commands of your word processor without difficulty. You can use Search and Replace to search for a <Carriage Return><Carriage Return> and replace it with a <Carriage Return>. Also, to make editing easier, you can reverse the process by searching for a <Carriage Return> and replacing it with a <Carriage Return><Carriage Return>.

ENTERING OTHER CONTROLS

You can also enter the codes Xerox Ventura Publisher uses for anchors, footnotes, hidden text (comments), and index entries with your word processor.

Anchors

To enter anchor information, type:

<$&anchorname>	to place the frame on the same page as the anchor.
<$&anchorname[v]>	to place the frame below the anchor position.
<$&anchorname[^]>	to place the frame above the anchor position.

Footnotes

To enter footnote information, type <$FContent of the footnote>.

Hidden Text

To enter hidden text, type <$!Content of hidden text>.

Hidden text is used for comment lines. You never see the hidden text on the screen or in the final Xerox Ventura Publisher printout. You see it only when you open the text file with your word processor.

Index Entries

To enter index entries, type:

<$IPrimary Entry[Sort Key];Secondary Entry[Sort Key]>	for a regular index entry.
<$SPrimary Entry[Sort Key];See Reference[Sort Key]>	for a "See Also" entry.

Appendix D

COMMAND KEYS

Many of the commands available within Xerox Ventura Publisher can be accessed by using keyboard shortcuts. Most of the commands are accessed by pressing and holding the Ctrl key and then pressing another key. These are designated in this book as Ctrl-? where ? is the name of the key to press in combination with the Ctrl key.

For some Xerox Ventura Publisher keyboard commands, you must press two keys in combination with the Ctrl key. For example, to create the copyright symbol (C), you must press and hold the Ctrl key, the Shift key, and then letter C.

Finally, sometimes you need only press a single key on the keyboard to execute a command. For example, press End to go to the last page in your Xerox Ventura Publisher document.

The keyboard commands and their keys in alphabetical order by command name are:

Command	*Key*	*Command*	*Key*
Add frame, tag, or set font	Ctrl-2	Go to Last Page	End
Assign function keys	Ctrl-K	Go to Next Page	PgDn
Bring to Front	Ctrl-A	Go to previous Page	PgUp
Cancel (from dialog box)	Ctrl-X	Graphic Mode	Ctrl-P
Copy	Shift-Del	Insert Special Item	Ctrl-C
Copyright	Ctrl-Shift-C	Line Attributes	Ctrl-L
Cut	Del	Non-breaking space	Ctrl-Spacebar
Delete < – of the cursor	Backspace	Normal View	Ctrl-N
Delete – > of the cursor	Del	Paragraph Mode	Ctrl-I
Delete Selection line text	Esc	Paste	Ins
Discretionary Hyphen	Ctrl--	Recall Last Dialog Box (or Cancel)	Ctrl-X
Double Quote, closed	Ctrl-Shift-]	Redraw screen	Esc
Double Quote, open	Ctrl-Shift-[	Reduced View	Ctrl-R
Edit Special Item	Ctrl-D	Registered trademark	Ctrl-Shift-R
EM dash	Ctrl-]	Renumber Chapter	Ctrl-B
EM space	Ctrl-Shift-M	Save	Ctrl-S
EN dash	Ctrl-[	Select All (graphics)	Ctrl-Q
EN space	Ctrl-Shift-N	Send to Back	Ctrl-Z
Enlarged View	Ctrl-E	Show/Hide Side Bar	Ctrl-W
Figure Space	Ctrl-Shift-F	Show/Hide Tabs & Returns	Ctrl-T
Fill Attributes	Ctrl-F	Text Mode	Ctrl-O
Frame Mode	Ctrl-U	Thin space	Ctrl-Shift-T
Go to Page	Ctrl-G	Trademark	Ctrl-Shift-2
Go to First Page	Home	Update Tag List	Ctrl-K

Appendix E
CHARACTER SETS

This appendix contains the characters and their decimal equivalents that can be displayed and printed with Xerox Ventura Publisher. There are three character sets—one for regular letters (Alpha), one for mathematical and scientific characters (SYMBOL), and one for special typographic characters (dingbats). The regular letters are called International and contain many special characters needed for most Romance languages, including English, Spanish, French, Italian, and German.

To use one of these special characters:

1. Locate the desired character and determine the decimal equivalent from the chart.
2. Press and hold Alt and enter the decimal equivalent using the keyboard numeric keypad. Do not use the numbers above the letters.
3. After the number has been entered, release Alt. The character appears on the screen.
4. Select text, then select Set Font in the Side Bar and set the font to Symbol or Dingbat.

The type of printer, as well as available fonts, determines the final result.

You can also insert the special character into your text with the word processor. To do so, type the decimal equivalent of the special character between the left and right angle brackets. For example, suppose you wanted to display the copyright symbol. Simply type <189>. When Xerox Ventura Publisher formats the text, the copyright symbol will be placed in the document.

Decimal	International	Symbol	Dingbat
32	space	space	space
33	!	!	✁
34	"	∀	✂
35	#	#	✃
36	$	∃	✄
37	%	%	☎
38	&	&	✆
39	'	∍	✇
40	(	(	✈
41	)	)	✉
42	*	∗	☛
43	+	+	☞
44	,	,	✌
45	-	−	✍
46	.	.	✎
47	/	/	✏
48	0	0	✐
49	1	1	✑
50	2	2	✒
51	3	3	✓
52	4	4	✔
53	5	5	✕
54	6	6	✖
55	7	7	✗
56	8	8	✘
57	9	9	✙
58	:	:	✚
59	;	;	✛
60	<	<	✜
61	=	=	✝
62	>	>	✞
63	?	?	✟
64	@	≅	✠
65	A	Α	✡
66	B	Β	✢
67	C	Χ	✣
68	D	Δ	✤
69	E	Ε	✥
70	F	Φ	✦
71	G	Γ	✧
72	H	Η	★
73	I	Ι	✩
74	J	ϑ	✪
75	K	Κ	✫
76	L	Λ	✬
77	M	Μ	✭
78	N	Ν	✮
79	O	Ο	✯

Decimal	International	Symbol	Dingbat
80	P	Π	✰
81	Q	Θ	✱
82	R	Ρ	✲
83	S	Σ	✳
84	T	Τ	✴
85	U	Υ	✵
86	V	ς	✶
87	W	Ω	✷
88	X	Ξ	✸
89	Y	Ψ	✹
90	Z	Ζ	✺
91	[	[	✻
92	\	∴	✼
93	]	]	✽
94	^	⊥	✾
95	_	_	✿
96	‘	‾	❀
97	a	α	❁
98	b	β	❂
99	c	χ	❃
100	d	δ	❄
101	e	ε	❅
102	f	ϕ	❆
103	g	γ	❇
104	h	η	❈
105	i	ι	❉
106	j	φ	❊
107	k	κ	❋
108	l	λ	●
109	m	μ	❍
110	n	ν	■
111	o	ο	❏
112	p	π	❐
113	q	θ	❑
114	r	ρ	❒
115	s	σ	▲
116	t	τ	▼
117	u	υ	◆
118	v	ϖ	❖
119	w	ω	◗
120	x	ξ	❘
121	y	ψ	❙
122	z	ζ	❚
123	{	{	❛
124	|	|	❜
125	}	}	❝
126	~	~	❞
127			

Decimal	International	Symbol	Dingbat
128	Ç		
129	ü	ϒ	❡
130	é	′	❢
131	â	≤	❣
132	ä	⁄	❤
133	à	∞	❥
134	å	ƒ	❦
135	ç	♣	❧
136	ê	♦	♣
137	ë	♥	♦
138	è	♠	♥
139	ï	↔	♠
140	î	←	①
141	ì	↑	②
142	Ä	→	③
143	Å	↓	④
144	É	°	⑤
145	æ	±	⑥
146	Æ	″	⑦
147	ô	≥	⑧
148	ö	×	⑨
149	ò	∝	⑩
150	û	∂	❶
151	ù	•	❷

Decimal	International	Symbol	Dingbat
152	ÿ	÷	❸
153	Ö	≠	❹
154	Ü	≡	❺
155	¢	≈	❻
156	£	…	❼
157	¥	|	❽
158	¤	—	❾
159	ƒ	↵	❿
160	á	ℵ	➀
161	í	ℑ	➁
162	ó	ℜ	➂
163	ú	℘	➃
164	ñ	⊗	➄
165	Ñ	⊕	➅
166	ª	∅	➆
167	º	∩	➇
168	¿	∪	➈
169	“	⊃	➉
170	”	⊇	➊
171	‹	⊄	➋
172	›	⊂	➌
173	¡	⊆	➍
174	«	∈	➎
175	»	∉	➏

Decimal	International	Symbol	Dingbat
176	ã	∠	❼
177	õ	∇	❽
178	Ø	®	❾
179	ø	©	❿
180	œ	™	➔
181	Œ	Π	→
182	À	√	↔
183	Ã	·	↕
184	Õ	¬	➘
185	§	∧	➙
186	‡	∨	➚
187	†	⇔	➛
188	¶	⇐	➜
189	©	⇑	➝
190	®	⇒	➞
191	™	⇓	➟
192	. „	◊	➠
193	…	〈	➡
194	‰	®	➢
195	•	©	➣
196	–	™	➤
197	—	∑	➥
198	°	⎛	➦
199	Á	⎜	➧

Decimal	International	Symbol	Dingbat
200	Â	⎝	➨
201	È	⎡	➩
202	Ê	⎢	➪
203	Ë	⎣	➫
204	Ì	⎧	➬
205	Í	⎨	➭
206	Î	⎩	➮
207	Ï	⎪	➯
208	Ò		
209	Ó	〉	➱
210	Ô	∫	➲
211	Š	⌠	➳
212	š	⎮	➴
213	Ù	⌡	➵
214	Ú	⎞	➶
215	Û	⎟	➷
216	Ÿ	⎠	➸
217	ß	⎤	➹
218	Ž	⎥	➺
219	ž	⎦	➻
220	/	⎫	➼
221		⎬	➽
222		⎭	➾
223			

Appendix F
VENTURA EXERCISES

1. About This Book
   a. What is a module?
   b. What hardware is required to use Xerox Ventura Publisher?
   c. Describe the contents of the modules.
   d. Is a mouse required to use Xerox Ventura Publisher?
   e. What other programs should you be proficient with before you begin learning Xerox Ventura Publisher?

2. Xerox Ventura Publisher Overview
   a. What is desktop publishing?
   b. What is a "camera-ready" document?
   c. How is Xerox Ventura Publisher equal to a graphic designer's layout table?
   d. What type of documents can be produced with Xerox Ventura Publisher?
   e. Describe how the author views learning Xerox Ventura Publisher.
   f. What is WYSIWYG?
   g. Is there such a thing as true WYSIWYG?
   h. Describe at least one laser printer limitation.
   i. How do you install Xerox Ventura Publisher?
   j. How do you start Xerox Ventura Publisher?
   k. List ten of the thirteen parts of the Xerox Ventura Publisher screen.
   l. Can Xerox Ventura Publisher be operated under Windows?
   m. What is the title bar?
   n. Describe the scroll bars, how they can be used, and where they are located.
   o. What is a Side Bar?
   p. Name the five typical mouse operations.
   q. How many different mouse cursor shapes are there in Xerox Ventura Publisher?
   r. What is a frame?
   s. What is a paragraph tag?
   t. What are Xerox Ventura Publisher pull-down menus?
   u. What is a dialog box?
   v. Describe a pica and a point.
   w. What is a style sheet?
   x. What are Xerox Ventura Publisher's modes of operation?

3. Sample Session
   a. What is the purpose of the Sample Session?
   b. Why should Xerox Ventura Publisher not be used as a word processor?
   c. Why must a specific extension be used as a filename extension on a text file?
   d. What is the VP.INF file?
   e. Why was VP.INF removed?
   f. Describe the procedure to load a text file.
   g. Describe the procedure to select Text Attributes.
   h. Describe the procedure to alter the style sheet.
   i. Describe the procedure to use another style sheet.
   j. Describe the two methods of changing views.
   k. Describe how to insert a new page in a Xerox Ventura Publisher document.
   l. How is a Xerox Ventura Publisher chapter saved?
   m. Describe how to quit Xerox Ventura Publisher.
4. Abandon
   a. What is the Abandon command?
   b. Where is the Abandon command located?
   c. When would you use the Abandon command?
5. Add/Remove Fonts
   a. What is a width table?
   b. When is the Add/Remove fonts command used?
6. Alignment
   a. Name the four types of alignment available in Xerox Ventura Publisher.
   b. What is a relative indent?
   c. What is an outdent?
   d. What is an indent?
   e. Where is the Alignment command located in Xerox Ventura Publisher?
   f. What effect can rivers of white space have on your documents?
7. Anchors & Captions
   a. What is the difference between an anchor and a caption?
   b. Can an anchor and caption be assigned to the underlying page frame?
   c. What is the Table Counter and the Figure Counter?
   d. How is the Anchors & Captions command accessed?
   e. Describe the procedure for setting an anchor.
   f. Describe the procedure for creating a caption.
8. Attributes Overrides
   a. What is the purpose of having an Attributes Overrides command?
   b. List five attributes that can be added with the Attributes Overrides command.
   c. Describe the procedure for changing text attributes by using the Attributes Overrides command.

9. Auto-Numbering
    a. What is auto-numbering?
    b. Can auto-numbering be assigned to text located in frames?
    c. List five different numbering schemes Xerox Ventura Publisher can create.
    d. What paragraph tag is created for auto-numbered text?
    e. Describe the procedure for changing the text attributes of auto-numbered text.
    f. Describe the procedure for setting auto-numbering in a Xerox Ventura Publisher chapter.
    g. How is the Renumber command related to the auto-numbering command?
    h. Where is the Auto-Numbering command located?

10. Box Character
    a. What is a box character?
    b. Why is the box character available in Xerox Ventura Publisher?
    c. Where is the box character command located?
    d. What is the keyboard shortcut to access the command to create a box character?

11. Breaks
    a. What is a break?
    b. What is the difference between a line break and a paragraph break?
    c. Where is the break command located?
    d. When would column breaks be used?
    e. What is Allow Within as it pertains to Breaks?
    f. Describe why and how breaks are used to force a paragraph to the top of a new page.

12. Bring to Front, Send To Back
    a. What can be sent to the back or brought to the front in Xerox Ventura Publisher?
    b. What is the keyboard shortcut to Send to Back?
    c. What is the keyboard shortcut to Bring to Front?

13. Chapter Menu
    a. List 8 of the 12 commands available in the Chapter menu.
    b. What was the Chapter menu called in earlier versions of Xerox Ventura Publisher?
    c. Where are the Page Layout, Auto-Numbering, Chapter Typography, and Footnote settings stored?

14. Chapter Typography
    a. What is chapter typography?
    b. What is a widow?
    c. What is an orphan?
    d. What is the difference between Chapter Typography and Frame Typography?
    e. What is a baseline?
    f. What is column balance?

15. Cut/Copy/Paste
    a. What are the Cut/Copy/Paste commands used for in Xerox Ventura Publisher?
    b. What is the function of Cut?
    c. What is the function of Paste?
    d. What is a clipboard?
    e. How many clipboards are used by Xerox Ventura Publisher?
    f. How is the Shift key used with Cut/Copy/Paste?
    g. What are the keyboard shortcuts used to access Cut/Copy/Paste?
    h. Describe how Copy/Paste can save you time when working with Xerox Ventura Publisher.

16. Define Colors
    a. Name the three elements that color can be assigned to in Xerox Ventura Publisher.
    b. What determines the color of your final printed page?
    c. What mode must Xerox Ventura Publisher be in before Define Colors can be accessed?

17. Desk Menu
    a. What important information is located within the Desk menu?
    b. Describe how to locate the hidden diagnostic information in the Desk menu.

18. DOS File Operations
    a. What is a File Spec?
    b. Describe how to delete a directory from within Xerox Ventura Publisher.
    c. Explain how a directory can be created with the DOS File Ops.

19. Edit Menu
    a. Describe the Edit menu and how it changes options when Xerox Ventura Publisher is in different modes.
    b. What options are available in Edit menu when Xerox Ventura Publisher is in Paragraph mode?

20. File Menu
    a. List eight of the eleven commands available in the File menu.
    b. Categorize the main functions of the commands available in the File menu.

21. File Type/Rename
    a. What is the File Type/Rename command?
    b. Describe the procedure for using this command.

22. Fill Attributes
    a. What is fill?
    b. What is Fill Attributes?
    c. What is the keyboard shortcut used to access the Fill Attributes dialog box?
    d. Where is the Fill Attributes command located?
    e. What is a transparent graphic?

23. Font
    a. Define font.
    b. Where is the Font command located?
    c. What can be selected in the Font dialog box?
    d. What is a strike-thru?

24. Footnotes
    a. What is a footnote?
    b. What is a number template?
    c. Name the tags Xerox Ventura Publisher creates for use with footnotes.
    d. Where is the footnote information stored?
    e. Where is the Footnote command located?

25. Frame Background
    a. Define Frame Background.
    b. What two attributes can be selected in the Frame Background dialog box?
    c. Explain what a screen is.

26. Frame Menu
    a. List 8 of the 11 commands available in the Frame menu.
    b. What mode must Xerox Ventura Publisher be in before the commands in the Frame menu are available for selection?

27. Frame Settings
    a. What is the Frame Setting command?
    b. How many files can be placed within a frame?
    c. Describe the underlying page frame.
    d. What shape is a Xerox Ventura Publisher frame?
    e. Describe the differences and similarities between a frame and the underlying page frame.
    f. Once placed, can a frame be moved?
    g. Once placed, can a frame be resized?
    h. Can text flow from one frame to another?
    i. Can a frame be dragged from one page to another?
    j. How can a frame add white space to your documents?

28. Frame Typography
    a. What is Frame Typography?
    b. Define Move Down to 1st Baseline By.
    c. When is the Frame Typography command used?

29. Go To Page
    a. What is the Go To Page command?
    b. Name the two ways available to access the Go To Page command.
    c. List the four keyboard shortcuts available to help move between pages.
    d. How do you stop the execution of a Go To Page command?

30. Graphic Menu
    a. List five of the seven commands available in the Graphic menu.
    b. What mode must Xerox Ventura Publisher be in before the various commands in the Graphic menu can be accessed?

31. Grid Settings
    a. What is a grid?
    b. Where is the Grid Settings command located?
    c. What is Grid Snap?
    d. What is Vertical Spacing in a grid?

32. Headers & Footers
    a. What is a header?
    b. Name the three parts of each header and footer in a Xerox Ventura Publisher document.
    c. Describe the procedure for inserting a page number in a footer on both left and right pages.
    d. Can Header information be copied to a Footer?
    e. Explain how the text attributes can be added to a Footer.

33. Image Settings
    a. What is an Image Setting?
    b. Define Halftone.
    c. What is a screen angle?
    d. Explain the term Lines Per Inch.
    e. What is TIFF?
    f. Define gray scale image.

34. Insert Cross Reference
    a. What is a Cross Reference?
    b. Where is the Cross Reference option located?
    c. Describe the procedure to insert a Cross Reference.

35. Insert/Edit Anchor
    a. What is a frame anchor?
    b. Describe the procedure to insert a frame anchor.
    c. What is the advantage of using frame anchors?
    d. How is the Insert/Edit Anchor option used?

36. Insert/Edit Index
    a. What is an index?
    b. Describe the use of the Insert/Edit Index command.
    c. What is a two-level index?
    d. Why should the index information be placed at the end of a paragraph?

37. Insert/Edit Special Item
    a. What is a special item?
    b. What mode must Xerox Ventura Publisher be in to use the Insert/Edit Special Item command?
    c. What is the keyboard shortcut to access the Insert/Edit Special Item command?

38. Insert Fraction
    a. What advantage does the option Insert Fraction provide you?
    b. Name the two types of fractions that can be created in Xerox Ventura Publisher.
    c. Describe the procedure to create a fraction.

39. Insert/Remove Page
    a. Describe the procedure to remove a page.
    b. Where is the Insert/Remove Page command located?

40. Line Attributes
    a. Define the term Line Attributes.
    b. What is the keyboard shortcut to access the Line Attributes command?
    c. Explain Defaults in the Line Attributes dialog box.
    d. Describe the procedure to assign color to a previously created line.

41. Load Different Style
    a. Explain when the Load Different Style command is used.
    b. Where is the Load Different Style command located?

42. Load Text/Picture
    a. Describe the purpose and use of the Load Text/Picture command.
    b. What is the Assignment List?
    c. Name the three general types of files that are loaded with this command.
    d. What should you do with a text file before you use the Load Text/Picture command?

43. Margins & Columns
    a. What is the Margins & Columns command?
    b. What is the maximum number of columns permitted in a frame or column?
    c. Where is the Margins & Columns command located?
    d. What is the difference between Calculated Width and Actual Frame Width?

44. Multi-Chapter
    a. What is the Multi-Chapter feature of Xerox Ventura Publisher?
    b. What is a PUB file?
    c. Where is the Multi-Chapter located?
    d. Describe the procedure to make an index in a Multi-Chapter.
    e. Describe how to copy a chapter with the Multi-Chapter command.

45. New
    a. Where is the New command located?
    b. Describe when New is used.

46. Open Chapter
    a. What is a chapter?
    b. Describe the procedure to open a chapter in Xerox Ventura Publisher.
    c. What is the filename extension that Xerox Ventura Publisher recognizes as a chapter?
    d. Where is the Open Chapter command located?

47. Options Menu
   a. List 9 of the 13 commands available in the Options menu.
   b. How are the commands available within the Options menu different from commands in other Xerox Ventura Publisher menus?

48. Page Size & Layout
   a. Describe the purpose of this command.
   b. What is the difference between landscape and portrait page orientation?
   c. Where is the Page Size & Layout command located?

49. Paragraph Menu
   a. List 9 of the 13 commands available in the Paragraph menu.
   b. What mode must Xerox Ventura Publisher be in before the commands in the Paragraph menu can be accessed?

50. Paragraph Tagging
   a. What is the purpose of tagging paragraphs?
   b. What is a tag?
   c. Where are paragraph tags saved?
   d. Can the Body Text tag be deleted?
   e. Describe the procedure to assigning text attributes to a paragraph tag.

51. Paragraph Typography
   a. What is Paragraph Typography?
   b. How does Paragraph Typography differ from Frame Typography and Chapter Typography?
   c. List five options available in the Paragraph Typography dialog box.
   d. What is automatic kerning?
   e. Define Letter Spacing and how and why it is used.
   f. What is tracking?
   g. What is an em?
   h. Define Grow Inter-Line to Fit.

52. Quit
   a. Describe the purpose of the Quit command.
   b. Where is Quit located?
   c. What effect does Quit have on the VP.INF file?

53. Re-Anchor Frames
   a. What does the Re-Anchor Frames command do when executed?
   b. How is an anchor created?
   c. Why should each page be checked after executing the Re-Anchor Frames command?

54. Remove Text/File
   a. Explain the use of the Remove Text/File command.
   b. Where is the Remove Text/File command located?
   c. When a file is removed, is it deleted from the disk?
   d. Explain why an unused file should be removed from the Assignment List.

55. Renumber Chapter
    a. Define the purpose of the Renumber Chapter command.
    b. Where is the Renumber Chapter command located?

56. Repeating Frame
    a. What is a repeating frame?
    b. Explain why a repeating frame is used.
    c. Describe the procedure for assigning captions to a repeating frame.
    d. Where is the repeating frame command located?
    e. Describe the procedure for creating a repeating frame.

57. Ruling Line Above, Line Below, Box Around
    a. What do the Ruling Line Above, Ruling Line Below, and Box Around commands do?
    b. What is the maximum amount of ruling lines available in these commands?
    c. What is the purpose of the display area in the Ruling Line dialog box?
    d. Describe the procedure to change the ruling lines to dashes.

58. Save
    a. What is the Save command?
    b. What is the keyboard shortcut to access the Save command?
    c. Where is the Save command located?
    d. What does Xerox Ventura Publisher do when the Save command is executed?

59. Save As
    a. What is the Save As command?
    b. What does Xerox Ventura Publisher do when the Save As command is executed?
    c. Where is the Save As command located?

60. Save As New Style
    a. Describe the purpose of the Save As New Style command.
    b. Why should a changed or modified style sheet be saved under a new name?
    c. What is the filename extension Xerox Ventura Publisher uses to identify a style sheet?
    d. Where is the Save As New Style command located?

61. Select All
    a. What is the Select All command, and how is it used?
    b. What is the keyboard shortcut to Select All?
    c. What mode must Xerox Ventura Publisher be in before Select All can be accessed?

62. Set Preferences
    a. What is Set Preferences command?
    b. What is greeking?
    c. How can Xerox Ventura Publisher make backup copies of your files?
    d. Describe the procedure to adjust the double click speed.
    e. What is on-screen kerning?
    f. What is a generated tag?

63. Set Printer Info
    a. What three things does the Set Printer Info command select?
    b. What is a screen font?
    c. Which are more precise: printer or screen fonts?
    d. What is a width table?
    e. How is the printing to disk option used?

64. Set Ruler
    a. What is the Set Ruler command?
    b. Which menu contains the Set Ruler command?
    c. What is a pica?
    d. What is a point?
    e. How many points are in an inch?
    f. How many picas are in an inch?
    g. How many points are in a pica?
    h. What is the zero point?
    i. How is the zero point moved?

65. Show/Hide Side Bar, Rulers, Column Guides, All Pictures, Tab & Returns, Loose Lines
    a. What is the Show/Hide Rulers command?
    b. What is the Show/Hide Side Bar command?
    c. What is the Show/Hide Column Guides command?
    d. What is the Show/Hide Loose Lines command?
    e. What is the Show/Hide All Pictures command?
    f. Does Xerox Ventura Publisher run faster or slower when the pictures are shown?
    g. What is a Side Bar?
    h. What is the keyboard shortcut to Hide/Show the Side Bar?

66. Sizing & Scaling
    a. What does the Sizing & Scaling command do?
    b. Which mode must Xerox Ventura Publisher be in to access the Sizing & Scaling mode?
    c. What is vertical padding?
    d. How can the mouse be used to scale a picture?
    e. What are the settings to make sure a picture prints exactly as scanned?
    f. How can the Sizing & Scaling command be used to exactly position a frame on a page?

67. Spacing
    a. What is leading?
    b. What is a temporary margin?
    c. What mode must Xerox Ventura Publisher be in to access Spacing?
    d. What is an Inter-Line?
    e. Define how and when the In From Right and In From Left options should be used.
    f. What happens when a paragraph has been over-leaded?
    g. What happens when a paragraph has been under-leaded?

68. Special Effects
    a. What two special effects are available in Xerox Ventura Publisher?
    b. What mode must Xerox Ventura Publisher be in before Special Effects can be accessed?

69. Tab Settings
    a. What is the maximum amount of tabs that can be set in Xerox Ventura Publisher?
    b. What must be at the end of a line of tabs?
    c. What is a leader tab?
    d. Name the four types of tabs available in Xerox Ventura Publisher.
    e. Why is justification not used for text lines with tab settings?
    f. Define leader spacing.

70. Text Editing
    a. What operations can be completed when in Text Editing mode?
    b. What is Subscript?
    c. Describe the procedure for creating a block of text.
    d. What is the keyboard shortcut to access Text Editing mode?
    e. What does Normal do when selected in the Side Bar?

71. To Print
    a. List five options available in the To Print dialog box.
    b. Define collated copies.
    c. What are crop marks?
    d. Describe Spot Color Overlays.
    e. Define Shrink & Overlap.
    f. Describe the procedure for printing only page 7 of a 20 page chapter.

72. Turn Column/Line Snap On/Off
    a. Define Column Snap.
    b. Define Line Snap.
    c. Where are the Column and Line Snap commands located?
    d. How does the grid affect Column and Line Snap?

73. Turn Header/Footer On/Off
    a. What is a header?
    b. What is a footer?
    c. What does the Turn Header Off command do?
    d. What does the Turn Footer On command do?
    e. Where are the Turn Header/Footer On/Off commands located?

74. Update Counters
    a. What is the primary purpose of this command?
    b. List six different number formats available.
    c. Explain Update Method.

75. Update Tag List
    a. List four of the five tools available in the Update Tag List dialog box.
    b. Why are function keys assigned to tags?
    c. Describe the procedure to remove a tag.

76. Vertical Rules
    a. What is a vertical rule?
    b. Describe the procedure for setting a vertical rule in Xerox Ventura Publisher.
    c. Describe the procedure for precisely positioning the vertical rule within a frame.
    d. Where is the Vertical Rules command located?

77. Views and Mode Changes
    a. How many different views are available within Xerox Ventura Publisher?
    b. List the keyboard shortcuts for the various views available within Xerox Ventura Publisher.
    c. What is a mode?
    d. Name the two methods of changing Xerox Ventura Publisher's modes.
    e. What is a facing page?
    f. Can frames be dragged from one page to another when in facing page?

78. Widows & Orphans
    a. What is the difference between a widow and an orphan?
    b. Why are widows and orphans eliminated from most documents?
    c. What is the normal number settings for widows and orphans?

Index